RACIAL
CASTRA-
TION

PERVERSE

MODERNITIES

A series edited by

Judith Halberstam

and Lisa Lowe

RACIAL CASTRA- TION

MANAGING MASCULINITY IN ASIAN AMERICA

DAVID L. ENG

DUKE UNIVERSITY PRESS

Durham and London

2001

© 2001 Duke University Press
All rights reserved
Printed in the United States of America
on acid-free paper ∞
Designed by Amy Ruth Buchanan
Typeset in Scala by Tseng Information
Systems, Inc. Library of Congress
Cataloging-in-Publication Data
appear on the last printed
page of this book.

CONTENTS

_____

PREFACE, vii

INTRODUCTION, 1
Racial Castration

ONE, 35
I've Been (Re)Working on the Railroad:
Photography and National History in
China Men and *Donald Duk*

TWO, 104
Primal Scenes: Queer Childhood in
"The Shoyu Kid"

THREE, 137
Heterosexuality in the Face of Whiteness:
Divided Belief in *M. Butterfly*

FOUR, 167
Male Hysteria—Real and Imagined—in
Eat a Bowl of Tea and *Pangs of Love*

EPILOGUE, 204
Out Here and Over There: Queerness and
Diaspora in Asian American Studies

NOTES, 229

BIBLIOGRAPHY, 267

INDEX, 283

PREFACE

Arnold Genthe was a German doctor of philosophy who immigrated to the United States in 1895 and settled in San Francisco as the tutor to the son of a wealthy baron. An avid photographer, Genthe took hundreds of photos on glass negatives of San Francisco's Chinatown before the devastating 1906 earthquake and fires leveled it to rubble and ashes. Indeed, Genthe's well-known images of Chinatown's "bachelor society" helped to establish his long and prosperous career as an acclaimed landscape and portrait photographer. Ross Alley, or "The Street of Gamblers (by day)," the cover image of *Racial Castration,* might be said to describe an encounter between two immigrant groups in America: the German doctor from Hamburg and his anonymous Chinese male subjects. In this encounter between the photographer and the photographed a world appears. This world emerges in the instant of a flash—in the image of a photograph captured for history and preserved for time. *Racial Castration* explores the creation and management of images—visual and otherwise—that configure past as well as contemporary perceptions of Asian American male subjectivity.

This book has had numerous supporters to whom I owe much gratitude. First, I would like to thank those family, friends, colleagues, and mentors whose limitless generosity, warmth, kindness, humor, and brilliance provide an enabling supply of personal inspiration and intellectual support: Bernard Arias, Christina Bernstein, Judith Butler, Deborah Cheung, Lily Chinn, Deborah Dowell, Connie Eng, Carolina González, Elizabeth Grainger, Shinhee Han, David Hirsch, Alice Y. Hom, Michele Hong, JeeYeun Lee, Lisa Lowe, Sanda Lwin, Farhad Karim, David Kazanjian, Holly Kim, Sharon Liebowitz, John Martin, Susette Min, Rob Miotke, Mae Ngai, Judith Oh, Catherine Prendergast, Eric Reyes, James Runsdorf, Teemu Ruskola, Josie Saldaña, Tazuko Shibusawa, Kaja Silverman, Gayatri Chakravorty Spivak, Kendall Thomas, Sophie, Leti, and Serena Volpp, Priscilla Wald, Eric Wallner, Dorothy Wang, Timothy Watson, Deborah White, Sau-ling C. Wong, and Stephen Wong.

At Columbia, I have a remarkable group of colleagues whose encouragement makes my daily work not just possible but enjoyable: Rachel Adams, Victor Bascara, Ritu Birla, Marcellus Blount, Julie Crawford, David Damrosch, Suzanne Daly, Jewelnel Davis, Gina Dent, Ann Douglas, Robert Ferguson, Joan Ferrante, Gayatri Gopinath, Joy Hayton, Ursula Heise, Robert Hanning, Jean Howard, David Kastan, Karl Kroeber, Amy Martin, Martin Meisel, Jodi Melamed, Christia Mercer, Edward Mendelson, Michael Mallick, Rosalind Morris, Zita Nunes, Gary Okihiro, Robert O'Meally, Margaret Pappano, Sonali Perera, Julie Peters, Kate Ramsey, Chandan Reddy, Jim Shapiro, Sandhya Shukla, Isabel Thompson, Cynthia Tolentino, Elliott Trice, Gauri Viswanathan, and Alan Yang.

I am lucky to be part of several inspiring community-based and political organizations in New York City, among them the Asian American Writers' Workshop (AAWW) and the Center for Lesbian and Gay Studies (CLAGS). In addition, I have the remarkable good fortune to belong to an enchanting downtown queer reading group, whose members include Henry Abelove, Ed Cohen, Douglas Crimp, Ann Cvetkovich, Lisa Duggan, Licia Fiol-Matta, Beth Freeman, Phillip Brian Harper, Janet Jakobsen, Martin Manalansan, Anna McCarthy, José Muñoz, Ann Pellegrini, and Patricia White. Finally, I would like to thank some wonderful interlocutors for their sustaining conversations in in-between spaces: Mark Chiang, Yvette Christiansë, Jeffrey Fort, Judith Halberstam, Grace Hong, Anne McKnight, Linda Norton, Karen Su, and Eric Zinner.

I am grateful for the excellent research assistance of Nick Boggs, Judith Goldman, Ziv Neeman, and Naomi Reed, who also prepared the index, as I am indebted to Esra Ackan and Jack Tchen for their help with the images for this book. Chapter three and the epilogue were published previously in different forms. Chapter three appeared in *Q & A: Queer in Asian America*, edited by David L. Eng and Alice Y. Hom (Philadelphia: Temple University Press, 1998): 335–65; and the epilogue appeared in *Social Text* 52–53 (fall-winter 1997): 31–52. In addition, a small portion of chapter two appeared in *Critical Mass: A Journal of Asian American Cultural Criticism* 1.2 (spring 1994): 65–83. I thank Temple University Press, *Social Text*, and *Critical Mass* for allowing me to include this revised material, as well as the Columbia University Council for Research in the Humanities, which provided a summer grant toward the completion of this book. Finally, I would like to thank my editors at Duke University Press, Ken Wissoker, Katie Courtland, and Jon Director, for piloting this project, as well as Amy Ruth Buchanan for her beautiful design and Jan Opdyke for her meticulous copyediting. This book is dedicated to my parents, Philip B. and Lucy W. H. Eng, for their love and support of my scholarly dispositions.

INTRODUCTION

Racial Castration

> I am an Oriental. And being an Oriental,
>
> I could never be completely a man.
>
> SONG LILING, *M. Butterfly*

Being Oriental: the antithesis of manhood, of masculinity? So declares Song Liling to the judge, to the law, under oath, and in a suit. The derobed Chinese opera diva/transvestite/spy attempts to explain to the pontificating bureaucrat how it is that Gallimard, the white male diplomat, can mistake him less for a rug than a woman: "The West thinks of itself as masculine—big guns, big industry, big money—so the East is feminine—weak, delicate, poor."[1] Such is the particular crossing of sexual and racial fantasy that compels Gallimard's colonial world order, a fantastic reality in which the *Oxford English Dictionary* would define *Oriental* as "submission," as "weakness," as "woman." Such is the fantasy that makes *Oriental* and *masculine* antithetical terms in Gallimard's universe, a place in which an "Oriental . . . could never be completely a man." In such marvelous narratives of penile privilege, the Westerner monopolizes the part of the "top"; the Asian is invariably assigned the role of the "bottom." For twenty-five years, *Aiiieeeee!* editors Frank Chin, Jeffery Paul Chan, Lawson Fusao Inada, and Shawn Wong have bemoaned the predicament of Asian American masculinity in similar terms: "It is an article of white liberal American faith today that Chinese men, at their best, are effeminate closet queens like Charlie Chan and, at their worst, are homosexual menaces like Fu Manchu."[2] In "Looking for My Penis," Richard Fung summarizes the phenomenon even more bluntly: "Asian and anus are conflated."[3]

Racial Castration: Managing Masculinity in Asian America explores this conflation of *Asian* and *anus* through a group of cultural productions—literature, drama, and film—focused on representations of Asian American masculinity. Investigating the intersection of racial and sexual differences, stereotypes, and fantasies, this book considers from numerous angles the impact of gender and sexuality on the racial formations of Asian American men. Even more, it insists that sexual and racial difference cannot be understood in isolation. What the example from David Henry Hwang's 1988 Tony-award-winning drama *M. Butterfly* so incisively illustrates is the impossibility of thinking about racism and sexism as separate discourses or distinct spheres of analysis. Rather, Song's statement insists that racial fantasies facilitate our investments in sexual fantasies and vice versa. As such, they must be understood as mutually constitutive, as drawing their discursive legibility and social power in relation to one another.

Racial Castration—the book's title derives from my reading of *M. Butterfly*—brings together analyses of masculinity in Asian American literary and cultural productions with psychoanalytic, feminist, queer, postcolonial, and critical race theories. This book analyzes the various ways in which the Asian American male is both materially and psychically feminized within the context of a larger U.S. cultural imaginary. In his 1927 essay "Fetishism," Freud states that the man, traumatized by the sight of female difference—of castration—creates a fetish—a surrogate penis—and projects it onto the female body in the guise of a substitute object: a plait of hair, an undergarment, a shoe.[4] From a slightly different perspective, fetishism describes a psychic process whereby the man attempts to obviate the trauma of sexual difference by seeing at the site of the female body a penis that is not there to see.

A psychoanalytic reading of *M. Butterfly* would seem, then, to insist upon an analysis of the drama through the logic of fetishism. While Gallimard's misrecognition of Song's anatomy indicates the white diplomat's abiding psychic investment in the protocols of the fetish, Hwang's drama also resists, reverses, and ultimately revises Freud's traditional paradigm by opening it upon a social terrain marked not by singular difference but by multiple differences. That is, rather than seeing at the site of the female body a penis that is not there to see, Gallimard refuses to see at the site of the Asian male body a penis that *is* there to see. The white diplomat's "racial castration" of Song thus suggests that the trauma being negotiated in this particular scenario is not just sexual but racial difference. As such, Gallimard's psychic reworking of fetishism challenges our conventional interpretation of the Freudian model by delineating a crossing of race with what is traditionally seen only as a paradigm of (hetero)sexual difference.

Figure 1 Not a rug but a woman: B. D. Wong and John Rubenstein in David Henry Hwang's *M. Butterfly*

Through this racial castration, Gallimard need not see Song as anything other than a woman. Through this distinct refashioning of fetishism, an Oriental "could never be completely a man." And through this elaborate exercise of mental gymnastics Gallimard can strive to maintain the tenuous boundaries of his own assaulted white male (hetero)-sexuality (fig. 1). Hence, in Gallimard's orientalist world fetishism cannot be understood as a scandalous perversion of the social order. Indeed, fetishism is naturalized, functioning as a normative psychic mechanism by means of which a ubiquitous sexualized and racialized vision of the feminized Asian American male emerges and takes hold.

Racial Castration investigates the numerous psychic and material crossings—the various political, economic, and cultural conditions—that solicit our view of Asian American masculinity in these particular and constrained ways. Especially focused on the critical intersection of psychoanalysis and Asian American studies, this book examines the less apparent and visible aspects of sexual and racial identifications that come together not only to construct Asian American male subjects but also to produce against these particularized images the abstract national subject of a unified and coherent national body. From another angle, then, *Racial Castration* might be described as a theoretical project examining the numerous ways in which articulations of national subjectivity depend intimately on racializing, gendering, and sexualizing strategies.

Analyzing critical works by Freud and Lacan in relation to cultural productions by Hwang, Maxine Hong Kingston, Frank Chin, Lonny Kaneko, Louis Chu, David Wong Louie, Ang Lee, and R. Zamora Linmark, among others, *Racial Castration* focuses primarily on Chinese American and Japanese American texts. I do not, however, want these particular readings to be construed as a universal prototype for Asian American male subjectivity. Indeed, the experiences of Asian American men are not easily homogenized. At times, they are seen as analogous (e.g., as racialized, exploitable, noncitizen labor), but in other historical moments they are configured as singular (e.g., Japanese internment during World War II).[5] As the individual chapters of this book illustrate, conceptions of Asian American masculinity are historically and psychically bound by the particularities of race, ethnicity, national origin, sexuality, gender, class, and age. I hope that the analyses I pursue here between specific Asian American cultural productions and particular psychoanalytic paradigms will serve as a modest albeit critical model for the continued interrogation of the commonalities that support, as well as the dissonances that qualify, coalitions among Asian American men.

Focusing primarily on the domain of the specular and the role of the imaginary, *Racial Castration* investigates both the psychic and the material limits circumscribing Asian American male subjectivity. Moreover, it undertakes a crucial examination of the numerous ways in which subjects, both mainstream and minority, remain invested in the normative identifications, stereotypes, and fantasies that maintain the dominant social order. It is, after all, only through Gallimard's sustained identifications with and Song's sustained investments in conventional stereotypes and fantasies of the Oriental geisha that Hwang's drama can unfold to its pitiable end. And it is only through a critical investigation of the production, dissemination, and reinscription of these sexual and racial identifications, stereotypes, and fantasies that we can begin to examine the ways in which Asian American cultural productions also help us to expose, confront, and dispute these significant representational burdens.

Psychoanalysis and Race in Asian America

From an alternate perspective, *Racial Castration* might be considered an extended theoretical meditation on the following question: can psychoanalysis be as useful to Asian American and ethnic studies as it has been to feminist and queer studies? Until recently, the answer to this query would have been an emphatic "no."[6] Detractors of psychoanalytic theory have justifiably noted that, in its insistent privileging of sexuality as the organizing principle of subjectivity and loss, psychoanalysis has had little to offer to the study of race or processes of racialization. Indeed, psychoanalytic, feminist, and queer theories traditionally have had the same conceptual blind spot: these are all critical discourses that emphasize sexual difference over and above every other type of social difference. Yet we need to ask whether (hetero)sexual difference is the only and primary guarantor of loss structuring our psychic lives. Is it (hetero)sexual difference that gives legibility to—indeed, sanctions the emergence of—our subjectivities?

Psychoanalytic theorists have been slow to consider the ways in which diverse social categories underpin, intersect, disturb, or disrupt their investigations of sexuality and sexual difference. Alternative markers of difference—race, ethnicity, class, nationality, language—are often uncritically subsumed into the framework of sexual difference. It is indispensable to incorporate socially and historically variable factors into what hitherto has been rather ahistorical and essentializing psychoanalytic formulations of the construction of subjectivity. This incorporation allows us to consider the ways in which multiple forms of difference underpin the genesis of subjectivity. How, for example, are racial boundaries secured or contested through symbolic norms as well as prohibitions on sexuality and sexual practices? How does the social regulation of sexuality produce—and how is it produced by—race? This type of critical inquiry advances an understanding of how psychoanalysis as a philosophical body of thought helps authorize and reinforce the (re)production of social hierarchies, such as sexuality and race, as the essentialized and naturalized order of things.

As our example from M. Butterfly unequivocally illustrates, we are at one and the same time, to borrow a phrase from Norma Alarcón, multiply interpellated subjects.[7] M. Butterfly underscores the fact that sexuality and race, often seen as disparate or independently articulated domains, are mutually constitutive and constituted. Gallimard's management of sexual difference through his exploitation of the fetish is a management of racial difference as well. In this regard, the sexual effects of the fetish are also racial effects, a reiterated racializing practice. Sexual and racial difference are legible—indeed, they are derived—in relation to one another. Hence, M. Butterfly not only suggests that castration is always a *racial* castration, but it also insists that the traditional ways in which scholars in feminist and queer studies have deployed psychoanalytic theory to deconstruct naturalizing discourses of sexual, and in particular heterosexual, difference must be rethought to include viable accounts of race as well.

This constitutive crossing of sexual and racial difference is not just found in Hwang's contemporary drama. Significantly, this crossing traces its critical genealogy to the psychoanalytic project itself. Any careful investigation of Freud's oeuvre reveals the numerous ways in which a racialized account of subjectivity is constitutive of the psychoanalytic project. From its very inception, psychoanalysis has systematically encoded race as a question of sexual development. As the privileged episteme of psychoanalytic theory, sexuality often comes to stand for—and serve as a displaced category of—racial difference in Freud's writings. At the same time, racial difference repeatedly operates as a proxy for normative and aberrant sexualities and sexual practices. Before moving on to a discussion of the status of sexuality in Asian American studies, I would like to illustrate briefly an emblematic instance of this constitutive crossing of sexuality and race in psychoanalytic theory: the convergence of two "pathological" Freudian characters, the figure of the primitive in *Totem and Taboo* (1912–13) and the figure of the homosexual in "On Narcissism" (1914). Commenting on the writings of Frantz Fanon, the black Algerian psychoanalyst, Diana Fuss writes in *Identification Papers* that "Fanon's remarks on homosexuality, while failing to challenge some of Freud's most conventional and dangerous typologies of sexuality, simultaneously question, at least implicitly, the ethnological component of psychoanalysis that has long equated 'the homosexual' with 'the primitive'" (155). I would like to trace explicitly the theoretical and political stakes of this conflation.

Totem and Taboo, a speculative treatise on the relationship between "primitive" sexual practices and "civilized" neuroses, provides a compelling account of the ways in which Freud's psychoanalytic project manages racial difference through a discursive strategy configured as the teleological evolution of normative sexual practices and "pathological" sexual perversions. Freud opens this volume by centering his discussion on the figure of the primitive. With the expressed purpose of tracing the "dark origins" of the contemporary European psyche, Freud writes in the opening pages of *Totem and Taboo* that primitive man

> is known to us through the inanimate monuments and implements which he has left behind, through the information about his art, his religion and his attitude towards life which has come to us either directly or by way of tradition handed down in legends, myths and fairy tales, and through the relics of his mode of thought which survive in our own manners and customs. But apart from this, in a certain sense he is still our contemporary. There are men still living who, as we believe, stand very near to primitive man, far nearer than we do, and whom we therefore re-

gard as his direct heirs and representatives. Such is our view of those whom we describe as savages or half-savages; and their mental life must have a peculiar interest for us if we are right in seeing in it a well-preserved picture of an early stage of our own development.[8]

"Savages" and "half-savages," standing in close proximity to primitive man, can be observed because they exist *during* Freud's time. However, these racially other savages and half-savages do not exist *in* Freud's time. Instead, they are securely positioned as temporally other to modern European man. That is, these contemporaneous savages not only exist in an indeterminate premodern past from which present-day European society has decisively emerged, but they are psychically frozen in this indeterminate past.

For Freud, white European man represents civilized man, or what he suggests to be primitive man's unrealized psychic potential. In insisting that there "are men still living who, as we believe, stand very near to primitive man, far nearer than we do, and whom we therefore regard as his direct heirs and representatives," Freud implies that these present-day savage races have fallen outside the chain of psychic evolution and human development. That is, these racialized groups are savage (and not only primitive) because they are not (nor can they ever be) in any process of psychic or social advancement. Locked in time, they are preindividuals and maldeveloped groups, undeveloped and undevelopable. This temporal congealing of Freud's figure of the savage with the primitive is evident in his assertion that in their mental life we see an atavistic image, a "well-preserved picture of an early stage of our own development." If, for Freud, ontogeny recapitulates phylogeny, then the development of the individual recapitulates the development of civilized mankind not only through a specifically sexualized form but through a specifically racialized valence.

The teleological evolution into and the claiming of civility by modern European man thus rely on the presumed incivility of the figure of the primitive who underpins the "dark origins" of Freud's narrative of white racial progress. If the figure of the primitive attests to a certain analytic transparency for Freud, this transparency is the result of an unquestioned faith in the steady progress of European civilization. It is crucial to point out that the primitive's presumed incivility is symptomatized by Freud precisely as a problem of sexual development. Freud focuses much of *Totem and Taboo* on an extended discussion of the multiple sexual prohibitions against incest found in primitive societies. He concludes the first chapter by stating that it is "therefore of no small importance that we are able to show that these same incestuous wishes, which are later destined to become unconscious [in us], are still regarded by savage peoples as immediate perils against which the most severe measures of defence must be enforced" (17).

Further honing what exactly constitutes the limits of the primitive psyche, Freud states that the primitive has no unconscious to speak of, that his thoughts and motivations are eminently one-dimensional, present, and transparent. Even more, Freud contends that what marks the primitive psyche as such, beyond all other distinguishing characteristics, is its propensity for sexual impropriety:

> We should certainly not expect that the sexual life of these poor naked cannibals would be moral in our sense or that their sexual instincts would be subjected to any greater degree of restriction. Yet we find that they set before themselves with the most scrupulous care and the most painful severity the aim of avoiding incestuous sexual relations. Indeed, their whole social organization seems to serve that purpose or to have been brought into relation with its attainment. . . . It must be admitted that these savages are even more sensitive on the subject of incest than we are. They are probably liable to a greater temptation to it and for that reason stand in need of fuller protection. (2, 9)

Freud's racial certainty forecloses the figure of the primitive from the category of the unconscious. Unable to banish forbidden sexual impulses to this inaccessible domain, primitive peoples are thus liable to the horrible seductions of incest. This foreclosure of the unconscious is symptomatized precisely as the failing of sexual decorum, the falling into excessive sexual temptation, represented by incest. For Freud, the fact that primitive societies have scrupulously regulated their sexual impulses does not function as collateral for their social restraint or as evidence of their civil progress. Rather, he reads this heightened sexual regulation back into primitive societies as pathognomonic of their susceptibility to such temptations and consequently as further proof of their incivility.

Freud hypersexualizes the primitive, racialized body. What emerges most clearly from this linking of the sexually voracious primitive with the failure of the incest taboo, then, is the inseparability of racial from sexual identity. By invoking the "dark origins" of these primitives, Freud clearly connects the savage tribes under discussion in *Totem and Taboo* with a type of visual darkness—with a type of visual marking, that of being dark-skinned. Yet, the legitimate mark and proof of racialization is ultimately to be found neither in the register of pigmentation nor in any system of visual authentication. To the contrary, this proof is established through Freud's depiction of the sexual practices and pathologies of primitive peoples.

In delineating the figure of the primitive in this particular manner, Freud thus links an explicitly psychosexual discourse with a Western anthropological tradition bound to eighteenth- and nineteenth-century epistemologies of European dominance and colonial expansionism. In "Notarizing Knowledge," David Kazanjian points out that the "argument that non-Europeans were pre-modern and atavistic was, of course, one of the most important justifications for many Euro-American colonialist and, later, imperial enterprises, because it allowed colonial and imperial exploitation to proceed under the guise of economic and/or cultural 'modernization.' "[9] Indeed, *Totem and Taboo* might be seen as a paradigmatic treatise on this sanctioning of colonial exploitation through a rhetoric of modernization—a rhetoric that takes the specific form of the regulation of sexual practices and propriety. In this regard, Freud's psychical theories of sexual development express what Fuss, in *Identification Papers,* describes as one of psychoanalysis's less studied historical genealogies, that of colonial imperialism. Writing about Fanon's investigation of the neurotic structure of colonialism, Fuss states that "Fanon's investigation of the dynamics of psychological alterity within the historical and political frame of colonialism suggests that identification is neither a historically universal concept nor a politically innocent one. A by-product of modernity, the psychoanalytic theory of identification takes shape within the larger cultural context of colonial expansion and imperial crisis" (141–42).

Freud concludes *Totem and Taboo* with an expanded discussion on the question of the unconscious and the manner in which the thoughts of the primitive are directly transformed into actions and deeds. Excluded from the repressive forces of the unconscious—its exacting symbolic norms and prohibitions—their thoughts assume a kind of omnipotent pretension: "Primitive men . . . are *uninhibited:* thought passes directly into action. With them it is rather the deed that is a substitute for the thought. And that is why, without laying claim to any finality of judgement, I think that in the case before us it may safely be assumed that 'in the beginning was the Deed' " (161; emphasis in original). Alongside the argument that the primitive lacks mental complexity and an adequate moral framework is this more pernicious, yet fundamental, conflation of sexual perversions with racial difference, a constitutive crossing motivated precisely by the absence of unconscious regulation. This merging of sexual and racial difference not only subtends Freud's account of the progressive evolution of European society from its "dark origins"; by embedding this racial narrative into his theory of the unconscious, the convergence of sexuality and race also comes to penetrate the central metapsychological structure of the psychoanalytic project itself.

Freud does nothing to problematize his observations on this privileged coupling of European racial progress with the advancement of normative sexual practices and the repressive standards of unconscious regulation. Throughout *Totem and Taboo,* Freud invokes his observations on the figure of the primitive with a positivist self-confidence not evident in his other writings. Freud's assertions that certain non-European savage tribes—the Akamba, Australian Aborigines, Barongos, Battas, Malays, Maori, Melanesians, Polynesians, Ta-Ta-thi, Zulas, and so on—have attained a level of sexual, psychic, and social development equivalent to that of the ancient ancestors of Europe are not based on firsthand observations. To the contrary, they are gleaned from a variety of secondary anthropological sources and written accounts by anthropologists such as J. G. Frazer, Anthony Lang, John Lubbock, E. B. Tylor, and Wilhelm Wundt. For this reason, Kazanjian observes, critics have often dissociated *Totem and Taboo* from the Freudian oeuvre proper as an unfortunate, but anomalous, foray into bad anthropology. In the same logical breath, the figure of the primitive is also disregarded as an incidental effect of this bad anthropology.

Although it clearly participates in a quotidian racist discourse of white superiority, the racial logic embodied in *Totem and Taboo* should not be dismissed as an aberrant example of a poor psychosocial analysis. Instead, the racial logic found in *Totem and Taboo* must be recognized as one that comes to inhabit and embed itself within the organizing structure of Freud's metapsychological theories—as a logic indicative of a problematic internal to the "proper" Freudian oeuvre itself. Attention to the bridging of this racial logic has far-reaching implications. It facilitates a more thorough understanding of the ways in which racial difference is both constitutive of and managed in the production of modern liberal subjectivity. At the same time, it forces us to consider the various ways in which race implicitly underpins the more explicit narratives of sexual development that permeate the psychoanalytic canon.

I conclude this section on psychoanalysis and race by turning to "On Narcissism: An Introduction," which was published one year after the appearance of *Totem and Taboo.* In this well-known essay—a cornerstone of Freudian metapsychology on individual development from narcissistic to "proper" anaclitic love attachments—Freud initially isolates the figure of the homosexual as an exemplary model of a stalled and pathological narcissism. He goes on to elaborate his observations on narcissism in terms of a libido theory that he connects to the mental lives of both children and primitive peoples. "In the latter," Freud observes, "we find characteristics which, if they occurred singly, might be put down to megalomania: an over-estimation of the power of their wishes and mental acts, the 'omnipotence of thoughts,' a belief in the thaumaturgic force of words, and a technique for dealing with the external world—'magic'—which appears to be a logical application of these grandiose premises."[10] Notions of the primitive—those whose mental thoughts pass directly into action—developed in *Totem and Taboo* return here embedded within the metapsychological narrative of "On Narcissism." Unlike children, who according to Freud naturally develop out of their narcissism during the process of psychic maturation, the primitive remains interminably trapped within a narcissistic loop, locked in an atavistic temporal prison.

Freud concludes "On Narcissism" by observing that

> [T]he ego ideal opens up an important avenue for the understanding of group psychology. In addition to its individual side, this ideal has a social side; it is also the common ideal of a family, a class or a nation. It binds not only a person's narcissistic libido, but also a considerable amount of his homosexual libido, which is in this way turned back into the ego. The want of satisfaction which arises from the non-fulfillment of this ideal liberates homosexual libido, and this is transformed into sense of guilt (social anxiety). Originally this sense of guilt was a fear of punishment by the parents, or, more correctly, the fear of losing their love; later the parents are replaced by an indefinite number of fellow-men. (101–2)

Freud's extension of the libido theory produces such a rich understanding of the ego ideal as the central mechanism of sexual regulation that "On Narcissism" ultimately concludes by expanding its claims beyond individual psychology and the Oedipal family romance to an analysis of group psychology and the emergence of the social sphere. The transformation of homosexual libido into heterosexual identification and esprit de corps—the turning back of homosexual desire as conscience and guilt—allows for the formation of a legible and legitimated heterosexual identity supported by parents and community ("an indefinite number of fellow-men") alike. The formation of a legitimated heterosexual identity through the sublimation of homosexuality into a sense of custodial dread is, according to Freud, essential to the advent of "the common ideal of a family, a class or a nation." This sublimation is governed by an exacting ego-ideal organized by a heterosexual imperative and its concomitant homosexual prohibition. In other words, the formation of the normative Freudian (male) ego depends upon the elimination of homosexuality. Desire for the father must be transformed into a desexualized identification with him.[11]

It is important to emphasize that Freud's formulation of modern psychic life and sociality through mechanisms of heterosexual production and homosexual interdiction are sanctioned in part by his initial observations on the narcissistic, stalled mental life of savages. However, while Freud's children have grown up to be functioning adults, the figure of the primitive has vanished by the conclusion of this essay, has fallen through, as it were, the cracks of Freud's civilized polity. Only the figure of the homosexual remains — remains, that is, to be banished. In "Notarizing Knowledge," Kazanjian notes that Freud's vision of this social formation "is not that of 'primitive peoples,' however, but one in which a paranoia like Schreber's [the repressed homosexual *Senatspräsident*] can exist and, presumably, can be resolved — that is, a 'civilized' social. Freud thus claims that modern, 'civilized' European political formations like family, class, and nation can be understood, in part, on the basis of the study of colonized subjects figured as pre-modern 'primitives.' Although they function as objects readily available to observation and interpretation, these 'primitive peoples' are excluded from the social formation they somehow inform" (104). As excluded native-informant, the primitive secures the fantasy of Freud's civilized European sociality. This is a civilized sociality that can seemingly exist and be (sexually) analyzed independent of colonialism and racial problematics. Constituting the external, atavistic prehistory of this civilized European sociality, primitive peoples, in their brief appearance on the scene of "On Narcissism," authorize and underwrite the analysis of homosexuals, children, and narcissism in its multiple psychic forms. Through exclusion, the banished figure of the primitive is thus positioned as the limiting condition of possibility for a psychoanalytic project that tracks the development of narcissistic subjects into functional, socialized, and neurotic citizens.

We might understand the proscription on homosexuality in "On Narcissism," then, as also coming to signify this expunging of racial difference. Freud's management and erasure of the figure of the homosexual are a simultaneous management and erasure of the figure of the primitive. As such, the sublimation of homosexual desire upon which Freud focuses in his concluding remarks to "On Narcissism" is itself predicated on the simultaneous sublimation of racial difference. The management and erasure of "primitive" sexual impulses are no longer figured here as the threat of incest but as the threatened return of same-sex desire. In this regard, a displaced racial otherness is made legible in the lexicon of pathological (homo)sexuality.[12]

In crossing *Totem and Taboo* with "On Narcissism," we witness a convergence of homosexuality with racial difference, a coming together of the homosexual and the primitive as pathologized, banished figures within the psychic landscape of the social proper. In this merging, the figure of the homosexual is racialized as the figure of the primitive is (homo)sexualized. To approach this issue from a slightly different angle, we come to understand that the troping of racial difference in *Totem and Taboo* as pathological sexual practices is reformulated in "On Narcissism" as the sublimation of a pathologized racial difference into a normative theory of (hetero)sexual development. It is through this management and erasure of racial difference that sexuality—specifically, a system of *compulsory heterosexuality*—gains its hold within psychoanalytic theory as a universal and ahistorical principle. Resisting this universalizing impulse, we must recognize that any discussion of sexuality within psychoanalytic theory not only signifies sexuality per se but necessarily accounts for racial difference as well.

Judith Butler remarks in *Bodies That Matter* that "it seems crucial to rethink the scenes of reproduction and, hence, of sexing practices not only as ones through which a heterosexual imperative is inculcated, but as ones through which boundaries of racial distinction are secured as well as contested. Especially at those junctures in which a compulsory heterosexuality works in the service of maintaining hegemonic forms of racial purity, the 'threat' of homosexuality takes on a distinctive complexity" (18). Butler challenges us to question the ways in which symbolic prohibitions against homosexuality and nonwhiteness secure the very boundaries by which subjects are granted a social legibility and cultural viability. In light of our present discussion, Butler's statement not only emphasizes the fact that a theory of heterosexual development cannot be easily dissociated from racial regulation but also suggests that heterosexuality gains its discursive power through its tacit coupling with a hegemonic, unmarked whiteness. At the same time, I would suggest, the "distinctive complexity" arising from the "threat" of homosexuality necessarily entails restoring to the psychoanalytic project its "dark origins": the return of the "threatening" racialized figure of the primitive, the return of race to psychoanalysis, and the return of psychoanalysis to race.

The investigation of the figure of the homosexual and the primitive underscores the theoretical necessity of further exploring the intersection of sexual and racial difference in psychoanalytic theory. It insists that we examine how one category cannot be constituted save through the other. It asks us to consider how the assumption of a normative social identity requires a heterosexualizing imperative bound to a hegemonic structure of whiteness—how the assumption of a "pathological" social identity is circumscribed by a homosexual prohibition bound to a racialized position. How might we understand homosexuality and race to converge at the outside limits of the symbolic domain governed by norms of heterosexuality and whiteness? These questions are especially relevant to our investigation of Asian American masculinity. If Asian American male subjectivity is psychically and materially constrained by a crossing of racial difference with homosexuality—what Fung describes as the conflation of "Asian" and "anus"—then its relation to these dominant social norms and prohibitions takes on a distinctive critical cast and an urgent critical dissonance. What types of identificatory routes—what types of ambivalent psychic detours—are impressed upon the Asian American male psyche to bring it to this particular social destination?

My examination of Asian American masculinity in terms of sexuality and race works against contemporary claims that dismiss the applicability of psychoanalysis to critical race studies. Moreover, it resists modern theories of self that configure subjectivity as a type of essentialized *sexual* subjectivity. As Ann Pellegrini notes in *Performance Anxieties,* feminist (and I would argue queer) projects aimed at analyzing the complex crossings of multiple social differences are implicated, for better and for worse, in psychoanalysis. Pellegrini writes that the solution to this theoretical impasse "is not to abandon psychoanalytic categories or theory—as if psychoanalysis (and Freud) could be so easily bracketed from the narrative frame of modernity and postmodernity" (3). Instead, as I have been arguing, we must recognize that psychoanalytic narratives are not only integral to but also are integrated into our contemporary sense of self as modern liberal (sexualized as well as racialized) subjects. As one of the most significant intellectual and cultural influences of the twentieth century, Pellegrini concludes, psychoanalysis provides "patterns of order and interpretation for telling, retelling, and making sense of life experiences, and this is no less the case when the story told emerges in reaction against psychoanalysis." What is called for "is the engagement of psychoanalysis on very altered terms" (3).

Psychoanalytic theory can help us understand the important lesson that sexuality is not natural—that it is resolutely cultural and constructed. We need to expand this valuable axiom into the field of Asian American and ethnic studies to insist that psychoanalysis also and at once describes, marks, and produces social differences other than sexuality. Feminism and queer studies—as both intellectual and political projects—cannot proceed without an active reengagement of psychoanalysis on these radically and racially modified terms. In this new form, psychoanalytic theory might provide a rich set of conceptual paradigms for the investigation of Asian American racial formation in relation to specific epistemologies of sexuality and sexual development. To bring the discourse of psychoanalysis to the field of Asian American studies is to consider explicitly questions of sexuality and gender as they impact the formation of Asian American male subjectivity. As one of the premier theories exploring the relationship between gender and sexuality, and between identifications and desires, psychoanalysis provides a set of critical paradigms that helps us to understand not only the multiple ways in which sexual and racial difference intersect to configure the Asian American male psyche but also the significant material effects of these productions. To account for the production of race, processes of racialization, and the naturalization of racism in psychic terms would be to provide potentially transformative methods of exploring how Asian American men are managed by, and in turn manage, their masculinities.

Sexuality in Asian America

The broadening of the psychoanalytic project to encompass a serious analysis of racial difference is imperative. However, insofar as psychoanalytic theory and criticism must be reexamined in relation to social formations other than sexuality, I might also stress with equal insistence that the investigation of racial formation in Asian American studies must include a systematic consideration of sexuality. Scholars in Asian American studies have typically paid great critical attention to the ways in which Marxist analyses of class underpin the emergence of racial identity.[13] Yet, to the extent that sexuality has been theorized in this field, it has often been seen as additive or adjunct and not primary in the constitution of Asian American racial formation.[14]

Moreover, while there has been substantial research done in Asian American studies—in both the humanities and the social sciences—on female subjectivity and gender, mother-daughter relations, and questions of feminism, less critical attention has been paid to the topics of masculinity and sexuality.[15] *Racial Castration* extends important scholarship in Asian American and women's studies on female subjectivity and gender to think specifically about the formation of Asian American male subjectivity and, in particular, homosexuality. In "The Woman Warrior versus The Chinaman Pacific," King-Kok Cheung evaluates from a fresh perspective the historical conflicts between seemingly divergent agendas of feminism and heroism in Asian American studies. Cheung observes that "the racist treatment of Asians has taken the peculiar form of sexism—insofar as the indignities suffered by men of Chinese descent are analogous to those traditionally suffered by women."[16] Hence, she admonishes, Asian American activists and critics must refrain from seeking antifeminist solutions to predicaments of Asian American masculinity. To do otherwise would reinforce not only patriarchy but white supremacy. Precisely because the feminization of the Asian American male in the U.S. cultural imaginary typically results in his figuration as feminized, emasculated, or homosexualized, we must vigilantly pursue the theoretical connections between queer studies—with its focus on (homo)sexuality and desire—and women's studies—with its focus on gender and identification—in relation to the production of Asian American male subjectivity.[17]

In the field of Asian American studies, the recent work of Lisa Lowe helps us to underscore the disparate ways in which race, gender, and sexuality come together in various configurations to secure and organize a genealogy of Asian American male subjectivity. Rehearsing the lengthy history of U.S. legal definitions of citizenship, Chinese immigration, naturalization, exclusion, detention, national antimiscegenation laws, and legislative bans on the entry of Chinese wives into the United States, Lowe observes in *Immigrant Acts* that collectively these juridical practices produced a "technology" of simultaneous racialization and gendering of the Asian American male subject (11). That is, for Asian American men racial identity was—and continues to be—produced, stabilized, and secured through mechanisms of gendering.

Lowe observes, for instance, that the rapidly industrializing U.S. nation-state in the nineteenth century required a cheap, abundant labor force for the construction and maintenance of a growing national infrastructure. The construction of the transcontinental railroad entailed the recruitment of over ten thousand Chinese male immigrant laborers for the completion of the western portion of its track. Commenting on the contradiction that emerged between the U.S. nation-state's economic imperative to procure cheap, flexible, Chinese immigrant labor and its political refusal to enfranchise these male workers as full citizen-subjects, Lowe concludes that

> [R]acialization along the legal axis of definitions of citizenship has also ascribed "gender" to the Asian American subject. Up until 1870, American citizenship was granted exclusively to white male persons; in 1870, men of African descent could become naturalized, but the bar to citizenship remained for Asian men until the repeal acts of 1943–1952. Whereas the "masculinity" of the citizen was first inseparable from his "whiteness," as the state extended

citizenship to nonwhite male persons, it formally designated these subjects as "male," as well. (11)[18]

Lowe analyzes the juridical exclusions through which Chinese American male immigrant laborers were barred, at once, not only from institutional and social definitions of maleness but from normative conceptions of masculinity legally defined as "white." In this particular crossing, let me emphasize that the nation-state's sustained economic exploitation, coupled with its political disenfranchisement, of the Asian American male immigrant is modulated precisely through a technology of gendering not adjunct but centrally linked to processes of Asian American racial formation. Indeed, Lowe concludes, there is no social contradiction that is not simultaneously articulated with other social contradictions. In this respect, Asian American male identity is historically and increasingly characterized by critical intersections in which racial, gendered, and economic contradictions are inseparable. They are mobilized by means of and through one another. Put another way, it might be said that the acquisition of gendered identity in liberal capitalist societies is always a racialized acquisition and that the exploitation of immigrant labor is mobilized not only through the racialization of that labor but through its sexualizing. Acknowledging these mutual imbrications is to understand the social emergence of masculinity and femininity as dependent on these fundamental constitutive intersections and crossings.

From another historical vantage point, the high concentration of Asian American male immigrants in what are typically thought of as "feminized" professions—laundries, restaurants, tailor's shops—further illustrates a material legacy of the intersectionality of gender and race.[19] Collectively, these low-wage, feminized jobs work to underscore the numerous ways in which gender is mapped as the social axis through which the legibility of a racialized Asian American male identity is constituted, determined, rendered coherent, and stabilized. Popular stereotypes connecting past and present Asian American male laborers to these types of professions are succinct and compelling illustrations of the ways in which economically driven modes of feminization cling to bodies not only sexually but also racially.[20]

Finally, important lessons from Asian American history teach us that the antimiscegenation and exclusion laws that interdicted, for example, the entry of Chinese wives into the United States (such as the Page Act Law of 1875) worked to produce Chinatowns as exclusive "bachelor communities," which exerted great influence on questions of sexuality.[21] The particular historical configuration of the bachelor society insists that we extend our theoretical study of the intersectionality of race and gender for Asian American male subjects into the domain of homosexuality. Physically, socially, and psychically isolated, these segregated bachelor communities might easily be thought of as "queer" spaces institutionally barred from normative (hetero)sexual reproduction, nuclear family formations, and entitlements to community. Collectively, these material and social conditions provide a compelling argument for the relevance of queer critiques of the normative and the deviant in formulating questions of Asian American historiography and epistemology.[22] Collectively, these numerous historical examples—of the legal definitions of citizenship, of the economic imperatives of professions, of the institutionalized productions of social space—link racial, gendered, and sexual constructs. Considered in relation to one another, they encourage us to understand that critical discourses on "deviant" sexuality do not affect merely those contemporary Asian American subjects who readily self-identify as queer, gay, or lesbian. Rather, discourses on deviant sexuality describe and encompass a far larger Asian American constituency whose historically disavowed status as full members of the U.S. nation-state renders them queer as such.

Lowe concludes her juridical critique of citizenship—its racial and gendered productions—with an observation on Chinese American male subjectivity before and after the Magnuson Act repealed immigration exclusion in 1943.[23] She notes that Chinese American male immigrants prior to this historical moment can be said to have occupied a "feminized" position in relation to the universalized national white male citizen and after this historical moment a "masculinity" whose "*racialization* is the material trace of the history of this 'gendering'" (11–12). Lowe's provocative statement insists that we investigate the ways in which the racialization of Asian American masculinity functions as an opaque screen. This screen obscures the complex histories of social organization through which categories of sexuality and gender gain their coherence and symbolic significance. From this particular angle, Asian American masculinity must always be read as an overdetermined symptom whose material existence draws its discursive sustenance from multiple structures and strategies relating to racialization, gendering, and (homo)sexualizing. In this regard, uneven national histories of anti-Asian discrimination might be described not only as being turned into the subject but also as being repressed and erased through the abstraction of that turn, the subjection of that subject. Disavowed histories turned inward are internalized in—and as—Asian American male subjectivity.

In our contemporary context, we cannot think of race as a fixed or singular essence; instead, we must view it as a constitutive formation in which multiple social contradictions converge to organize a socially dominant view of Asian American male identities. In other words, the conceptualization of racial and sexual difference as if they were distinct categories of analysis is a false construction that serves the political power, economic interests, and cultural hegemony of a mainstream social order. We cannot isolate racial formation from gender and sexuality without reproducing the normative logic of domination that works to configure these two categories as opposed, independent discourses in the first instance. Thinking about the ways in which gender and sexuality are inflected by race, and vice versa, *Racial Castration* brings together two fields of study—psychoanalytic theory and Asian American studies—that are typically seen as disparate in the humanities. This unorthodox pairing encourages not only a more comprehensive analysis of the psychic valences and material dimensions by means of which Asian American male subjectivity is constituted and sustained but also a more adequate understanding of the critical importance of sexuality and sexual difference to Asian American racial formation.

Stranded Identifications

Considering Asian American studies and psychoanalytic theory together yields a more comprehensive understanding of the historical intersections of race, gender, and sexuality that produce a dominant image of the Asian American male subject in the U.S. cultural imaginary. In addition, a critical focus on the vocabulary of psychoanalysis offers a compelling theory of identification that allows us to delineate the specific psychic processes by means of which the Asian American male subject internalizes these dominant images as processes of self-regulation. While Asian American studies has not widely embraced or acknowledged psychoanalytic theory as a viable or necessary discourse, I would like to point out that throughout the historical development of the Asian American studies movement numerous scholars and activists have borrowed critical concepts and vocabulary from psychoanalysis to describe the psychological predicaments, social parameters, and internal dimensions of Asian American identity. As a result, these critics stress, and even inadvertently argue for, the need for a more in-depth understanding of the processes of identification that both produce and constrain the psychic limits of Asian American male subjectivity.

Various contemporary critics of Asian American and ethnic studies lament the field's historical reliance on the social sciences and its exclusively materially based analyses of Asian American identity. These critics argue that Asian American studies' sociological emphasis on the "quantifiable" aspects of racism curtail the ability of scholars in the field to confront the more immaterial and psychological aspects of race and racism. This criticism is certainly nothing new. It was precisely those "qualities which are incapable of objective management" that formed the basis for the Supreme Court's decision in *Brown v. Board of Education* (1954) to abolish racial segregation in education.[24] Material considerations alone did not—and still do not—adequately encompass the full effects of race and racism, for, as the Supreme Court held in this landmark decision written by Earl Warren, they cannot capture "intangible considerations." Furthermore, while material considerations might be remedied, the Supreme Court believed that these intangible considerations affected the racialized subject psychologically "in a way unlikely ever to be undone." Yet, despite such passionate arguments, a divide remains between the psychoanalytic and the sociological.

Elizabeth Abel, Barbara Christian, and Helene Moglen, the editors of the recent *Female Subjects in Black and White,* point out that if "psychoanalysis has entered and been reconstituted within the academy under the aegis of the humanities, 'race' has been institutionally positioned as an object of primarily sociological inquiry" (5). I resist, along with these editors, any false opposition between the "psychological" trajectory of the humanities and the "material" emphasis of the social sciences. Instead, I argue that our conception of the real and the "reality" of race occurs not on one side of the psychic or on the other side of the material but at its very intersection.[25]

Let me note further that from the early days of the Asian American movement scholars and activists committed to material analyses of U.S. racism stressed the need to explore the psychological dimensions of Asian American identity. In the 1973 preface to *Aiiieeeee! An Anthology of Asian-American Writers,* for instance, the editors emphasized the necessity of thinking about the ways in which "legislative racism and euphemized white racist love have left today's Asian-Americans in a state of self-contempt, self-rejection, and disintegration."[26] In this manner, the *Aiiieeeee!* editors insisted on an understanding of the complicated ways in which the external conditions of race and racism—material structures productive of contempt and rejection by mainstream society—are internalized by Asian Americans and transformed through this movement from outside to inside as *feelings* of "self-contempt, self-rejection, and disintegration."[27]

In the example drawn from the *Aiiieeeee!* editors it is important once again to point out a continual and circular process of internalization and externalization, the ways in which internalized racial feelings of self-contempt, self-rejection, and disintegration are reexternalized, transformed, and displaced in the process as a war between the sexes. In their obsessive focus on—in their incredible anger over—the feminization, emasculation, and homosexualization of the Asian American male, the *Aiiieeeee!* editors advance an untenable solution for the redress of these exclusions. They argue that the rehabilitation of Asian American masculinity depends on the programmatic reification of a "pure" Asian martial tradition. Paradoxically, this reification of a strident cultural nationalism, with its doctrine of compulsory heterosexuality and cultural authenticity, mirrors at once the dominant heterosexist and racist structures through which the Asian American male is historically feminized and rendered self-hating in the first place. Not to question cultural nationalism's heterosexist discourse of authenticity, in other words, reinscribes the same mechanisms of identification that support oppression in the first instance.

This heralding of an Asian American cultural nationalist project often engenders displaced masculinist attacks against Asian American women socially for their "treasonous" romantic filiations with white men and politically for their lack of racial "authenticity."[28] This argument, indeed, establishes the political parameters of the enduring debate between Frank Chin and Maxine Hong Kingston over authenticity and fakeness. This see-saw between psychic forms of internalized self-hate and their externalized material effects raises yet again the issue of the intersectionality of race and gender. That is, racial problems consistently manifest themselves in questions of sexual relations between Asian American men and women, with the figure of the Asian American homosexual entirely banished from this heterosexual landscape. Indeed, Asian American cultural nationalism posits a slippery equation of homosexuality instead of a virulent homophobia with white racist agendas. As such, the *Aiiieeeee!* group obviates the possibility of undertaking an antiracist and antihomophobic agenda at once. This is a dynamic that lends an uncanny racial valence to Freud's provocative statement, slightly altered here, that—for Asian American men and women and Asian American straights and queers—"love is a phase apart."[29]

Writing in the same historical period as the *Aiiieeeee!* editors, but from the perspective of clinical psychology, Derald and Stanley Sue prefigure many of the political and social lamentations of the *Aiiieeeee!* editors in their concept of the "Marginal Man." In 1971, in the early pages of the new *Amerasia Journal,* the Sue brothers defined the "Marginal Man" as an Asian American male subject who desires to assimilate into mainstream American society at any cost (the psychological equivalent of the sociological phenomenon of the "Banana"). The Sues point out that this type of assimilation is purchased only through elaborate self-denial on the part of the minority subject of daily institutionalized acts of racism directed against him. In "Chinese American Personality and Mental Health," the two write about the complex psychological defenses that the Marginal Man must necessarily employ in order to function within a racist American society. The Marginal Man finds it "difficult to admit widespread racism since to do so would be to say that he aspires to join a racist society." [30] Caught in this untenable contradiction, the Marginal Man must necessarily become a split subject, one who exhibits a faithful allegiance to the universal norms of abstract equality and collective national membership at the same time that he displays an uncomfortable understanding of his utter disenfranchisement from these democratic ideals.

Ultimately, the untenable predicament of wanting to join a mainstream society that one knows clearly and systematically excludes oneself delineates the painful problem of becoming the instrument of one's own self-exclusion. This psychological paradox comes to mark not only Asian American male subjectivity but also all minority subjectivities in varying degrees of severity. Here, as Fuss points out in *Identification Papers,* the work of Frantz Fanon is particularly relevant: "Fanon asks us to remember the violence of identification, the material practices of exclusion, alienation, appropriation, and domination that transform other subjects into subjected others. Identification is not only how we accede to power, it is also how we learn submission" (14). A fuller understanding of this model of conflicted identifications requires, I argue, a more nuanced psychoanalytic vocabulary of repression, disavowal, and erasure. In other words, the minority subject must, in the vein of the fetishist, simultaneously recognize and not recognize the material contradictions of institutionalized racism that claim his inclusion even as he is systemically excluded. This formulation provides a rich psychological model for evaluating the contemporary model minority stereotype (a project I undertake in chapter four).

In this respect, I am not interested in psychoanalysis as some urtext of universal human development, pure individual truth, or absolute descriptive reality. Instead, I am interested in the ways in which it might be creatively deployed to leverage a more thorough understanding of the psychic burdens and material costs imposed on the Asian American male subject who aspires to assimilate into mainstream society. What is psychically required of the Asian American male subject who desires to be part of the dominant mainstream society? How is the Asian American male subject encouraged or coerced to see himself in a social order governed by race and racism? How does he unconsciously or unwittingly contribute to the perpetuation of his already contested existence?

The circular conflict traced here between external and internal and material and psychic contradiction is not dissimilar to Althusser's description of ideology as representing "the imaginary relationship of individuals to their real conditions of existence," a theoretical elaboration of Marx's notion of the ways in which estranged labor is lived out subjectively as alienation and assimilation into ideals of the dominant class.[31] In "Ideology and Ideological State Apparatuses," Althusser points out that it is on the level of the "imaginary," in the sense of both the psychological and the fictional, that the contradictions between the psychic and material are alternately negotiated, denied, and managed. Thus, for example, the ideology of American liberal pluralism posits an analogical identification between the individual and the democratic state. In light of American rhetoric of equality and freedom, questions of systematic exclusion are especially inadmissible, albeit widespread in all aspects of American political, economic, and cultural life. As we see through our discussions of the Marginal Man, the identifications of the particular, marked individual with the abstract national universal body require a continual, repressed recognition of difference and exclusion. While the formation of the minority Asian American subject takes place on the material terrain of disparate social relations, the processes through which the marked Asian American male subject is interpellated and stitched into the national fabric are sustained through the register of an imaginary whose force of seduction and lure of fantasy create a fiction of identification as seamless equivalence. This fiction of identification, Lowe points out in *Immigrant Acts,* "reveals and sutures the gap in the lived misidentification of difference as the same, [and] is responsible for the production of universalities, harmonies, and gratifications" (151).

While the *Aiiieeeee!* editors, the Sues, and Lowe all acknowledge the ways in which psychoanalytic theories of identification, and misidentification, might help us understand the ways in which Asian Americans live out imaginary relationships of equivalence to the otherwise unbearable contradictions of their everyday material lives, none of these critics pursues the development of a sustained psychoanalytic model. While the rhetoric of equality in American representational democracy suggests that all individuals, despite their particular circumstances and material situations, have equal access to political, economic, and cultural representation, the degree to which differential inequities continue to exist, particularly for the racially marked populations to whom that notion holds out the promise of national membership, is especially prevalent.

The color line, as W. E. B. Du Bois predicted at the turn of the last century, endures as the national predicament of this century.[32]

More work needs to be done in the field of Asian American studies in particular and ethnic studies in general to elaborate and specify the imaginary aspects of racial identification, the ways in which the more immaterial, invisible, or unconscious effects of racism are internalized by the minority subject as a social system of self-regulation and self-domination. *Racial Castration* takes up this project by isolating, in the key Asian American texts it analyzes, specific moments of lived (mis)identifications in which the fantasy of abstract equivalence breaks down and disintegrates for the Asian American male subject. Moreover, considering Asian American male subjectivity not only in relation to gender and (homo)sexuality but also in terms of black and white racial and sexual ideals helps us to triangulate what is admittedly still a national landscape of Manichean race relations. This analysis of the racialization of Asian Americans—a group alternately seen as the most foreign, racialized, and unassimilable in the era of exclusion (the myth of yellow peril) and the most invisible, colorless, and compliant in the post-1965 era (the model minority myth)—in the greater landscape of American race relations remains crucial. Such an investigation provides a better understanding of the Constitution and the continual project of U.S. nation building on the uneven liberal capitalist terrain of a sexually and racially diverse society.

Impossible Origins

Psychoanalysis provides us with a compelling theory with which to explore how marginal subjectivities are constituted across lines dividing outside from inside, abstract from particular, group from individual, and public from private. It allows us to explore, as Homi Bhabha observes, what is private in the public and what is public in the private.[33] This idea underscores a notion evident in our discussion of the Marginal Man: the individual subject can never be a fully autonomous or private "I." The I, in other words, is the result of hybrid mixing. Like Bhabha, Maxine Hong Kingston's narrator in *The Woman Warrior: Memoirs of a Girlhood among Ghosts* also points to the impossibility of fully separating what is private and particular from what is public and intrinsic to society at large. "Chinese-Americans, when you try to understand what things in you are Chinese," Kingston's narrator asks in a famous passage, "how do you separate what is peculiar to childhood, to poverty, to insanities, one family, your mother who marked your growing with stories, from what is Chinese? What is Chinese tradition and what is the movies?"[34] The quest for pure origins—for an unpolluted vision of Chinese tradition—compels Kingston's narrator to question the dream of authenticity, the impossible quest for a pure self.

Taken together, Bhabha and Kingston underscore the impossibility of purity for the individual subject. The clear understanding, then, that Asian American male subjectivity is the hybrid result of internalized ideals and lived material contradictions that were once external allows us a compelling qualification to historical debates about authenticity—realness and fakeness—in Asian American studies. Moreover, it forces us to make an explicit distinction between subjectivity and agency in Asian American politics. While questions of subjectivity preoccupy the theoretical project of psychoanalysis, the identity politics of race are historically more "thoroughly examined in terms of domination and agency rather than subjectivity." [35] They have, in other words, been predominantly motivated by questions of domination and agency as well as autonomy and self-will.

Our psychoanalytic discussions about the impossibility of purist subject positions warn us that the quest for a self-willed—an autonomous and transparent—subjectivity is an illusory goal. "Why on earth should we be on that impossible ahistorical quest for purist positions, that's about as non-materialist as could be," Gayatri Spivak contends: "Isn't it autonomy that is suspect?" [36] We must understand, in other words, that the subject is not the agent, that the two are never fully in alignment, and that the notion of a pure political agency is itself questionable. "If we persist in reductively defining black subjectivity as political agency," Claudia Tate suggests in *Psychoanalysis and Black Novels*, "we will continue to overlook the force of desire in black texts as well as in the lives of African Americans" (10). Departing from Tate, I might add that if we persist in reductively defining a "progressive" Asian American male subjectivity as pure political agency we will continue to overlook the vexing question of conflicted and stranded identifications in both Asian American politics and movements for social justice.

From a psychoanalytic point of view, the distinction between the subject and the agent might be usefully rethought of as the gap between identification and identity. In *Group Psychology and the Analysis of the Ego* (1921), Freud suggests that collective political action pivots on the individual's ties to the social group. To the extent that social groups are constituted through identifications between their individual members, through psychic bonds formed by the perception of common interests, ideas, and values, identification is a prerequisite for political action. Yet, as Fuss warns, our social "identity is continually compromised, imperiled, and one might even say *embarrassed* by identification" (10; Fuss's emphasis). Our psychic identifications, in other words, never quite align with our political or politicized identities.

In Asian American political struggles it is thus crucial that we do not conflate our conflicted identifications with our desired identities. To understand this distinction—to understand that identification is the mechanism through which dominant histories and memories often become internalized as our own—is to understand that we are all borrowers and thus not pure. It is to underscore that our social identities as well as our political intentions are not irreproachable, that political agency while a necessary goal must be continually interrogated for its slippages, thought of more as a variable process than a permanent position. To acknowledge that our identifications come from elsewhere—from overlapping and opposing communities—is to understand that our seemingly voluntary and self-willed political agendas are sometimes misaligned, compromised, or curtailed. As the subject can never be aligned with the agent, so, too, identity and identification never quite meet. All identifications are inevitably failed identifications, a continual passing as a coherent and stable social identity. Even the most orthodox of subject positions, finally, are ambivalent and porous.

To espouse such an understanding of subjectivity and agency, identification and identity, is not to place the politics of Asian American identity in the discourse of fracture—the discourse of injury and victimization that compels, as Wendy Brown points out, the identity politics of race and *ressentiment* in the late twentieth century.[37] Equally important, it is not to place the politics of Asian American identity in opposition to poststructuralist theory. Rather, it is to think of the two fields in a dialectic tension. Too often debates in social sciences and humanities assume the position that scholars in ethnic studies desire to recuperate a naive notion of wholeness and a pure ethnic identity that has been suppressed by mainstream racism. These debates often configure scholars in poststructuralist theory as having moved beyond this naive position to deconstruct the constructed notions of a pure and whole identity.[38] Put another way, the latter is all about abstraction and philosophical questions of being while the former is about a materiality based in transparent notions of experience. To cast the debate in these terms is to ignore the significant work of past and present Asian American activists and critics, in both the humanities and the social sciences, who have theorized the question of the autonomy of the subject in relation to abstract conditions and material concerns. It is also to place entirely at the doorstep of ethnic studies questions of purity, wholeness, and self-will. Let us remember that these concepts also trace their genealogy to discourses of universalism, Enlightenment theories, and the legacies of abstract liberal humanism that impose the burden of authenticity and essentialism upon racialized subjects even as they exclude and erase them.

To espouse an understanding of the distinction between subjectivity and agency, between identification and identity, is to understand structures of domination that inform and constrain our ability to act politically. We need to transpose this useful distinction to rethink not merely the limitations of our political agency but also the new political possibilities that this knowledge generates for the Asian American movement. At the very least, an understanding of the decentered subject allows us to interrogate the exclusionary mechanisms of our own identitarian claims.

To approach for a moment this issue from the point of view of queer studies, let us turn to Judith Butler's *Bodies That Matter*. As Butler writes of queer activism's desire to resignify a term of shame and degradation against its constitutive history of injury,

> if the genealogical critique of the subject is the interrogation of those constitutive and exclusionary relations of power through which contemporary discursive resources are formed, then it follows that the critique of the queer subject is crucial to the continuing *democratization* of queer politics. As much as identity terms must be used, as much as "outness" is to be affirmed, these same notions must become subject to a critique of the exclusionary operations of their own production: For whom is outness a historically available and affordable option? Is there an unmarked class character to the demand for universal "outness"? Who is represented by *which* use of the term, and who is excluded? For whom does the term present an impossible conflict between racial, ethnic, or religious affiliation and sexual politics? What kind of policies are enabled by what kinds of usages, and which are backgrounded or erased from view? In this sense, the genealogical critique of the queer subject will be central to queer politics to the extent that it constitutes a self-critical dimension within activism, a persistent reminder to take the time to consider the exclusionary force of one of activism's most treasured contemporary premises. (227; Butler's emphasis)

How might we appropriate the premises of poststructural theory not to oppose and deconstruct but to strengthen and democratize the community we claim under the label "Asian American"? As we must examine the ways in which a resignified and affirmative view of queerness presents "an impossible conflict between racial, ethnic, or religious affiliation and sexual politics," those of us working in Asian American studies must also consider the consequential operations of our own exclusions. As vital a term as "Asian American" has become in affirming a necessary political identity in the late twentieth century, it is imperative that we continue to examine the difficult definitions and tenuous coalitions of Asian American identity—the ways in which it is constructed and self-constructed, the ways in which it circulates and is sustained. If we cannot construct a political platform exclusively around the notion of a pure Asian American "I," we must adopt other strategies of community building, projects based on goals and participation, on becoming, rather than on exclusive notions of being. As the interrogation of the queer subject reveals a set of impossible identity conflicts relating to race, the interrogation of the Asian American subject, I have been arguing, reveals a set of impossible identity conflicts relating to gender and (homo)sexuality. What other exclusions might we interrogate?

Here we are back on the sticky terrain with which I began this introduction: the vexed crossing of sexual and racial difference in *M. Butterfly*. We must think of the political necessities for claiming Asian American identity. At the same time, we must also consider responsible methods of bringing together Asian American studies and psychoanalytic (and poststructuralist) theory to examine the ways in which their dialectic combination might yield a strengthened rather than a diminished sense of Asian American identity and community as well as Asian American coalitions and movements for social transformation. I do not think, in other words, that psychoanalytic theory and Asian American studies need to be thought of as mutually exclusive or opposed. In this sense, my specific focus in this book on psychoanalysis and the intersections of racial and sexual difference that form our conceptions of Asian American male subjectivity might be thought of as one particular study meant to open these larger and more pressing questions.

Managing Masculinity in Asian America

Racial Castration is a project at once descriptive and political: descriptive because it presents through psychoanalytic theory a method of analyzing the ways in which Asian American male subjectivity is formed, circulated, and sustained; and political because it is with this understanding that we are able both to reformulate and to transform the conditions under which we claim our identities and communities. In this manner, *Racial Castration* takes seriously the fact that we are both objects and subjects of racism, that we both manage and are managed by our masculinity. In other words, while we are continually subjected to institutional structures of material and psychic domination, we can also assert our rights as racialized subjects to contest and to alter these significant conditions.

The book is divided into four subsequent chapters and an epilogue. Chapters one through four focus on particular historical events or ruptures—the building of the transcontinental railroad, the internment of Japanese Americans during World War II, the era of cold war diplomacy, and the rescinding of immigration exclusion and the liberalization of immigration policy from 1943 to 1965—that have worked to shape a mainstream perception of the Asian American male as what Frank Chin derisively calls the "emasculated sissy." These chapters dialectically pair canonical and noncanonical Asian American texts focused on masculinity with several traditional psychoanalytic paradigms: photography and the dreamwork, the mirror stage and the primal scene, fetishism and the signification of the phallus, and male hysteria. Throughout *Racial Castration*, I pay particular attention to the influential status of the image and the ways in which visual representations significantly constitute our sense of everyday reality. In our current age of technology, these images and representations assume a ubiquitous power in their now global dissemination and speed. This project insists that psychoanalytic theory can teach us useful methods of reading to understand and to contest the ideologies of the dominant image-repertoire.

In this sense, I am less interested in the new historicist approach to psychoanalysis that reads its theoretical discourse as an anthropological chapbook on colonialism. Rather, I am interested in analyzing, deconstructing, and revising several major psychoanalytic paradigms in order to proffer some productive ways to read the intersection of race and racialization with gender and (homo)sexuality. If these Asian American literary texts seem to call for a psychoanalytic frame of reference, I suggest, they simultaneously demand a revision of psychoanalytic theory along very altered lines of racial difference. As such, I isolate not only textual moments in which the Asian American male subject is coerced and held to certain (de)idealized sexual and racial identifications but also instances when these identifications fail or threaten to break down. Collectively, then, these chapters trace the psychic methods as well as the material practices with which we attempt to manage, misremember, or forget historical events configuring Asian American male subjectivity in ways that challenge the exceptionalist American ideology of liberty, its rhetoric of abstract equivalence, and its convictions of integration and inclusion.

Chapter one, "I've Been (Re)Working on the Railroad: Photography and National History in *China Men* and *Donald Duk*," begins with an exploration of the relationship among Asian American masculinity, the photograph, and history. Pairing Maxine Hong Kingston and Frank Chin, two authors who initially seem to be unlikely critical bedfellows, I argue that both writers rework dominant narratives of national history through an emphatic shifting of the visual image. Photography's "reality effect," its status as transparent historical record and "truth," is insistently challenged. In *China Men* and *Donald Duk*, both Kingston and Chin critique the now infamous 10 May 1869 photograph taken at Promontory Summit, Utah. Commonly referred to as the "Golden Spike Ceremony," this photograph depicts the joining of the Central Pacific and the Union Pacific Railroads, often described as this nation's greatest technological feat of the nineteenth century. While more than ten thousand Chinese American male laborers were exploited in the building of the western portion of the Central Pacific track, not one appears in the photograph commemorating its completion.

For both Kingston and Chin, the irony of their visual project is this: there are no pictures of their railroad ancestors to be seen; "there is no record of how many died building the railroad."[39] Seeking a historical narrative for these men—fighting for those images that would "threaten to disappear irretrievably"—thus entails for Kingston and Chin radical new methods of looking.[40] Focusing on memory and the dreamwork— on the unconscious aspects of looking—Kingston and Chin teach us how to resist what Lacan terms "the given-to-be-seen" of the visual order so as to see something else: a history, an image, a historical reflection of Chinese America that should not be regarded as lost to itself. In its attention to the status of the visual image and history, chapter one not only begins, as it were, at the beginning of Asian American literary studies with a critical reading that brings together the matriarch and patriarch of Asian American literature; it also establishes a particular structure of vigilant looking that continues to be developed through the remainder of the chapters.

Chapter two, "Primal Scenes: Queer Childhood in 'The Shoyu Kid,'" explores the identificatory limits in Lonny Kaneko's short story of Japanese American male subjectivity during wartime internment. As opposed to the invisibility of the Chinese laborer during the nineteenth-century railroad building project, this chapter explores the hypervisibility of the Japanese American body during World War II. The need to fix and repeat hypervisible images of disloyal Japanese Americans—what Homi Bhabha describes as the paralyzing fixity of the stereotype—during World War II underwrote a national project in which media representations played an increasingly ascendant role. The lives of these Japanese American internees (two-thirds of whom were American citizens),

nominally recognized as citizens yet dispossessed of constitutional free-
doms and personal property, find their specular correlation in the inability of the Japanese American male to find or create a jubilant image
of self with which to identify.

Kaneko's short story follows the lives of four young Japanese American boys interned in the Minidoka concentration camp, one of whom—
the Shoyu Kid—is molested by a camp guard. The story is obsessed with
the psychic effects and seductions that normative white male heterosexual images exert upon the sexual and racial identifications of these
young boys. Ultimately, "The Shoyu Kid" presents a dense psychological commentary on these Japanese American boys' inability to maintain a coherent ego and thus a stable image of self. Their frustrated
attempts to change "face," to mimic and incorporate psychically those
idealized male images of "heterosexuality" and "whiteness" to which
they pay such great obeisance, resolutely fail. These images remain stubbornly exterior to them. Chapter two analyzes two fundamental mechanisms of psychic identification within the visual domain: Lacan's mirror
stage and Freud's primal scene. Placing these theories in critical dialogue, I analyze Itchy's witnessing of the Shoyu Kid's molestation by
a white soldier as a "sodomitical" primal scene. This reconfigured primal scene is one that ultimately encloses these young boys not within
a normative and jubilant identification with heterosexuality and whiteness but within a profoundly negative identification with homosexuality
and Japaneseness. This is a historical condition that clearly results in, to
return to the vocabulary of the *Aiiieeeee!* school, destructive feelings of
"self-contempt, self-rejection, and disintegration."

Chapter three, "Heterosexuality in the Face of Whiteness: Divided
Belief in *M. Butterfly*," the play by David Henry Hwang with which
we began our discussion, shifts its focus from the formation of Asian
American male subjectivity to consider the limits of conventional white
male heterosexuality during the era of cold war diplomacy. The chapter investigates how symbolic norms of whiteness and heterosexuality
coerce the material and psychic allegiance of Gallimard, the white male
diplomat from France, to these impossible paternal ideals. Analyzing
these patriarchal norms—what Lacan describes as the "Name-of-the-
Father"[41] in his essay on the signification of the phallus—in relation to
Gallimard's utter failure to approximate them discloses the inability of
even the most conventional of white male subjects to align securely their
identifications with their desired identities.

Hwang's drama ultimately exposes the production of whiteness as
a universal norm that attempts to project the burden of racial difference onto the Asian American male body. Moreover, it reveals how

this production of an unmarked and invisible whiteness is achieved only through its complicit intersection with a system of compulsory heterosexuality. Focusing on fetishism—perhaps Freud's most privileged visual mechanism for the management of sexual difference—I refigure this psychic category in terms of a racial castration, one demanding serious reconsideration of Freud's psychoanalytic paradigm along the lines of race. In the process, it becomes clear that Gallimard's appropriation of the fetish is meant to protect the integrity of heterosexuality and whiteness. Ultimately, the diplomat's failed attempt to arrest the trauma of (hetero)sexual difference commemorates the unsuccessful management of racial difference as well.

Chapter four, "Male Hysteria—Real and Imagined—in *Eat a Bowl of Tea* and *Pangs of Love*," delivers what is conventionally viewed as a female malady to the doorstep of the Asian American male. Given the long and formidable history of female hysteria, contemporary critics have been at a loss to account for a theory of male, or for that matter racial, hysteria. However, even the most cursory glance at Louis Chu's *Eat a Bowl of Tea* and David Wong Louie's short stories in *Pangs of Love* suggests the need to account for their male characters' recurring physical impotence through this locus of psychic trauma. How might we explain the shift of hysterical symptoms from the female body to the Chinese American male body? How might we explain the recurrence of Asian American male hysteria across two historical periods—the post–World War II late 1940s and the multicultural 1980s—before and after the easing of immigration exclusion, before and after desegregation and the civil rights movements, before and after the rise of the "model minority" stereotype, before and after the renewal of Chinatowns as dying bachelor communities?

Collectively these questions raise issues of sickness and health in relation to Asian American assimilation. As the state legally transforms the Asian alien into the Asian American citizen, it institutionalizes the disavowal of its history of racialized exploitation and exclusion through the promise of freedom, abstract equality, and inclusion in the nation-state. Placing illness and dis-ease, then, in the context of Asian American immigration, assimilation, and racialization opens up new ways of considering not only the limits of a teleological narrative of American progress but also the limits of Asian American male subjectivity in the age of citizenship and multiculturalism. Reworking Freud's theory of hysteria across lines of sexual and racial difference, this chapter considers the ways in which Asian American male subjectivity remains haunted by the enduring regulations of ghostly racial and sexual norms.

The epilogue, "Out Here and Over There: Queerness and Diaspora in Asian American Studies," shifts the book's emphasis from the domestic to the diasporic. In the process, it serves to bring the project of Asian American cultural politics to new locations outside the immediate borders of the U.S. nation-state. The psychoanalytic readings I undertake in the four previous chapters focus largely on stereotypical representations and images of a feminized and emasculated Asian American masculinity within the domestic borders of the United States. However, the question of how queerness and diaspora impact new formations of Asian American identity must be explored in our increasingly transnational era of global capitalism. Might Asian American identity be considered more appropriate to diasporic discourses of exile and emergence than domestic ideals of immigration and settlement?[42]

Beginning with a historical analysis of Asian American cultural nationalism's claiming of the domestic landscape through naturalized structures of compulsory heterosexuality, I argue for a new pairing of queerness and diaspora in a globalized age. Through a reading of queer diasporic immigrants in Ang Lee's *The Wedding Banquet* and R. Zamora Linmark's *Rolling the R's*, I suggest that the popular presumption in both Asian American and American studies that our intrinsic fields of inquiry are necessarily grounded in one location—limited to the domestic space of the United States—merits reconsideration through the lens of a more spatially and sexually encompassing theoretical framing. How might we theorize queerness and diaspora against a historical legacy that has unrelentingly configured Asian Americans as exterior or pathological to the U.S. nation-state? How might queerness and diaspora provide a critical methodology for a more adequate understanding of Asian American racial and sexual formation as it is shaped in the space between the domestic and the diasporic? What enduring roles do nations and nationalism play in the delineation of such a critical project? What new forms of community, identities, and representations emerge through a diasporic and queer challenge to the linking of home and the nation-state in an age of globalized sexual and racial formation?

Examining literature, drama, film, and other representations of Asian American masculinity, *Racial Castration* takes seriously the relationship between cultural production and the nation's political landscape. That is, it takes seriously the intimate connection between aesthetics and politics. Precisely because culture in our postmodern era of what Fredric Jameson has called "late capitalism" has been especially burdened with managing the contradictions of the nation-state, it is often on the terrain of culture that discrepancies between the individual and the state, politics and economics, and the material and the imaginary are resolved or, alternately, exposed.[43] The distance at which Asian American cul-

tural production is often positioned from the national culture constitutes it as an alternative location for political formation and resistance,
with Asian American male subjectivity as an especially contradictory
identity within discourses of national citizenry. Rather than constituting
a "failed" integration of Asians into the American political, economic,
or cultural spheres, this distance preserves the creative works of Asian
America as an alternative site where, as Lowe suggests, "the palimpsest
of lost memories is reinvented, histories are fractured and retraced, and
the unlike varieties of silence emerge into articulacy" (*Immigrant Acts,*
6). Thus, we begin our critical excavation of Asian American cultural
politics, a psychoanalytic project in which race and sexuality are integral and integrated, challenging and deconstructing the assumptions of
Being Oriental.

ONE

I've Been (Re)Working on the Railroad:
Photography and National History in
China Men and *Donald Duk*

The replicants are perfect "skin jobs," they look like
humans, they talk like them, they even have feelings and
emotions. . . . What they lack is a history. For that they have to be
killed. Seeking a history, fighting for it, they search for their
origins, for that time before themselves. Rachel succeeds.
She has a document—as we know, the foundation of
history. Her document is a photograph.

GIULIANA BRUNO, "Ramble City:
Postmodernism and *Blade Runner*"

Ah Goong does not appear in railroad photographs.

MAXINE HONG KINGSTON, *China Men*

Reviewers of Maxine Hong Kingston's *China Men* (1980) and Frank
Chin's *Donald Duk* (1991) typically point out the authors' attempts to
challenge and rework dominant historical narratives that exclude Chinese American men.[1] David Leiwei Li, for instance, notes that "Kingston

has unfolded in *China Men* more than a century of Chinese American experience and constituted an oppositional voice to official American history."[2] Commenting on the "satisfying" resolution of *Donald Duk*, Tom De Haven writes in a review of Chin's novel that "Donald and his pal Arnold Azalea . . . storm back into history class and fortified with documentary evidence, set the record straight. Better late than never."[3]

Indeed, by giving "voice" and visibility to generations of unrecognized Chinese American laborers who worked on the construction of the transcontinental railroad, on the sugar plantations of Hawai'i, in the canneries of Alaska, and in the laundries and restaurants of America's Chinatowns, *China Men* and *Donald Duk* collectively dispute the popular notion of democratic membership underpinning discourses of American exceptionalism.[4] Kingston's and Chin's focus on the disavowed, repressed, and invisible histories of Chinese American men from the mid–nineteenth century to the present day insistently critiques the striking contradiction between the U.S. nation-state's economic need to recruit cheap and exploitable Chinese immigrant labor and its political refusal to enfranchise these racialized laborers as citizens—to recognize them as "proper" subjects of the nation-state.[5] While I am certainly in agreement with these critical assessments of Kingston's and Chin's literary projects, in this chapter I focus on a thematic issue that has gone largely unremarked in the commentaries generated by these authors: that is, their efforts to rework dominant history through an emphatic shifting of the visual image.

In *China Men* and *Donald Duk*, photography's "reality effect"—its status as transparent historical record and "truth"—is insistently challenged. Both Kingston and Chin critique the now infamous 10 May 1869 photograph taken at Promontory Summit, Utah (fig. 2).[6] Commonly known as the "Golden Spike Ceremony," this photograph depicts the joining of the Central Pacific and Union Pacific railroads, often described as the nation's greatest technological feat of the nineteenth century. While more than ten thousand Chinese American male laborers were exploited for the building of the western portion of Central Pacific track, not one appears in the photograph commemorating its completion.

Roland Barthes tells us in *Camera Lucida* that history is constituted "only if we look at it."[7] The past, Walter Benjamin earlier observed, is "seized only as an image that flashes up at the instant when it can be recognized and is never seen again."[8] Yet for Kingston and Chin the irony of their situation is this: there are no pictures of their railroad ancestors to be seen; "there is no record of how many died building the railroad."[9] Like the replicants of the film *Blade Runner*, these Chinese American

Figure 2 The greatest technological feat of the nineteenth century: the "Golden Spike" ceremony, Promontory Summit, Utah, 10 May 1869 (photo by C. R. Savage; Union Pacific Museum)

male laborers lack official documentation—a history of visible images—a lack that threatens to consign their existence to oblivion. Seeking a history for these men—fighting for those images that would "threaten to disappear irretrievably"—thus entails for Kingston and Chin radical new methods of looking.[10]

This chapter begins with a discussion of writings by early and contemporary critics of photography. Collectively, these writings question the photograph's impulse toward a mimetic realism and historical truth. This chapter explores how Kingston and Chin resolutely work against notions of mimetic realism so as to look awry at what the visible image would have us most readily apprehend. That is, they train us to look askew at what Lacan labels as the "given-to-be-seen" of the visual domain and what Homi Bhabha describes as the paralyzing fixity of the stereotype. Focusing on personal memories and the dreamwork—on the *unconscious* aspects of looking—Kingston and Chin teach us how to resist both the given-to-be-seen and the stereotype in order to see something else: an image, a history, a reflection of Chinese America that should not be regarded as lost to itself.

A Mimetic Ideology of Realism

Whatever it grants to vision and whatever its manner,
a photograph is always invisible: it is not it that we see.

ROLAND BARTHES, *Camera Lucida*

Early critics of photography describe its departure from other mediums of art—its singularity as a "realist" form—in terms of unprecedented technological mastery over the visual domain. "Originality in photography as distinct from originality in painting," André Bazin writes in 1945 in *What Is Cinema?* "lies in the essentially objective character of photography."[11] Unlike painting, which depends upon the presence and literal hand of the artist, Bazin asserts, photography's uniqueness lies in the fact that for "the first time, between the originating object and its reproduction there intervenes only the instrumentality of a nonliving agent"—the mechanical apparatus of the camera (13).

Bazin thus attributes to photography a certain ontological status, arguing that the photograph "affects us like a phenomenon in nature, like a flower or a snowflake whose vegetable or earthly origins are an inseparable part of their beauty" (13). Bazin claims a privileged, essential connection between the photograph and the object it depicts, a phenomenal relationship he describes as sharing "a common being, after the fashion of a fingerprint" (15). This evidential quality of the photograph as fingerprint leads Bazin to insist that the viewer of a snapshot must necessarily "accept as real the existence of the object reproduced" (13).

Writing more than thirty years later in *Camera Lucida*, Roland Barthes also draws an analogy between photography and evidence, likening the photograph to a "certificate of presence" (87) and the photographer's show to that of a "police investigation" (85). He contends that the difficulty of penetrating beyond the photograph's connection with the "real" lies in the seductive allure of its evidential force. Barthes observes that "in the Photograph the power of authentication exceeds the power of representation" (89) and describes it as a literal "emanation of the referent," suggesting that the photograph serves as an "umbilical cord link[ing] the body of the photographed thing to my gaze" (81).

In a 1985 essay entitled "Photography and Fetish," Christian Metz elaborates upon this phenomenological aspect of the photographic image, invoking a metaphor of surgical penetration.[12] Metz describes the relationship between the photograph and the object it depicts as "a cut inside the referent" (158), as an incision and subsequent abduction of a piece of the real. Metz thus reprises Walter Benjamin's suggestive comparison of the photographer with the surgeon in "The Work of Art in the Age of Mechanical Reproduction." While "the painter maintains in his work a natural distance from reality," Benjamin writes in this famous 1936 essay, "the cameraman penetrates deeply into its web."[13]

I offer this quick theoretical survey of photography as evidence and the photograph as "a cut inside the referent" in order to illustrate a brief critical history of photography's impulse toward what Eduardo Cadava describes as a "mimetic ideology of realism."[14] This ideology underwrites the popular belief that the photographic image comes about only by seizing upon a piece of the real. The singularity of photography thus lies in the perception that it is a medium in which the distance between the referent and its signifier is collapsed. This is a medium, in other words, in which the boundary separating representation and "reality" blurs.

Deconstructing the Photograph

Early in *Camera Lucida*, Barthes describes the joining of signifier and referent in photography as a process of lamination: "The Photograph belongs to that class of laminated objects whose two leaves cannot be separated without destroying them both" (6). Barthes emphasizes throughout *Camera Lucida* the inseparable quality of these two laminated leaves: of the photograph and the real. We might note, however, that by describing this lamination process as a fatal one in which the two leaves of image and object cannot be "separated without destroying them both," he also offers us a way of deconstructing the photograph's mimetic impulse toward reality. The lamination process, Barthes insists, enacts an inevitable destruction of the image and object, which ultimately encourages us to think of the photograph not as an ontological incision into the real but as a representation of the real.[15] How might we deconstruct photography's reality impulse both temporally and spatially?

Temporally, we must keep in mind, the photographic image is secured only by arresting the object in time. If the photograph captures a piece of the real it does so only by freezing and fixing the object in a moment irretrievably past. The successful lamination of image and object, Barthes reminds us, is the joining together of two leaves that finally presupposes the untimely destruction of the referent. Barthes describes this temporal event as a kind of improper death: "For the photograph's immobility is somehow the result of a perverse confusion between two concepts: the Real and the Live: by attesting that the object has been real, the photograph surreptitiously induces belief that it is alive, because of that delusion which makes us attribute to Reality an absolutely superior, somehow eternal value; but by shifting this reality to the past ('this-has-been'), the photograph suggests that it is already dead" (79). If "reality" implies an eternal, interminable, present, the temporal "this-has-been" aspect of the photograph tells us that reality is no longer with us, that the real—the live—of the photograph is impossible, that it has slipped away and is no longer. Barthes labels this process the "mortifying effect" of photography, suggesting that the abduction of the object by the camera lens—its memorialization through the representational frame of the photographic image—results not in its final capture but in its ultimate loss.

Rather than faithfully and perfectly giving the viewer the moment it depicts, the photographic image thus presents the "posthumous character of our lived experience."[16] Thus, we might consider the two leaves of Barthes's lamination process not just as the joining together of signifier and referent but temporally as the instantaneous capture and destruction of the referent. It is this simultaneous, paradoxical preservation and annihilation of the object through its photographic memorialization that leads Barthes to declare photography a "bizarre *medium*," one that negotiates between two phases of time, and a "mad image, chafed by reality" (115; Barthes's emphasis). According to Barthes, to believe in the reality of a photo is finally to buy into a type of "temporal hallucination," for "whatever it grants to vision and whatever its manner, a photograph is always invisible: it is not it that we see" (6).

Not only does the temporal convergence of the "past this-has-been" with the present reality of liveness at the site of the photographic image work to confuse the status of the medium as decisively representational, but the mimetic allure of the photograph also involves a spatial misrecognition as well. It is important for us to remember that the "reality effect" of the photographic scene that unfolds before our eyes depends on the collapse of a three-dimensional object into a two-dimensional plane. In this regard, Barthes's lamination metaphor also suggests the flattening of the three-dimensional space of reality into the two-dimensional space of representation. Lamination thus becomes a progressive attempt to close the gap between these two domains by searing them together. While lamination suggests the spatial convergence of object and image, this process is finally an impossible project. The two leaves of signifier and referent exist in parallel universes. As closely aligned as they might be in the photograph, there will always remain a space between image and object that can never be entirely eliminated.

Furthermore, as viewers of the photograph, we, too, must establish a certain distance from it in order to apprehend its contents. It is crucial to note that the reality of the scene that unfolds before our eyes in the photograph depends, like cinema, upon our stereoscopic vision being aligned with the monocular camera lens. Theorists of the cinema describe this process of joining (and flattening out) as "suture."[17] Elaborating upon the viewer's identification with the perspective of the camera lens, Kaja Silverman observes that the "camera designates the point from which the spectacle is rendered intelligible, [and] the maintenance of perspectival illusion is assumed to depend on a smooth meshing of the spectator with that apparatus."[18] An unconscious identification with the filmic apparatus, in other words, positions the viewer in an ideal spatial location from which the contents of the photograph can then, and only then, be mastered. To apprehend—to "get"—the picture, the spectator must necessarily occupy what in the eleventh seminar Lacan calls a pregiven "geometral point," that location designated by the lens of the camera from which a photograph's contents are most easily perceived.[19] And, as many critics of the visual image have observed, photography's geometral point—the one given over most readily to the photograph's mimetic ideology of realism—is based upon the laws of Renaissance perspective and the optical tenets of the Cartesian *cogito*.[20]

Theorists of suture in film repeatedly point out the viewing pleasure afforded to the subject who identifies with the camera lens.[21] By unconsciously occupying the camera's pregiven geometral point of view, this stitching together—this lamination—of the human and mechanical eye, the subject gains illusory control over the field of vision. Primary identification with the camera lens, and with the reality it depicts, thus places the spectator in a pleasurable but dependent relationship with the apparatus. Hence, the reality of the visible field that seems to appear effortlessly before the spectator's eyes is only possible through the subjugation of the human eye to the camera lens. Epistemological mastery over the field of vision lies not intrinsically within the capacity of this eye but only in the eye's unconscious alignment with and subjection to the photographic apparatus as its functionary. In this respect, the geometral point of the photograph determines the spatial positioning that the spectator must necessarily occupy as much as any personal point of view that the spectator might bring to the visual image. Photography's impulse toward a mimetic ideology of realism consequently demands from the viewer a particular concession, a particular self-placement, and a particular geometral point of view—one given in advance, more determining *of* the spectator than determined *by* the spectator.

Earlier in this discussion, I set the words *reality* and *real* in quotation marks, for what our critique of the photograph's mimetic ideology of realism shows is that, far from being an absolute phenomenon directly accessible to an all-seeing Cartesian subject, reality is a process properly belonging to the realm of representation and perception. In the photographic apparatus, our apprehension of reality lies not intrinsically within our selves—in an all-powerful I/eye—but externally in a social relation between this I/eye and the placement of the camera lens. Hence, the ideal geometral point from which we perceive reality is not merely a physical but an ideological positioning. How does the imperative to see the world from a particular temporal, spatial, *and* ideological location— to accept its reality from a particular *social* point of view—intersect with the domain of history?

The Given-to-Be-Seen

More urgently than other early theorists of the visual image, Siegfried Kracauer and Walter Benjamin challenge us to think about the ways in which photography functions as both a system of representation and a network of material practices. Observing that the rise of modern photography and the academic discipline of history coincide with the ascension of capitalism, Kracauer notes that photographic and historical reality are both a means of alienation for the masses.[22] He writes in *History: Last Things before the Last* that one "may define the area of historical reality, like that of photographic reality, as an anteroom area. Both realities are of a kind which does not lend itself to being dealt with in a definite way. . . . They share their inherently provisional character with the material they record, explore and penetrate."[23] Together, photography and history are implicated in their mutual task of creating an entire temporal and spatial course of events meant to sustain the prevailing political beliefs of the time. "Historicism," Kracauer writes, "is concerned with the photography of time."[24]

Elaborating upon the erroneous ways in which photography underwrites a privileged historical narrative of capitalism and fascism, Benjamin warns us that there "is no document of civilization which is not at the same time a document of barbarism" ("Theses," 256). While "nothing that has ever happened should be regarded as lost for history" (254), Benjamin laments, the "true picture of the past flits by" (255). Historicism, the tool of the ruling class, invariably supports the historical narratives of the victor. To reformulate Kracauer's and Benjamin's concerns in terms closer to our present discussion: how might the pregiven geometral point from which a spectator ideally views a photograph exist not only as a spatial location but as an ideological point of view? How does the representational logic of the photograph intersect with the dominant historical conditions of its time?

To explore these issues, I suggest we turn to the *Four Fundamental Concepts of Psycho-Analysis,* in which Lacan delineates three categories: gaze, look, and screen.[25] In this eleventh seminar, Lacan insistently separates the look from the gaze, placing the latter on the side of Otherness and unapprehensibility while attributing the former to the human eye, to the activity of seeing, to desire, to memory, and to lack (83). Like language, the gaze not only exceeds all human subjectivity but it provides the imaginary camera click necessary for the conferral of that subjectivity. Lacan writes that "in the scopic field, the gaze is outside, I am looked at, that is to say, I am a picture. . . . What determines me, at the most profound level, in the visible, is the gaze that is outside. It is through the gaze that I enter light and it is from the gaze that I receive its effects. Hence it comes about that the gaze is the instrument through which light is embodied and through which—if you will allow me to use a word, as I often do, in a fragmented form—I am *photo-graphed*" (106; Lacan's emphasis). Lacan suggests that it is the function of the gaze to put me in the "picture." It is through the imaginary click of the camera that I am not only "photo-graphed" and symbolically ratified as a subject but also given a particular set of specular coordinates through which I am constituted and apprehended as a social subject within the visible field.

While it is through the metaphor of the camera that Lacan most consistently delineates his concept of the gaze, he is quick to emphasize that the gaze or camera in and of itself does not determine how the subject will ultimately be seen, or what form he or she will assume as a picture within the field of the visible. The gaze or camera, in other words, determines neither how the subject will apprehend his or her reality nor under what material conditions. For this process, Lacan reserves the category of the screen—the field of representations and the image-repertoire of visual perceptions. Intervening between the human look and the gaze, the screen is comprised of ideologically marked and pregiven images through which the subject is captured as a picture within the visual domain. It is these pictures, from television, cinema, and print media, that permit subjects to assume their social—for example, racial, sexual, economic, and national—identities (97). If I am anything, Lacan insists, it is in the form of the screen.

Lacan goes on in this eleventh seminar to connect the images of the screen with a category he labels the "given-to-be-seen." The given-to-be-seen is that group of culturally sanctioned images against which subjects are typically held for their sense of identity (80). Like the spatial point of view from which a photograph's contents can most easily be viewed, the screen images of the given-to-be-seen provide the ideological point of view from which the spectators are encouraged to identify with those pregiven representations that would most easily accord with the dominant sociopolitical ethos of their time. (In our present era, the given-to-be-seen would most clearly be those visual images affirming the tenets of whiteness, heterosexuality, and liberal capitalism.) It is at the level of given-to-be-seen that our normative sense of reality is established.

The frozen images of the given-to-be-seen not only provide the mainstream viewer with a sense of identificatory pleasure and psychic stability over time, but they are also foundational to the formation of punitive and static stereotypes of the other. These mortifying images are what Homi Bhabha describes as one of the prevailing features of colonial discourse and an example of its "dependence on the concept of 'fixity' in the ideological construction of otherness." [26] Like Lacan and Bhabha, Barthes focuses on the collective power of these generalized images, concluding *Camera Lucida* with the observation that "'nowadays the images are livelier than the people.' One of the marks of our world is perhaps this reversal: we live according to a generalized image-repertoire" (118)—the laminated object, the given-to-be-seen, the stereotype. The fixity of these pictures—of the various representations comprising the given-to-be-seen—establishes reality by providing a dominant image-repertoire through which individuals are repeatedly encouraged over time and space to "see" not only themselves but others.

Since the given-to-be-seen from which the viewer most easily apprehends the image is based on a temporal and spatial hallucination, this perceived reality is always already overwritten by an ideological and a social positioning. Kaja Silverman warns us in *Male Subjectivity at the Margins* that it is crucial to "insist upon the ideological status of the screen by describing it as that culturally generated image or repertoire of images through which subjects are not only constituted, but differentiated in relation to class, race, sexuality, age, and nationality. The possibility of 'playing' with these images then assumes a critical importance, opening up as it does an arena for political contestation" (150). How might a spectator play with the images of the screen? How might the viewer contest the dominant historical view of the given-to-be-seen?

It is crucial to point out that the reality of the given-to-be-seen is neither inevitable nor inviolable. The given-to-be-seen is ultimately dependent upon collective affirmation of those images comprising it. Far from being absolute or static, the given-to-be-seen is finally dependent on widespread ratification of its repertoire of conventional images. Despite the normative allure of the given-to-be-seen, how might individual viewers withhold their visual sanctioning of its pregiven images? How, in other words, might the spectator look awry at the given-to-be-seen of the photograph, look away from the dominant historical narrative that it proffers to be validated? I turn to *China Men* and *Donald Duk* in order to investigate the methods by which Kingston and Chin teach us to resist a given-to-be-seen that would obliterate the existence of their Chinese immigrant ancestors.

China Men *and Cultural Vision*

The men posed bare-chested, their fists clenched,
showing off their arms and backs. The artists sketched them
as perfect young gods reclining against rocks, wise expressions on
their handsome noble-nosed faces, long torsos with lean stomachs,
a strong arm extended over a bent knee, long fingers holding a pipe,
a rope of hair over a wide shoulder. Other artists drew faeries with
antennae for eyebrows and brownies with elvish pigtails; they
danced in white socks and black slippers among
mushroom rings by moonlight.
MAXINE HONG KINGSTON, *China Men*

In an article focusing on photography in *China Men*, Carol E. Neubauer observes that it is through looking at the family photo album that Kingston "achieves a final synthesis that captures the *truth* of her family's immigration to and life in America."[27] While it is certainly the case that the author of *China Men* constantly turns to both personal and historical photographs as a source of creative provocation, far from giving Kingston the truth of her family's experience in America, these images present her with a stream of continual doubts: the photographs constantly display uncertainties about the visual reality they ostensibly portray.

For instance, Kingston writes about relatives in the United States and China whose exchanges of photographs and poses in front of the camera are meant to portray for the faraway viewer a certain type of reality: the scholar father who dons expensive suits and hats so as to present a false sense of affluence in America, one that belies his lowly status as laundry man (64); Mad Sao's mother and Ah Po in China, who send their emaciated snapshots (doctored by venal Communists?) as testimonies to their poverty so as to demand that hard currency be remitted at once (172, 249). Throughout *China Men*, Kingston presents us with a battery of visual images whose mimetic authority she continually challenges through her critical attention to the fixing of the pose. Once "I feel myself observed by the lens, everything changes," notes Barthes: "I constitute myself in the process of 'posing,' I instantaneously make another body for myself, I transform myself in advance into an image" (10).

Kingston not only questions the truth of the pose in personal photographs that are consciously manipulated to achieve a certain affect. She also notes how larger social differences—racial and sexual—often overdetermine the ways in which we are given-to-be-seen. In a chapter entitled "The Brother in Vietnam," she writes about an ophthalmology student, "an American of Japanese Ancestry," who is stationed on the brother's battleship. Surprisingly, this student of scientific vision does not espouse any absolute optical tenets; instead, he advocates a philosophy of visual relativity, one resolutely tied to racial difference. Speaking proudly of his epicanthic fold, he tells the narrator's brother that "ethnic Asians have a naturally faraway focus":

> "If we lived in Asia," he said, "where everything is arranged according to our eyesight, we wouldn't need glasses." Clarity was a matter of preference and culture. "Americans zone cities and make billboards for Caucasian eyes," he said. "Blackboards are set so many feet from the students' desks, traffic signals at such a size and distance, newspapers and books in a certain size type. If we AJA's [Americans of Japanese ancestry] with our epicanthic eyes and peculiar focus went back to Japan, we wouldn't need glasses any more." The brother had American 20–20 vision, but didn't notice things getting either blurrier or sharper in Taiwan. That eye doctor trainee was a crackpot. (294–95)

In his comments on the epicanthic fold of AJAS, the ophthalmology student's opinions may seem initially to veer toward an essentializing genetic determinism. Kingston, however, refuses to associate the student's "crackpot" views with any absolute biologism about Asians or Caucasians. The brother, who has American 20/20 vision, sees as clearly on one side of the Pacific as on the other. Here, perhaps, the category "Asian American" serves to resist the absolute division of cultures—Asian or American, East or West—calling attention to the mobility of cultures as well as the relational basis of the concept "20/20" itself.

Kingston thus places the crackpot student's theory of optics squarely within the realm of social construction—"Clarity was a matter of preference and culture"—as well as within the shifting spatial locales of Asia and America. Nevertheless, by pointing out how billboards, blackboards, traffic signals, newspapers, and books in the United States are made for Caucasian eyes this passage speaks to a given-to-be-seen that is racially motivated. It suggests that the dominant visual images created and manufactured in the United States are culturally targeted to white consumers, just as those in Asia are produced and marketed for the specific audiences there. The fact that the brother in Vietnam is able to see both sides clearly not only indicates the presence of multiple and conflicting bodies of images and ideologies but also points to his over-lapping identifications with them.

In addition, Kingston implies that our perception of "reality" not only depends on our racial backgrounds but on a deliberate material racism that underpins the visual domain itself. In an earlier interchapter entitled "The Wild Man of the Green Swamp," she reveals a given-to-be-seen that is motivated by virulent and willful racism. She writes of two "wild men"—one Chinese, the other black—who are described by the authorities as dangerous and insane. The Chinese wild man, who "terrorized" residents on the edge of Green Swamp, Florida, for eight months and "made strange noises," is at first not seen at all by the officers of the law but labeled a mass hallucination and thus rendered altogether absent from the visual domain (221). Upon his capture, the police discover that the strange noises are in fact Chinese and his burlap bag is neither a bag nor burlap but "a pair of pants with the legs knotted," (222). The wild man is merely a homesick sailor stuck on a Liberian freighter as low-wage transnational labor. When told by the U.S. Border Patrol that he will be sent back to China, he commits suicide.

Kingston describes his photograph as it appears in the tabloids: "In the newspaper picture he did not look very wild, being led by the posse out of the swamp. He did not look dirty, either. He wore a checkered shirt unbuttoned at the neck, where his white undershirt showed; his shirt was tucked into his pants; his hair was short. He was surrounded by men in cowboy hats. His fingers stretching open, his wrists pulling apart to the extent of the handcuffs, he lifted his head, his eyes screwed shut, and cried out" (223). The narrator's perception of the visual object of the "wild man" clearly diverges from the dominant picture of him painted by the authorities—his shipmates, the residents of Green Swamp, the fish and game wardens, the sheriff's deputies, the medical doctors and psychiatrists, and the Border Patrol. Collectively, their elaborate, fanci-ful, and alarming speculations contradict the mundane self-descriptions he offers to the authorities upon his apprehension: "He said that he was thirty-nine years old, the father of seven children who were in Taiwan. To support them, he had shipped out on a Liberian freighter" (222).

Here Kingston offers two incommensurate versions of reality. These opposing realities hinge upon a racist failure to read correctly certain cultural codes such as the Chinese language, a type of "reverse halluci-nation," a refusal to see what is obviously there to be seen.[28] Moreover, this misreading of the Chinese language extends beyond the immediate jurisdiction of the U.S. authorities to affect even distant homelands. The ultimate reason for the wild man's suicide is questionable. Perhaps his life as an illegal immigrant and fugitive in the Florida swamps drives him insane, or perhaps his death is the result of a poor translation. His family, he tells us, is after all in *Taiwan*. Yet twice the authorities insist that they will return him to *China*. Kingston suggests that this conflation of Taiwan and China as one and the same—a spatial version of "all Asians look alike"—leads to the Chinese man's vertiginous loss of self-control: "They had driven him to the airport, but there he began screaming and weeping and would not get on the plane. . . . He became hysterical. That night, he fastened his belt to the bars, wrapped it around his neck, and hung himself" (222–23). Indeed, something is always lost in translation.

Whatever the source of his "madness," this we know: the China man from Taiwan begins his quest for economic survival aboard a Liberian freighter and ends his life on the Gold Mountain as a "wild man," a barbarian, an escaped lunatic, a swamp dweller.[29] (That he was on a Liberian freighter is ironic. Liberia, established as an independent state in 1847, began as a settlement for freed American slaves, who continued to migrate there until the end of the American Civil War.) Looking at the newspaper picture, the narrator insists that the wild man "did not look very wild" at all. Kingston presents the unequivocal material consequences of these two opposing visual regimes: death. In this particular example, the Taiwanese sailor's literal demise is one that precedes the narrator's witnessing his capture and death within the celluloid frame of representation. For Kingston, the mortifying newspaper snapshot assumes an emphatic racial valence, an emphatic racial violence.

Kingston ends "The Wild Man of the Green Swamp" with a short paragraph that brings him closer to events at home: "There was a Wild Man in our slough, too, only he was a black man. He wore a shirt and no pants, and some mornings when we walked to school, we saw him asleep under the bridge. The police came and took him away. The newspaper said he was crazy; it said the police had been on the lookout for him for a long time, but we had seen him every day" (223). Again, there is a visual disjunction between what the narrator sees on a daily basis—a homeless man asleep under a bridge—and what the dominant eyes of the law and the newspaper are able or willing to perceive—a crazy and elusive fugitive. In these two examples of "wild men," racial difference becomes that privileged category through which a punitive visual reality is constituted. Far from being neutral, these pictures of the Chinese and black wild men assume the frozen immobility of the stereotype. That is, the images fix the ways in which these two minority fugitives will be apprehended and emasculated as less than men—both unable to wear pants—by the authorities in comparable ways. Once again, the black wild man's racialized reality has tangible and predictable effects. Like his Chinese counterpart, the homeless black man not only is deemed insane but also taken away and incarcerated by the police, his freedom and perhaps his life duly compromised through this visual ordering.

It is crucial to note that there is nothing absolute, inevitable, or intrinsic about the ways in which the dominant eyes of the law categorize these two men. Indeed, the punitive visual ordering that freezes and arranges both the authorities' and mainstream public's tarnished views of the Chinese and the black man is constructed through the arrangement of a number of arbitrary images and unrelated documents—police records, public testimonies, medical records, and newspaper stories, images, and captions—into a unified and naturalized totality. Collectively, these random images and documents are organized by a logic that attempts to form a coherent whole and to frame a fixed historical narrative. This organizing of disparate components into a narrative totality forms what Michel Foucault describes as the structure of the modern archive. The document, Foucault writes in *The Archaeology of Knowledge,*

> is no longer for history an inert material through which it tries to reconstitute what men have done or said, the events of which only the trace remains; history is now trying to define within the documentary material itself unities, totalities, series, relations. History must be detached from the image that satisfied it for so long, and through which it found its anthropological justification: that of an age-old collective consciousness that made use of material documents to refresh its memory; . . . history is one way in which a society recognizes and develops a mass of documentation with which it is inextricably linked.[30]

In bringing together a mass of unrelated documentation, the archive constructs a historical narrative—a historical alibi—that comes to assume the status of an inviolable statement. The very condition of possibility for this transformation of random material into an enunciative statement lies not in the intrinsic nature of its elements but in the method of its arrangement—that is, in the organizing of these elements into unities, totalities, series, and relations. "A series of signs," Foucault insists, "will become a statement on condition that it possesses 'something else' . . . a specific relation that concerns itself—and not its cause, or its elements" (89). The possibility of this reinscription and transcription, Foucault adds, lies not in the realm of ontology but in the order of material institutions (103).

What is strikingly clear, then, about the archive that is constructed around these two wild men is its relational arrangement through a particularized racial logic that finds its material expression in legal institutions such as the police, medical institutions such as the clinic, and social institutions such as the newspaper. If the archive does not merely record identities already in existence but rather creates them through a performative act of cataloging and camouflaging, then Kingston's example of these two men works to undo what hides beneath such naturalized manifestations. In the process, it exposes the racist logic through which cataloging and camouflaging are mobilized.

Throughout *China Men*, Kingston points out the cultural variables and material dangers underpinning the spectator's relationship to the discursive power of the dominant given-to-be-seen and the archive. However, she is not content with ascribing a wayward process of looking merely to racial difference. She also illustrates how sexual difference comes to affect the visual domain and the cataloging of its images. For example, in an interchapter entitled "On Mortality," Kingston writes of Tu Tzu-chun, who is given three white pills by a Taoist monk:

> "Swallow these," he said, pouring him a cup of wine. "All that you'll see and feel will be illusions. No matter what happens, don't speak; don't scream. Remember the saying 'Hide your broken arms in your sleeves.' "
>
> "How easy," said Tu as he swallowed the pills in three gulps of wine. "Why should I scream if I know they're illusions?" (119–20)

As Tu descends into the various levels of hell, he is presented with horrifying visual images: decapitations, the torturing of his wife, and even his own bodily dismemberment. Throughout the ordeal, he neither speaks nor screams, reminding himself that what he sees as the reality before him is only a hallucinatory illusion.

As his journey through hell continues, Tu is reborn as a deaf-mute female. It is at this point in his journey that his perception of the same illusory images he had earlier viewed as a male suddenly changes. Married to a man who tires of his silence, Tu is threatened by the husband, who demands that he speak. Threatening to dash their child's head against the rocks, the husband picks up the infant and swings:

> Tu shouted out, "Oh! Oh!"—and he was back with the Taoist, who sadly told him that at the moment when she had said, "Oh! Oh!" the Taoist was about to complete the last step in making the elixir

for immortality. Now that Tu had broken his silence, the formula was spoiled, no immortality for the human race. "You overcame joy and sorrow, anger, fear, and evil desire, but not love," said the Taoist, and went on his way. (121)

As a female, Tu's perception of visual reality and illusion are reversed. Finding the vision of his child being killed too cruel and all too real, Tu protests with a short "Oh! Oh!" and thus condemns the human race to death. The ostensible moral of the traditional Chinese fable upon which "On Mortality" is based blames the female sex for the loss of immortality. It configures woman as the weaker sex due to her inability to maintain silence. However, as King-Kok Cheung points out, for "a mother to scream at the wounding of her child is hardly a weakness . . . [for] the maternal anxiety [Tu] experiences attests to the superiority of human love over the abnegation of [male] emotion."[31] As such, not only is the visual reality and superiority of Tu's male world questioned from an alternative female viewing position but the relational logic of the dominant patriarchal norms and mores underpinning this gendered order are exposed, critiqued, and rendered illusory from Tu's female perspective.

While Kingston emphasizes that racial and sexual difference greatly influence the ways in which the viewing subject perceives reality, she also stresses in the examples of the ophthalmology student, the wild men, and Tu Tzu-chun that it is possible to look awry at the given-to-be-seen each time one apprehends its visual images. It is possible, as Foucault writes, that "each discourse contains the power to say something other than what it actually says" (118). For instance, even though the "brother in Vietnam" thinks the relativizing optical philosophy of the ophthalmology student is crackpot, his own relationship to a group of photographs presented before his departure for the Vietnam War belies a constant visual flux that defies any stable notion of reality. Showing to his five classes the slides of a former student who is now fighting in the Vietnamese jungles, the brother can neither understand nor reconcile how the horror he experienced upon his first viewing of these images — "puff of orange smoke . . . row of tanks . . . and shit-colored helicopters" — can give way to visions of happiness and contentment upon later viewings of the same photographs: "The third of fourth time around, the pictures seemed very happy, very attractive: Alfredo, grown, not lonely, almost married to a large and happy leopard-skinned wife. The sun shining orange in their cottage. Smoking an after-dinner cigarette while children played at his feet. Children laughing around his head, all their faces catching the light. Many friends, compadres. In winter Alfredo had jungles, not leafless trees in concrete. Even the prisoner was smiling.

A lovely day. Sunshine and palm trees. The old woman held up half a potato and laughed" (282).

The very orange puffs of artillery fire that horrify the brother in his initial examination of Alfredo's snapshots become brilliant orange sunsets in his third and fourth viewings, a serene Asian landscape unsullied by the ravages of modernization, Western neo-imperialism, and military conflict. The sullen Vietnamese prisoner of war inexplicably becomes a jolly comrade, an amiable native informant and cultural tour guide. Terrorized children amid a heinous military invasion become kids laughing and playing at the feet of American GIS, a veritable "Kodak moment."

What Kingston illustrates through these various examples are the shifting realities that the viewer of the photograph invariably detects — perhaps desires to detect — every time he or she looks at the visual image. In *China Men*, racial and sexual differences serve to position Kingston's spectators in a dissonant relationship with a dominant society's given-to-be-seen. In each instance, however, these various spectator's looks and personal points of view also oppose through their visual wanderings what would pass as pregiven reality. This errancy of the human look, in other words, equips the spectator with the capacity to view with suspicion what the dominant society would proffer as real. What allows the human look to wander in such a manner?

Unreliable Memory and the Given-to-Be-Seen

In a chapter entitled "The Making of More Americans," Kingston describes an "uncle, a second or third cousin maybe, who went back to China to be a Communist" (189). Uncle Bun—whose name could be a pun in Chinese, meaning "Uncle Stupid"—is extremely talkative and quick to point out that not only do "white demons" oppress Chinese immigrants in the United States, but also "upper-class Chinese made their money off lower-class ones" in Republican China (192). Through his critical views of American as well as Chinese society, Uncle Stupid (as he is sometime called by his relatives) clearly stands outside the conventional point of view of both the Western free market system and the eastern "feudal" order.

Uncle Bun's unorthodox views extend beyond the realm of politics and economics. Suspicious of the nutritive value of "white" foods— eggs, bread, milk, vanilla ice cream, flour, sugar, and white beans—all of which he believes to be poisonous, Uncle Bun eats only wheat germ (that brown embryo of the wheat kernel used as a concentrated source of vitamins before it is polished into the artificial whiteness of flour).

He espouses its digestive merits and even connects its salubrious qualities to communism, a somewhat comical linking of the corporeal body with the body politic ("Amazing! His two big ideas—wheat germ and Communism—connected" [194]).

Kingston's vignette leaves us with a serious lesson in the ramifications of moving away from the dominant given-to-be-seen—Uncle Bun's "stupid" resistance to and departure from the dominant political views of American as well as Chinese society. Considered mad by his relatives, he is ostracized by his own immigrant community, prevented from entering their houses, and more often than not ignored by their children. Furthermore, he is under suspicion by authorities of the Immigration and Naturalization Service for supporting Red China.

From her own liminal point of view, Kingston's narrator remains uncertain about Uncle Bun's insanity, pointing out the virtues of his unconventional political beliefs and his decision to return to China: "He talked about how he was using only a part of his money for passage and giving the rest to new China. If they were suspicious of his years in America and did not let him in, he would sneak in from Hong Kong" (200). As thousands of Chinese refugees flee the Communist regime by escaping into Hong Kong and Taiwan, Uncle Bun makes the opposite journey back to mainland China, challenging again the Western anticommunist political sentiments of the time.

It is crucial to note that Kingston's narrator connects Uncle Bun's unconventional politics with the notion of a questionable return to China: "'Returning' is not to say that he necessarily had ever been there before" (200). This return is not only an uncertain physical journey back to a mainland China no longer the same, a China under Communist not Republican rule; it is also an uncertain psychic journey whose final destination is punctuated by the unreliability of personal memory. "The day he left," Kingston writes of Uncle Bun,

> he spoke to my youngest sister, who was about three years old. He bent over so that she could hear and see him very well. "Don't forget me, will you?" he asked. "Remember I used to play with you. Remember I'm the man who sang songs to you and gave you dimes. What's my name?" She laughed that he would ask her such a silly, easy question. Of course, she knew his name. He coaxed her to say it several times for him. "You won't forget? Tell me you won't forget."
>
> "I won't forget," she said. He seemed satisfied to leave, and we never saw him or heard from him again.
>
> For a while I reminded my sister, "Do you remember Uncle

Bun, the bald fat man who talked a lot? Do you remember him asking you not to forget him?"

"Oh, yes, the funny man, I remember."

I reminded her periodically. But one day, I noticed that I had not asked her for some time. "Do you remember the funny man who talked a lot, the one who smuggled himself into Red China?"

"Who?" she asked.

"Uncle Bun. Remember?"

"No," she said. (200–1)

With this closing "no," the narrator not only marks her younger sister's faulty memory of Uncle Bun but simultaneously ends her own uneven recollection of the uncle "who went back to China to be a Communist." By concluding her reminiscence of Uncle Bun—alternately described as the funny, bald, and fat man—on this note of unreliability, Kingston thus connects his unorthodox political views with a certain errancy of personal memory.

Uncle Bun's unusual return to China provides a larger lesson in how to read the visual images of *China Men.* To stand in a position outside conventional society's given-to-be-seen necessarily entails a certain lapse of memory, an acceptance of its unreliability, an embracing of its wayward impulses. In *Camera Lucida,* Barthes writes about the "punctum," the unconscious prick, of a photographic detail—a dirty fingernail, a necklace, a shoe—that punctures and bruises the "studium," that visual quality of the photograph that is invested not only with the obviousness of dominant cultural codes (the given-to-be-seen) but with "sovereign consciousness" (26–27). The studium, Silverman explains, might be thought of as the result of a contract between "the creators and consumers of culture to perpetuate those 'myths' which are synonymous with normative representation."[32] The studium, in other words, is what we see when we apprehend the world through a particular image-repertoire and from a position that is given in advance, the given-to-be-seen.

In *Camera Lucida,* Barthes ultimately associates the punctum not with the detail itself but with memory (42). He concludes that the punctum activates unconscious aspects of personal memory that allow him to resist the cultural normativity of the studium. In this manner, the punctum grants him a second look at the photograph (53), a type of visual alterity that allows him to detect what is marginal and insignificant to others but personally meaningful to himself. In a passage of radical cultural prelapsarianism, Barthes insists that under the sway of the punctum "I am a primitive, a child—or a maniac; I dismiss all knowledge, all culture, I refuse to inherit anything from another eye than my own" (51). The punctum pricks Barthes and transports him elsewhere in the picture, dislodging him from the traditional viewing position of the studium—of the given-to-be-seen—and placing him in a new relationship with the visual images before him. The punctum thus unfreezes the mortifying moment of the photographic image, releasing the viewer into the present tense of memory.

Like Barthes, Kracauer elaborates upon the ways in which personal memory stands in opposition to the historical project of photography. As he writes in his essay "Photography":

> *Memory* encompasses neither the entire spatial appearance nor the entire temporal course of an event. Compared to photography memory's records are full of gaps. . . . Memories are retained because of their significance for that person. Thus they are organized according to a principle that is essentially different from the organizing principle of photography. Photography grasps what is given as a spatial (or temporal) continuum; memory-images retain what is given only insofar as it has significance. Since what is significant is not reducible to either merely spatial or merely temporal terms, memory-images are at odds with photographic representation.[33]

In their particular significance for each individual, personal memories provide an oppositional force to the master narrative that historical images of the given-to-be-seen attempt to create, fix, and impose on a society. Indeed, if photography works to dominate the spatial or temporal perception of an object through an ideological master narrative, personal memory works to restore the occluded contours of that object's "history" that this narrative would efface.[34]

Barthes's description of the punctum—of the unconscious prick and second look it engenders—as well as Kracauer's analysis of history and photography provide a useful commentary on Kingston's view of personal memory as it structures her narrator's permutating remembrances of Uncle Bun. It is only by allowing memories to wander, Kingston insists, that traditional views can be displaced. To be pricked by the unconscious reservoirs of memory gives rise to the creation of new psychic pathways whose final destinations "return" the viewing subject not to an old location or a conventional point of view but to someplace new— be it a new China or a new political positioning. It is in this way that we must understand Kingston's lesson of psychic return as not necessarily bringing us to a place where we have been before.

The errant and unpredictable quality of personal memories leads

Barthes to insist in *Camera Lucida* that the photograph is "never, in essence, a memory (whose grammatical expression would be the perfect tense, whereas the tense of the Photograph is the aorist), but it actually blocks memory, quickly becomes a counter-memory" (91). Expanding upon the temporal discrepancy that emerges between the past tense of the photographic image and the present tense of memory as it emerges from the domain of the preconscious, Silverman adds that whereas "photography performs its memorial function by lifting an object out of time and immortalizing it forever in a particular form, memory is all about temporality and change. It apprehends the other less as a clearly delineated object than as a complex and constantly shifting conglomeration of images and values" (*Threshold,* 157). Working under contravening impulses to photography's project of historical reality, memory's errant wanderings not only provide a means of moving away from the fixity of the given-to-be-seen, and the fixity of the stereotype, but also help us to apprehend reality in ways that cannot be predicted in advance.

In *The Threshold of the Visible World,* Silverman points out the fundamental tenet of psychoanalysis that every memory involves a simultaneous impulse to return to as well as depart from a particular phantasmic scene or object. "The potentially productive uses to which memory can be put reside not in the imperative to return, but, on the contrary, in the interlocking imperative to displace," she writes. "Because the backward path ostensibly leading to gratification is blocked, as Freud puts it in *Beyond the Pleasure Principle,* we have no choice but to move forward; repression dictates that the desired object can only be recovered or 'remembered' in the guise of a substitute. There can thus be no return or recollection which is not at the same time a displacement, and which consequently does not introduce alterity. The productively remembering look is one in which the imperative to displace has come to supersede the imperative to return" (181). Because the psychoanalytic conditions under which a subject remembers prohibits any final recovery of either a phantasmic scene or an object, the faithful return demanded by the given-to-be-seen to one particular viewing position—to the fixity of the stereotype—becomes an impossible psychic journey. As a consequence, each return to the given-to-be-seen is an approximation of—or a displacement from—an "original" point of view. In this sense, the given-to-be-seen, like the stereotype, is not just underpinned by fixity and stasis but is undermined by a profound psychic ambivalence and instability. The stereotype, Bhabha reminds us, "connotes rigidity and an unchanging order as well as disorder, degeneracy and daemonic repetition.... [It] is a form of knowledge and identification that vacillates between what is always 'in place,' already known, and something that must be anxiously repeated" (*Location of Culture*, 66). Vacillating between fixity and infidelity, the viewer's faithful return to the given-to-be-seen is in no way guaranteed. Memory's psychic return, in other words, can bring us to a place where we have never been before.

If memory in this psychoanalytic sense is inherently unreliable and unstable, this constraint need not be seen in a negative light. Silverman proposes that the truly productive look is one that maximizes memory's impulse to displace, allowing personal recollections continually to overwrite and reconfigure a subject's relation to the stereotypical images of the given-to-be-seen. Moving out of a dominant viewing position necessarily requires that memory's imperative to displace has come to supersede the imperative to return to an original object, scene, or way of looking. Consequently, Silverman concludes, the productive look is one "in which the movement forward is no longer at the service of a return, but has developed an independent momentum" (*Threshold*, 181). In other words, the productive look remains continually open to the independent wanderings of memory and thus resistant to the absolute tyranny of those visual limitations of the given-to-be-seen that would determine how and what the spectator would apprehend from a pregiven point of view.

Throughout *China Men*, Kingston displays the potential uses of memory's wanderings through a vertiginous doubling of titles, myths, legends, and laws that do not return us to an original narrative or image but bring us to a place where we have never been before.[35] By offering two (and sometime three) versions of every story she presents—for example, the twelve interchapter myth stories, the numerous possible ways in which "the father from China" entered the United States (49, 237), and the beating episode of the two sisters at the hands of BaBa (253)—Kingston highlights an emphatic departure from the "original." This departure is even grammatically relevant to the book's title. David Leiwei Li points out that the original epithet "Chinaman Chink" was used to insult Chinese male laborers in America from the late nineteenth century (484). Kingston's departure from—and revision of—this term comes in the form of a pluralization and a space between the two words *China* and *Men*. By opening this space between *China* and *Men*, she unlocks the term for potential resignification. That is, she acknowledges in her unfaithful repetition of the epithet both its punitive history and the possibility of viewing it from alternative perspectives neither entirely constrained nor completely given in advance by its prior historical meanings.

Kingston's emphasis on the productive uses of memory finds its most powerful potential for opposition in its resistance to those widely circulated visual images that would attempt to portray one particular historical reality. However, she is careful to warn us throughout *China Men* of the difficulties of moving into an alternate viewing position. The material consequences involved in looking awry at the given-to-be-seen are often deadly. Before we turn to her critique of the Promontory Summit photograph, let us briefly examine her interchapter on "The Ghostmate" in order to elaborate upon the material costs of moving outside the parameters of the visually normative.

Vanitas and Death

In her rewriting of "The Ghostmate," a traditional Chinese folktale, Kingston illustrates the difficulty encountered by the marginalized Chinese male subject in attempting to occupy not only the dominant given-to-be-seen but a viewing position outside of it. In this version, Kingston recounts the tale of a wandering scholar, farmer, or artisan who encounters on his return journey to his village a beautiful noblewoman. A widow, she invites him into her splendid house, feeding and entertaining the young fellow for what seems to him to be only a short period of time. When the young scholar finally takes leave of his gracious host and resumes his travel toward his home, his "appearance startles the townspeople" (80), who flee from him in terror.

The wandering scholar is no longer youthful but sick and haggard looking: death warmed over. Encountering a fellow villager, who mentions his long absence, they return to the site of the noblewoman's house:

> He remembers a beautiful lady he met in a previous incarnation or a dream last night.
>
> The closer he comes to where the house had been, the more the home village becomes the dream. "Look," says his friend. "A grave."
>
> Where a front door stood is the marker for the noblewoman's grave. The rain and wind have not quite rubbed the dates and the strange emblems off. She has been dead for years, centuries.
>
> Fear burns along the young man's spine, and he runs from the lonely spot where no paths meander, no house looms, no peacocks or dogs stalk among the lilac trees. His friend dashes after him, not to be left by himself at the grave. (81)

Kingston's closing line of this interchapter—"Fancy lovers never last"—points to the illusory quality of the young man's lavish days spent with the noblewoman ghost whom he remembers as a beautiful lady met "in a previous incarnation or a dream last night." (It also functions as an allegory for the initial illusory and then soured love affair that Ed, the "Father from China," has with the United States.) Yet, as the scholar re-approaches the noblewoman's house with his fellow villager, his home village also becomes a dream. Hence, Kingston suggests, both realities—his village life as well as his days with the noblewomen—are over-determined by an illusory force. Both visual positions prove mutually problematic. In which reality, then, should the young scholar invest his belief?

In the *Four Fundamental Concepts of Psycho-analysis*, Lacan concludes his chapter "Anamorphosis" by discussing a 1533 Hans Holbein painting entitled *The Ambassadors*. He observes that Holbein encodes in *The Ambassadors* two points of view: a traditional geometral point based on Renaissance perspective, depicting the two ambassadors of the painting's title, and an anamorphic point of view outside the given-to-be-seen, depicting a skull.[36] Lacan indicates that the traditional viewing position from which one apprehends the two ambassadors is based on *"vanitas"* and misrecognition. Caught in the perspectival space of the given-to-be-seen, the viewing subject cannot construe the meaning of the anamorphic image. It is only when looking at the painting from the far edges of the picture frame—looking at it anamorphically—that the viewing subject is dislodged from traditional perspectival space and can thus encounter death in the form of the skull.

Commenting upon Lacan's discussion of the Holbein painting, Silverman writes in *The Threshold of the Visible World* that "the painting also provides a model both for understanding normative vision, and for imagining how it might be possible to see in a way which is not entirely given in advance. It shows that the same image can look very different depending upon the vantage-point from which is it observed. . . . *The Ambassadors* thus suggests that the geometral point is only one site from which to apprehend the image—or, by extension, the cultural screen—and that the screen can appear very different depending upon where one 'stands'" (177–78). While Lacan analyzes Holbein's skull as an example of symbolic castration, Silverman discusses this same image as teaching us that a normative viewing position is not inevitable. To state the case from a slightly different perspective, the anamorphic viewing position designates a position apart from the dominance of the geometral point. It marks a viewing position from which the same representational field may be apprehended from another angle and from which something other may be seen. But what are the material constraints under which subjects can move from one viewing position to another?

Kingston's example of "The Ghostmate" suggests the extreme material difficulty of occupying either a normative or an anamorphic viewing position. When the young man is apart from dominant reality and in the splendid home of the noblewoman, he sees the world as vibrant, beautiful, and alive. Yet this anamorphic viewing position outside the given-to-be-seen is an illusion that proves not merely unsustainable in the larger society but ultimately damaging to the well-being of the young man himself. On the other hand, when the wandering scholar returns to a traditional viewing position the world is dull and mundane. Death and a gravestone replace the beauty of his earlier illusion.

While Holbein's painting equates the dominant viewing position with the misrecognized splendor and vanitas of European imperialism and an anamorphic viewing position with death, Kingston proposes in "The Ghostmate" the opposite scenario. Only when he is outside a normative viewing perspective does the young man experience the beauty of the world. Upon his eventual return to reality and village life all the scholar sees around him is overwritten by a gravestone and dis-ease. Kingston's reversal points to a certain untenability of existence for the Chinese male subject both inside and outside the given-to-be-seen.

This untenability of existence becomes especially relevant when it is recontextualized in terms of the Chinese American male immigrant in the United States. Throughout *China Men,* Kingston repeatedly describes Chinese immigrant men—from the father from China to the wild man of the Green Swamp, to Uncle Bun—who are altogether unable to sustain a comfortable relationship with a dominant American point of view that excludes them. This is a punitive visual and material ordering that constitutes them as madmen. As such, they cannot be seen as proper members of the nation-state—a state that nevertheless is eager to exploit their noncitizen labor on the railroads, sugar plantations, and farms and in canneries, laundries, and restaurants. Disempowered to move outside this punitive ordering, their lives are constrained by the material violence of a visual regime that threatens both their psychic and bodily existence.

Let us turn now to Kingston's elaborate description of her grandfather in "The Grandfather of the Sierra Nevada Mountains," perhaps the "maddest" of all her forefathers. In this chapter, Kingston provides an extended and detailed exploration of the most charged historical image of Chinese American absence: the exclusion of Chinese American laborers from the Golden Spike ceremony that marked the joining of the Union Pacific and the Central Pacific Railroads.

A Materialism of Absence

There are no visual records, Kingston tells us, of the ten thousand Chinese male laborers who built the transcontinental railroad; "there is no record of how many died" (138), risking life and limb by blasting through the Sierra Nevada Mountains while enduring Arctic-like winters living in the tunnels they excavated—self-made graves. In "The Grandfather of the Sierra Nevada Mountains," Kingston emphatically states that "Ah Goong does not appear in railroad photographs" (145). She thus provides a terse and immediate corrective to the infamous 1869 photograph of "The Big Four" robber barons—Huntington, Hopkins, Stanford, and Crocker—who are depicted hammering in the Golden Spike.[37]

Ah Goong knows that the railroad he is building "would not lead him to his family" (129). Because of American exclusion laws against immigration, naturalization, miscegenation, and citizenship, the railroad he is building will not bridge the distance that separates Ah Goong from his family in a distant land. The capitalist American economy, Yen Le Espiritu writes, "wanted Asian male workers but not their families. To ensure greater profitability from immigrants' labor and to decrease the cost of reproduction—the expense of housing, feeding, clothing, and educating the workers' dependents—employers often excluded 'nonproductive' family members such as women and children."[38] The China man is not needed for his reproductive but for his labor power. His presence is not intended to populate the barren landscape of the Wild West with Chinese families but to build the national economic infrastructure supporting westward expansion. Indeed, the joining of the Union Pacific and the Central Pacific Railroads to form the first U.S. transcontinental railroad marked not only the fulfillment of westward expansion but the achievement of the doctrine of Manifest Destiny. It made the journey across the country—and thus settlement from coast to coast—far easier than it had been before.

It is important to note, however, that while Manifest Destiny required the actual movement of the white population westward—the "civilizing" mission of westward expansion—it would not have been possible without the concomitant movement of goods and the racialized labor of immigrants. Historian Sucheng Chan reports that the conditions under which Chinese railroad laborers toiled were particularly harsh. She notes that "six days a week, the Chinese toiled from sunrise to sundown, while subject to whipping by overseers and forbidden by the company to quit their jobs."[39] In *Strangers from a Different Shore*, Ronald Takaki tells the terrible story of the winter of 1866 when Central Pacific managers, determined to accelerate construction, forced Chinese laborers to work in the bitter cold: "The snowdrifts, over sixty feet in height, covered construction operations. The Chinese workers lived and worked in tunnels under the snow, with shafts to give them air and lanterns to light the way. Snowslides occasionally buried camps and crews; in the spring, workers found the thawing corpses, still upright, their cold hands gripping shovels and picks and their mouths twisted in frozen terror."[40]

The development of industrial capitalism and the shoring up of a nationalist racial project of westward expansion were not merely ends achieved through the completion of the transcontinental railroad. Indeed, capitalism and racism were intertwined as a means, becoming a self-perpetuating cycle so that the success of industrial capitalism—typified by the labor practices of the Big Four robber barons—depended on the abuse of cheap and flexible labor that was *racialized*. The Big Four racialized their labor force through wage differentials, paying white laborers more than nonwhites for identical (if not easier) work. Sucheng Chan notes that during the building of the transcontinental railroad Chinese workers received 30 dollars a month without board, compared to unskilled European American workers, who received 30 dollars a month with board, which was worth approximately 75 cents to a dollar a day (*Asian Americans,* 81). These wages were paid regardless of which tasks the workers performed or how many hours they worked. Takaki cites similar statistics, stating that Chinese workers were paid $31 dollars a month for their labor. According to Takaki, had the Central Pacific Railroad Company "used white workers it would have had to pay them the same wages plus board and lodging, which would have increased labor costs by one third" (85).

Hence, these examples serve as historical illustrations of the ways in which American industry refined capitalist practices in the nineteenth century through the racialization of its labor forces. Lowe writes in *Immigrant Acts* that "in the history of the United States, capital has maximized its profits not through rendering labor 'abstract' but precisely through the social productions of 'difference,' of restrictive particularity and illegitimacy marked by race, nation, geographical origins, and gender. The law of value has operated, instead, by creating, preserving, and reproducing the specifically racialized and gendered character of labor power. These processes of differentiation have provided the means for capital to exploit through the fracturing and segmentation of different sectors of the labor force" (27–28). It is important to emphasize, then, that the historical division of labor into white and nonwhite racialized groups in the nineteenth century first required a new codification of white ethnic groups. For instance, many laborers on the eastern portion of the Union Pacific track were Irish immigrants. Their incorporation into "whiteness"—from which they had consistently and often violently been barred since their arrival in the United States—relied on a redefinition of the term.[41] For industrial capitalism, the extension of "whiteness" to include the Irish was useful because it effectively divided labor racially—making union organizing more difficult and the extraction of greater surplus value from workers possible.

Given these historical conditions, it is safe to say that Ah Goong not only recognizes that the railroad "he is building would not lead him to his family" (129) but that the narrative of industrial development that exploits the China man's labor will surely exclude and displace him from its historical achievements. Excluded from all official historical records, these Chinese American railroad laborers threaten to disappear irretrievably, as Roy Batty laments in the closing moments of *Blade Runner*, like "tears in rain." To articulate the past historically, Benjamin states, "means to seize hold of a memory as it flashes up at a moment of danger" ("Theses," 255). Recognizing, with Benjamin, that the "state of emergency" overshadowing her Chinese American ancestors is not the exception but the rule, Kingston relies upon personal memory to apprehend something other than that which is given-to-be-seen in the Promontory Summit photograph. This photograph thus provides a culminating occasion for the convergence of errant memory, a critique of a racially motivated given-to-be-seen, and the historical recuperation of this Chinese American visual absence.

If this particular return—to family and to history—is an impossible one, Kingston nevertheless makes us understand that it offers the possibility of bringing us elsewhere. During the construction of the Central Pacific, the Chinese workers strike for shorter hours and increased pay.[42] They attract the attention of newspaper editors, who send their artists up the Sierra Nevada mountains to record this daring event. Writing about the strike, which "began on Tuesday morning, June 25, 1867," Kingston not only points out the complicity of these newspaper artists, who render a certain view of the China male laborers into historical "reality," but she offers a different way of looking at this reality: "The men posed bare-chested, their fists clenched, showing off their arms and backs. The artists sketched them as perfect young gods reclining against rocks, wise expressions on their handsome noble-nosed faces, long torsos with lean stomachs, a strong arm extended over a bent knee, long fingers holding a pipe, a rope of hair over a wide shoulder. Other artists drew faeries with antennae for eyebrows and brownies with elvish pigtails; they danced in white socks and black slippers among mushroom rings by moonlight" (141–42). Here, Kingston's imaginings give over to two opposing portraits of Chinese American masculinity: young handsome gods or "elvish" faeries, feminized and emasculated. While some artists clearly sympathize with the plight of the China men, depicting their fight for economic justice through their visual rendering of "bare-chested, fists clenched . . . perfect young gods," those less sympathetic highlight the stereotyped characteristics of an orientalized Chineseness: "faeries with antennae for eyebrows and brownies with elvish pigtails."

Hence, the historical reality of the railroad strike can be as easily reframed into an image of valor as it can be configured as a picture of cravenness. Yet, because it is the latter historical image that dialectically endures, Kingston simultaneously warns that any visual image that would pretend to depict historical reality is always already written over by ideological content and value. Refusing to grant visual sanction to this image of cravenness, Ah Goong attempts to negotiate a punitive American image-repertoire by assimilating its masculine criteria: "Ah Goong acquired another idea that added to his reputation for craziness: The pale, thin Chinese scholars and the rich men fat like Buddhas were less beautiful, less manly than these brown muscular railroad men, of whom he was one. One of ten thousand heroes" (142). While Kingston provides through Ah Goong's visual recalcitrance a blueprint for shifting the given-to-be-seen, she is also careful to note how his dissonant point of view is met with resistance not only by white Americans but by his fellow Chinese laborers who equate his fanciful visual notions with insanity. Ah Goong's valorization of the Chinese laborers as "brown muscular railroad men" speaks to an alterior view not easily reconcilable with either the dominant visual regime of white Americans or traditional Chinese ways of seeing. Once again, we witness the extreme material difficulty of looking awry at culturally coded image-repertoires: Ah Goong precedes a long line of male progeny whose visual wanderings garner them the institutional and cultural label "madmen."

Kingston exposes the ideological content of the given-to-be-seen that depicts the Chinese American laborer as a demonic faerie. At the same time, she is careful to note the material circumstances that not only make it difficult for the Chinese laborer to oppose this punitive visual ordering but also threaten to obliterate his presence from railroad history entirely. Writing about the visual absence of China men from the Promontory Point photograph, Kingston attempts to seize their fleeting images at this moment of danger. She emphasizes the "driving out" that culminates in Ah Goong's erasure from the visual field:

The transcontinental railroad was finished. They Yippee'd like madmen. The white demon officials gave speeches. "The Greatest Feat of the Nineteenth Century," they said. "The Greatest Feat in the History of Mankind," they said. "Only Americans could have done it," they said, which is true. Even if Ah Goong had not spent half his gold on Citizenship Papers, he was an American for having built the railroad. A white demon in a top hat tap-tapped on the gold spike, and pulled it back out. Then one China Man held the real spike, the steel one, and another hammered it in.

While the demons posed for photographs, the China Men dispersed. It was dangerous to stay. The Driving Out had begun. Ah Goong does not appear in railroad photographs. (145)

Like stuntpeople in Hollywood action films, the China Men function as body doubles — performing hard labor — only to be replaced by a universalizing whiteness, the faces of the robber baron "stars": Huntington, Hopkins, Stanford, Crocker. Kingston's doubled contrast of the white demon's "tap-tapping" of the golden spike, which is then "pulled . . . back out," against the China Men's hammering in of the real steel spike underscores the splitting of the real from representation, of reality from the ways in which it is reconfigured in the laminating photograph that memorializes this event. Again, Kingston presents two different ways of viewing this event, two possible returns of memory to this famous photographic scene.

Focusing on the stunning contradiction between Ah Goong's economic exploitation and political disenfranchisement, Kingston insists that "even if Ah Goong had not spent half his gold on Citizenship Papers, he was an American for having built the railroad." Yet the explicit connection that Kingston makes between Ah Goong's economic exploitation for the "Greatest Feat of the Nineteenth Century . . . the Greatest Feat in the History of Mankind . . . [which] only Americans could have done" with his deserving political enfranchisement as a citizen is an impossible conjunction.[43] *American* emphatically does not include *Chinese,* as the China Men are driven out and their racialized labor is transformed into an abstracted whiteness — a catastrophe, as Benjamin would describe it, of progress. The driving out marks the China Man's visual absence from this historical archive — an absence mobilized precisely through the threat of his physical elimination:

Ah Goong would have liked a leisurely walk along the tracks to review his finished handiwork, or to walk east to see the rest of his new country. But instead, Driven Out, he slid down mountains, leapt across valleys and streams, crossed plains, hid sometimes with companions and often alone, and eluded bandits who would hold him up for his railroad pay and shoot him for practice as they shot Injuns and jackrabbits. . . . In China bandits did not normally kill people, the booty the main thing, but here the demons killed for fun and hate. They tied pigtails to horses and dragged china-men. (146)

A fugitive like the wild man of the Green Swamp, Ah Goong's method of survival is ensured only by his self-erasure, a mandate of invisibility. His self-erasure is necessary and inevitable not only to avoid further economic sanction but to evade racial antipathy—white demons who killed "for fun and hate." To reinsert the China Man's rightful place in the historical event culminating at Promontory Summit requires, then, the deferred envisioning of official history from a radically divergent perspective. It requires us to look "east," in other words, against a visual tide of westward expansion.

In *Immigrant Acts,* Lisa Lowe analyzes the U.S. nation-state's rapid industrial expansion from 1850 to World War II and its history of recruiting cheap Asian labor to meet the needs of development. According to Lowe, the contradiction between the needs of the economic sphere for cheap noncitizen labor and the refusal to recognize or enfranchise this labor in the political arena "was *sublated* through the legal exclusion and disenfranchisement of Chinese immigrant laborers" (13; Lowe's emphasis). This historical period of exclusion was a time when popular stereotypes of Chinese as unassimilable heathens, economic sojourners, and "yellow peril" prevailed. The abstraction and consolidation of the nation's citizenry as an imagined community of whiteness in the nineteenth century depended not only on the rhetoric of these injurious stereotypes; the relative success of the nation-state in negotiating the economic and political contradictions that arose from a racially diverse population also relied, as Kingston's story of Ah Goong illustrates, upon the strict management of the cultural terrain and visual apparatus. Kingston's story exemplifies how the contradiction between Ah Goong's economic exploitation and his political disenfranchisement as a full subject of a "democratic" nation-state is resolved visually through his erasure from the Promontory Summit photograph. The photograph functions, then, not just as a questionable historical image but as an ideological apparatus that attests to the ways in which contradictions among the political, economic, and cultural spheres are reconciled through the visual management and racialization of the figure of the China Man.

Ah Goong returns to China with his pittance of railroad pay and then goes back to San Francisco, where in typical fashion Kingston relates two different versions of his fate: "Some say he died falling into the cracking earth," while others claim that "the family went into debt to send for Ah Goong, who was . . . a homeless wanderer" (150). She qualifies these separate returns, however, stating that "maybe he hadn't died in San Francisco, it was just his papers that burned; it was just that his existence was outlawed by Chinese Exclusion Acts" (151). It is both fitting and ironic, then, that in "The Grandfather of the Sierra Nevada Mountains" Kingston concludes with a description of the earthquake and fire of 1906, which burned San Francisco's Hall of Records and all its "Citizenship Papers . . . Certificates of Return, Birth Certificates, Residency Certificates, passenger lists, Marriage Certificates—every paper a China Man wanted for citizenship and legality burned in that fire" (150; fig. 3). Like the elimination of a single term in a sign chain, the burning of the Hall of Records—the literal destruction of these particular documents— demands a subsequent shift in meaning, a shift in the relational terms that attempt to shore up the historical ruins of the archive. Hence, as a result of this fire, Kingston tells us, an "authentic citizen" had no more legal papers—no more claim on America—than an "alien," and every "China Man was reborn out of that fire a citizen" (150).

In Fae Myenne Ng's *Bone*, I would like to recall for a moment, it is a false identification paper, which Leila discovers in Leon's "suitcase of lies," that finally satisfies the skeptical authorities at the Social Security Agency. "Leon was right to save everything," Leila concludes. "For a paper son, paper is blood. . . . I'm a stepdaughter of a paper son and I've inherited this whole suitcase of lies. All of it is mine. All I have is those memories, and I want to remember them all."[44] Like the Chinese male laborer's visual absence in the Promontory Point photo, it is through this absence of "authentic" legal documentation that the exploited China Men could finally claim citizenship and their rightful place within a narrative of America and American history as "paper sons." A certificate of fiction, a dis-appearance, a type of absent presence, paper sons are overdetermined by the material conditions and visual images that would not have them. Yet, in turn, they force new meaning into national history as they create unexpected paths of affiliation and kinship for their progeny, like Leila, to remember, "to remember them all."

Figure 3 "It was just his papers that burned": "San Francisco, April 18, 1906," by Arnold Genthe (U.S. Library of Congress)

Donald Duk *and the Proper Name*

> The true picture of the past flits by. The past can be seized only
> as an image which flashes up at the instant when it can be recog-
> nized and is never seen again. . . . For every image of the past that is
> not recognized by the present as one of its own concerns
> threatens to disappear irretrievably.
>
> WALTER BENJAMIN,
> "Theses on the Philosophy of History"

> Donald Duk sleeps, dreams, wakes, panics through the books and
> pictures looking for Chinamen from out of the past.
>
> FRANK CHIN, *Donald Duk*

Like Maxine Hong Kingston, Frank Chin harbors strong suspicions
about the dominant images of the given-to-be-seen and the historical
reality they proffer to the viewer. In *Donald Duk,* Chin opposes the
truth value of those dominant visual images, which exclude Chinese
American men. He does so not only by resignifying the proper name
but by dislodging mainstream representations and offering up a new
set of images and points of view. Like Kingston, Chin relies upon the
errancies of memory to effect this linguistic and visual displacement.
In particular, Chin turns to Donald Duk's dreams—perhaps the psychoanalytic category most immediately connected to memory—in order to
conjure forth a collection of substitute images and meanings from the
domain of the young boy's unconscious.

Donald Duk begins with an extended meditation on the proper name
of its eponymous protagonist. Like Kingston's orthographic insertion of
a space between the epithet "Chinaman" and her pluralized *China Men,*
Chin's omission of the letter *c* in Donald Duk's surname marks an infidelity to the original Walt Disney icon, Donald Duck—an immediate
connection between the shifting of language and the shifting of image.
Chin's adulterated citation of the proper name endeavors not only to
undercut the authenticity and symbolic power of this immensely famous icon of American popular culture; it also highlights the possibility
of going to a place we have never been in the larger cultural imaginary
and national screen. Put in slightly different terms, Chin's orthographic
displacement effects not a faithful return to but an unfaithful departure
from the conventional meanings typically associated with Walt Disney's
Americana. Chin attempts to resignify this powerful American icon to
include the figure of the Chinese American boy, to accommodate, that
is, an affirmative vision of racial difference within the influential image-
repertoire of American popular culture.

Throughout *Donald Duk*, Chin presents the reader with a vertiginous doubling, deformation, and expansion of the proper name. Several other racially marked characters in the novel sport appellations that are noticeable not only for their snappy alliteration—Daisy Duk, Larry Louie, and the Fong Fong Sister—but for their insistent and disjunctive pairing with popular white media icons. Thus, we are told, Daisy Duk is the Chinese Betty Crocker (46) and Larry Louie is the Chinese Fred Astaire (50). In addition, the Chinatown Frank Sinatra, the Chinese Richard Avedon, and the Chinese Marilyn Monroe (134) make guest appearances in Donald's Chinatown world.[45] Furthermore, Chin creates a series of "body doubles" in the form of female twins. Donald's own sisters, Penelope and Venus Duk—from whose demure mouths spouts a constant stream of Freudian pop psychology—challenge in their Chinese American corporeal presence those classical visions of ancient Western Greek and Roman female beauty that their proper names necessarily evoke.

While Kingston exploits the errancies of memory to rewrite popular Chinese and American myths, legends, and fables of origin, Chin locates his point of departure and resistance at the site of American popular culture. In their whitewashed omnipresence in national (and now global) media, the largely static yet immensely influential images of the American cultural screen shape our collective perception of identity and reality while acquiring in their repetitive circulation the status of truth value.[46] We must note, however, that Chin's resignifying project—his attempt to fold an affirmative vision of racial difference into mainstream popular culture—works against a long historical tide of punitive media images of Asians. In *Donald Duk* and nearly everything else he has written, Chin rails against the pathological absurdity of familiar Hollywood stereotypes such as Charlie Chan (e.g., *Donald Duk*, 121), Fu Manchu, and Hashimura Togo.[47]

In this respect, Chin's efforts to resignify the definitional limits of an image like Donald Duck are not unlike recent attempts by activists and progressive scholars to rework the historical significance of the term *queer* in order to turn against and expand its authorized meanings. Yet, as Judith Butler asks, what are the social and discursive limits of resignifying a term historically deployed as a paralyzing slur—an accusing taunt of sexual degradation and shame—with a new and affirmative set of meanings? Butler writes of this significant reappropriation and reversal: "Does the reversal reiterate the logic of repudiation by which it was spawned? Can the term overcome its constitutive history of injury? Does it present the discursive occasion for a powerful and compelling fantasy of historical reparation? When and how does a term like 'queer' become subject to an affirmative resignification for some when a term like 'nigger,' despite some recent efforts at reclamation, appears capable of only reinscribing its pain?"[48] Chin's attempts to rework our vision of American popular culture through the figure of the Chinese American boy must be placed within the recurring and virtually naturalized history of disparaged images of the "chinaman chink." The possible affirmative resignification of the sign-chain "Donald Duck" to include a racialized version of "Donald Duk" exists only in relation to the accumulated historical force of the negative effects and prior injuries of these disparaged images. If "Donald Duk" demands a startling turn against a constitutive history of damaging Asian stereotypes, what are the formidable limits and constraints on Chin's unfaithful citation of this particular proper name? Throughout the novel, Chin makes it abundantly clear that this project of resignification is by no means an easy task. To the contrary, the refunctioning of the privileged, authorized, and institutionalized meanings of Disney's Donald Duck threatens the very material existence and psychic dissolution of Chin's Chinese American protagonist.

Donald's Self-Hate

In the midst of his attempts to resignify the proper name, Chin questions the efficaciousness of his project. While he opens the novel with a meditation on the possibilities of Donald's adulterated sobriquet, Chin is also careful to emphasize the material consequences of this vexed pairing of Donald Duk with his Disney namesake: "Who would believe anyone named Donald Duk dances like Fred Astaire? Donald Duk does not like his name. Donald Duk never liked his name. He hates his name. He is not a duck. He is not a cartoon character. He does not go home to sleep in Disneyland every night" (1). Chin not only indicates that Donald hates his name but also that the dominant white society holds him in contempt of the "original": who would believe that a Chinese American boy named Donald Duk could dance like Fred Astaire? Chin's citational departure from the proper name not only garners ambivalent political results but often scorn and ridicule. While his modified vision of the Disney character challenges the boundaries of popular American culture that would exclude the Chinese American boy, any potential political subversion of the cultural screen is neutralized by mainstream society's reluctance to see or ratify Donald in this particular guise. Chin's attempted displacement of Magic Kingdom reality thus cannot be easily accommodated. To rephrase a famous line of the film theorist Laura Mulvey, Donald is set adrift to shift restlessly in his borrowed Disney clothes.

Chin's deformative reiteration of the proper name Donald Duk results neither in an upheaval of symbolic norms and sanctioned meanings nor in the dissolution of the Disney original. Instead, it is Donald's own psychic and material stability that is eroded and threatened. At his expensive private school, Donald "avoids the other Chinese here. And the Chinese seem to avoid him. This school is a place where the Chinese are comfortable hating the Chinese. 'Only the Chinese are stupid enough to give a kid a stupid name like Donald Duk,' Donald Duk says to himself. 'And if the Chinese were that smart, why didn't they invent tap dancing?' " (2). Daily, Donald finds himself in an institutionalized space of learning where the "Chinese are comfortable hating the Chinese" (2). He is compelled by this racial (self-)hatred: he resents the fact that his parents are so detached from mainstream popular culture that they could name their only son after a ridiculous cartoon character, "that barebutt cartoon duck in the top half of a sailor suit and no shoes" (7) — a Du(c)k, in other words, with no pants. He relentlessly complains that "his own name is driving him crazy! Looking Chinese is driving him crazy!" (2) — another Chinese madman. Hence, he associates his intense hatred for Chinese culture and the Chinese community with his own name and finally his own self. As a result, his ability to be comfortable hating the Chinese is purchased only at the expense of an internalized self-loathing and a subjectivity that is radically split. To reinvoke a statement from the *Aiiieeeee!* group, Donald is infused with feelings of "self-contempt, self-rejection, and disintegration."[49]

Donald's fractured psyche is accompanied by an insistent yet failed identification with whiteness, what might be described as a melancholic form of racialized subjectivity. Despising his name and attempting to displace his Chinese identity with one that is typically American, he looks, ironically, to American popular culture for an alternative sense of identity. Donald obsessively views Fred Astaire films, occupies all his spare time with tap-dancing lessons, and hangs posters of his hero all over his bedroom walls. Donald idolizes Fred Astaire and tap dancing. ("And if the Chinese were that smart, why didn't they invent tap dancing?") Ironically, in the United States tap dancing traces its genealogy not to whiteness but to nineteenth-century minstrel shows. Donald impersonates his hero and invests all of his psychic belief in dominant white images of the silver screen that will not have him. King Duk, Donald's father, observes his son's slavish mimicry of white culture with disappointment: "He's acting strange. . . . He's jumpy and jittery, tapping his toes and clicking his heels all the time like someone with a palsy. . . . He finds some old movie on a late-night channel and lets some dead guy in black and white be him" (89, 104). In this Manichean world of white and black, there is clearly no space for the yellow boy.

Donald's psychic self-splitting and utter lack of racial self-respect comes to poison all his relationships with his family members and friends. His father, in particular, demurs at his son with the unmitigated frustration of effaced paternal pride. He criticizes Donald's antipathy for the Chinese as well as his relentless assimilatory drive. Bringing Donald to a Chinese herb doctor to be exorcised of his vexed identifications with whiteness, King Duk laments: "He steals from me and lies, and treats the Chinese like dirt. . . . I think that I may have accidentally taken home a white boy from the hospital and raised him as my own son. And my real son is somewhere unhappy in a huge mansion of some old-time San Francisco money. . . . I can't believe I have raised a little white racist. He doesn't think Chinatown is America" (89–90).

Donald's racial self-loathing also poisons every aspect of his material life. Ultimately, his lack of confidence and self-esteem becomes so extreme that it overshadows even his postural schema. At the beginning of the novel, King Duk abruptly wakes his son in the middle of the night to kvetch: "You walk like a sad softie. . . . You look like you want everyone to beat you up" (3). King Duk criticizes Donald's slouching shoulders, his pouting face, his grasping hands. Donald's distinctly passive and feminine character gives pause to his father's paternal anxieties. King Duk notes that his son seems "scared" (4), and he fears that this lack of confidence will make Donald "look like a sissy" (5) in front of the gangs of Chinatown. Donald's emphatic confirmation of his father's anxieties— "I am scared!" (4)—does nothing to assuage King Duk's paternal dismay.

In an ultimate act of self-loathing that marks the inexorable fissures of his split subjectivity, Donald must laugh at himself in order to fend off the verbal and physical taunts of Chinatown gang members, who like to beat him because of his compromised moniker. Since Donald cannot defend a part of himself that he hates with such great intensity, and since "he doesn't know how to fight," he, too, must participate in his own self-denigration:

> "Don't let these monsters take off my pants. I may be Donald Duk, but I am as human as you," he says in Chinese, in his Donald Duck voice, "I know how to use chopsticks. I use flush toilets. Why shouldn't I wear pants on Grant Street in Chinatown?" They all laugh more than three times. Their laughter roars three times on the corner of Grant and Jackson, and Donald Duk walks away, leaving them laughing. . . . Donald Duk does not want to laugh about his name forever. There has to be an end to this. There is an

end to all kidstuff for a kid. An end to diapers. An end to nursery rhymes and fairy tales. There has to be an end to laughing about his name to get out of a fight. Chinese New Year. Everyone will be laughing. He is twelve years old. (7)

By laughing at himself, along with the ridicule of others, Donald actively and repeatedly rejects his Chinese American identity. His mimicry of Disney's cartoon duck—his actions and his voice—results not in the final subversion of this cultural icon but ultimately in his own self-parody, his spiritual pantsing and emasculation, as it were. This unrelenting objectification and hatred of the self causes the twelve-year-old no uncertain physical and psychic pain: "He does not want to laugh about his name forever. There has to be an end to this." Yet in the world of Chin's Chinatown there are no alternative images of self with which Donald can easily identify. When he spies himself in a window at night, it resembles a "tarnished mirror" (57). Slouched and hunched over, he "looks like he's about to cry. . . . 'How depressing,' Donald Duk says at the sight of himself" (57). For the Chinese boy, the cultural screen is a meager source of self-confidence. Unlike Lacan's jubilant and narcissistic infant in front of its mirror image, Donald experiences little joy at the sight of his reflection (a disidentification and loss of jubilance that will be explored in chapter 2).

If Donald's adulterated surname cannot on its own extend the boundaries of the American cultural imaginary to include the young Chinese American boy, what can? Chin suggests that the shifting of both the word and the images of screen—a shift that would alleviate the self-loathing and suffering that grip his protagonist—must be found elsewhere. He thus turns to the level of the unconscious—to Donald's dreamwork—in order to provide his protagonist with a new set of affirming images and meanings with which to identify. It is only through these new images and meanings, Chin suggests, that Donald can begin to challenge the repetitious damages of history.

The Damages of History

We cannot be surprised that Donald relentlessly identifies with dominant images of whiteness at the same time that he disparages his Chinese heritage. The racial self-loathing that characterizes his daily life is continually taught to him at his private school and reinforced by this material environment of "learning," where, Chin reminds us, "the Chinese are comfortable hating the Chinese" (2). We also must remember, along with Lowe, that "education is a primary site through which the narratives of national group identity are established and reproduced, dramatizing that the constructions of others—as *enemies*—is a fundamental logic in the constitution of national identity" (*Immigrant Acts*, 56). The passive demeanor that King Duk despises in his son finds one of its more influential genealogies in this institutional setting, one rooted in the psychic life of an impressionable childhood. For Donald, the demand to turn against this constitutive space of national indoctrination seems insurmountable.

During a history lesson, Donald is presented with a group of historical narratives that shape a dominant national view of Chinese American men as passive and feminized. The history teacher poses a direct institutional challenge to any deviation from mainstream society's point of view. Mr. Meanwright, whose very name invokes at once a malignancy of spirit and a "do-good" liberalism, is a staunch promoter of a faithful vision and reiterated version of the Chinese in American history:

> The teacher of California History is so happy to be reading about the Chinese. "The man I studied history under at Berkeley authored this book. He was a spellbinding lecturer," the teacher throbs. Then he reads, "The Chinese in America were made passive and nonassertive by centuries of Confucian thought and Zen mysticism. They were totally unprepared for the violently individualistic and democratic Americans. From their first step on American soil to the middle of the twentieth century, the timid, introverted Chinese have been helpless against the relentless victimization by aggressive, highly competitive Americans. (2)

Mr. Meanwright personifies Benjamin's suspect historiographer, who provides not a flitting but an eternal image of the past. Benjamin warns us that the "good tidings which the historian of the past brings with throbbing heart may be lost in a void the very moment he opens his mouth" ("Theses on the Philosophy of History," 255). When Mr. Meanwright "throbs" on about the Confucian thought and Zen mysticism that characterize the passive and nonassertive qualities of the introverted Chinese in America, he perpetuates a particular tradition of storytelling that Benjamin stringently eschews. He regurgitates a brand of static history perpetuated by his "spellbinding" professor at Berkeley and the line of orientalist scholars who precede him. He attempts to transfer this fixed history to future and impressionable generations of unquestioning and spellbound students.

By describing the Berkeley history professor as spellbinding, Chin suggests the illusory and make-believe quality of the image that is presented by Mr. Meanwright as indisputable historical reality. Furthermore, he also suggests that this spellbinding history garners its truth value only through its continual citation and repetition over time of a set of static images and meanings. Mr. Meanwright offers his spellbound class the unadulterated version of history that he was given. The nature of these lectures, one after another, requires the unqualified transfer of truth from one generation to the next. That he quotes directly from the history book written by his mentor suggests that Mr. Meanwright is less the author or owner of historical reality than the citational mouthpiece of the particular fixed historical narrative he summons. As such, he derives his authority as a teacher precisely through his faithful citation and repetition of a conservative, institutionalized version of history. He is captivated by his own blindness, mesmerized by the history he cites. Indeed, this version of history succeeds only to the extent that it echoes former citations, accumulating its force of authority through its repetition of a prior, authoritative set of practices.[50] It preserves a distorted view of the sojourning and victimized Chinese in America that continues to fuel the present-day needs of American ideology—that continues to suit the contemporary demands of American exceptionalist notions such as *democracy, individualism, competitiveness, free market,* and *capitalism.*

For example, Mr. Meanwright notes that "one of the Confucian concepts that lends the Chinese vulnerable to the assertive ways of the West is 'the mandate of heaven.' As the European kings of old ruled by divine right, so the emperors of China ruled by the mandate of heaven" (2). In comparing the nonassertive Chinese to individualistic and aggressive Americans, Mr. Meanwright ultimately reiterates a historical view that judges the eternally superior and democratic founding qualities of white America against the wanting and static characteristics of prior as well as contemporary generations of Chinese. Ironically, while the era of divine right has unequivocally become a relic of the past for its European progeny, the mandate of heaven still seems to grip the atavistic Chinese. Mr. Meanwright, we cannot help but notice, pontificates in the present tense: "One of the Confucian concepts that *lends* the Chinese vulnerable to the assertive ways of the West is 'the mandate of heaven.'" Lost in the splendor of this comparison, Mr. Meanwright, not unlike Freud in his vision of the atavistic primitive, fails to recognize the temporal slippages of his erroneous analogy. By aligning the era of absolute rule with the contemporary Chinese in America, Mr. Meanwright not only helps to fill Donald's childhood with institutional abuse but fails to recognize this history as one that motivates dominant ideologies and beliefs.[51]

In his unmitigated passion for his version of history, Mr. Meanwright loses sight of the Benjaminian historicism that he imparts with such gleeful ignorance. His image of the Chinese in America is one that maintains its status as history only by inspiring an illusory belief in the truth of its fixed images, repetitively passed down from spellbinding teachers to spellbound pupils, generation after generation: "The teacher takes a breath and looks over his spellbound class. Donald wants to barf pink and green stuff all over the teacher's teacher's book" (2–3). Indeed, that Donald wants to barf all over this history suggests a hysterical desire to reject the version of history he is being force-fed at his expensive private school. This is a history that injures him, psychically and materially, a history that is in no small way responsible for his lack of self-regard. Yet Donald's resistance to the overwhelming and constitutive force of Mr. Meanwright's official vision of history involves the daunting project of undoing a vast network of sanctioned beliefs. In the end, Donald himself is compelled to lend his voice to this particular citational vision. Asked by his pal Arnold Azalea what Meanwright is saying, the boy replies, "Same thing as everybody else—Chinese are artsy, cutesy, and chickendick" (3).

Given the authoritative force of Mr. Meanwright's dominant image of the Chinese, how might Donald begin to turn against the constitutive injuries of this history? I turn now to the dreamwork and investigate Chin's psychic prescription for undoing this vast network of historical beliefs.

Donald's Dreamwork

Chin ultimately suggests that it is only on the level of the unconscious that Donald can oppose conscious mainstream views of the Chinese as "chickendick." He suggests that the omnipresent screen images of American popular culture, as well as the dominant historical narratives they impart, can only be displaced by turning to an alternate set of dream images that appear as Donald slumbers. Chin navigates Donald's movement away from the pervasive images of the given-to-be-seen through a series of opposing dream visions—unconscious images of heroic Chinese laborers that flash up at the instant when they can be recognized and then threaten never to be seen again. Impelled by a family photograph album given to him by his uncle, Donald begins to dream against the dominant historical reality and narratives that configure the Chinese American male laborer as passive or absent. Not surprisingly, these images depict a myriad of wizened Chinese faces as they lay down tracks for the railroad.

In the *Interpretation of Dreams*, Freud observes that dreams represent the unconscious reworking during sleep of waking perceptions.[52] In this topographical model, stimuli (primarily visual or auditory) penetrate the psyche, pass inward through its reservoir of mnemic traces to enter the domain of the unconscious. After being processed by the unconscious, these stimuli return outward, traveling to the level of the preconscious, finally to arrive again at a state of conscious perception—what Freud labels the manifest content of the dream.[53] The preconscious, organized by the rules of language, is governed by social norms and prohibitions. As such, it acts not only as the cultural anteroom and clearinghouse for unconscious desires and impulses to emerge into conscious thought but as a psychic censor, binding through language the meanings that the images of the dream-thoughts can consciously assume. In this manner, the forbidden impulses and affects (of the primary process) running rampant on the level of the unconscious are linguistically dampened and controlled (by the secondary process) so that their emergence into consciousness will not threaten the order of things. (Here again we see the intimate connection between images and words.)

In the process of weaving its associative webs, the unconscious, unlike the preconscious, manifests a striking indifference to the question of what is conventionally assumed to be important or worthless at the level of the given-to-be-seen. The unconscious often displaces psychic value from one term to another on the basis of what would, in waking life, seem to be a completely "inapposite analogy."[54] Indeed, Freud glimpsed in the dreamwork the ego's potential for promiscuous mobility; the dreamwork reveals that psychic life is astonishingly mobile even if lived experience is not. This flexibility and seemingly random transfer of psychic value becomes necessary because of the censoring mechanism that governs the secondary operations of the preconscious. That is, the complex networks of signifying chains that are created at the level of the unconscious are formed in order to facilitate the disguised expression of a prohibited desire, object, or scene that cannot be named directly at the level of the preconscious.

In other words, it is the duty of the unconscious, through condensation and displacement, to attach censored images to permissible ones that would allow them to persist and reappear in the preconscious. Governed by the imperative to recover an interdicted fantasy, the dreamwork circuitously emerges into conscious thought through the laws of substitution. Under the pressure of preconscious surveillance, the unconscious must resort to alternate representations. It must mobilize signifiers that are capable of disguising their signifieds while at the same time speaking for them. In this manner, a seemingly innocent substitute object (on the level of the preconscious) is invested with the affect and intensity that properly belongs to another taboo object (on the level of the unconscious). By attaching its prohibited desire to this acceptable object, the dreamwork, Freud explains, evades censorship and thus becomes a wish fulfillment in disguise as it returns to consciousness.

Like memories, the dreamwork's return cannot be an authentic recovery. It is never the same since the laws of repression dictate that the tabooed desire, scene, or object can only be recuperated in the guise of a substitute object that is acceptable to the social prohibitions governing the linguistic systems of the preconscious. In this respect, the dreamwork's substitutions not only offer the psychic blueprint for the evasion of censorship but also, at one and the same time, suggest a potential way of renegotiating regulatory norms and prohibitions by introducing difference back into our conscious, waking lives. In other words, by introducing forbidden differences on the level of the unconscious, and by disguising these prohibited differences on the level of the preconscious, the dreamwork offers the possibility of departure from conventional norms and prohibitions. It thus introduces the possibility of alterity back into the domain of social life. As condensed and displaced desires, objects, and scenes of the dreamwork emerge into consciousness, they not only expand the field of representation and meaning but they simultaneously refigure the social boundaries of difference that govern our waking lives. In this manner, dreams harbor the potential to reform our conscious notions of reality by continually contesting and permutating what would conventionally pass as real. In their disguised form, the substitute images of the dreamwork—these memories—recalled during the light of day have the political potential to take us someplace where we have never been before.

We might characterize this push and pull method of looking—the visual and linguistic tension between unconscious and preconscious ways of seeing—as *Nachträglichkeit,* or "deferred action."[55] Freud uses the term in relation to issues of psychic causality and temporality, as does Barthes, who claims in *Camera Lucida* that the punctum is revealed "only after the fact" (53). *Deferred action* describes a psychic process by means of which conscious views and meanings are revised at a later time to accommodate new experiences that emerge from unconscious thoughts and experiences. As such, conscious memories and views do not develop in any strict linear or chronological fashion. Instead, they are continually subjected to a fresh rearrangement of meaning in accordance with new psychic and material circumstances. The retroactive and reciprocal quality characterizing deferred action, Laplanche and Pontalis point out, suggests "a conception of temporality which was brought to the fore by philosophers and later adopted by the various tendencies of existential psycho-analysis: consciousness constitutes it own past, constantly subjecting its meaning to revision in conformity with its 'project.'"[56]

Bringing together Freud's idea of *Nachträglichkeit* with our discussion of the dreamwork, we might describe the introduction of alterity into consciousness through the disguised objects of the dreamwork as a deferred method of productive looking. To resignify the images of the given-to-be-seen, Silverman points out, requires a double method of productive looking that must be written under the psychic registers of both consciousness and the unconscious. Silverman suggests that deferred looking entails a psychical process in which we consciously rework the terms under which we unconsciously look at the objects comprising our visual landscape. This unconscious looking involves a perpetual struggle first to recognize our involuntary acts of incorporation and repudiation, and our implicit affirmation of the given-to-be-seen, and then to look once more in an alternative way: "The ethical becomes operative not at the moment when unconscious desires and phobias assume possession of our look, but in a subsequent moment, when we take stock of what we have just 'seen,' and attempt—with an inevitably limited self-knowledge—to look again, differently" (*Threshold*, 173).

For instance, while mainstream society would consciously reject the resignifying potential of Donald Duk's proper name, by altering society's unconscious ways of seeing this popular cartoon character we could hope to effect a gradual shift in the meaning of this image on the level of the conscious. In other words, the introduction of alterity into waking life through the deferred visual action of the dreamwork provides a method of productive looking—an introduction of unconscious, prohibited views into consciousness—that would help to expand the field of representation and meaning by encouraging us to depart from traditional and conscious ways of seeing. Conscious resignification requires, then, unconscious support. By introducing the forbidden material of unconscious prohibitions into consciousness, individuals as well as the larger society around them can come to revise and accept on a conscious level what they would normally reject as incommensurate with society's prevailing beliefs.

"What I can name," Barthes avers, "cannot really prick me" (*Camera Lucida*, 51). The method of double looking described here provides a new set of images and meanings that not only pricks the viewer with its unconscious and yet to be named novelty but also dislodges the traditional narratives of the given-to-be-seen in politically productive ways. By giving voice to—by naming—these unconscious images as they emerge into consciousness, the viewer can displace the traditional meanings of old signifiers to endow them with new significance. Reconfiguring visual images on the level of the unconscious and reintroducing them into our conscious waking lives, the dreamwork retroactively alters our conventional ways of seeing, our conventional narratives and histories. The dreamwork provides a new battery of images and meanings with which Donald Duk can identify in order to rework the restrictive parameters of his daytime life.

The Optical Unconscious

Throughout *Donald Duk,* the eponymous protagonist wavers between waking and sleeping life. Indeed, many of the most unforgettable scenes in Chin's novel take place while Donald is slumbering. As a consequence, the reality of Donald's conscious daytime existence is explored and qualified on the level of the unconscious dreamwork. In his dreams, Donald appears as a young boy who works with older Chinese laborers to build the transcontinental railroad. In this regard, history rearranges itself against the dominant historical narrative presented to Donald by the spellbinding Meanwright, placing him in direct contact with a group of nineteenth-century workers. Accepted, not ridiculed or scorned, by these men, Donald is presented with a visual affirmation of self. Moreover, he finds himself part of a larger racialized community that, unlike his private school, ratifies his existence as a Chinese American subject. A repository of new images and meanings emerges from Donald's unconscious dreams—an evolving image-repertoire that initiates the difficult task of resignifying the static pictures of the given-to-be-seen. This project of visual displacement begins the crucial undoing of Donald's psychic network of self-hate—a task contiguous with the material, backbreaking labor of the railroad workers.

However, this project also causes Donald no uncertain anxiety. It is a slow and painstaking process; the evolution of Donald's image-repertoire is by no means direct or unimpeded. Indeed, it is marked by *Nachträglichkeit* and remains highly precarious, for the moment of historical accessibility is decisively fleeting. While forbidden images of heroic Chinese laborers make their direct appearance in his dreams, Donald nearly loses sight of this past. "The true picture of the past flits by," Benjamin warns. "The past can be seized as an image which flashes up at the instant when it can be recognized and is never seen again" ("Theses," 255). Donald's dreams flash by while he is asleep. Lost in a bevy of competing images, these dream visions are in danger of vanishing as quickly as they appear. As soon as Donald wakes, his "dream is already nothing but a fading feeling. But how? And why? Donald Duk closes his eyes and covers his head with his pillow" (99). When his mother inquires about this odd behavior, Donald replies, "I'm trying to remember" (99). Truth for Donald, like Tiresias, emerges from the dark.

Even when some of Donald's dream visions manage to endure and persist in his waking life, they quickly meet the regulating mechanism of preconscious censorship. Initially, Donald himself rejects the narrative of his dream visions as incommensurate with his pregiven reality: the dreams "are all bad because they are all about Chinese he does not understand" (25). However, as he comes to accept the significance of these countervisions, the pressure of bringing his forbidden dreams into a mainstream culture resistant to their point of view nearly forces these alternative historical interpretations into miscarriage. What he learns about the Chinese railroad workers in his dream visions clearly contradicts the lessons proffered within the institutionalized space of the classroom. Encountering an increasing number of these contradictions, Donald faces a personal crisis. He valiantly attempts to follow the narrative momentum of those departing images, which take him away from the official tracks of history, a historical "Calgon moment," as it were.

In one particular dream vision, Donald witnesses before his eyes the multitude of Chinese laborers who set a track laying record on Thursday, 29 April 1869. Yet just as he beholds this important event Donald also sees a "reporter with the telescope" deliberately ignoring the historical feat. Refusing to acknowledge the presence of these China Men, the white reporter asks Strobridge, the Central Pacific foreman: "By the way, what are the names of the eight Irishmen unloading the rail?" (111). The disparity between Donald's unconscious dream vision and the official records of the event he encounters in another institutionalized space— the archive of the local library—revolves precisely around the reporter's telescopic vision, his exclusion of the Chinese from this occasion. Reading the caption that accompanies the picture memorializing this incident, Donald calls out to his friend Arnold Azalea. "Look at this," he tells his pal. *"At rail's end stood eight burly Irishmen, armed with heavy track tongs. Their names were Michael Shay, Patrick Joyce, Michael Kennedy, Thomas Dailky, George Elliot, Michael Sullivan, Edward Killeen, and Fred McNamara.* Not one Chinese name" (122; Chin's emphasis). Absent in both image and proper name, the Chinese laborers are erased from this historical event. In a similar historical continuum, the racially marked Donald Duk is also absent from contemporary images comprising the screen of American popular culture.

While Donald is rather surprised by the contradictions between the personal images of his dreamwork and the dominant images of the history book, he is initially reluctant to look awry at the truth value of the official photographic image. King Duk admonishes his son: "The truth came looking for you in the dreams. You go look for the truth in the library. You know what is true. You know what is true. . . . That makes your life hard, kid. You have the choice. If you say Chinese are ching chong, you have to choose to do it and lie about what you know is true" (139). Despite his father's caveat, Donald hesitates to look against the given-to-be-seen, to dismiss the institutional weight of the historical narrative that emerges from the venerable archives of library records. It is not until the force of contradiction between his dream images and the static pictures of official history lessons accumulate to the point of what Althusser describes as "ruptural unity" that a new vision of historical truth can emerge to oppose the dominant history of the ruling classes.[57]

Only when the accumulated effects of these contradictory visions begin to affect Donald's sense of self does he begins to view history as what Benjamin labels a "state of emergency" ("Theses," 257). Donald comes to understand that the fleeting images of his dream visions need to be, as Benjamin emphasizes, "recognized by the present as one of its own concerns" (255). It is only at this moment of crisis, at this point of ruptural unity, at this formative juncture of a dis-appearing history that he begins to understand the urgency of King Duk's admonitions. The continuous pressure of his alternative dream visions begins to force its way into his consciousness, and Donald learns through these deferred visions how to look differently at the dominant historical images and narratives before him.

A category of memory, the dreamwork (unlike the photographic image) is always given in present tense. Rather than vague lectures about atavistic Chinese and the mandate of heaven, Donald directly experiences in his dreamwork a tangible history of deprivation that addresses his present concerns: the difficulties of hard labor, the lack of food, the exploitation of low-wage labor. These material hardships become concrete, practical concerns for the young boy. Donald wakes up with the other laborers, works grueling hours to lay a world record's worth of track, and witnesses the effacement of this historical feat in the official pages of daily newspapers and history books. He beholds the foreman Kwan's courageous interactions with the robber baron Crocker. He overhears a heated exchange between Crocker and the foreman, who demands better working hours and wages on behalf of Chinese collective.

Donald's dreamwork thus provides a pregnant moment for the birth of a new national history, a countervision of Chinese Americans in the

United States. Just as Donald's dreams are in danger of disappearing, the history of Chinese participation in the building of the transcontinental railroad is in danger of being lost forever. Donald's dreams are closely connected to this crisis of history; in order for this truth to be revealed to a new generation, he must be able to grasp the fleeting images of his dream, connect them to his present concerns, and use them to look against the historical reality before him. Focusing directly on this question of use value, Fred Astaire suggests to Donald in one of his nighttime visions that dreams may serve as the privileged psychic mechanism by which one can shift the dominant visual images of the given-to-be-seen: "If you forget who you are in your dreams, maybe, then maybe, that is what dreams are for" (126). Dreams provide the occasion for going somewhere else, the occasion for creating new psychic parameters and pathways that transform both others and finally the self. In this regard, the dreamwork opens decisively upon the territory of fantasy—a fantasy that according to psychoanalytic axiom has the most tangible effects on the shaping of our sense of reality.[58]

Donald comes to understand that dreams are those privileged psychic vehicles through which subjects not only are allowed to abandon their traditional bodily coordinates but are permitted to resignify their waking perceptions. As Kwan and his fellow Chinese laborers' heroic feats become increasingly palpable in his nighttime visions—as these feats come to fulfill Donald's present needs for psychic sustenance and material survival—the threat of their conscious loss is diminished. Donald, initially passive and along for the ride, becomes increasingly active in protecting the integrity of his personal visions. As he witnesses Kwan's leadership skills, admires the courageous demeanor of his comrades, and directly participates in the hard labor of this historical event, Donald's unconscious dreams come to mark a conscious shifting of his entire waking life, demeanor, and attitude.

Like *China Men, Donald Duk* culminates with the protagonist's displacement of the given-to-be-seen of the infamous Promontory Summit photograph. Immediately following his conversation with Fred Astaire, Donald witnesses the completion of the Central Pacific track by the Chinese laborers, whose last railway tie is pulled up by Irish crew members in preparation for the Golden Spike ceremony. "I reckon twenty or thirty newspapers and magazines have sent their writers and artists" (131), T. C. Durant tells Crocker, ignoring the angry protests of the excluded Chinese laborers. Like Kingston, Chin highlights the material dangers responsible for the visual absence of Chinese Americans from the photograph:

Your candor is most refreshing and appreciated, sir. I promise you, Mr. Durant, there will not be a heathen in sight at tomorrow's ceremonies. I will, with your permission, post riflemen up on the locomotives and the telegraph poles to warn us of the approach of any uninvited Celestial and keep them away, with force of arms if need be. The Golden Spike. The Silver Spike. The Last Spike will be hammered home, the telegram sent, our photograph made to preserve a great moment in our nation's history, without the Chinese. Admire and respect them as I do, I will show them who built the railroad. White men. White dreams. White brains and white brawn. (131)

While Crocker admits that the Chinese are integral to the railroad's completion, he also understands the need to manage a racialized history specifically through the power of the visual image. He shifts the truth of this historical event by claiming that the railroad project is one of pure white imagination, of "White men. White dreams. White brains and white brawn," thus erasing the presence of the China Men. Crocker's monomanic repetition of *white* highlights the ways in which this particular historical event has been racially whitewashed for the specific needs of a white nationalist supremacy and history. Like Kingston's parable of Ah Goong, Chin reveals a certain truth about the contradictions between the nation-state's inability to rationalize abstract labor with the doctrine of citizenship and equal opportunity. His example, in Lowe's words, illustrates how in the "history of the United States, capital has maximized its profits not through rendering labor 'abstract' but precisely through the social productions of 'difference,' of restrictive particularity and illegitimacy marked by race, nation, geographical origins, and gender" (*Immigrant Acts*, 27–28). Like Kingston, Chin shows how the visual apparatus—specifically configured here as the camera lens—is mobilized to dissociate the China Man from the nation's official history.

Crocker recognizes the historical importance of Promontory Summit to the nation's self-imagining. Consequently, through the production of whiteness as an abstract yet tangible social difference, the fulfillment of Manifest Destiny—as well as the progressive and sanctioned expansion of the U.S. nation-state from east to west—is configured as a function of white self-determination. According to Crocker's rhetoric, this spiritual and physical movement across the continent—this abstraction of whiteness—necessarily excludes the "heathen" Chinese, whose deviance immediately disqualifies them. This disqualification depends upon the erasure of the figure of the China Man from the visual screen. As in

Kingston's analysis of the Golden Spike photograph, the contradictions between the economic and political exploitation of the Chinese American laborer are resolved in the domain of images: an explicit racialized logic thus configures the China Man's absence from this photograph, coercing his ghostly disappearance.

Grasping the material violence of this particular dream vision, Donald again encounters the waking reality of a whitewashed historical image. And once more he is presented with alternative ways of looking, a splitting of conscious belief and unconscious resistance. This epistemological crisis finally resolves its contradictions through Donald's conscious shifting of and looking away at the given-to-be-seen:

Are there any Chinese in the old photos snapped at Promontory on May 10, 1869? One Chinese face? One glimpse of a long black braid of hair? Are the dreams so much poisoned poof? If there are none, does it mean the dreams are flashbacks to the real, to his ancestral first Lee come to American as a paper Duk? . . . He has the books with the pictures from the library. Big books. Big old pictures. . . . None of the photos posed and snapped from the ground or from the tops of the locomotives shows anything, anyone Chinese. (132)

Through the battery of fleeting visual contradictions that flash before him on the level of his unconscious, Donald is finally able to bring forth in waking life a new vision of history. Deferred looking begins when he initiates a search for new material evidence to corroborate his unconscious visions: "Donald Duk sleeps, dreams, wakes, panics through the books and pictures looking for Chinamen from out of the past" (133). More importantly, he begins to regard the dominant historical images around him with renewed suspicion while endowing familiar objects with entirely new significance. In Benjamin's words, Donald thus "regards it as his task to brush history against the grain" ("Theses," 257).

He begins to connect the opposing images from his sleep to look differently at the daily images around him. The railroad foreman of his dreamwork finds significance with regard to the present: "Donald Duk pads along the hall carpet with expert silence to look at Kwan Kung, robed on his left side like a scholar. His right side shows an exposed general's armor. . . . He has the eyes of Kwan the foreman" (78). Donald draws a silent but important connection between the visions of his unconscious and the shifting views of his conscious reality, the former coming directly to affect the significance of the latter. Inspired by Kwan the foreman, he endows the wooden statue of Kwan Kung with renewed meaning, an importance that finally reshapes the difficult personal relationship he has with both Chinese culture and his own father. Kwan the foreman bears a striking resemblance to the mythic hero, who bears a striking resemblance to the hero of the Chinatown opera, played by none other than Donald's own father—the circuitous renewal of an assaulted patrilineage. The past and the present, at first seemingly irreconcilable, begin to merge, and Donald begins to see his waking world differently. In the end, King Duk's role as Kwan Kung reorients Donald's position with a rehabilitated paternal line. For Chin and the Duk family, the possibility of racial harmony and self-worth is recovered.

Donald gradually transfers psychic investment from the frozen and static images of the given-to-be-seen to the dream visions that he has brought into the present. Bombarded with the aging, cellophane-wrapped posters of Fred Astaire lining the walls of his bedroom, Donald notices that Fred has taken on a strange and eerie pallor. The hero of his black-and-white screen world seems inordinately dull in comparison with the colorful world of Donald's dreams: "All over the walls are Donald Duk's aging movie posters and glossy stills from Fred Astaire's movies. Each Fred Astaire wrapped tight in a shiny transparent plastic wrap makes a lot of strange eyes looking out of the shadows and the jittery shine of things in the room. Donald Duk realizes where he is and wants back into the dream" (99). The once alluring images of American popular culture that entranced the self-hating Donald become stagnant, laminated images whose dull luster now encloses and suffocates Chin's protagonist in their paralyzing fixity. Torn between his initial unwillingness to abandon his conscious prejudices of the Chinese as "chicken-dick" and his present desire to be an integral member of his Chinese (dream) community, Donald finally forces his unconscious visions into waking reality. As a sense of movement and excitement is brought to Donald's world of dreams, the work of bringing Donald's unconscious visions into waking reality is slowly accomplished.

Donald's dreamwork thus provides a psychic road map by means of which the individual look can work against a tide of collective vision. In the gradual push-and-pull process of displacing old visions with new images—of a model of deferred, productive looking—Donald experiences an increasing desire to identify with the pictures of Chinese men he has consciously rejected for so long. Ultimately, railroad visions, and not his monomanic obsession with the static screen images of Fred Astaire, reunite Donald with a renewed and an affirmative sense of self. Deciding that he no longer wants to go to school, he tells his gathered family that "they don't like Chinese" there. "Since when did you like Chinese?" Venus asks. "Tell them they don't like Chinese," Donald's father responds, "not me. I have no problem with Chinese people. You're going to school" (150). In the end, Donald returns to the institutionalized space of the classroom. However, he brings with him a consciously different notion of history, a significantly altered image of historical reality.

The Shifting of the Screen

Donald Duk begins as it ends with a Meanwright history lesson. As the culmination of the Chinese New Year, the history teacher presents a Promontory Summit slide show from which the heroic feats of the Chinese laborers are predictably absent. These slides, depicting similar images that haunt Donald in his dreams, present a dominant historical narrative that Donald has worked through repeatedly during the course of his nocturnal labors. The chickendick vision of the Chinese in American history is one that the young boy can no longer accept as true. Instead, he airs his unconscious visions in the light of day.

During Meanwright's lugubrious lecture, Donald's attention is captured by one of the slides. Squinting, he begins to look awry at its visual truth by seeing something that is not immediately apparent to the others: "There is a face that might be Donald Duk's. Donald Duk sees and looks harder as Mr. Meanwright recites on" (151). As Donald stares at the slide to conjure forth and find his own mirror image, he recalls a heroic memory that causes him to "look harder" at this image and claim it as his own. He is "surprised he's flashing hot blood and angry now at what he hears all the time" (150). In contrast to his earlier mutterings, Donald speaks out clearly this time, "louder than he expects":

> "You are . . . sir, Mr. Meanwright, not correct about us being passive, noncompetitive. We did the blasting through Summit Tunnel. We worked through two hard winters in the high Sierras. We went on strike for back pay and Chinese foremen for Chinese gangs, and won. We set the world's record for miles of track layed [sic] in one day. We set our last crosstie at Promontory. And it is badly informed people like you who keep us out of the picture there." Donald jerks his chin up to look down his face with killer eyes at the slide of the Last Spike ceremony, still easy to see, like a faded painting projected on the wall. Everyone in the room avoids Donald Duk's eyes but follows his gesture to the screen. The slide changes back to an old grainy shot of the Chinese in the Sierra Nevadas, in the first year, working above the snowline. The white

foreman standing to the side of work on the right of way is lost behind his beard, fur hat and puffy bearskin coat. (151–52)

The literal insertion of his Chinese American male body on top of Mr. Meanwright's slide—the superimposition of his corporeal frame over the projected image—speaks to a conscious redress of the material absence of Chinese laborers from the Promontory Summit photo. Donald's earlier fusion with this historical image on an unconscious level gives him a sense of self-confidence in waking life with which he can consciously oppose that which is given-to-be-seen. Donald refutes Mr. Meanwright's claims about Chinese passivity and noncompetitiveness as false; he defends his Chinese ancestors through the strategic deployment of a collective "we." Indeed, his repeated use of "we" and "us" indicates a newly claimed group identification with the Chinese once absent and unavailable to the young boy.

This plural "we" thus solidifies a conscious identification with his ancestors of the past. It begins to heal the injurious psychic wounds of self-hate that marked the younger, isolated Donald through a new and future sense of group belonging. Donald's claiming of his place in the Chinese community occurs now in the bright light of day, not in the darkened realm of nocturnal dreams. Thus, he brings what he has learned from his unconscious dreamwork into consciousness. Significantly, Donald's vision is no longer maligned as pathological or individual; nor is he isolated in exceptional singularity. It is through other (white) classmates such as Arnold Azalea, who share Donald's unconscious dream visions, that the young Chinese boy's views are neither dismissed with derision on the part of his peers nor finally looked upon with self-contempt.

Their collective participation in this particular dream vision ultimately provides the psychic ratification and political support that Donald requires to resignify his proper name and expand the boundaries of the American cultural imaginary. The enduring corporeal presence of Donald Duk's body over Mr. Meanwright's slide image thus dislodges an effete version of American history to present an alternative view from which to look awry at the infamous Promontory Summit photograph. Through an optical unconscious, Donald learns how to look against the dominant historical images before him. The truth of the photograph is challenged as its mimetic impulse toward reality is slowly eroded. There is a literal shifting of the screen as the familiar photographic image dissolves, transformed into a "faded painting" on the wall.

The Remains of History: (Homo)sexuality and the Given-to-Be-Seen

The historical materialist leaves it to others to be drained
by the whore called "Once upon a time" in historicism's bordello.
He remains in control of his powers, man enough to blast
open the continuum of history.

WALTER BENJAMIN,
"Theses on the Philosophy of History"

Like two old China Men, they lived together lonely with no
families. . . . They were white men, but they lived like China Men.
MAXINE HONG KINGSTON, *China Men*

I took tap dancing when I was a kid. It was my second choice.
I wanted to take ballet. Isn't that what every father wants to hear?
I wanna take ballet! But he wouldn't let me take ballet because he was
scared that if I did, I'd turn out to be a big homo. Which is ridiculous.
Ballet won't turn you into a big homo. Tap dancing will.
ALEC MAPA, "I Remember Mapa"

To begin our study of Asian American masculinity by pairing Maxine
Hong Kingston and Frank Chin seems at first to be a somewhat unorthodox gesture. Despite their respective statuses as spiritual matriarch and
apoplectic patriarch of Asian American literature, Kingston and Chin are
an unlikely critical couple given their long-standing historical feud over
the public roles and personal responsibilities of Asian American writers
to their ethnic community.

Ever since the 1976 publication of Kingston's highly acclaimed *The
Woman Warrior: Memoirs of a Girlhood among Ghosts,* Chin has directed
at Kingston a steady and vitriolic stream of criticism.[59] Accusing her of
pandering to a mainstream, parochial white readership by reinforcing
injurious stereotypes of Chinese men as publicly passive and effeminate yet privately abusive and patriarchal, Chin and fellow *Aiiieeeee!* editors Jeffrey Paul Chan, Lawson Fusao Inada, and Shawn Wong denounce
what they consider to be Kingston's "twisting" of traditional Chinese
mythologies that portray Chinese American men as excessive and misogynist wimps.[60] These male editors—Asian American studies' own
"gang of four"—describe Kingston's oeuvre in such typical fashion: "The
China and Chinese America portrayed in these works are the products
of white racist imagination, not fact, not Chinese culture, and not Chinese American literature." [61] Chin, all the more virulent—and virulently
sexist—in his personal reprovals, states that writers who reinforce white

stereotypes of Chinese males are whores, while the large commercial publishing houses that print their works are "pimps hanging out at the Port Authority looking for pretty faces they can sell." (This latter statement might indeed hold a grain of truth.) [62]

Chin's self-appointed role as the "authentic" gatekeeper of the Chinese American cultural flame, compounded by his undisguised contempt for "fake," "phony," and "fraudulent" feminist writers, would seem to disqualify him immediately as a critical bedfellow of the author of *The Woman Warrior*. Nonetheless, despite Chin's public denunciations— and in spite of the apparent ideological gulf separating these two writers —Chin's and Kingston's creative works clearly converge around a common set of historical anxieties and theoretical concerns regarding the truth status of the photographic image. [63]

Through their attention to the limits of collective vision, Kingston and Chin explore the psychic and material dangers surrounding photography, the visual image, and the establishment of national history. In *China Men* and *Donald Duk*, the two authors focus on the ways in which the political imperatives, economic needs, and cultural representations of the nation-state collectively configure the Chinese American male subject as an absent presence in the domain of the visual, erasing his crucial role within the industrial development of the U.S. nation-state and his legitimate place in national history. Benjamin remarks in "Theses on the Philosophy of History" that historicism claims that whatever remains as the dominant account of history is truth: "Historicism gives the 'eternal' image of the past" (262). Both Kingston and Chin challenge historicism's account of an absolute, fixed past. Through their attention to the errancies of personal memory, they teach us to recognize history as a tool of the ruling classes, to view it through the lens of emergence and emergency: "A historical materialist cannot do without the notion of a present which is not a transition" (262).

Ultimately, Kingston and Chin create a form of visuality that problematizes the visual order itself. Both authors endow their protagonists with the politically productive capability of looking awry at the dominant images of the given-to-be-seen. Following the errancies of their memories or the unconscious visions of their dreams, Kingston's and Chin's protagonists not only learn to seize those images of the past that unexpectedly appear, in Benjamin's words, "to man singled out by history at a moment of danger" (255). Moreover, they discover a way to resignify the dominant images of the given-to-be-seen so as to recuperate a repudiated history of their Chinese ancestors. Looking awry at the domain of the visible through the lens of a repressed Chinese American historical materialism, these protagonists discover a new version of Chinese American history that is not immediately detectable, that "flashes up at the instant it can be recognized and is never seen again" (255). By capturing these fleeting images and wresting "tradition away from a conformism that is about to overpower it" (255), Kingston and Chin endow the individual look with the conscious agency to enact historical change. The individual look, they teach us, need not accept the dominant images of the screen as inevitable; it can learn to resist the dominant remains of history as incontestable truth.

Kingston's and Chin's political projects in *China Men* and *Donald Duk* are thus justifiably comparable—a critical convergence largely overlooked by critics in Asian American studies. Both seek to recuperate a repressed history of Chinese American laborers on the railroad through the shifting of visual images. Ultimately, however, the two authors diverge on the question of *how* to achieve their critical goals. While both Kingston and Chin might be said to have arrived at a common destination in relation to their critique of race and the visual image, they have differing itineraries for getting there. Their critical projects diverge most strikingly on questions of sexuality and its intersection with racial difference. In particular, the authors hold opposing views on the role of sexuality as it crosses and underpins a more progressive vision of Asian American racial formation.

In both novels, the authors recognize that the U.S. exclusion and miscegenation laws emasculated Chinese men by restricting their access to heterosexual norms and ideals such as nuclear family formations. Ah Goong, Kingston reminds us, knows that the railroad "would not lead him to his family" (129). In addition, they recognize the ways in which economic hardships feminize Chinese American men by forcing them into professions typically associated with women: cook, waiter, tailor, and laundryman. For the China Man in America, losing his place in national history is intimately tied to the compromise of traditional notions of masculinity. In this respect, the erasure or recuperation of the Chinese laborer's place within national history is leveraged through the management of his sexuality. That is, sexuality is not adjunct but central to the reenvisioning of a suppressed Asian American racial history. While both Kingston and Chin recognize the complex intersection of race and sexuality that underpins the formation of Asian American male subjectivity, they harbor contrary views about the best way to rectify this crisis of masculinity. The critical conflict that emerges between Kingston and Chin largely revolves around what meanings the sexual images of the given-to-be-seen will come to assume in relation to the racial formation of Chinese American masculinity.

Asian American critics have noted that Chin's oeuvre is unapologetically homophobic and misogynist. Railing against mainstream stereotypes that depict Asian American men as "completely devoid of manhood," Chin notes that "our nobility is that of an efficient housewife." He spits bile toward a mainstream society that configures the Asian American man as contemptible: "womanly, effeminate, devoid of all the traditionally masculine qualities of originality, daring, physical courage, creativity."[64] While his more recent pronouncements and cultural productions have been tempered somewhat, Chin's early essays and creative works consistently denigrate not only women but men who are in any way "feminine." Elsewhere, Chin explicitly describes this problem as one in which white racism has produced the yellow man as "gay": "It is an article of white liberal American faith today that Chinese men, at their best, are effeminate closet queens like Charlie Chan and, at their worst, are homosexual menaces like Fu Manchu."[65]

Chin and his *Aiiieeeee!* colleagues constantly invoke the stereotype of the homosexual to describe how the yellow man is seen by white society. Although this image of gay Asian American male subjectivity is something that Chin categorically deplores, his work displays an intense anxiety over the possibility that this is something he has become. Chin insists throughout his works that white racism has unfairly imputed to the Asian American male this gross homosexual desire, and he rejects those yellow men who would seem to display any willingness to subordinate themselves to the white man whom mainstream culture deems superior. Yet, Chin's fury over the hegemonic norms of mainstream society are often mixed with a frustrated and loving obsession with the iconic image of white manhood, a melancholic longing for the heterosexual propriety and the concomitant entitlement it represents.

While this ambivalent hatred of, yet identification with, dominant images of white masculinity underpins all of Chin's early essays and dramas, these vexed affiliations are somewhat transformed in *Donald Duk*. While an ambivalent identification with whiteness almost certainly accounts for Donald's initial self-hatred, the young boy does not develop into an embittered character. In this respect, Donald is unlike many of Chin's earlier and older male protagonists, whose conflicted identifications with both mainstream and Chinese culture remain in deadlock. Instead, Donald gradually learns to embrace and accept Chinese culture with what Sau-ling Cynthia Wong describes as the "warm glow of ethnic pride."[66]

Chin himself admits a conscious attraction to such a recuperative project and utopian resolve. In a 1996 interview with Robert Davis, he noted that he composed *Donald Duk* to work against the prevalent Asian American "autobiographical" tradition, which characterizes "the Chinese family or Japanese family in America as dysfunctional. . . . Where was the portrait of the functioning Chinese-American family? How did all these people grow up in America—I am fifth generation—without committing suicide? . . . I wrote it to demonstrate that I could tell a story with everything in it that would not be seen as an angry book."[67] The dreamwork, I argue, is key to the transformation of the "angry book." By providing a psychic mechanism with which to challenge the problematic images of the given-to-be-seen, the dreamwork allows Donald a way to transform his self-loathing into a narrative of social restitution and psychic fortitude.

While Chin's employment of the dreamwork ultimately transforms Donald's self-hatred and ambivalent identifications with whiteness into the "warm glow of ethnic pride," we must note that this psychic turn is dependent upon its unstated yet unwavering connection to heterosexuality. Donald's movement into racial self-acceptance comes only with his resolute pledge to heterosexual norms and ideals. When King Duk criticizes Donald's lack of racial pride in front of the herb doctor, the father makes repeated references to Donald's "womanish" behavior, thus associating his son's failure of racial pride, as well as his desire to be white, with the lapse of a traditionally accepted masculinity. The doctor asks the prepubescent Donald if he has a girlfriend:

"No."
"Do you think about girls a lot?"
"No."
"Hmmmmm. Hmmmmm." The herb doctor looks up from his notes again. "Do you think about boys the way boys think about girls?"
"No."
"Whew!" Dad says. (90–91)

The specter of feminization and homophobia that haunts this conversation between father and son, and doctor and patient, represents the precarious balance on which Chinese American history rests. Chin ties his project of racial recovery to the success of heterosexuality, associating proper Chinese male pride with normative masculine desire. In this scenario, heterosexuality emerges only negatively—by default—through Donald's disavowal of the doctor's disavowal of an unstated homosexuality: "Do you think about boys the way boys think about girls?" When Donald comes to embrace Chinese culture, he ultimately seeks nothing more than to confirm what his father initially desires—a rescripting of paternal power through the unimpeded transmission of a masculinized Chinese culture.

King Duk tutors Donald into an acceptance of Chinese culture precisely through his aggressive masculinization of it. The father valorizes the Chinese martial tradition. He exposes Donald to dominant Chinese myths through his building of stick and paper model airplanes that represent each of the 108 heroes of the legendary Chinese folktale *Outlaws of the Marsh*. He thus combines an entertaining childhood activity with war stories, seeking to replace a dominant American tradition of cowboys and Indians with one distinctly Chinese.

King Duk even masculinizes the traditionally feminized realm of food preparation. A renowned chef, he often mentions food in connection with the mythic Kwan Kung, "the most powerful character in the opera" (67). He emphasizes the culinary discipline governing his own performance of Kwan Kung in the Chinese opera, ultimately associating this self-control with the mandate of heaven: "When I play Kwan Kung I eat nothing but vegetables three days before the performance. . . . I bring my water in a bottle. I bring my own food. I soak dried oysters, dried vegetables, dried seeds and fruit and bean threads to make Monk's delight. The water restoring the dried things and the cooking of the restored mummied things makes up all the five elements and the mandate of heaven" (68–69). Weaving together the Chinese martial arts tradition with his duties as cook, King Duk alters the feminized status of his profession. Cooking becomes an essential element not just for the survival of Chinese culture but for the perpetuation of masculinity itself.

King Duk's actions might be described as the conscious substitution of masculine images from a dominant Chinese cultural imaginary for those comprising a dominant American cultural imaginary. This substitution contravenes the historical figuration of the Chinese American male as feminized and passive. King Duk presents these unedited substitutions, gleaned from Chinese mythology and folklore, without troubling their heterosexist assumptions. Initially, these paternal exchanges have no tangible effect on Donald. That is, King Duk's lessons assume no immediate significance until they affect Donald's dreams, until they dislodge the images of self-hate that circulate on the level of his unconscious.

Donald's dreamwork, I must note, is also consistently aligned with heterosexuality. For instance, in his first dream Donald encounters the son of Yin the Magician. Yin's son functions as Donald's alter ego; the two physically resemble one another and are the same age. However, while Donald idolizes the Western image of Fred Astaire, Yin's son honors the Chinese image of Kwan Kung, wielding a copy of his halberd during his kung fu exercises. During the course of Chin's novel, Donald slowly transfers his psychic investments from Fred Astaire to Kwan

Kung. However, the ultimate success of Donald's identification with Yin's son as well as with Kwan Kung's heroic narrative comes about largely through the catalytic presence of the twin sister of Yin's son. Donald reacts to her presence with surprised joy: "She is so pretty!" (29), he repeatedly exclaims. This young girl consistently appears in Donald's dreams, her physical beauty and graceful movements used to attract the protagonist's prepubescent attention and desire. She pays Donald special heed, tutoring him in king fu and validating his sense of self. She makes Chinese culture alluring for Donald with the promise of reciprocity and the fulfillment of heterosexual desire: "The dream was so real. Her eyes were happy to see him. He wants to stay asleep and dream" (29).

As such, Chin's unconscious dreamwork accomplishes its racial project by attaching its goals to a normative heterosexual fantasy. Donald's ultimate willingness to look differently at the Chinese is inextricably tied to this heterosexual satisfaction. As both an object and a subject of desire, the young girl affirms Donald's role as heterosexual agent. This sexual affirmation encourages Donald to rethink his initial renunciation of Chinese culture as well as his ambivalent identification with whiteness. Heterosexuality transforms Donald's self-hate and his dismissal of Chinese culture into self-acceptance by luring the young boy's psychic investments through the force of its appealing desire. Put otherwise, Chinese racial identity is reconsolidated as positive through an affirmation of heterosexuality and a disavowal of homosexuality.

Once Donald's sense of a Chinese self is established on the level of his unconscious, the image of his dreams comes to merge with the conscious reality of his father's world. In the epilogue to Chin's novel, Donald participates in the New Year's dragon parade, just as he had participated earlier in his dreamwork's lion dance. For the first time, Donald takes on an active role: "Year after year Donald Duk sees it all. But this is the first time he's run in the dragon" (170). Inside the dragon, Donald hears the "thumping running shoes, the thumping hearts roll a pattering fleshy thunder tuned to the dragon's drums and tooth-chattering brass" (170). He unites with the larger Chinese community, culture, and tradition through the social collective powering the dragon. He identifies, as Freud notes in *Group Psychology*, "On Narcissism," "On the Mechanism of Paranoia," and elsewhere, with a social group—this particular one based on racial difference and its implicit connection to heterosexuality: That is, through the psychic bonds formed by the common perception of racial group interests, ideas, and values, erotic friendship is managed and homosexual desire is sublimated into heterosexuality and an abstract sense of esprit de corps.[68]

Predictably, the girl from Donald's dreams makes a guest appearance to mark this transformation from the optical unconscious to an optics of conscious belief. Donald spies her and "walks fast, intent on keeping up with the dragon and seeing if the girl is the girl from the dreams" (170). The girl's presence provides a heterosexual bridge between the unconscious world of Donald's dreamwork and the conscious world of his waking reality. Donald's new image-repertoire is reinforced through heterosexual continuity between these two worlds. Heterosexuality thus remains a constant in both domains, and it is only with this heterosexual continuity that the dreams abate and the legacy of Promontory Summit is finally put to rest: "He's glad the dreams are gone. He believes the dreams are gone. The last spike—the photos snapped slowly on glass plates—seems the end of the story. Donald Duk looks into the crowd for faces he knows. The white sweatshirts and black pants make sense now" (170).

Chin's version of Chinese American history is an admittedly masculinized one. His recuperation of a lost racial history is, at one and the same time, a leveraging of normative (hetero)sexuality—the recuperation of a heterosexual tradition and an aggressive masculinity. "History is war, not sport!" King Duk tells Donald. "You gotta keep the history yourself or lose it forever, boy. That's the mandate of heaven" (123). While Chin rescues his young narrator from a future of self-loathing and racialized self-hate and anger, this psychic recovery is purchased only through its concomitant and committed relationship to heterosexuality. In limiting Donald's racial pride to the development of a normative heterosexuality, Asian American women and gay men are left out of Chin's vision—left out, as it were, of the picture. Consequently, they are the figurative mules who bear Donald's psychic burdens.

Chin does not recognize that women and homosexuals are not the major source of the racist and sexist treatment that Chinese males suffer in a white America that is organized around patriarchal systems of power. The masculinized substitutions of a conservative heterosexist Chinese tradition for a conservative heterosexist American tradition cannot viably redress the problems facing either Asian American men or women. It cannot account for King-Kok Cheung's admonition that "precisely because the racist treatment of Asians has taken the peculiar form of sexism—insofar as the indignities suffered by men of Chinese descent are analogous to those traditionally suffered by women—we must refrain from seeking antifeminist solutions to racism. To do otherwise would reinforce not only patriarchy but also white supremacy" ("The Woman Warrior Versus The Chinaman Pacific," 244).

While Chin's analysis reveals the ways in which race and sexuality intersect one another—how Asian American men come to be feminized in dominant white culture—Chin does not investigate how this strategic recovery might address not only issues of racism but also feminist and queer concerns. To the contrary, Chin's vision is decidedly misogynistic and homophobic. Against this point of view, we must ask whether feminization and homosexuality inevitably signify racial subordination and loss of agency for the Chinese male. Chin's failure to consider how heterosexuality and whiteness work in unison to limit Chinese American male subjectivity replaces one patriarchal lineage with another. *Donald Duk* challenges the racist feminization of Chinese men by inserting its young protagonists into a dominant (and according to Chin authentic) Chinese tradition. This insertion valorizes heterosexualized myths and martial culture in its attempts simply to reverse the feminization process to which Asian American men have been subjected in the U.S. cultural imaginary. Sau-ling Cynthia Wong aptly summarizes Chin's works, noting that they bring out "the intoxicatingly destructive aspects of mechanized locomotion, the sexual violence implied in the male imagery of continental penetration, and the intense contradictions involved in creating a Chinese American mobility myth around the symbol of the railroad" (*Reading*, 146).

For Kingston, the railroad cannot be recuperated as a macho myth; reclaiming it as a symbol of masculine power and heterosexual prowess will not bring Ah Goong back to his family or to heterosexuality. In contrast to Chin, Kingston's shifting of the given-to-be-seen accounts for the possibility of resisting not just white supremacy but its interlocking patriarchal support. In other words, Kingston's literary project interrogates the relationship between heterosexuality as it underwrites a project of white racial oppression.

Like Chin, Kingston invents a form of visuality that problematizes our ways of seeing. For Kingston, however, the recuperation of national history for the China Man need not be organized around martial violence and the patriarchal oppression of women and homosexuals. As Kingston explores the ways in which we are given-to-be-seen, she avoids prescribing a new (hetero)sexual content to replace the old. She leaves the question of sexuality open, introducing the possibility of resignifying Asian American masculinity in new and unprecedented ways. Her rewriting of Chinese patriarchal myths with different or open endings has attracted intense criticism from Chin. Given the fact that Chin's project of racial recuperation, as we witness it in *Donald Duk*, depends precisely upon "authentic" and hierarchical relations between the sexes, his reprovals are not surprising.

In *China Men*, Kingston's "Grandfather of the Sierra Nevada Mountains" represents, to borrow a phrase from Kaja Silverman, male subjectivity at the margins. Emasculated in America by political, economic, and cultural laws feminizing the Chinese man, Ah Goong, we must remember, voluntarily eschews patriarchal privileges even in China, where he supposedly has unimpeded access to them. "Dumbfounded that he had four sons, all in his old age" (*China Men*, 16), he continually questions the role of his penis. Disappointed by its inability to produce a daughter, Ah Goong happily trades his fourth son, a promising scholar, for a neighbor's female infant:

> He walked slowly, adoring the peachy face. He sat by the side of the road to look at her. He counted her pink toes and promised that no one would break them. He tickled her under the chin. She would make his somber sons laugh. Kindness would soon soften the sides of their mouths. They would kneel to listen to her funny requests. They would beguile her with toys they'd make out of feathers and wood. "I'll make you a doll," he promised her. (20)

Ah Goong has little regard for the traditional propagation of the paternal line from father to son. The conventional connection of heterosexuality—the utilitarian purpose of the penis as a vehicle for the reproduction of male heirs—to the continuance of patriarchal norms is a historical lesson lost on Ah Goong. He willingly takes on the feminine role of seamstress in order to fabricate a doll for his precious daughter. In a later episode, after the "driving out," Ah Goong encounters a young child on a farm road. As the youngster "climbed into the hollow of his arms and legs," Kingston presents an even more radical vision of gender, the dream of epicene progeny: " 'I wish you were my baby,' he told it. 'My baby.' He was very satisfied sitting there under the humming sun with the baby, who was satisfied too, no squirming. 'My daughter,' he said. 'My son' " (147).

Ah Goong's fabrications come to a grinding halt, however. In Kingston's world of indeterminate gender roles, it is left to Ah Goong's wife, Ah Po, to enforce the patriarchal rules that her husband relinquishes. When Ah Po learns that he has traded their son for a daughter, she immediately redresses Ah Goong's "foolish" actions by "snatching" her baby back from the "swindling" neighbors. Ah Goong is lost in tears, as the narrator contemplates:

> Perhaps it was that very evening and not after the Japanese had bayoneted him that he began taking his penis out at the dinner table, worrying it, wondering at it, asking why it had given him four sons and no daughter, chastising it, asking it whether it were

yet capable of producing the daughter of his dreams. He shook his head and clucked his tongue at it. When he saw what a disturbance it caused, he laughed, laughed in Ah Po's irked face, whacked his naked penis on the table, and joked, "Take a look at *this* sausage." (21; emphasis in original)

Ah Goong chastises his member for its inability to produce the daughter of his dreams, taking personal responsibility for the burdens of sexual difference. The chromosomal *xy* responsibility, we must note, is typically associated not with males but with females in a patriarchal culture. In attempting to fabricate new lines of kinship, Ah Goong treats this privileged organ as a separate entity, not with traditional awe but with surprising contempt. The prestige of his male organ, rendered as a sausage, is given over to a frightening display of disappointment and disdain.

In America, unlike China, Ah Goong is subject to harsh immigration and miscegenation laws that involuntarily emasculate him. Kingston is careful to note the ways in which these laws force the China Men to waste their lives and their seed. However, she is also careful to connect her critique of white racial supremacy with patriarchal norms through Ah Goong's sustained attention to the penis. Suspended from a wicker basket, Ah Goong digs holes into the mountainside, placing gunpowder and fuses into them. He witnesses a number of fellow China Men fall from their baskets to unsightly deaths at the bottoms of ravines. He watches as a number of fellow workers are blown to bits in gunpowder accidents. One day, Ah Goong urinates out of his basket, calling to the wind: "Look at me . . . I'm a waterfall." And on another day, "dangling in the sun above a new valley, not the desire to urinate but sexual desire clutched him so hard that he bent over in the basket. He curled up, overcome by beauty and fear, which shot to his penis. He tried to rub himself calm. Suddenly he stood up tall and squirted out into space. 'I am fucking the world,' he said" (132–33).

Here Ah Goong uses his penis to make a statement of racial protest. He laughs in the face of death, sending his waste down where other China Men have sent their lives. While he intentionally pulls down his pants to urinate out of the basket, when Ah Goong desires to "fuck the world" he loses all control. Clutched by desire and "overcome by beauty and fear," he ejaculates suddenly and helplessly into the empty air. Kingston ties this loss of control to Ah Goong's devalued racial position in America. Associated with urine—his waste—Ah Goong's reproductive seed is thus also rendered unproductive. Instead, the power of his labor is harnessed to build the railroad, whose paternity is then attributed to the white suits who appear in the photograph commemorating its completion. His desire to be seen and recognized is unrequited. As far as national history is concerned, only white men are the fathers of the railroad. In this respect, the China Men who gave their bodies and lives to build it are cut off from its paternal legacy. Ah Goong is right to be suspicious of patriarchal lineage.

In the face of the racist laws that "fuck" the China Man and place him outside the sphere of social recognition, Ah Goong continues to question the role of the penis and its privileged place in a male world. He constitutes the male penis as the source and site of oppression. The masturbatory scene in the basket does not assert traditional notions of virility, nor is it productive in conventional ways. After completing the railroad, Ah Goong continues to berate his penis, taking it out from "under his blanket" or baring it "in the woods." He "also just looked at it, wondering what it was that it was for, what a man was for, what he had to have a penis for" (144). Kingston, of course, never answers these questions. She does not prescribe new content to replace the old. Instead, she presents the predicament of masculine privilege endured by the racialized China Man in America and teaches us to look at it differently. Released from patriarchal norms, the unmanned China Man offers the possibility not only of resignifying Asian American masculinity but of envisioning a new set of gender roles outside traditional boundaries.

In a passage near the end of *China Men*, Kingston raises the possibility that a resignified masculinity might remake the world in a kinder image, cognizant of both racial hierarchies and sexual oppression. Kingston describes two white men who lived with one another like a married couple:

> Like two old China Men, they lived together lonely with no families. They sat in front of stores; they sat on their porch. They fenced a part of the slough for their vegetable patch, which had a wooden sign declaring the names of the vegetables and who they belong to. They also had a wooden sign over their front door: TRANQUILITY, a wish or blessing or the name of their house. They gave us nickels and quarters; they made dimes come out of noses, ears, and elbows and waved coins in and out between their knuckles. They were white men, but they lived like China Men. (243)

Kingston compares the plight of China Men in America to that of a gay white couple, who "live together lonely with no family." Both disappear in the dominant images of the given-to-be-seen. In contrast to Chin, Kingston has no interest in subsuming the China man to a dominant Chinese heroic and heterosexual tradition. Comparing them to this gay couple, she critiques the sexual as well as the racial given-to-be-seen. She suggests that one cannot be thought of outside its relation to the other and that one cannot be redressed without redressing the other.

Predictably, Kingston teaches us to look at the white men who live like China Men in new ways. Although they may seem "lonely with no family"—outside of traditional heterosexual norms—they are together in their affiliation and mutual commitment. Their domestic life is marked by a striking tranquility, harmony, and peace. Like paper sons, they reconstitute a new form of family life and kinship with the Chinese narrator and her siblings. The hidden nickels, dimes, and quarters that appear out of noses, ears, elbows, and knuckles make no visual sense; they are optical illusions, sleights of hand. Yet, as Kingston implies through her attention to these visual antics, it is only by shifting the visual order that the hidden racial and sexual histories of both China Men and this couple can emerge from invisibility. In linking together racial difference and homosexuality, Kingston not only critiques American racism but heterosexual privilege across races, cultures, and national borders. She gestures toward a necessary consideration of the ways in which multiple axes of social difference come to overdetermine Chinese American male subjectivity while imagining a type of masculinity that could be feminist and antihomophobic as well. While Chin eliminates any social space for homosexuality and feminism, Kingston envisions a world in which homosexuality and racial difference need not have an inverse or adversarial relation. Kingston acknowledges multiple and intersecting social injuries and attempts to rework them simultaneously.

Resignifying categories such as race, gender, and sexuality is no small task. The affirmative resignification of the term "queer," as discussed earlier, demands a turn against a long constitutive history of shame. And, as much as this identity term must be used, and as much as outness is to be affirmed, "queer" must also be subjected to a thorough critique of its exclusionary operations of production. As we resignify "Asian American masculinity" against its long history of feminization and invisibility in national history, we might ask who is presently included and who is decidedly excluded in its contemporary usage. "Queer" as it is deployed today may present an impossible conflict for a concurrent and equal vision of racial justice. We cannot wish a similar fate for "Asian American." "Asian American masculinity" should not come to eliminate the occasion for a complex consideration of a progressive sexual politics that is both antiracist and antihomophobic.

Ultimately, Chin's vision in *Donald Duk* resembles Benjamin's historical materialist approach to history, which "blasts a specific era out of the homogenous course of history" ("Theses," 263). Benjamin's discourse of "shock" and violence suits Donald's dreamwork well insofar as

Chin marks all of the young boy's discoveries by a strong masculine and heterosexualized power. As workers blast through the Sierra Nevadas, so, too, does historical materialism blast the lost history of the Central Pacific Railroad into Donald's consciousness, leaving it to others to be drained by the whore called "once upon a time." Yet, as Kingston warns, these blasts are not without their fatalities. In creating a space for the railroad, and a space in national history for the China Man, these blasts also threaten the precarious existence of Ah Goong himself.

TWO

Primal Scenes: Queer Childhood in "The Shoyu Kid"

"What are you, Itchy, some kind of queer or something?

Don't you know you're supposed to have a hard-on when

you see a naked girl?" Jackson was getting wound up on

his favorite subject. I sneaked a look at Jackson,

and I think he was lying.

LONNY KANEKO, "The Shoyu Kid"

Strangers from a Different Shore

Unlike the imposed invisibility of Chinese American male laborers at Promontory Summit, the political rhetoric advocating the mass incarceration of persons of Japanese ancestry during World War II turned precisely on a question of visibility. In a 7 November 1941 report on the West Coast situation forwarded to President Roosevelt, Curtis B. Munson, a well-to-do Chicago businessman enlisted by John Franklin Carter, a highly placed Roosevelt intelligence adviser, states: "The Japanese are hampered as saboteurs because of their easily recognized physical appearance. It will be hard for them to get near anything to blow up *if it is guarded*. . . . We do not believe that they would be at least any more disloyal than any other racial group in the United States with whom we went to war."[1] Despite Munson's opinion—and the concurring views of numerous other intelligence sources—that the ethnic Japanese posed a very limited risk to national security and should not be detained en masse, President Roosevelt, swayed more by "public and political pressure rather than on factual data,"[2] came to a divergent conclusion and signed Executive Order 9066. Authorized on 19 February 1942, the order permitted the forcible removal and exclusion of any person deemed undesirable from designated military areas.[3] General John L. Dewitt, head of the Western Defense Command based in San Francisco's Presidio, implemented Executive Order 9066 for the immediate detention, relocation, and incarceration of more than 112,000 people of Japanese ancestry on the Pacific coast, roughly two-thirds of whom were American-born citizens.

In contrast to Americans of German and Italian ancestry, the Roosevelt administration reasoned, the Japanese—"strangers from a different shore"—while distinct as a racial group, were difficult to distinguish from one another as individuals.[4] This visual justification for internment was largely based on opinions held by military commanders in the War Department such as Dewitt, who strongly advocated incarceration of the Japanese. In a conversation between Dewitt and John J. McCloy, a special assistant and then assistant secretary of war, the general stated that "all Japanese look alike and those charged with the enforcement of the regulation of excluding alien enemies from restricted areas will not be able to distinguish between them."[5] While those of German and Italian descent could be individually monitored, "the Occidental eye [could not] easily distinguish one Japanese resident from another."[6] Sucheng Chan concludes that as a result of this Euro-American failing, the mass evacuation of persons of Japanese ancestry became inevitable (*Asian Americans*, 124). "Look in the mirror, Richie," directs Misa Wakatsuki to her perplexed son in Jeanne Wakatsuki Houston's memoir of wartime internment, *Farewell to Manzanar*. Responding to Richie's queries as to why German and Italian Americans have not been similarly detained, Wakatsuki states, "We can change our names, but we can never change our faces."[7]

Historically, certain Japanese and Japanese Americans, attempting to disguise their racial identities, did change their surnames after America's entry into World War II. Moreover, there is at least one documented case of a Japanese American citizen—Fred Korematsu—who altered his face through plastic surgery in an effort to pass as other than Japanese.[8] Korematsu's effort proved fruitless, as did his two subsequent legal hearings before the U.S. Supreme Court contesting the constitutionality of the government's evacuation orders.[9] Arguing that membership in the American union requires certain burdens, Justice Hugo Black wrote in the six-to-three *Korematsu v. United States* (1944) decision: "All citizens alike, both in and out of uniform, feel the impact of war in greater or lesser measure. Citizenship has its responsibilities as well as its privileges, and in time of war, the burden is always heavier."[10]

Ironically, this national inability to distinguish one Japanese American from another depended on the revision of the competing perception that "all Asians look alike." Directly after the bombing of Pearl Harbor, both the popular press and U.S. military published advice columns on how to distinguish the Japanese from other "friendly Asiatics" (fig. 4). For instance, in their 22 December 1941 issues, *Time* and *Life* printed handbooks for "Americans" under the headlines "How to Tell Your Friends from the Japs" and "How to Tell Japs from the Chinese."[11] These publications offered an array of sweeping visual, material, ideological, sartorial, and anthropological comparisons:

> Some Chinese are tall (average: 5 ft. 5 in.). Virtually all Japanese are short (average: 5 ft. 2½ in.). . . . Japanese—except for wrestlers—are seldom fat; they often dry up and grow lean as they age. The Chinese often put on weight, particularly if they are prosperous (in China, with its frequent famines, being fat is esteemed as a sign of being a solid citizen). . . . Most Chinese avoid horn-rimmed spectacles. . . . Although both have the typical epicanthic fold of the upper eyelid (which makes them look almond-eyed), Japanese eyes are usually set closer together. . . . Those who know them best often rely on facial expressions to tell them apart: the Chinese expression is likely to be more placid, kindly, open; the Japanese more positive, dogmatic, arrogant. . . . Japanese walk stiffly erect, hard-heeled. Chinese, more relaxed, have an easy gait, sometimes shuffle. (*Time,* 22 December 1941, 33)

During this time of Japanese American isolation and internment, one can only imagine why the Chinese appeared to be more relaxed.

Examples drawn from the popular press and military publications thus evidence a historical moment in which the political management of race worked to shift dominant stereotypes of Asian Americans as difficult to distinguish from one another by attempting to atomize them into specific ethnic groups and national identity types. This diversification of the specular realm depended on a new battery of stereotypical images. While disloyal Japanese Americans were characterized as monstrous, hard-heeled, dogmatic, and arrogant, this frightful portrait drew much of its negative ideological reinforcement from a contrasting portrait of Chinese Americans as placid, loyal, and domesticated—feminized attributes associated with their easy gait and occasional shuffle.[12] In the divide-and-conquer logic of this visual management of race, Japanese Americans and Chinese Americans were polarized as bad and good, dis-

Chinese   *Japanese*

HOW TO TELL YOUR FRIENDS FROM THE JAPS

Of these four faces of young men (*above*) and middle-aged men (*below*) the two on the left are Chinese, the two on the right Japanese. There is no infallible way of telling them apart, because the same racial strains are mixed in both. Even an anthropologist, with calipers and plenty of time to measure heads, noses, shoulders, hips, is sometimes stumped. A few rules of thumb—not always reliable:

▶ Some Chinese are tall (average: 5 ft. 5 in.). Virtually all Japanese are short (average: 5 ft. 2½ in.).

▶ Japanese are likely to be stockier and broader-hipped than short Chinese.

▶ Japanese—except for wrestlers—are seldom fat; they often dry up and grow lean as they age. The Chinese often put on weight, particularly if they are prosperous (in China, with its frequent famines, being fat is esteemed as a sign of being a solid citizen).

▶ Chinese, not as hairy as Japanese, seldom grow an impressive mustache.

▶ Most Chinese avoid horn-rimmed spectacles.

▶ Although both have the typical epicanthic fold of the upper eyelid (which makes them look almond-eyed), Japanese eyes are usually set closer together.

▶ Those who know them best often rely on facial expression to tell them apart: the Chinese expression is likely to be more placid, kindly, open; the Japanese more positive, dogmatic, arrogant.

In Washington, last week, Correspondent Joseph Chiang made things much easier by pinning on his lapel a large badge reading "Chinese Reporter—NOT *Japanese*—Please."

▶ Some aristocratic Japanese have thin, aquiline noses, narrow faces and; except for their eyes, look like Caucasians.

▶ Japanese are hesitant, nervous in conversation, laugh loudly at the wrong time.

▶ Japanese walk stiffly erect, hard-heeled. Chinese, more relaxed, have an easy gait, sometimes shuffle.

Chinese   *Japanese*

Carl Mydans, Black Star

Figure 4 "How to Tell Your Friends from the Japs" (*Time*, 22 December 1941)

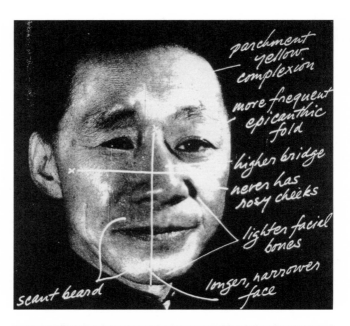

Figures 5 and 6 "How to Tell Japs from the Chinese" (*Life,* 22 December 1941)

loyal and loyal, subjects of the nation. We might note that in the contemporary context a similar logic endures in the mainstream ordering of race that largely characterizes African and Asian Americans as problem and model minorities, respectively, in the public sphere.

These brief examples—drawn from an array of historical, juridical, literary, journalistic, and military materials—of the hypervisibility of the Japanese American body during World War II underscore the crucial role that the specular played in isolating, regulating, and demonizing a particular racial group following the bombing of Pearl Harbor. In contrast to the heightened visibility of Japanese Americans, the refusal of the U.S. government to grant citizenship to Chinese immigrant male laborers, whose cheap and flexible labor was indispensable to the economic success and political stability of a rapidly industrializing nation-state, worked to enforce their invisibility within the political realm, to dissolve their group history, and ultimately to erase them from the specular domain. In examining these particularized, opposing portraits of Japanese and Chinese Americans, however, we immediately realize that neither invisibility nor visibility guarantees Asian American subjects access to or membership in the nation-state. Homi Bhabha observes that the stereotype "is a form of knowledge and identification that vacillates between what is always 'in place,' already known, and something that must be anxiously repeated . . . as if the essential duplicity of the Asiatic or the bestial sexual license of the African that needs no proof, can never really, in discourse, be proved."[13]

Considering the history of the stereotype in specific relation to differing Asian American ethnic groups, Lisa Lowe observes further:

> Throughout the twentieth century, the figure of the Asian immigrant has served as a "screen," a phantasmatic site, on which the nation projects a series of condensed, complicated anxieties regarding external and internal threats to the mutable coherence of the national body: the invading multitude, the lascivious seductress, the servile yet treacherous domestic, the automaton whose inhuman efficiency will supersede American ingenuity. Indeed, it is precisely the unfixed liminality of the Asian immigrant—geographically, linguistically, and racially at odds with the context of the "national"—that has given rise to the necessity of endlessly fixing and repeating such stereotypes.[14]

The need to fix and repeat newly specific and hypervisible images of Japanese American disloyalty during World War II underwrote a national project in which media representations played a crucial role. Ultimately, I argue, invisibility and visibility are not opposed but are two sides of one representational coin. That is, visibility is not necessarily better or more positive than invisibility, and visibility is not necessarily indicative of a more evolved or progressive political state of being for Asian Americans.[15]

What we come to understand from a comparison of stereotypes of the Chinese American male laborer during westward expansion and the Japanese American male body during wartime internment is that invisibility and visibility work in historical tandem to configure and reconfigure the Asian immigrant as the phantasmatic screen on which the nation projects its shifting anxieties of coherence and stability. Invisibility and visibility work to fix, shift, and refix the figure of the Asian immigrant according to the particular political exigencies and historical demands of the nation-state. The battle for control of this representational currency has serious material effects as to which Asian American ethnic groups will or will not be—how they will or will not be seen—in the national political, economic, and cultural life.

The visual apartheid enacted against Americans of Japanese descent during World War II points to a larger phenomenon by which racial difference is insistently managed and figured in relation to visual stereotyping. The effects of the specular domain on Asian American male subjectivity are expanded upon in this chapter through a focus on the visibility of the Japanese American male body during wartime internment. In particular, Lonny Kaneko's "The Shoyu Kid," which is set in Idaho's Minidoka concentration camp, exposes and reworks—indeed, "shows you"—the mechanisms of this specularity.[16] A semiautobiographical short story published in *Amerasia Journal* in 1976, "The Shoyu Kid" follows a day in the lives of four young boys, one of whom, dubbed the Shoyu Kid by the others, is molested by a white camp guard. Throughout the course of the day, the three boys, Jackson, Itchy, and Masao, race around the internment camp playing cowboys and Indians. Refusing to adopt the part of "colored" Indians, however, they gang up on the Shoyu (meaning "soy sauce" in Japanese) Kid, forcing him to assume the abject brownness of this colored role. The three boys reserve the role of cowboy for themselves, attempting to identify with a group of Hollywood screen icons (John Wayne and Humphrey Bogart most notably) through their slavish imitation of these cinematic idols.[17]

Kaneko's short story is obsessed with the realm of the visible and the psychic effects that normative white male heterosexual images have upon the sexual and racial identifications of the four youngsters. Ultimately, "The Shoyu Kid" presents a dense psychological commentary on these young Japanese American boys' frustrated attempts to change "face." While they mimic and attempt to incorporate idealized male images of American heterosexuality and whiteness, these images remain stubbornly exterior to them. Their psychic obeisance toward these unattainable images proves not only frustrating but debilitating.

My analysis of "The Shoyu Kid" relies upon two fundamental mechanisms of identification within the visual domain: Lacan's mirror stage, in which the infant forms its primordial sense of self through seeing its reflection in a looking glass; and Freud's primal scene, described by Jean Laplanche and Jean-Bertrand Pontalis as a retroactive childhood fantasy of origin.[18] The goal of this chapter is to explore how sexual and racial identifications mutually inform the genesis of Japanese American male subjectivity. As such, I will draw on Kaja Silverman's theory of the self-same body as a way to read productively social difference into the mirror stage. Placing the mirror stage, the self-same body, and the primal scene in critical dialogue, I then analyze Itchy's witnessing of the Shoyu Kid's molestation by the white soldier. I argue that Kaneko configures this spying incident as a "sodomitical" primal scene. This primal scene ultimately encloses these young boys not within a normative identification with heterosexuality, whiteness, and Americanness but within a profoundly negative identification with homosexuality, racialization, and alienation from the U.S. nation-state.

The Mirror Stage and the Self-Same Body

In "the mirror stage as formative of the function of the I as revealed in psychoanalytic experience," Jacques Lacan describes the infant's original encounter with its "self" in the reflective surface of a mirror.[19] According to Lacan, the ego and the sense of self are created through this specular act of identification, which entails the infant's instantaneous mental apprehension of its reflected bodily form (what Lacan terms the *imago*). According to the logic of the mirror stage, sense of self is introduced from the outside in, through an "other" in the form of this external image. The I "finds its unity in the image of the other," Lacan remarks in *Seminar II.* "And it is jammed, sucked in by the image, the deceiving and realised image, of the other, or equally by its own specular image. That is where it finds its unity." [20]

The mirror stage thus revises the doctrine of Cartesian humanism by qualifying the sanctity of the *cogito*—"I think therefore I am"—and by challenging the principle that subjectivity emanates from the inside out through an all-seeing I/eye. For Lacan, the ego and sense of self does not result from an internal act of enlightened will. Instead, it comes only from the outside in, from the infant's identification with its external image: "Unable as yet to walk, or even to stand up, and held tightly as he is by some support, human or artificial . . . he nevertheless overcomes, in a flutter of jubilant activity, the obstructions of his support and, fixing his attitude in a slightly leaning-forward position, in order to hold it in his gaze, brings back an instantaneous aspect of the image" ("Mirror Stage," 1–2). Unable as yet to walk, and still lacking anything remotely resembling full motor capacity, the jubilant infant nevertheless tips forward, aggressively separating itself from its supporting mother, in an attempt to merge with its imago. Considering the theoretical vocabulary of the previous chapter on photography in relation to this particular scenario, we might characterize the infant's forward-leaning movement as indicative of an irrepressible desire to become one with its mirror reflection—to laminate body and image together. Kaja Silverman extends this notion of lamination, arguing that the sense of self in Lacan's mirror stage depends not merely on the infant's identification with its specular image but on its successful mapping of this external imago onto its corporeal coordinates, a phenomenon she describes as the "self-same body."

In *The Threshold of the Visible World*, Silverman argues that the self-same body is created through the successful alignment of two distinct egos—one bodily (or sensational), the other visual.[21] Her observations on the role of the sensational ego—gleaned from Freud's famous statement that the ego is "first and foremost a bodily ego"[22]—offer, then, a critical qualification to Lacan's theory of self-discovery and development as a purely specular transaction. Although Lacan does not directly suggest that the infant's recognition of its self in the mirror stage depends upon this mapping of bodily and visual ego, Silverman writes that his "curious reliance in his account of the mirror stage on a tableau in which the visual image seems a direct extension of the physical body of the child . . . implies as much" (17). Hence, it is only with the smooth mapping of the (Lacanian) visual imago onto the (Freudian) bodily ego that the infant is able to gain a sense of self-sameness and coherent identity—to secure psychic presence, hereness, and ultimately jubilation.

That the infant moves aggressively toward and not away from its mirror image suggests that the reflection encountered in Lacan's looking glass enchants rather than horrifies, seduces rather than repels. Lacan and his commentators repeatedly stress the fictional quality of the mirror stage, and they are quick to point out that the infant's infatuated love of its image is a tragic misrecognition—a self-love compromised by "*méconnaissance*." The coherence of the visual imago that captures the infant's attention is at heart a misplaced belief in the permanence of a unified image of the self.[23] For Lacan, from its moment of inception, the ego (and human desire) are oriented in a "fictional direction" ("Mirror Stage," 2), alternating between jubilant identification with and paranoid dissolution of the specular imago. On the one hand, the infant experiences jubilation and narcissistic ecstasy (*jouissance*) by tipping into the image to find its self in the mirror reflection. On the other hand, the infant is beset with poisonous anxiety and jealous aggressivity at the discovery that the image is precisely not "I," that it is a misrecognition (méconnaissance), an unmappable specular illusion, remaining, as Mikkel Borch-Jacobsen observes, at a stubborn distance "over there"—rigid, elusive, frozen, "unshakable [and] fixed for eternity."[24]

While much of the critical commentary generated by Lacan's short essay revolves around the alienating effects of this jubilant/identification and paranoid/misrecognition see-saw dynamic of human subjectivity, little has been said about the specific ways in which this psychic transaction is socially determined. That is, while Lacan warns that the infant's identification with its imago is finally a tragic misrecognition of self, he nevertheless implicitly assumes that there is always a moment of jubilant identification for the infant. He does not suggest that there might be situations in which jubilation is an impossible prospect.

Might subjects experience jouissance in dissimilar ways? Does the mirror stage necessarily and invariably entail moments of joyful identification given over to the constitutive formation of the ego and the psychic reinforcement of the sense of self? How can we understand the subjectivity of those who do not have the initial jubilance of Lacan's infant against which méconnaissance works? How might sexual and racial difference intersect this drama of self-discovery in the mirror stage to trouble the smooth alignment and identification of bodily ego and visual imago? How might sexual and racial difference disturb the productions of self-sameness, leading the infant less to joy than to profound sadness and bitter dejection? While Lacan offers no direct comments on the presumed (white) racial status of the generic (male) child he describes in "The Mirror Stage," we must pause to consider whether the white male and the Japanese American child experience their images before the mirror in similar ways. That is, we must rethink the question of méconnaissance in terms of less than jubilant identifications.

The Mirror Stage and Social Difference

We come to understand how social differences—sexual and racial—encourage or impede the formation of the self-same body when we understand that the joining of the infant's bodily ego with its imago is not a two-way imaginary but a three-way symbolic transaction. The successful alignment of bodily ego and imago requires the presence of a symbolic third term, providing social sanction, ratification, and support. This particular point is clarified when we consider Lacan's description of the infant's initial capture of its image as being triangulated from the outside by "some support, human or artificial" ("Mirror Stage," 1).

The mother, for example, who holds the baby up to the frame of the mirror not only supports the infant in a literal sense; she also supports in a figurative sense the cultural expectations that invariably precede and psychically inform the image of self that the infant first encounters and then assumes in its specular reflection. "Look, junior, you doctor, you lawyer, you fireman," coos the mother. Her acoustic invocations and bodily gestures thus work in tandem with the mirror image of the infant to laminate it to its sense of self while conveying a pregiven set of social (gendered, racial, and class) expectations. Here we not only find a merging of the bodily ego and imago socially facilitated by the mother; we come to understand that what is already there lying in wait for the child within the frame of the mirror are the demands, hopes, and intentions of others—social ideals and imperatives. Read metaphorically, Lacan's essay is thus as much about an encounter of the infant with images from the place of others—the images and expectations of other subjects—as it is about an encounter of the infant with the images of self.

Silverman observes that the reliance of the self-same body—this mapping of bodily ego with visual imago—on social validation becomes all the more evident when we substitute for the imago Lacan's category of the screen, that cultural image-repertoire of external visual representations by means of which identity is constructed.[25] These screen imagos —images from photographs, the print media, television, and cinema, for example—act as metaphorical mirrors in which individuals are continually (re)constituted as subjects. "All sorts of things in the world," Lacan reminds us in Seminar II, "behave like mirrors" (49). And here we must remember that neither the mirror stage nor entry into the visible world happens only once. In its metaphorical capacity, the mirror stage must be continually (re)negotiated if the subject is to have a stable and coherent sense of identity over time. In other words, identity comes to be profoundly dependent not merely on the "original" image of self encountered in the mirror frame (primary identification) but on a constant stream of socially sanctioned representations that comprise the visual screen (secondary identifications).

Lacan tells us in The Four Fundamental Concepts of Psycho-Analysis that in order to emerge within the field of the visible the subject must not only align himself or herself identificatorily with the images of the screen but must also be recognized and validated in that guise by multiple others (in the form of an unapprehensible "gaze").[26] In the specular drama of "The Mirror Stage," the mother's look plays that pivotal role of social validation and gendered support, standing in for what no one look can actually approximate: the gaze. Lacan's theory of look, screen, and gaze thus qualifies and delimits, as Silverman maintains, the fashionable concept of a perpetually mobile subject able to identify freely with a plurality of heterogeneous images.

Considering for a moment Lacan's *Four Fundamental Concepts of Psycho-Analysis* in light of his essay "The Mirror Stage," we come to understand that our psychic experience of the self-same body does not necessarily follow from our voluntary or self-willed identification with the imago. On the contrary, any jubilant sense of identification with an external image hinges on collective social affirmation. In other words, it is only when the cumulative looks of others provide symbolic validation and social support that the subject can gain access to the desired image. Without this collective affirmation, the imago cannot be successfully mapped onto the bodily ego to produce any feeling of psychic triumph or self-sameness.[27]

Silverman proceeds to note that in our present-day social organization of the field of vision those images traditionally idealized in society—masculinity, heterosexuality, and whiteness—cannot be readily available to all. Indeed, idealized images are available only to those whose bodily egos are somehow culturally authorized to see themselves within them. Consequently, one's psychic identifications with these prized images is not only dependent upon a self-willed identification; it is also dependent upon cultural norms and prohibitions that regulate the circulation of these idealized representations. That is, one can neither simply choose through a singular act of will how to be seen nor can one freely conjure up those idealized images with which one would like to be aligned. Without widespread social validation, the concomitant mapping of bodily ego and imago that produces a feeling of self-sameness cannot be sustained. Psychic "presence" is forfeited; jubilant identification is impossible; and the subject is left with a profound sense of fragmentation, disunity, and loss.

In this regard, we must remember that idealized images such as masculinity, heterosexuality, and whiteness also imply an obverse set of images such as femininity, homosexuality, and racialization. These culturally devalued images are ones that socially marked subjects are encouraged to loath. Even more, they are encouraged to disidentify with these images. When held to these unpleasant and devalued identifications, the subject experiences them as external impositions, which leads to a negative sense of self and a psychic sense of dislocation. Numerous cultural critics have pointed to Frantz Fanon's rich commentary on the profound feelings of fragmentation that result from the black male subject's ambivalent relation to pejorative, stereotypical images of black-ness—as savage, as criminal, as unlovable—that circulate around and dog him.[28] In *Black Skin, White Masks*, Fanon writes eloquently about the ways in which stereotyped cinematic portrayals and print represen-tations of the "dirty nigger" lead to a "consciousness of the body [that] is solely a negating activity."[29] Sitting in the darkness of a movie the-ater, Fanon waits anxiously for his image to appear on the screen, rep-resentations that not only frighten little white children (112) but leave the black man "forever in combat with his own image" (194). Fanon's struggle with this culturally compromised racial imago leads not to jubi-lant identification but to a strong desire to maintain as much psychic distance from it as possible. Inevitably, such a compromised relation-ship with this negative image of blackness results in feelings of dehis-cence, as Fanon's bodily schema fragments and crumbles into a myriad of psychic pieces: "I burst apart" (109).

From an Asian American perspective, we need to remember Misa Wakatsuki's admonition to her son in Houston's *Farewell to Manzanar:* "Look in the mirror, Richie. We can change our names, but we can never change our faces." Wakatsuki's statement allows us to understand the virtual impossibility for Asian American subjects not only to achieve a sense of psychic coherence but to control the ways in which they are apprehended. Houston's example shows us that it is not possible for all mothers to provide the kind of social validation and gendered sup-port that Lacan's generic mother in "The Mirror Stage" is presumed to offer her joyful infant. The male infant's separation from his mother— his overcoming "in a flutter of jubilant activity, the obstructions of his support"—speaks immediately to a drama of self-discovery that hinges on sexual difference (male separation from the mother into the public sphere of the father). What Fanon's and Houston's examples provide us with are alternate ways of thinking the racial dynamics that implicitly underpin the mirror stage as well.

Before turning to "The Shoyu Kid," I raise one final example that de-velops this complex relationship between sexual and racial difference in the mirror stage. The recent work of filmmaker Pamela Tom encour-ages us to consider further the ways in which sexual and racial differ-ence are constitutive of one another for their discursive legibility. Tom's sophisticated and stylized *Two Lies* is a short film that provides a com-pelling account of the intersection of sexual and racial difference as it impinges upon the mirror image and overdetermines the genesis of a lovable ego.[30] The film explores plastic surgery and the popular Asian American female practice of getting "eye jobs" to create a Caucasian double eyelid from a single epicanthic fold. The mother in *Two Lies* epitomizes the culturally marked Chinese American female subject whose tortured relations to deprecated images of femininity and Asianness cause her to mutilate her body. Her surgery is a futile and grotesque corporeal attempt to approximate the idealized images of white female beauty that she encounters in magazines and film. The mother's botched surgery scars her physically and psychically. Her bandaged eyes—a literal and metaphorical wound at the site/sight of identification—provide a sad and bitter commentary on the torturous difficulty of the Chinese female's ever gaining a sense of self-sameness and psychic stability. It is impossible for Tom's mother either willingly to identify with the devalued images of Asian femininity that she eschews or successfully to close the psychic gap between her bodily ego and the pervasive images of idealized white femininity to which she is drawn. In particular, *Two Lies* attests to the inability of the Chinese American female to exist in a comfortable relationship with valorized images of not just female but specifically white female beauty. Here sexual and racial difference work in conjunction to bar the Chinese American female from any possibility of jubilant identification. Idealized representations of sexual and racial beauty that demand and receive the mother's identificatory investments cannot be thought of separately in Tom's film. Indeed, for Tom's mother, they come into existence in a negative relation with one another.

While Lacan has little to say about the specific ways in which the psychic transactions in the mirror stage are socially determined, Fanon, Houston, and Tom provide compelling testimonies as to how both sexuality and race intersect in the mirror stage to produce social subjects constituted through multiple axes of social difference. Prized representations of whiteness and femininity prove inimical to these minority subjects, whose access to psychic coherence, presence, and jubilance are summarily dispensed with again and again. Fanon, Houston, and Tom underscore the ways in which dominant images of the cultural screen prohibit the psychic production of a lovable bodily ego in which the racialized subject can even provisionally invest.

Let us turn now to "The Shoyu Kid," a story in which cinematic images of whiteness and heterosexuality also remain stubbornly exterior to the Japanese American boys. Unable to identify with popular cinematic idols and to be socially ratified in connection with them, the youngsters in the story are held instead to devalued images of Japaneseness and homosexuality—visual representations that involuntarily mark them as alien others. These disparaged images provide little narcissistic gratification, are experienced as external impositions, and prove to be toxic representations with which the boys refuse to identify psychically. How is this failure of the self-same body charted through the events of Kaneko's short story? And how does this psychic failure revise the very phantasmatic consistency of the origins of an interned Japanese American childhood to mark it as both racialized and queer?

"The Shoyu Kid" and the Self-Same Body

An intensely visual text, "The Shoyu Kid" provides a virtual disquisition on the Japanese American male subject's overdetermination by images of the screen in wartime internment. Placed under "preventative detention," Japanese Americans during this particular historical period were not only presumed to be guilty and disloyal but were legally barred from keeping anything Japanese—books, pictures, clothes, artifacts, even scriptures—in their households.[31]

It comes as no surprise that under this assumption of disloyalty —the "No-No Boy" phenomenon—the youngsters in Kaneko's short story, Jackson, Masao, and Itchy, resist identifying with anything Japanese.[32] Instead, they gravitate toward idealized male images of whiteness. The three boys passionately mimic Hollywood icons John Wayne and Humphrey Bogart as well as an ancillary cast of generic white masculine ideals who exemplify American loyalty: soldiers in war movies, cowboys, cavalry colonels, and police investigators. These reified white male images populate Kaneko's short story from beginning to end, constituting the very phantasmatic limits of the three boys' identificatory framework. All three—and in particular Jackson—are imaginatively fixated on these American movie idols, self-consciously imitating their on-screen speeches, poses, bravado, and swagger. As such, their behavior illustrates the coercive power that these culturally idealized images of whiteness and masculinity possess in eliciting both psychic faith in and bodily mimicry of their representations.

In an attempt to keep disparaged Japaneseness at a distance, the three boys gang up on the Shoyu Kid in their games of cowboys and Indians, forcing him to play the abject role of Indian—alien other, foreign enemy, intruding burglar, prisoner of war, spy.[33] In adopting the role of cowboys, the three youngsters might also be viewed as enacting a fantasy of nationalism and citizenship, a battle for westward expansion and the patriotic duty of conquering the frontier from disenfranchised Indian hands. In waging this "good" war, Jackson attempts physically to displace his own racial brownness elsewhere by rubbing onto the Shoyu Kid's arm an "Indian burn" during a mock interrogation (7). In this patent move to disavow the similitude of their bodily egos, Jackson attempts to shore up his own dissonant relationship to valorized white male images of the cowboy by displacing, projecting, and marking racial difference elsewhere on the body of his intended victim.

However, this willful attempt to (re)define themselves outside a chain of Japanese signifiers proves futile. The boys' aspirations to identify with idealized images of white masculinity are not only undermined by their physical incarceration in Minidoka as enemies of whiteness but are qualified by a gaze that refuses to affirm them in such a particular guise. Their slavish mimicry of white male imagos results in neither the smooth psychic mapping of these hip-shooting images onto their own bodily egos nor the production of a coherent psychic sense of self-sameness. Instead, it produces what Homi Bhabha describes as a hapless doubling, a partial "*metonymy of presence,*" a result that is "*almost the same but not white.*"[34]

In yet another effort to dispatch loathed racial representations elsewhere, the three boys exchange their Japanese names for more Euro-American-sounding ones (e.g., Hiroshi becomes Jackson and Ichiro becomes Itchy). However, by persistently calling the boys by their Japanese monikers, the *obasans* (aunties/old ladies) of the camp refuse to provide the cultural sanction necessary for them to see themselves in a guise other than Japanese. Jackson's negative reaction to their hailing—he "would make a face or thumb his nose as soon as they turned their backs" (2)—underscores the tortured and ambivalent relationship that minoritarian subjects have with the racialized images that would mark them as disparaged alien others.

Here we are reminded of Althusser's description of interpellation in "Ideology and Ideological State Apparatuses," in which the subject comes about only through recognition by the police of his or her trespass against the law. Althusser suggests that the hailing moment is productive of both subjectivity and subjection, stigmatizing the individual from the initial hailing and holding him or her to a type of social criminalization.[35] Jackson's negative response to the obasans' scenario of naming suggests the ambivalent relationship the marginal male subject has with this social interpellation of Japaneseness. The resulting psychic tension to which this racial identification holds Jackson produces in him a loss of "presence" and an unlovable bodily ego, one in which he refuses to invest psychically.

Thus, when Jackson threatens to tear the Shoyu Kid "limb from limb" (7) during a mock interrogation, his John Wayne impersonation works less to close the gap between his own bodily ego and dominant images of white masculinity than to highlight the ironic distance between Jackson's own corporeal schema and this idealized imago. It is important to note that Kaneko's short story presents no coherent image of Japanese

American masculinity with which the boys can even potentially identify. The fathers of the camp, we are told by the narrator Masao, are off fighting a fire in the desert (can deserts catch fire?), their specular presence banished by means of this textual detail (9). The only Japanese male body within the visible realm of the Minidoka camp is the fractured image of cousin Aya's aged grandfather. Masao describes his crumpled body as "scurrying between the hollyhocks, leaping awkwardly every now and then as if he were stepping on nails. He was a skinny old man whose feet seemed to be moving in two directions at once while his body was heading in a third. His arms, weighted by a heavy, blunt spade, seemed to be confused about moving in a fourth direction" (5). Going in four directions, the grandfather's corporeal schema breaks down, fractures, and dissolves—to borrow a phrase from Lacan—into "bits and pieces."[36] This body, the only available Japanese American male body with which the boys can potentially identify, acquires in its fragmented state an abhorrent value. It is not surprising that, given this grotesque image of "mature" Japanese American manhood, the three boys resist identifying with anything Japanese. In their repudiation of the grandfather's repellent image, in their reluctance to allow any mapping of this disparaged Japanese American imago onto their bodily egos, they thus forfeit any potential for psychic coherence, presence, or "self-sameness."

The boys resist the Japanese names by which the obasans of the camp address them as willfully as they renounce any identification with the fragmented body of the aged grandfather. Nevertheless, Jackson, Itchy, and Masao are held to an uncomfortable identification with these Japanese names and images. Kaneko's description of the grandfather comes at a moment when he is engaged in an unsuccessful hunt for a rodent that has scurried under the barracks' floor. The question of whether the animal is a rat or a rabbit persists through the story. The ambiguous identity of the hunted animal is significant in its association with the pursuit of the Shoyu Kid, with Jackson (in the final lines of the story), and ultimately with the internees in general. Are Japanese Americans rats or rabbits, disloyal or loyal?

This unsuccessful hunt not only gestures to the radical difficulty of these questions; it also echoes the opening passage of Kaneko's short story in which the three boys fail to capture the Shoyu Kid. In their collective inability to subdue either rodent or "Indian," the discombobulated grandfather and the three boys are thus figuratively and thematically intertwined. The boys' homage to cinematic images of white American male potency results not in their alignment with John Wayne or Humphrey Bogart but finally in their alignment with the disparaged image of the old Japanese American grandfather. Their divestment from valorized masculine images of the visual domain permeates the short story from beginning to end.

Queer Expectations

There is something decidedly "queer" in the world of Minidoka, queer not just in the sense of the epithet, the slur of sexual shame that is continually hurled from one youngster to another, but queer in the sense that visual authority is consistently thwarted in the moment of its anticipated fulfillment. The story opens with just such a queer turn of events: the shifting of specular control away from the three young boys in the form of a botched ambush. The narrator, Masao, describes a game of cowboys and Indians in which the Shoyu Kid is meant to play the role of the Indian and the intended victim:

> We were ready for him. The three of us were crouched in the vines *expecting* the Kid to come stumbling into the garden. Itchy was to my right trying to tell me about what he'd seen earlier in the morning. Something about the sun rising from the wrong direction. I was too busy looking for the Kid to pay much attention. Jackson was in front of Itchy, ready to close off the Kid's escape in case he should see us before we could jump him. He came this way every day. . . . The Kid had stopped about six feet in front of Jackson, still too far away for Jackson to nab him. I heard him drawing the snot back into his nose. It was his trademark, that sniffing. . . . We waited a long time. When I looked up, the Kid was gone. (1–2; my emphasis)

As we join their ambush *in medias res,* Jackson, Itchy, and Masao are diligently—mechanically—enacting the role of cowboy, preoccupied with their surveillance of the Kid. Yet the world of Minidoka is full of unpredictable reversals, both cosmic and mundane. Not only does the Idaho sun seem to be rising from the "wrong direction" at this particular moment but the meticulous battle strategy of the three youngsters is subjected to a similar logic of reversal as well. Although the Kid, Masao tells us, "came this way every day," their plan backfires at its moment of predicted fulfillment. A mere six feet away and sniffling up an acoustic storm, the Kid appears—sounds—at first to be an easy target to nab. Yet as the three boys turn their eyes upon their intended victim he suddenly disappears. Instead of looking *at* him, they end up looking *for* him. The three are left in a state of bewilderment: "When I looked up, the Kid was gone."—"Hey, where'd he go?"—"I donno."—"That way. Around the building" (2).

The boys' attempt to play the active role of "looker" and aggressor is thus undercut through an estrangement of their specular control. Expecting to catch the Kid unawares, Jackson, Itchy, and the narrator are caught in their own voyeuristic confusion, as their "looks" are rendered impotent in this sudden moment of reversal. Unable to establish any visual authority in this game of cat-and-mouse, the boys cannot locate the object of their attention, the target of their attack. In this manner, they are left resembling their intended victim—more, that is, like an Indian than a cowboy. In a disconcerting instant, expectations are curiously frustrated, vision is blurred, and subject and object are rendered indeterminate.

Moreover, this moment of specular divestment is accompanied by a structural focusing of the literary text upon the lookers themselves. Eluded by the object of scrutiny, the narrator's attention comes to rest upon Jackson in what I would describe as the textual equivalent of a cinematic zoom. Unlike most filmic zooms, however, this textual zoom centers not on the supposedly passive object of their hunt—the Shoyu Kid, after all, is nowhere to be found—but on the ostensibly active stalkers of the scenario:

> Jackson was up and flying down the edge of the garden with Itchy and me not far behind. At the corner of the building, he pulled up, flattened himself against the wall and like a soldier in a war movie, peered around the corner. We pulled up behind him, puffing, and he turned and put a finger to his lips and inched an eye like a periscope around the corner. His body relaxed, and he turned back to us. "He's gone." (2)

Once again, their pursuit of the Kid proves futile from the start because the three cowboys never manage even to sight their Indian. Unable to locate the Kid, Masao's narrative delivers instead a detailed description of Jackson, the "soldier in a war movie." And while the narrative configures him as an all-seeing and flexible eye—a rotating "periscope" of vision— Jackson's inability to spot the Kid only compounds his ironic miscasting as the one who looks. In this manner, the story's textual zoom on Jackson not only constitutes a reversal of one of the conventional signifiers of vision—a zoom in on what is seen—but focuses its attention upon the looker rather than the object at which he seeks to look.

Consequently, this is a textual zoom that transports the looker emphatically into the domain of the visible and the realm of spectacle. It delivers up not the object of the three boys' attention but the boys themselves. As such, it draws attention to the impotence of their specular pretensions by placing their marked bodies squarely within the field of the visible. Any attempt on the part of the youngsters to identify with the position of cowboy—with the active role of the one who looks and stalks—is undermined and qualified by this abrupt inversion of the scopic drive. Hence, this textual zoom not only attests to the Japanese American boys' inability to fix their object, but the specular reversal also divorces them from traditional scopic regimes (discussed by feminist film theorists such as Laura Mulvey) in which visual authority is normally granted to the male subject, a crossing of race with a gendered visual differential.[37]

This opening passage of "The Shoyu Kid" provides a virtual gloss on the function of the gaze, as it prevents the three boys from looking with any visual authority while prohibiting their identification with culturally prized images of white masculinity. Like Sartre's voyeur at the keyhole—interrupted and surprised by a noise behind him—Jackson, Itchy, and Masao are disturbed by a gaze that suddenly overwhelms them and reduces them to a "feeling of shame."[38] Unlike Sartre's male voyeur, however, the shame that marks these three young boys is produced not only through the arrogance of aligning oneself with the gaze but through being seen in deidealizing ways—the shame of being looked at. Ultimately, the shame that marks these youngsters is produced and circulated within the historical, racialized space of the Minidoka concentration camp—in the face, that is, of virulent national anti-Japanese sentiment. As such, this opening scene of "The Shoyu Kid" does not merely establish that the young boys who look are less subject than subjected; it also suggests that their subjection is historically marked and culturally motivated by the particular racializing conditions under which they are seen as disloyal and suspect and thus incarcerated by the U.S. government.

The illustrated cover of the 1976 *Amerasia Journal* in which "The Shoyu Kid" was first published speaks to this intersection of the visual, psychic, and historical. In yet another gesture toward the story's specular and cinematic themes, the graphic box surrounding the figure of a slouching and sullen-looking Kid resembles the frame of a photograph (fig. 7). Unlike the jubilant infant capturing his image before the frame of Lacan's mirror, the reflected image of the Japanese American male body in this illustration is permeated with a profound sadness. Moreover, this frozen image of the Shoyu Kid does not exist in an unmarked physical space but is framed by the material environment of the internment camp. The cramped and makeshift barracks encroach upon and bleed into the borders of the frame. They enclose the image of the Shoyu Kid, as three indistinct and shadowy figures (presumably Jackson, Itchy, and Masao) emerge from the bottom of the illustration to echo this in-

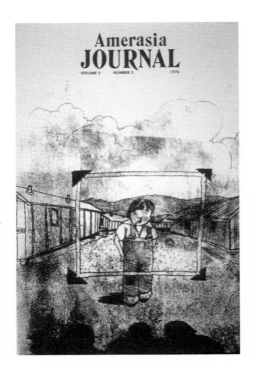

Figure 7 Cowboys and Indians: "The Shoyu Kid," cover of *Amerasia Journal* 3.2 (1976)

trusion visually. Both the opening passages of Kaneko's short story and the cover illustration establish, then, the historical and cultural parameters of this World War II period through which *all* the boys—far from being able to identify freely with the position of cowboy—are ultimately framed and forced to identify with one another in their role of victimized prisoner, Indian, and spy.

Thus far we have focused primarily on the racial foreclosures of Japaneseness underpinning Kaneko's text of literal wartime enclosure. How do these devalued racial images intersect with queerness—with homosexuality—in Kaneko's text? Sau-ling Cynthia Wong suggests that queerness works with racialization to configure Japanese American male subjectivity as weak. Wong observes that throughout Kaneko's story a "simple code, constantly reinforced by mutual egging-on, underlies [Jackson, Itchy, and Masao's] feeble gestures of defiance: avoid appearing weak—that is, Japanese and 'queer'—at all costs."[39] The boys' inability to identify with privileged racial images of whiteness manifests itself most profoundly in its intersection with the failure of a sexual ideal: a heterosexual norm. Collectively, these failures reconfigure the very phantasmatic limits of their unconscious psychic lives. I would like to examine

Itchy's primal scene, his witnessing of the Shoyu Kid's molestation by the white soldier.

Primal Glances

Let us return, then, to a scene of discovery, an old scene, a scene of seduction. Spying on the molestation of the Shoyu Kid behind the garage, Itchy at once discovers the source of the boy's coveted chocolate bars and witnesses a spectacle that I would describe as nothing less than primal. The narrator, Masao, tells us that "Itchy was already peering around the corner like an Indian from behind a tree, when his body went stiff. He motioned us back, but he stayed fixed at the corner for another minute; then he took off past us running as hard as he could" (3). Itchy's witnessing of the molestation is not—cannot be—overtly described by the narrator. Instead, it acquires meaning by means of its subsequent (re)construction through the psychical mechanism Freud labels as *Nachträglichkeit*—deferred action. This is a psychical process through which the importance of a memory is assigned only after the fact, its significance becoming clear through its juxtaposition with a latter series of events.

Kaneko's use of the past imperfect—"was already peering"—suggests through its indefinite grammar the temporal unresolvability as well as the psychic confusion of this primal scene as Itchy witnesses it. As the three boys race around the internment camp searching for the Shoyu Kid, their movement through space dissolves into a vertiginous frenzy—out of focus, untrackable, and suspended in time. Jean Laplanche observes in *Life and Death in Psychoanalysis* that, because of its skewed temporality, the primal scene is initially disempowering for the infant, who watches and overhears its parents in the act of copulation with little comprehension. In a passive and masochistic position, the infant, Laplanche writes, is like "Ulysses tied to the mast [of] Tantalus, on whom is imposed the spectacle of parental intercourse."[40] When Itchy spies on this unorthodox primal scene—this act of pedophilia—he, too, occupies the passive and masochistic position described by Laplanche. He is excluded from the action, witnessing rather than participating in the stream of events.[41] Stripped of his earlier role of cowboy and aggressor, Itchy stands behind the tree "like an Indian," a subject looking illicitly. In a similar manner to Laplanche's infant in the crib, he watches and listens passively with little visual or auditory control over the incidents he views. Moreover, he is physically placed in a marginal position—occupying a space on the edge of the scene as a silent witness—with respect to the framing of the main actions.

At first, Itchy reacts to this primal scene with mixed fascination and horror: "his body went stiff. He motioned us back, but he stayed fixed at the corner for another minute" (3). Like the infant who is at first unable to comprehend the meaning of parental intercourse, Itchy's subsequent reaction to the scene he observes is one of patent disavowal. Incapable of comprehending the significance of this physical assault, he flees in a confused panic: "Then he took off past us running as hard as he could. Jackson and I turned and ran too. Itchy turned the corner of the garage, cut across the street, zagged past the second row of barracks and cut into the walkway in front of the third, almost hitting the old women and stumbling over one of the girls with the rope. We followed as fast as we could" (3). Itchy races past Jackson and Masao, who chase after him in dumbfounded pursuit. However, despite the continual prodding of his unsuspecting pals, Itchy refuses to recount—for he cannot apprehend— what he has just witnessed. "Hey, Itchy, what were we running for?" the two boys query. His emphatic response: "Nothing" (3). Following upon the suspended temporal logic of the past imperfect, as well as the vertiginous topography of their pursuit, the boys' conversation at this moment dissolves into a similar pattern of indeterminacy. Their voices are a rebounding chorus of overlapping questions and answers: "Nothing." "Nothing?" "C'mon, what happened?" (3)

Because of its initial opacity, Laplanche characterizes the primal scene—its staging of fantasy and its inception of sexuality in the infant— as a traumatic "taking behind" of the ego (*Life*, 47). The primal scene, as well as the sexual knowledge it imparts to the young child, occurs both too early and too late, for it defines "a psychic experience in which the most crucial and constitutive dramas of human life are those that can never be viewed head on, those that can never be taken in frontally, but only, as it were, approached from behind."[42] In its *après coup* logic, the primal scene "occurs not so much in 'reality' as in fantasy . . . it is a construction after the fact, subsequent to an event with which it is by no means commensurate. The primal scene, in other words, never actually 'happens' as such, but is either constituted through a deferred action . . . or constructed as a fantasy on the basis of some remembered detail. It is consequently 'marked' as an image."[43] The primal scene has no existence as a scene of psychic trauma until it is marked as an image, (re)constituted, (re)presented, and (re)produced at a later time through deferred action. Yet the image and the meaning that the primal scene eventually assumes cannot be underestimated, for it provides what Freud labels the "stereotype plate" of our dreams, our "ready-made" unconscious fantasies, our object choices, and our desires.[44] In its retroactive form, the primal scene provides the psychic fodder of our phantasmatic life.

It is indeed not until after Itchy is initiated into the world of (hetero)-sexual difference that he becomes equipped with the knowledge to impute meaning to the earlier event he witnesses. Running away from the scene of molestation behind the garage, Itchy encounters yet another traumatic image: the naked body of Joyce Furata being bathed by her mother. His subsequent exchange with Jackson—an object lesson on the anatomical distinction between the sexes—is worth quoting at length:

> "C'mon what happened?"
>
> "Did you see Joyce?" Itchy was changing the subject. "Little girls are sure funny to look at, aren't they?"
>
> "Itchy, you act like you ain't never seen a naked girl before."
>
> "Well, have you? I mean really seen one, Jackson? Seen what kind of prick they have?"
>
> "They don't have one."
>
> "That's what I mean. Do you know what to do with it?"
>
> "Everyone knows. You get this hard-on, see, and . . ."
>
> "Jackson, you got a hard-on?" Itchy's face was tight.
>
> "Yeah, don't you? You're supposed to."
>
> "N-no."
>
> "What are you, Itchy, some kind of queer or something? Don't you know you're supposed to have a hard-on when you see a naked girl?" Jackson was getting wound up on his favorite subject. I sneaked a look at Jackson, and I think he was lying. (3–4)

Indoctrinating the reluctant Itchy into the protocols of (hetero)sexual difference, Jackson not only provides a summary lecture on female castration—the having and not having of the penis—but he also imparts to his two companions the imperatives of compulsory heterosexuality: "You get this hard-on, see." Curiously enough, Jackson's (hetero)sexual directive and his deprecation of the "queer" do not produce a commensurate anatomical response. Masao sneaks a look at Jackson's penis and believes him to be lying. Jackson's verbal affirmation of mainstream and compulsory heterosexual norms does not produce a stiff bodily reaction adequate to its stated ideals. In this case, Jackson's attempted identification with dominant images of heterosexuality emphatically slips away from his desired identity. For Jackson, identification and identity do not easily align.

Equipped with the social lessons of compulsory heterosexuality, Itchy is thus able to (re)evaluate the earlier event behind the garage. How does

Itchy's retroactive understanding of this incident stray from the normative protocols of compulsory heterosexuality? How does this scene of seduction come to intersect with whiteness, to mark Itchy and the other Japanese American boys as both queer and racialized?

Queer Childhood

Discussing the fluid identifications underpinning the primal scene, Freud observes in his 1925 essay "Some Psychological Consequences of the Anatomical Distinction between the Sexes" that the infant identifies as easily with the mother as the father in this psychic scenario.[45] Put another way, the primal scene encourages identification with both versions of the positive—heterosexual—and negative—homosexual—Oedipus complex. In a positive Oedipal trajectory, the male infant identifies with the father and desires the mother, while in a negative Oedipal trajectory he identifies with the mother and desires the father. The psychic fluidity emblematic of the primal scene confounds any easy distinction between identification and desire. As such, it "disposes of anatomical lack in ways that are profoundly disruptive of conventional masculinity."[46]

In his case history on the "Wolf Man" (1918), Freud states in unequivocal terms the nature of this intolerable disruption: by identifying with the position of the mother, the little boy desires to be used from "behind," as he perceives she is by the father.[47] In his piecing together of the Wolf Man's primal scene, Freud thus stumbles upon a scandalous supposition inimical to the norms of conventional male heterosexuality: a sodomitical fantasy of homosexual desire whose psychic roots form the foundational basis for the emergence of normative heterosexual masculinity.[48] By conceding the imaginative priority of a homosexual identification underpinning the primal scene, Freud, Lee Edelman notes, allows us to understand that male heterosexuality is retroactively produced as a "narcissistic compromise that only painfully and with difficulty represses its identification with the so-called 'passive' position in that [primal] scene so as to protect the narcissistically invested penis from the fate that is assumed to have befallen the penis of the mother"—castration.[49]

It is through the Law of the Father and the law of castration that the (re)construction of the primal scene is given over to a retroactive process of belated heterosexual revision. The traumatizing knowledge of the primal scene for the heterosexual male viewing it in hindsight—already, that is, within a compulsory heterosexual framework—is precisely the sodomitical trajectory of his earlier muddled queer identifications and desires. Hence, the emergence of normative male heterosexuality within the field of the visible depends upon the strict repression of these sodomitical traces and their belated revision into strict heterosexual forms of identification and desire. Edelman comments:

> Indeed, the sodomitical spectacle, when viewed from this perspective, cannot fail to implicate the heterosexual male situated to observe it since it constitutes an affront to the primary narrative that orients his theory of sexuality. From such a vantage point it generates a response that can be interpreted as the negative counterpart or inversion, as it were, of fetishism and the fetishistic overesteeming of the object: for if the problem engaged in the fetish is that of affirming a belief in presence of and against the knowledge of loss, the problem produced by the scene of sodomy is that of affirming a belief in loss over and against the knowledge of presence. (107)

According to Edelman, the primal scene—in its first instance perceived as sodomitical—must necessarily undergo a retroactive process of psychic revision and homosexual erasure in order for the Law of the Father and the (positive) Oedipal complex to make sense. Because the sodomitical spectacle threatens the Law of the Father by undoing the logic of castration, its presence proves intolerable to the conventional norms of heterosexuality. This sodomitical spectacle must therefore be repressed through a belated (re)configuration of the primal scene that heterosexualizes the young boy's identifications and desires. Coerced by the bogey of castration, the little man is terrorized into a type of psychic amnesia, the putting behind of his ambivalent erotic desires for the father in favor of an identification with him. Governed by the primacy of compulsory heterosexuality, the normative (re)construction of the primal scene through *Nachträglichkeit* thus necessitates the reworking of a homosexual presence into a homosexual absence and the strict segregation of identification and desire. We might characterize this psychic scenario, along with Edelman, as a type of reverse fetishism or reverse hallucination: not seeing what is there to see. (This revised psychoanalytic concept is central to the discussion of *M. Butterfly* in chapter three.)

How does racial difference come to intersect this primal narrative of belated heterosexualization? How do "queerness" and "Japaneseness" come together to mark Itchy's witnessing of the white soldier's sexual assault on the Shoyu Kid as a primal scene not heterosexually but homosexually as well as racially circumscribed? What we must consider in Freud's description of the belated heterosexual narrative of the primal scene is the fact that it is a racialized narrative at the same time. If, as I suggested in my earlier discussion of the self-same body, sexuality and race gain their discursive legibility in relation to one another, then the belated heterosexualization of the male infant's identifications in the primal scene can never simply be a heterosexual revision. Indeed, any retroactive reimagining of compulsory heterosexuality is made possible through its privileged relationship to a hegemonic whiteness.

That is, the principle of the self-same body teaches us that certain prized images of whiteness and heterosexuality are simultaneously barred for racially marked subjects culturally unauthorized to see themselves within them. If idealized images of whiteness and heterosexuality are inextricably bound together in our present-day cultural imaginary, then whiteness necessarily works in tandem with heterosexuality to regulate which subjects will or will not have retroactive psychic access to sexual as well as racial normativity in the primal scene. In other words, together whiteness and heterosexuality regulate who can or cannot have access to a lovable bodily ego and a coherent sense of self.

In their failure to incorporate successfully the cinematic images of white American masculinity exemplified by John Wayne and Humphrey Bogart, the Japanese American boys in "The Shoyu Kid" are thus retroactively closed off from heterosexual identifications as well. As he witnesses the white soldier's assault on the Shoyu Kid, Itchy is described by the author as observing "like an Indian from behind a tree" (3). Itchy's disempowerment is not merely structural in the sense of Laplanche's disenfranchised infant, who watches and listens passively to the events around him from the enclosure of the crib. In addition, Itchy's witnessing of this molestation illustrates a material reworking of a primal narrative in which whiteness structurally works in tandem with compulsory heterosexuality to foreclose the Japanese American youngster's psychic access to sexual normativity, masculine activity, and the Law of the (white) Father. Itchy's failure to become culturally validated in the image of whiteness thus manifests itself most insistently in this primal tableau through its intersecting failure with a concomitant heterosexual ideal. This intersection is the psychic correlation of Wong's earlier contention that "a simple code, constantly reinforced by mutual egging-on, underlies [Jackson, Itchy, and Masao's] feeble gestures of defiance: avoid appearing weak—that is, Japanese and 'queer'—at all costs" (Reading, 100).

Unable to identify with his white screen heroes, Itchy cannot make heterosexual sense of his primal scene. In its intersection with a foreclosed domain of whiteness, Itchy's primal scene is retroactively racialized in addition to being homosexualized. Instead of undergoing the belated heterosexualization (and ascendancy into male privilege and social empowerment) typical of Freud's male infant, Itchy's primal scene opens upon the psychic territory of the negative Oedipus complex. This is a primal scene whose trajectory of desire holds him at once to an unpleasurable identification with queerness as it holds him to an insistent identification with Japaneseness.

Going "behind" the tree, Itchy watches the Shoyu Kid going "down" on the white camp guard.[50] This depiction of a sodomitical primal scene gains its full psychic significance—its historical and social consequence—only after Itchy's initiation into the protocols of compulsory heterosexuality and only with our understanding that the availability of any retroactive heterosexual meaning in this scene is contingent upon its hegemonic collusion with whiteness. According to Freud, the primal scene necessarily opens upon both a negative and a positive Oedipal trajectory. In the maturation of the young (white) male infant from boy to man, heterosexuality and the Name of the (white) Father work to repress and to erase all traces of homosexuality. Itchy's sodomitical primal scene, however, suggests how racial difference intersects this Freudian narrative of retroactive heterosexuality by barring heterosexual identification for the Japanese American male. Itchy's primal scene works, then, to revise and render queer the very phantasmatic origins of Japanese American childhood during wartime internment. Japaneseness and homosexuality come to inscribe the psychic limits by means of which Japanese American male subjectivity is molded, formed, and constituted in queer childhood.

Psychic Infection

Before the discovery of the Shoyu Kid's molestation, Jackson, Masao, and Itchy are able to function more or less as a single psychic unit, mutually reassuring one another in their slavish imitations of cowboys, of white American heterosexual cinematic ideals. It is after Itchy's witnessing of the molestation of the Shoyu Kid, and his retroactive configuration of it as both a racially and a homosexually circumscribed primal scene, that the psychic implications of this discovery come to infect and implicate the three youngsters in reverse: from Itchy to Jackson to the narrator. This psychic chain reaction is brought to a resolution with the final pantsing episode of the Shoyu Kid:

> "No," the Kid was saying, "I didn't do anything. I just played with his chimpo like he asked."
>
> Jackson stopped, his mouth dropped open. "You what? You whore! Queer!" He was shouting "Queer! Queer!" and yanking at the pants at the same time and there staring at us with its single

eye squinting in Jackson's face was a little white prick like a broken pencil between equally white but shapeless thighs. Jackson was immobilized, his face slack in surprise, and Itchy moved away. (8)

As in the opening of the story, Jackson is forced yet again into an uncomfortable confrontation with an unwanted image of self. Through his admonishments of the Shoyu Kid, Jackson attempts to distance himself from this repellent image of homosexuality ("queer") and feminization ("whore"). The single eye of the Kid's penis, however, returns Jackson's look, implicating him in a circuit of shame and immobility. Though it is described as a broken pencil, the presence of the Shoyu Kid's prick does not fully conform to the Law of the (white) Father, which demands castration as the punishment for homosexuality. In its broken presence, the Shoyu Kid's penis elicits surprise from Jackson, who futilely attempts to yank it off: "And then Jackson was at him again. 'You played with the sonofabitch soldier? Goddam queer!' and Jackson's hands were fumbling for the Kid's prick and he was pulling as if he were going to pull it off and the Kid was convulsing on the ground, trying to roll away, his face smeared brown" (8). The emphatic contrast of the "white" prick on the Shoyu Kid's "smeared brown" body serves as an anatomical reminder of the sodomitical primal scene Itchy had witnessed earlier. The penis has not yet been cut off, as the Law of the (white) Father would demand of the normative (white) male subject. Jackson cannot serve as the enforcer of the Law of the (white) Father; his attempted identifications with heterosexual white male ideals—his attempts to punish and castrate the Shoyu Kid—are doomed to failure. Instead, the continued presence of the white and "broken" prick on the Shoyu Kid's smeared brown body serves as a symbolic marker of a sodomitical submission—a continual material reminder of the abhorrent racial and homosexual identification to which all these Japanese American boys are involuntarily held.

Itchy's witnessing of the Shoyu Kid's molestation forces us to consider the status of racial difference as underpinning the traditional heterosexual narrative of the primal scene. We discover through our analysis of this classic psychic paradigm a shifting backward of both homosexual and racial difference to an unconscious psychic arena that underpins fantasies of queer self in Japanese American male childhood. Yet I must emphasize that these fantasies of queer self are, if nothing else, historically constituted. Commenting upon the mutual connections of individual and group history, Teresa de Lauretis reminds us

that if the primal or original fantasies can be understood as a structure in the subject's prehistory . . . it is in the sense of a "prestructure which is actualized and transmitted by the parental fantasies." Thus the original fantasies lie "beyond the history of the subject but nevertheless in history—a kind of language and a symbolic sequence, but loaded with elements of imagination; a structure, but activated by contingent elements." The fantasies of origin, in other words, are historically structured as well as structuring of the subject's history; that is to say, the constitutive role of fantasy in subjectivity is both structural and historically motivated, historically specific.[51]

In its provocative exploration of a historical and psychic era of intense U.S. anti-Japanese sentiment, "The Shoyu Kid" provides an exemplary case study for a critical analysis of the ways in which wartime policies and prevailing national attitudes configure psychic structures—such as the mirror stage and the primal scene—through contingent historical events. It is through this mixing of the material and the psychic that Japanese American male subjectivity is formed, limited, and constrained. Throughout "The Shoyu Kid," Kaneko reminds us that identification is never outside history. Identification names the sexual and racial history of the subject while it is itself implicated in and through specific historical events.

I close this chapter by returning to the domain of the visible, to that symbolic treat of the brown chocolate bar that the white soldier ironically bestows upon the Shoyu Kid at the moment of his sodomitical violation. The chocolate bar provides a provocative closing image, crystallizing not just the psychic or historical aspects of Itchy's primal scene but its constitutive (homo)sexual and racial foreclosures. In its gooey brownness, the chocolate bar denotes not only sodomy and anal penetration but the process of racialization itself: "The Kid always had that heavy snot dripping from his nose. Like a perpetual cold. Except that the snot was the color of soy sauce. Jackson's older brother told him the reason the Kid had brown snot was because he used too much soy sauce, and it just dripped out of his nose. We all stopped using shoyu when we heard that" (5). The three boys think that the revolting brown snot comes from the use of too much *shoyu* (soy sauce) and is thus a congenital trait of Japaneseness. They therefore unanimously agree to avoid the use of this seasoning, refusing yet again to identify themselves with deprecated racial images and objects.

The events of Itchy's primal scene suggest, however, that the older brother's account of the Shoyu Kid's "brownness" is in fact more complex. Far from being an ontological marker of race, the brownness of the Shoyu Kid's snot could very well be attributed to the chocolate bestowed upon him by the white camp guard in return for sexual services. In this sense, race and racialization cannot be read as an ontological phenomenon. On the contrary, it must be read as a historically motivated event. As a marker of the soldier's material and psychic violation of the Shoyu Kid, the chocolate bar comes to displace any ontological racial pretensions associated with soy sauce. As Masao subsequently remarks, "Later, I thought it was the chocolate that made the Kid's snot brown because it didn't used to be when he trailed after us" (5). Hence, the chocolate bar serves not only as a marker of these continuous homosexual violations; it also signifies the racialized and homosexualized otherness that historically structures the identificatory limits of the Shoyu Kid's as well as the three other Japanese American boys' psychic lives.

Finally, it must be noted that the image of the chocolate bar carries another historical inflection as well, serving to comment upon the larger question of U.S. military aggression and neoimperialism. The image of the chocolate bar, Wong suggests, "recalls numerous propaganda photographs and film clips of friendly American GI's overseas giving out candy to eager, undernourished children. It evokes at once the enviable plenty of America—that which attracts immigrants from all corners of the world—and the concomitant power that makes domination possible abroad or at home" (48).[52] As a dominant image of the U.S. propaganda machine, the chocolate bar squarely occupies that cluster of idealized representations of "Americanness"—of American benevolence, sovereignty, and freedom. Yet, in an opposing capacity as symbolic marker of those racial and (homo)sexual identifications forced upon the Japanese American male subject, the chocolate bar also qualifies the rhetoric of abstract equality—of American democracy, liberal pluralism, and equal access to representation. At a particular historical moment in which Japanese Americans had to be seen as enemies of the nation at all costs, the chocolate bar functions as an overdetermined image through which multiple national anxieties are enacted and displayed. The image of the chocolate bar thus serves to mark the psychic distance of both the Shoyu Kid as an individual from a stable, coherent, or lovable identity and of Japanese American males as a social group from national ideals of proper citizenship and inclusion.

The American GI who bestows upon the Kid this ideological treat is also, after all, the pointer of the gun, the enforcer of the law, the gatekeeper of the nation's borders. "There's something strange about that guy," Itchy observes. "I mean that's the same red-headed soldier who used to stand there at the fence and point his gun at me like he was going to shoot" (4). As simultaneous guard and molester, it is this soldier with the shooting gun who patrols not just the material but the psychic and ideological fences around which Kaneko's short story both begins and concludes:

> "Jeez." Itchy was talking more to himself than to Jackson or me. "I thought the guy was just taking a leak behind the garage. Goddam queers. Jeezus, everyone's queer." He stood up and threw a rock at the Off Limits sign we had taken. And missed. He picked up another and missed again. "Do you think the kid will squeal?"
>
> "Nyaa. Who cares." Jackson's voice was quiet, almost a curse. He threw a stone at the other sign. It hit the wood above the words MINIDOKA RELOCATION CENTER. Jackson continued to stare at the red glow, his face pale in the spotlight from the fence a hundred yards off. He was sitting very still, and his eyes were soft and wide like a rabbit's. (312)

Itchy's verbal circumscription of Japanese American male subjectivity—"Jeezus, everyone's queer"—provides a final commentary on the homosexual and racial limits of these young boys' identifications and psychic sense of self. The dominating signs of white America that the three boys attempt to steal and at which they hurl stones in frustration are not theirs to use—are ultimately "off limits" to them. Instead, the youngsters are visually overdetermined by that "other" historical sign, MINIDOKA RELOCATION CENTER, which textually dominates this closing paragraph and resists through its foreboding specular presence their ability to define or control the images that would historically and psychically overshadow them. In this respect, "The Shoyu Kid" prefigures a significant and compelling group of subsequent Asian American works such as R. Zamora Linmark's *Rolling the R's*, Shyam Selvadurai's *Funny Boy*, and Norman Wong's *Cultural Revolution*, all of which expand upon queer male childhood through an insistent critique of the failure of national ideals and imaginings of abstract equivalence in the nation-state.[53]

It is always open season on gay kids, Eve Sedgwick notes in her essay "How to Bring Your Kids up Gay: The War on Effeminate Boys." She adds that the "presiding asymmetry of value assignment between hetero and homo goes unchallenged everywhere: advice on how to help your kids turn out gay, not to mention your students, your parishioners, your therapy clients, or your military subordinates, is less ubiquitous than you might think. On the other hand, the scope of institutions whose programmatic undertaking is to prevent the development of gay people is unimaginably large."[54] The primal scene Kaneko presents to us in "The Shoyu Kid" relies not, as Sedgwick poses, on the disregarded question of how in America to "bring your kids up gay." Instead, it hinges on the pressing question of how in Japanese American male childhood during wartime internment it could possibly be otherwise.

Yet Sedgwick's analysis neglects the fact that in the war on effeminate boys some racialized communities are indeed produced precisely as feminized, homosexualized, queer. In "The Shoyu Kid," the heterosexual stability of the patriotic white American male icon emerges only in contrast to the resolute linking of queerness with Japaneseness. In this manner, normative masculine self-representation constitutively depends upon the sexual "perversion" and pathologizing of the racialized masculine subject. The solution to such warfare on a racialized and effeminized Japanese American childhood, however, cannot be to reify or aspire toward those normative masculinized images underwritten by mainstream society—a version of Frank Chin and his *Aiiieeeee!* group's political prescription. We cannot place our psychic hopes in this type of so-called limited, positive imagery; we cannot place our political hopes in the extension of masculine, patriarchal privileges to these Japanese American youngsters. In the final analysis, we must not conserve but proliferate the idealized images of the screen.

The struggle to recompose the psychic and material body of the racialized masculine subject can often result in the ascribing of conservative norms to emancipatory political projects. For instance, Fanon—in reconstructing the black male body that has "burst apart"—has often been criticized by feminist and queer commentators for building his incisive critique of French colonialism on the reassertion of woman as lack and on the linking of racism with homosexuality rather than homophobia.[55] Countering stereotypes of Asian American male subjectivity as the conflation of "Asian" and "anus" by valorizing whiteness and heterosexuality would not only serve to reinforce the racist and homophobic logic that produces these limited and debilitating roles from the onset but also sanction the racist and homophobic logic that understands Japanese American internment as having been both legitimate and necessary in the first place. Psychic salvation for the Asian American male cannot be the monopoly of a masculinist compulsory heterosexuality. To accept this racial and (hetero)sexual logic—to aspire to the presumed material rewards it offers—amount to what Angela Y. Davis calls "accepting a bribe"—an illusory compensation for powerlessness.[56] Redeeming Japanese American queer childhood does not require, then, material and psychic strategies to maintain the dominant order of things. On the contrary, it requires renewed material and psychic challenges to the structures of domination altogether.

THREE

Heterosexuality in the Face of Whiteness:

Divided Belief in *M. Butterfly*

White is a color—it is a pastel. . . .

In a place where it doesn't belong, on Michael,

that same pastel remains a flaming signifier.

<small>EVE SEDGWICK, "White Glasses"</small>

For some time now, critics in gender, ethnic, queer, and cultural studies have stressed the importance of giving disenfranchised subjects— women, people of color, gays, and lesbians—"voices," full subjectivities, visibilities in the face of invisibilities.[1] In my discussion of photography and national history in *China Men* and *Donald Duk,* I noted the great psychic and material difficulties encountered by marginal Asian American male subjects who attempt to emerge from a domain of silence and invisibility into an order of speech and visibility. However, this emergence into history, as it were, is only one part of a larger cultural politics of difference. My analysis of the hypervisibility of the young Japanese American male during wartime internment in "The Shoyu Kid" expands my critique of the discursive mechanisms by means of which Asian Americans continue to be rendered speechless and invisible despite their appearance in the visual field. Chapter two takes into consideration the particular historical conditions of World War II to explore the psychic constraints under which Japanese American male subjectivity is allowed to emerge within the realm of the visible. Chapter two concludes with a caveat on the false promises of investing in a dominant ideology of heterosexuality and whiteness, the psychic costs of valorizing this hegemonic pairing instead of making a concerted attempt to contest and dismantle it. The present chapter extends the critique of heterosexuality and whiteness from yet another perspective. Reading *M. Butterfly* allows us to discover the costs of heterosexuality and whiteness not just from the Asian American male's point of view but from that of the putatively normative, straight white male.

Kobena Mercer provides an initial entry point for this investigation by insisting that we initiate a critical examination of whiteness and its strategic occlusion from the visible domain. For "all our rhetoric about 'making ourselves visible,'" he asserts, "the real challenge in the new cultural politics of difference is to make 'whiteness' visible for the first time, as a culturally constructed ethnic identity historically contingent upon the disavowal and violent denial of difference."[2] Mercer's intervention is significant. Whiteness—in its refusal to be named and its refusal to be seen—represents itself as *the* universal and unmarked standard, a ubiquitous norm from which all else and all others are viewed as a regrettable deviation.

I would like to take up Mercer's challenge to make whiteness visible, then, by investigating not only its conditions of possibility but its moments of failure. Consider the remarkable closing scene of David Henry Hwang's Tony-Award-winning drama *M. Butterfly*, which takes place moments before the demise of the French diplomat. Donning the robes of the forsaken Japanese geisha Cio-Cio-San (memorialized in Puccini's 1904 opera *Madama Butterfly* and its numerous antecedents),[3] René Gallimard commits seppuku, but only after uttering these final words: "There is a vision of the Orient that I have. Of slender women in chong sams and kimonos who die for the love of unworthy foreign devils. Who are born and raised to be the perfect women. Who take whatever punishment we give them, and bounce back, strengthened by love, unconditionally. It is a vision that has become my life."[4] I read this final scene of the drama in contrast to the unveiling of opera diva Song Liling's penis at the opening of act III. Gallimard is so committed to Puccini's *Madama Butterfly* fantasy of "the submissive Oriental woman and the cruel white man" (17) that it is impossible for him to imagine an alternative outcome to this dreary story of heterosexual domination and white supremacy. Indeed, because he cannot relinquish his colonial fantasy of "slender women in chong sams and kimonos who die for the love of unworthy foreign devils," the diplomat must "turn somersaults" (60) in order to protect the psychic integrity of his farce.

Vigilant in his desire to maintain this particular vision of a submissive Orient, Gallimard is forced to counter the disrobed diva with a transvesting act of his own: now that Song is publicly the man, Gallimard must publicly become the woman. "Get away from me!" he orders Song petulantly. "Tonight, I've finally learned to tell fantasy from reality. And, knowing the difference, I choose fantasy" (90). Rejecting the psychoanalytic axiom that posits a constitutive relationship between fantasy and reality—that what is most real to the subject is fantasy—the diplomat refuses to face the real world effects of his geisha dream. He assumes the sartorial role of Cio-Cio-San and thus recedes into the imagined realm of his *Madama Butterfly* fantasy by "straightening" his relationship to the exposed Chinese man. He returns it once again, in the realm of his imagination and in the domain of the visible, to a normative heterosexual union. This concluding scene is of course an ironic rendering of Puccini's dictum that "death with honor is better than life . . . life with dishonor" (92; Hwang's ellipsis), for the price of Gallimard's phantasmatic sartorial conversion—the death of the white man—is materially high. Gallimard commits suicide, but he dies with his orientalist fantasy intact and, most importantly, as a nominal member of the acceptably heterosexual community.

I would like to isolate a striking visual detail emphasized in this concluding scene both in Hwang's stage version and in David Cronenberg's film adaptation of the drama. Before Gallimard dons his wig and kimono, he carefully—even methodically—applies a thick layer of white makeup to his face, appearing literally in whiteface (figs. 8 and 9). Several commentators have read this cosmetic transformation as a faithful rendering of the aesthetic protocols of Japanese theater, relating Gallimard's application of whiteface to the traditional makeup of the *onnogata* in Kabuki theater.[5] Majorie Garber, however, expands the possible interpretations of this critical moment by analyzing the diplomat's bad makeup job in the confluence of various ethnic channels:

> The whiteness of the makeup is traditional in Japanese theater as a sign of the ideal white complexion of the noble, who can afford to keep out of the sun, and the pallor of the protected young woman (or trained geisha) even today. We might note that in *Chinese* opera face-painting participates in an entirely different sign system, in which white on an actor's face symbolized treachery, as red does loyalty, yellow, piety, and gold, the supernatural. In this story of spies and treason the Chinese and Japanese significations are at odds with one another, and Song has already warned Gallimard not to conflate the two.[6]

Although Garber's analysis of this scene largely focuses on Gallimard's egregious misreading of disparate East Asian cultural aesthetics—the conflation of Chinese chong sams and Japanese kimonos—she subsequently appends a final and provocative interpretation: "The white

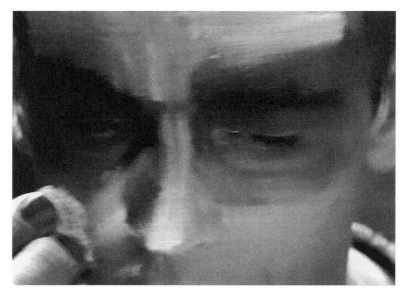

Figures 8 and 9 Heterosexuality in the face of whiteness: Jeremy Irons in David Cronenberg's *M. Butterfly* (Warner Brothers)

makeup has yet another significance, since [Gallimard] is continually described as a 'white man' throughout the play, even in France, where 'There're white men all around'" (244).[7] Garber proffers a triple reading of Gallimard's bad makeup job through this condensed cultural survey, but I would like to elaborate on her final point: Gallimard is continually described by Song as a white man; the visible face underscoring Gallimard's failures, demise, and swan song appears to us literally as a white face; the Orientalist and heterosexist fantasy for which Gallimard ultimately dies is achieved only in the face of whiteness.

Judith Butler insists that we must begin to theorize the compulsory regimes of the symbolic order—the numerous interpellations and coercive prohibitions by which individuals are rendered legible as subjects—through the lens not only of (hetero)sexual but also racial difference. "The symbolic—that register of regulatory ideality—is also and always a racial industry, indeed, the reiterated practice of *racializing* interpellations." She continues:

> Rejecting those models of power which would reduce racial differences to the derivative effects of sexual difference (as if sexual difference were not only autonomous in relation to racial articulation but somehow more prior, in a temporal or ontological sense), it seems crucial to rethink the scenes of reproduction and, hence, of sexing practices not only as ones through which a heterosexual imperative is inculcated, but as ones through which boundaries of racial distinction are secured as well as contested. Especially at those junctures in which a compulsory heterosexuality works in the service of maintaining hegemonic forms of racial purity, the "threat" of homosexuality takes on a distinctive complexity.[8]

Butler asks us to consider how sexual and racial norms intersect to produce viable and recognizable subject positions and to consider how the homosexual and racial prohibitions that underpin the foundations of the symbolic order interdict a spectrum of repudiated social identities. If the symbolic order is always also a set of racializing norms, it becomes impossible to speak of the heterosexual matrix apart from racial distinctions. The articulation of such a "colorless" category would assume a priori the ontological presumption of sexual over racial difference while denying race any constitutive role in the formation of a legible subjectivity.

Moreover, the assumed primacy in this model of the sexual over the racial would imply that sexual difference is in effect "*white* sexual difference, and that whiteness is not a form of racial difference."[9] In producing whiteness as an unnamed and invisible category, the symbolic order projects the burden of racial difference onto those bodies outside a universalizing discourse of whiteness. In other words, if a symbolic system of compulsory heterosexuality depends on the occlusion of whiteness as a racial category—drawing its discursive potency in and through this concealed alignment—then it is imperative that we insist on making whiteness emphatically visible as a culturally constructed and racialized category.

Furthermore, we must begin to consider the multiple ways in which this universalizing of an unmarked whiteness works to authorize at one and the same time the naturalizing power of heterosexuality. This attention to the discursive erasure of whiteness is a necessary amendment to the critical ways in which feminism and queer studies have hitherto framed issues of gender and sexuality. To deconstruct a system of compulsory heterosexual privilege (as psychoanalytic critics in feminist and queer studies have worked so hard to do) without considering racial difference—to fail to understand whiteness through the perspective of racial formation—would be to concede from the very outset that "whiteness . . . is yet another power that need not speak its name." [10] It would in effect allow the discursive pretensions of whiteness as a universalizing and unmarked racial category to continue unchecked and unqualified.

Granted that the consolidation of the symbolic order is contingent upon unstated norms of heterosexuality and whiteness, as well as prohibitions against homosexuality and nonwhiteness, we must note that this consolidation has functioned largely as a regulatory standard hitherto invisible within the field of the visible and unremarked in the protocols of social discourse. In their "ideal" form, heterosexuality and whiteness maintain their compulsory power by remaining veiled and undisclosed. Furthermore, they work in collusion, drawing their discursive force in and through their smooth alignment. If, as Eve Sedgwick says of her friend Michael Lynch—a gay, white male—whiteness somehow "doesn't belong" on him, remaining a "flaming signifier," it is because the crucial and mandatory combination of heterosexuality and whiteness has been violated and transgressed. [11] In his "flaming" queerness, the whiteness of Michael Lynch is suddenly brought into relief, rendered visible and disconcerting.

Consequently, I read Gallimard's phantasmatic sartorial conversion as a frantic attempt to maintain the normative sexual and racial stipulations of the symbolic order, as a desperate effort to maintain heterosexuality in the face of whiteness. Unable to occupy the position of the domineering European imperialist following Song's morphological unveiling, Gallimard is so invested in heterosexuality and whiteness that he ultimately elects to occupy the position of the "other" so as to guarantee the structural integrity of his *Madama Butterfly* fantasy. In a grave sense, then, the symbolic appeals of heterosexuality that impel the death of—and Gallimard's death as—Cio-Cio-San can be realized only in a white face. And it is, of course, this dual presumption of a (hetero)sexual and racial positioning that the French diplomat vigilantly struggles to maintain but fails miserably to preserve.

Gallimard's self-sacrifice must finally be read not only as a visible failure of heterosexuality and whiteness but as a hyperbolic illustration of the homosexual and racial anxieties that underpin the abject borders of the symbolic domain. Nevertheless, the overwhelming majority of commentaries generated by *M. Butterfly* do not account for this complex nexus of (homo)sexual and racial regulation. They focus exclusively on Song Liling's dramatic male to female crossing rather than on the possibility of Gallimard's passing between an acceptable white male heterosexuality and an abjected white male homosexuality. *New York Times* theater critic Frank Rich, for instance, claims that Hwang is not "overly concerned with how the opera singer . . . pulled his hocus-pocus in the boudoir." [12] Rich dismisses the possibility that Gallimard's blunder over Song's anatomy might be explored through the lens of a closeted or self-denying homosexuality. Moira Hodgson, in her summary of the drama for the *Nation*, emphatically concurs with Rich's latter point: "Hwang never gets to the bottom of Gallimard's character. He doesn't question whether the Foreign Service officer knew that Song Liling was in fact a man ('It was dark and she was very modest'), nor does he make him into a self-deluded homosexual." [13] Collectively, much of this criticism is so thoroughly transfixed by *M. Butterfly's* bizarre (homo)sexual story that the drama's incisive racial critique is in danger of vanishing.

Furthermore, when race is discussed, commentators by and large refuse to investigate the (hetero)sexual limits of white male subjectivity. Instead, they focus their critical attention solely on the "multicultural" issues of the drama: Asian American political agendas, assimilation, the model minority myth, and artistic license. [14] John Simon's bitter dismissal of *M. Butterfly* in *New York* magazine, for instance, attacks Hwang as the "son of affluent Chinese Americans [who] has scores to settle with both America and the new China, the former for making him embarrassed about his ethnicity, the latter for repudiating his bourgeois status and Armani suits." [15] Deflecting his attention away from the inherent qualities of the drama itself, Simon dislodges Hwang from the position of the disembodied artist. That is, Simon refuses Hwang the site of liberal subjectivity and artistic license, conflating the playwright with his opera diva. Hence, Simon's review largely focuses on the motivations and failures of Hwang as a frustrated, self-loathing Asian American dramatist, insisting instead on the "burden of liveness" for this artist of color. Ironically, while Simon conflates Hwang with Song, he resolutely disidentifies with Gallimard's cognitive inadequacies and avoids giving any serious consideration to the failures of conventional white masculinity that inform the play.[16]

These asymmetries remain unchallenged by critics, even though Song bluntly reminds Gallimard of these racial and sexual inequities from the very beginning of the play. At their first encounter, the diva challenges the diplomat's enthusiastic praise of his performance as Cio-Cio-San, responding with a sharp rejoinder: "Consider it this way: what would you say if a blonde homecoming queen fell in love with a short Japanese businessman? He treats her cruelly, then goes home for three years, during which time she prays to his picture and turns down marriage from a young Kennedy. Then, when she learns he has remarried, she kills herself. Now, I believe you would consider this girl to be a deranged idiot, correct? But because it's an Oriental who kills herself for a Westerner—ah!—you find it beautiful" (17). Song's *Madama Butterfly* parable—his cultural inversion of spurious sexual and racial asymmetries—seems to be a critical point lost on both Gallimard and his commentators.[17]

Hwang's drama allows us to consider the methods through which symbolic norms and prohibitions coerce Gallimard's phantasmatic allegiance to ideals of heterosexuality and whiteness. *M. Butterfly* ultimately exposes the production of whiteness as a universal norm that projects the burden of racial difference onto the Asian (American) male body. Moreover, it reveals how this production of an unmarked and invisible whiteness is achieved only through its complicit intersection with a system of compulsory heterosexuality. Focusing on fetishism—perhaps Freud's most privileged mechanism for the management of difference—I refigure this psychic category in terms of a "racial castration," one that demands serious reconsideration of Freud's paradigm along very altered lines of race.

What exactly is the "enchanted space" of the prison cell, ruled by the "work of fairies," that Gallimard describes in his opening monologue (2)? What are the queer and racial phantasms that order and control the white diplomat's psychic blunders and material failures? I turn my critical attentions to Gallimard in order to consider how for more than twenty years he could have been ignorant of Song's anatomical sex. "Did Monsieur Gallimard know you were a man?" (81) persists the officious judge, swinging the all too familiar juridical gavel as he interrogates the Oriental diva. In his desire to categorize and stabilize the foundational terms of the symbolic order for which he is a citational mouthpiece, the judge's obsessive question (Hodgson's question, too) emerges as the central concern of the drama. Yet psychoanalysis would tell us that there is no clear-cut answer to the judge's query, that to know and not know, that to *not* see what is apparently there for us *to* see, is a perfectly explicable condition in the realm of the psyche.

"An Almost Artful Dealing with Reality"

In "The Dissection of the Psychical Personality" (1933), Freud provides a visual map of the structural relations between the ego, the id, and the superego and the psychical territories of the repressed, the unconscious, the preconscious, and the perceptual-conscious systems.[18] This "final topography" is a structural elaboration of a comparatively schematic "late topography" developed in *The Ego and the Id*. In contrast to the late topography, in which the ego is seen to occupy a less capacious area of the psyche, the final topography illustrates a definitive expansion of the ego's psychic territory as it comes to occupy areas in the preconscious, the unconscious, and the territory of the repressed. As such, the final topography is notable because it visualizes a point repeatedly underscored in *The Ego and the Id:* a "part of the ego, too—and Heaven knows how important a part—may be unconscious, undoubtedly is unconscious."[19] If the ego is the seat of both (pre)conscious knowledge and unconscious resistance, then the final topography provides us with a visual representation of the divided subject, one who can know and not know at the same time.

The notion of the divided ego is most fully elaborated in one of Freud's posthumously published works, "Splitting of the Ego in the Defensive Process," written in 1938. In this essay, Freud explains that under the sway of a powerful instinctual demand whose satisfaction is threatened by the danger of an encroaching reality the ego is forced to decide "either to recognize the real danger, give way to it and do without the instinctual satisfaction, or to repudiate reality and persuade itself that there is no reason for fear, so that it may be able to retain the satisfaction."[20] Unable to make this no-win decision, the ego pursues both possibilities simultaneously through a defensive maneuver that results in two "contrary reactions": on one hand, the ego refuses reality and its constraints on instinctual satisfaction; on the other hand, it recognizes the danger of reality and attempts to divest itself of this fear. The "two contrary reactions to the conflict persist," Freud maintains, "as the centre-point of a splitting of the ego."[21]

Freud goes on to describe the paradigmatic psychic mechanism for this simultaneous gratification of instinctual demand and obedience to social prohibition as fetishism. A little boy caught masturbating is subject to the threat of castration not only by the father's admonishments but by the traumatic sight of female "castration," the absence of a penis on the girl.[22] Because the boy is reluctant to give up masturbation, and because the danger of an encroaching reality—the potential loss of his privileged organ—is effective only insofar as the threat of castration by the father is coupled with and reinforced by this frightening visual affirmation of absence, the boy creates a fetish that disavows the girl's lack and thus circumvents the paternal threat. Consequently, he carries out his denial of female castration by finding a substitute that can be projected in its place: a shine on the nose, a plait of hair, an undergarment, a shoe. The fetish serves, then, as a paradigmatic example of divided belief. Its very existence both denies and attests to female castration: it says that she does and does not have a penis. Freud maintains that the fetish serves as an ingenious mechanism that "almost deserves to be described as [an] artful" means of dealing with reality.[23] Through the fetish, the boy confronts the exigencies of psychic life and the redoubtable threats of the father. In this way, the little boy not only eludes paternal prohibition but facilitates a method by means of which he can continue undisturbed in his gratifying sexual activities.

In both "Splitting of the Ego in the Defensive Process" and "Fetishism," Freud provides us with a model of divided belief that explains how Gallimard could, at once, both know and not know Song's anatomical sex. Extending for a moment fetishism's logic of female castration to the Asian male body, might Gallimard's psychic appraisal of Song's corporeal endowments also fall into simultaneous affirmation and disavowal? Moreover, the defensive splitting of the ego explains how on a *conscious* level the diplomat could not see what he had already perhaps acknowledged on an *unconscious* level: Song's penis. We come to understand, through the diplomat's simultaneous disavowing and affirming of the presence of this male organ, how he could at once be and not be a (self-denying) homosexual.

Although Freud relishes his description of fetishism as a means of instinctual satisfaction and the evasion of paternal constraint, he leaves us with a foreboding caveat: "But everything has to be paid for in one way or another, and [the boy's] success is achieved at the price of a rift in the ego which never heals but which increases as time goes on." [24] The fetish, which "*almost* deserves to be described as [an] artful" means of dealing with reality, is secured at the cost of a split ego whose misrecognitions only grow larger with time. Castration inevitably comes back to haunt the ego in frightening and unpredictable ways. How does this promised homecoming of castration plague Gallimard in *M. Butterfly*? And what are the social conditions under which the diplomat is first coerced into such a state of divided belief?

Lotus Blossom Fantasy

"We were worried about you, Gallimard," remarks an envious Manuel Toulon, ambassador extraordinaire of the French embassy. "We thought you were the only one here without a secret. Now you go and find a lotus blossom . . . and top us all" (46; Hwang's ellipsis). In one fell swoop, Toulon assuages his worries about Gallimard through the reassuring articulation of the diplomat's heterosexuality. For Toulon, the secret of Gallimard's illicit affair with Song Liling is perfectly "straightforward"—filtered, that is, through symbolic imperatives of heterosexuality and whiteness and framed by a historical legacy of colonialism. As a consequence, Gallimard's secret is really no secret at all but a projection of Toulon's own proleptic confusions and orientalist dreams: the secret affair of the cruel white man and the Oriental "lotus blossom." Put otherwise, because Toulon's own fantasies are played out in and projected onto his imaginings of Gallimard's illicit affair, the ambassador is blind to the circular logic whereby Gallimard's relationship with Song proves his heterosexuality at the same time that Gallimard's heterosexuality proves his affair with Song.

The *Madama Butterfly* tableau that Toulon enjoys is a fantasy reinforcing and reinforced by the foundations of the colonial order—its demarcation of distinct sexual and racial borders materially fortified by a long history of European imperialism. I must emphasize that Toulon's "recognition" of Gallimard's perceived heterosexuality in this scene of economic, political, and cultural domination is facilitated through the diplomat's perceived possession of the Oriental butterfly—the sexual and racial exploitation of the little brown woman upon whom white male subjectivity in the colonial order is built. Indeed, Toulon's (mis)recognition of the diplomat's affair with the Oriental lotus blossom—Gallimard's racialized heterosexuality, as it were—speaks to a colonial structure of knowledge in which sexual and racial difference gain a new and full significance in relation to one another. Ultimately, this lotus blossom fantasy is neither private nor personal but an open secret that is passed down in time from one colonial bureaucrat to another, from one colonial administration to the next. In the process, it becomes, like Puccini's *Madama Butterfly* tableau, the same old story through its continuous reprisals and compulsive rescriptings.

That Hwang chooses to set *M. Butterfly* during the cold war and Vietnam War eras as well as the late 1980s (at the end of Reagan's "evil empire" discourse) is significant.[25] Gender scholars of the cold war era, such as Robert Corber and Lee Edelman, note that this was a historical period when a triumphant U.S. exceptionalism spearheaded the movement to contain the threat of communism on the international level. At the same time, it also labored on the domestic front to consolidate its "democratic" ideals as leader of the so-called free world through the codification of middle-class family values and the (re)consolidation of strict gender norms.[26] This historical era of the Red scare—of *Father Knows Best,* the witch-hunts of the House Un-American Activities Committee, and the shift from production to consumer capitalism—witnessed the interpenetration of nationalism with new figurations of sexuality. These included the development of the "organization man," the rise of corporate culture, and the suburbanization of the efficient middle-American housewife.

In *Homosexuality in Cold War Culture,* Robert Corber writes that in this historical context homosexuality "was understood as a form of psychopathology that undermined the nation's defenses against Communist infiltration. The politicization of homosexuality was crucial to the consolidation of the Cold War consensus. The homosexualization of left-wing political activity by the discourses of national security enabled Cold War liberalism to emerge as the only acceptable alternative to the forces of reaction in postwar American society" (3). In the national imaginings of the cold war era, heterosexuality is linked to national health and security while homosexuality is connected not only to the threat of communist infiltration but to the figure of a foreign and racialized other.[27] The national paranoia ensuing from this double threat, it is important to note, arose precisely as a problem of visuality. The possibility that homosexuals could escape detection by passing as heterosexuals linked them in the cold war political imaginary to unidentified and undetected communists who were thought to be conspiring against U.S. government interests.

Given this particular historical context, Toulon's lotus blossom fantasy might be also said to illustrate the vexed crossings between psychoanalysis and an ascendant Western neoimperialism. It is worth remarking that many of Freud's psychic paradigms rely heavily on metaphors of economic domination and compensation. As was noted earlier, for instance, in "Splitting of the Ego in the Defensive Process," Freud states: "But everything has to be paid for in one way or another, and this success is achieved at a price of a rift in the ego which never heals but which increases as time goes on" (275–76). In *M. Butterfly,* the economics of colonialism as well as an ascendant neoimperialism intersect with these economic metaphors of the psyche in ways that demand the historicizing of psychoanalysis and the psychologizing of colonialism and its contemporary legacies. In the context of *M. Butterfly*, such crossings indicate that, like any other commodity in the imperial system, Toulon's knowledge of Gallimard's open "secret" circulates as a kind of "intellectual" property undergirding the rise of Western neoimperialist interventions across the globe, often configured as the political containment of communism.

If Toulon's secret *Madama Butterfly* fantasy is less an individual than a collective fantasy of Western domination, then its articulation serves not merely to describe the conditions of a culturally acceptable heterosexual and white colonial desire but, more importantly, to produce these symbolic ideals in its very utterance. In this structuring of the social order, colonial ideals of heterosexuality and whiteness acquire their efficacy only in and through a reiterative structure of citationality and a material structure of the circulation of commodities, capital, and knowledge on the global stage. As such, Toulon's gleeful utterances function as a kind of colonial performative, hailing Gallimard into its ideological web. Toulon — subject of and subjected to the symbolic norms and prohibitions of the colonial order — becomes a spokesperson for this exclusive club, another cog in the wheel, as it were.

That the presumptuous Toulon and the pontificating judge ("Did Monsieur Gallimard know you were a man?") are scripted by Hwang to be played by the same actor works to underscore their collective psychic and material investments in the colonial regime they mindlessly extol. The very fabric of the social world dramatized in *M. Butterfly* thus gains its psychic and material resilience through the homogeneous fantasies of corporate players like Toulon and juridical tools like the judge. Collectively, their primary responsibilities to their particular domains of economics and politics involve the repeated interpellations of bureaucratic tools such as Gallimard into this old boy network.[28]

The French ambassador's gleeful statement — "We were worried about you, Gallimard. We thought you were the only one without a secret. Now you go and find a lotus blossom . . . and top us all" — is an optative hailing of the bumbling diplomat into a compulsory network of heterosexuality and whiteness and into an economic and a political structure of colonial privilege. Hence, the performative utterance by which Toulon transforms and renders Gallimard's little secret public functions as the reiterative mechanism through which the colonial legacy strives to secure its psychic investments, bind its political entitlements, and guarantee its economic inheritance. How well does Gallimard recite the prescriptive norms of this collective lotus blossom fantasy?

In "Fetishism" (1927), Freud describes the fetish as a psychic process by means of which a little boy gives the female a penis substitute so as to disavow her "lack" and difference and make women "tolerable as sexual objects."[29] Freud thus implies that fetishism serves as a compensatory psychic mechanism through which the trauma of female sexual difference is managed and heterosexual relations between men and women are normalized. Since fetishes are "easily accessible and [the fetishist] can readily obtain the sexual satisfaction attached to [them]" (154), Freud offers this psychic process as an everyday means of facilitating a normative heterosexual relationship between the sexes.

Classic fetishism, according to Freud, plays itself out along lines of sexual difference. The male fetishist refuses to acknowledge female castration by seeing on the female body a penis that is not there to see. In *M. Butterfly*, however, we encounter a strange reversal of this psychic paradigm, a curious reconfiguration of the fetish beyond what Freud's essay explicitly offers. With Gallimard, we do not witness a denial of sexual difference and lack resulting in the projection onto the body of a female a substitute penis that is not there to see. Instead, we encounter the opposite, a "reverse fetishism," so to speak: Gallimard's blatant refusal to see on the body of an Asian male the penis that *is* clearly there for him to see. How might we account for this strange reconfiguration of the fetish and its *avowal* of castration?

At this juncture, it is necessary to consider racial difference in the formulation of any potential explanation since in Gallimard's reconfiguration of the fetish, castration is not denied but stringently affirmed—and affirmed not at the site of the white woman but at the site of the Asian man. How might this racial castration—this curious crossing of castration with race—make possible the heterosexual relationship between the white man and white woman on which Freud implicitly centers his discussions? In this particular psychic scenario, what kinds of differences and lacks are being denied, shorn up, and rendered invisible?[30]

To begin our exploration, let us turn to an example of racial dynamics offered by Kaja Silverman in *The Threshold of the Visible World*. In her discussion of the different ideological and cultural values conferred upon the black and white male penises, Silverman delineates a social structure in which the black penis works to disturb the sexual relations between white man and white woman: "The differentiation of the white man from the black man on the basis of the black man's hyperbolic penis consequently reverberates in disturbing ways within the domain of gender. It places the white man on the side of 'less' rather than 'more,' and, so, threatens to erase the distinction between him and the white woman. This is the primary reason, I would argue, why the body of the black man disrupts the unity of the white male corporeal ego."[31] The putatively hyperbolic black male penis threatens the unity of the white male ego by placing him in the position of being less masculine, thereby endangering the structural distinction between him and the white woman.

In *M. Butterfly*, however, we encounter the opposite situation: a white male is placed into the position of being more masculine through his disavowal of the Asian penis—a triangulating of American race relations beyond the conventional Manichean relationship of black and white.[32] In other words, by denying the penis that is clearly there for him to see, Gallimard psychically castrates the Asian male, placing him in a position of lesser masculinity to secure for himself a position of greater masculinity—a material illustration of Richard Fung's contention that in the Western imaginary "Asian and anus are conflated."[33] The white diplomat's racial castration of the Asian male works, then, not to disturb but to stabilize the distinction between him and the white woman—a reversal of the psychic anxiety he conventionally faces with the black male body. Indeed, this model of racial castration—of "reverse fetishism" and its denial of the Asian penis—might be seen as an attempt to produce and normalize heterosexual relations between the white couple. In *M. Butterfly*, racial castration comes to reinforce the very structures of normative fetishism described by Freud: the myth of the sufficient white male and the lacking white female is upheld and strengthened. Put otherwise, a gendered distinction between the white man and the white woman is stabilized and secured through racial difference.

The French diplomat's reconfiguration of Freudian fetishism in this particular manner, then, works less to problematize than to reiterate the prescriptive norms of the colonial order—the emasculation of the Asian male functioning through not only a material but a psychically enforced orientalist framework. In this particular example of reverse fetishism, the Asian male is psychically emasculated, foreclosed from an identification with normative heterosexuality, so as to guarantee the white male's claim to this location. As such, the potential trauma of sexual difference is not arrested at the site of the female body (as in the case of classic fetishism). Instead, sexual difference is managed through the arrest, disavowal, and projection of racial difference at the site of the Asian male body. Hence, Gallimard's racial castration of Song presents a psychic scenario in which sexual and racial differences intersect and are simultaneously managed in attempts to affirm and stabilize the diplomat's subjectivity. Gallimard's refusal to see the Asian penis before him thus illustrates the complex manner in which Asian, white, and black male identity circulate in a psychic economy of racial as well as sexual differences, gaining their discursive legibility in relation to one another. In this particular instance, Gallimard's racial denial of Song's penis facilitates the smooth alignment of heterosexuality and whiteness. This is an invisible alignment that, in its refusal to be named or seen, attempts to secure heterosexuality and whiteness as universal norms in a colonial world order.

Gallimard's use of reverse fetishism in an effort to shore up his flagging masculine position illustrates a definitive instance in which racial difference must be discussed in terms of sexual difference. The white diplomat's racial castration of Song exemplifies a distinct psychic process through which whiteness and heterosexuality work collectively to articulate and secure their universal status in relation to a devalued Asian racial positioning. Through Gallimard's psychic revision of classic fetishism, the potential trauma of racial difference is deflected away from the white male body and projected elsewhere. In his continual defense against the potential threats of numerous social differences, Gallimard's reworking of classic fetishism both manages and erases race. In this respect, we might recall our introductory discussion of Freud and psychoanalysis's management and erasure of the figure of the primitive to assert that castration is in every case racial castration. This administration of sexuality and race simultaneously reveals the gaps while suturing the fissures through which various material incongruities and lived misidentifications are not psychically experienced as discrepant. Racial castration thus functions for Gallimard and the colonial legacy he represents as a psychic mechanism that, in its protectionist veiling of heterosexuality and whiteness, is "responsible for the production of universalities, harmonies, and gratifications."[34] In this manner, conventional white male subjectivity, as well as a normative heterosexual relationship between the (white) sexes, is scripted and sustained through a specified racial distinction and loss.

Anatomical Weenies and Epic Fiction

Freud describes classic fetishism as serving to normalize the white heterosexual relations on which the paternal legacy is built through the management of female sexual difference and the simultaneous denial of female castration and lack. Reconfigured by Gallimard, fetishism also manages anxieties of racial difference by facilitating a normative white heterosexual relationship through the affirmation of a castrated Asian male body that serves to reinforce white male sufficiency. However, as we come to see in M. Butterfly, this psychic mechanism turns out to be a profound disappointment for the diplomat. *M. Butterfly* qualifies Gallimard's call to normative white masculinity by charting a series of notable (hetero)sexual reversals.

Ambassador Toulon's attempts to interpellate Gallimard into a colonial matrix of whiteness and heterosexuality through their shared lotus blossom fantasy, as well as the diplomat's own attempts to shore up his flagging masculine position through his racial reconfiguration of classic fetishism, are qualified in the course of the drama by a long history of repeated failures with white women: the pinup girl, Helga, and Renée. If the purpose of the Freudian fetish is to remake the (white) female body into a viable sexual object through the denial of her sexual difference and the projection of a penis substitute, then Gallimard's relationships with these three white women come to be marked by a strange psychic reversal. The trauma of castration is not neutralized at the site of the female body. Indeed, it returns to wash over the white male body.

The diplomat's history with white women—before, during, and after his relationship with Song—is highlighted by the continued failure of the heterosexual imperative. In the young Gallimard's *Playboy* fantasies, we witness the first instance of this washout. His onanistic activities are rapidly short-circuited by uncooperative anatomy:

GALLIMARD: I first discovered these magazines at my uncle's house. One day, as a boy of twelve. The first time I saw them in his closet . . . all lined up—my body shook. Not with lust— no, with power. Here were women—a shelfful—who would do exactly what I wanted.

The "Love Duet" creeps in over the speakers. Special comes up, revealing, not Song this time, but a pinup girl in a sexy negligee, her back to us. Gallimard turns upstage and looks at her.

GIRL: I know you're watching me.
GALLIMARD: My throat . . . it's dry.
GIRL: I leave my blinds open every night before I go to bed.
GALLIMARD: I can't move.
GIRL: I leave my blinds open and the lights on.
GALLIMARD: I'm shaking. My skin is hot, but my penis is soft. Why?
. . . .
GIRL: I can't see you. You can do whatever you want.
GALLIMARD: I can't do a thing. Why? (10–12)

Within the confines of the avuncular "closet," Gallimard's reactions seem atypical of most pubescent heterosexual males. Although the diplomat's identification with paternal power is definitively aroused, his penis remains permanently soft. On one hand, Gallimard is thoroughly excited by the prospect of phallic control—enthralled by the power to make "women . . . do exactly what I wanted." On the other hand, he lacks the necessary equipment and is racked by performance anxieties about his heterosexual adequacy. Despite the pinup girl's self-proclaimed inability to return Gallimard's look, the young diplomat is overwrought by seeing and being seen. He is, moreover, disturbed by the visible failure of his privileged organ: "I'm shaking. My skin is hot, but my penis is soft. Why? . . . I can't do a thing. Why?" Gallimard, the young voyeur, is thus himself caught at the peephole, subjected to the power of an unapprehensible and terrorizing gaze. Since the diplomat literally occupies center stage at this particular moment, the visible failure of his organ comes under intense scrutiny, its flaccid presence given our full cinematic attention.

As a "queer" adolescent, the diplomat's struggle to identify with the position of the father—with a position of heterosexuality and whiteness—comes to be haunted by the masculine dis-ease of his organ. Just as Gallimard's racial reconfiguration of fetishism in relation to Song suggests a logic of reversal—the affirmation of the "castrated" Asian male—here, too, we witness a further inversion. Castration is not disavowed and projected onto the white female body but emphatically returns to wash over the white male body. Gallimard—the white male, not the white female—becomes the locus of insufficiency. Hence, we witness in this *Playboy* phantasmatic an incipient pledge to a white and heterosexual paternal order, one strongly qualified by a dissonant trajectory of desire. Penis and phallus work toward opposite ends, a slippage of phallic power from anatomical control.

At this point, it seems appropriate to invoke recent feminist debates on the distinction between phallus and penis and the displacement of a differential "lack" and "castration" onto the female body. Silverman, for instance, delineates two separate castrations experienced by all subjects: the entry into language (primal repression) and the paternal metaphor (the Oedipus complex). If primal repression and the paternal metaphor can be thought of as two separate events, Silverman argues, we can understand the Freudian castration complex "as the metaphoric reinscription and containment of a loss which happens much earlier, at the point of linguistic entry—as the restaging with a 'difference' of a crisis which would otherwise prove inimical to masculinity."[35] Silverman's critique of Freud's inequitable distribution of a prior linguistic castration onto a "lacking" female (and, in Gallimard's instance, racial) body finds an unwitting ally in the diplomat. Gallimard's inability to place his flaccid penis within a phantasmatic scene of tumescent phallic plenitude suggests that there is nothing inevitable, after all, in the connection between anatomical male penis and symbolic phallus. The diplomat's failures with white women, as well as with Asian men, emphatically illustrate that he is also—and most hyperbolically—a subject of sexual and racial lack.

Gallimard's psychosexual inadequacies are further elaborated in his "arranged" marriage to Helga, the Australian ambassador's daughter. Their conjugal union exemplifies the continuous rescripting of a divided allegiance between white paternal authority and heterosexual desire. To begin with, the couple's marriage is overshadowed by Gallimard's "vow renouncing love . . . for a quick leap up the career ladder" (14). Moreover, the political, economic, and social gain enjoyed by Gallimard through this union is subsequently qualified by a noticeable absence of progeny, the material failure of what we might call, in a contemporary context, "family values." That their marriage remains childless is, as Helga contends, not of her doing. Gallimard's loyalties to a white and heterosexual symbolic order appear yet again to be undermined by a slippage between the psychic and the material. Although he identifies with the privileges of paternal, colonial power, the diplomat is immobilized by the performative requirements this power demands.

This rift between phallic authority and bodily penis finds its most resonant example in Gallimard's interactions with Renée, the assertive Danish coed. If the male René Gallimard's patronym, which invokes one of France's largest publishing houses, indicates an inherited legacy of paternal privilege, his first name qualifies this presumption through its relationship to his female *doppelgänger*. Renée's presence, perhaps more than that of any other white woman in the drama, works to the utter ruination of Gallimard's identifications with a colonial regime of privilege. To begin with, the diplomat's extramarital affair with the Danish coed is marked by a reversal of gender norms. She is a woman who is "*too* uninhibited, *too* willing . . . too masculine" (54; Hwang's emphases). Furthermore, Renée's discourse on anatomical "weenies" and epic fiction attests to the slippage of male penis from symbolic phallus, bringing the male René face to face with his sexual insufficiency:

> RENÉE: I—I think maybe it's because I really don't know what to
> do with them—that's why I call them "weenies."
> GALLIMARD: Well you did quite well with . . . mine.
> RENÉE: Thanks, but I mean, really *do* with them. Like, okay, have
> you ever looked at one? I mean, really?

GALLIMARD: No, I suppose when it's part of you, you sort of take it for granted.

RENÉE: I guess. But, like, it just hangs there. This little . . . flap of flesh. And there's so much fuss that we make about it. Like, I think the reason we fight wars is because we wear clothes. Because no one knows—between the men, I mean—who has the bigger . . . weenie. So, if I'm a guy with a small one, I'm going to build a really big building or take over a really big piece of land or write a really long book so the other men don't know, right? But, see, it never really works, that's the problem. I mean, you conquer the country, or whatever, but you're still wearing clothes, so there's no way to prove absolutely whose is bigger or smaller. And that's what we call a civilized society. The whole world run by a bunch of men with pricks the size of pins. (*She exits*)

GALLIMARD (*To us*): This was simply not acceptable. (55–56)

René Gallimard's horrified reaction to the female Renée's disquisition on the separation between anatomical weenies and their symbolic manifestations—wars, epic fiction, large buildings—clearly results from her unwelcome incursion into the realm of paternal privilege and her appropriation of its most powerful tool: language. Renée is completely dominant, physically and psychically. In bed she is in charge, quite literally on top, as Gallimard admits in saying "you did quite well with . . . mine" (his penis). Outside the bedroom, she assumes a position of discursive authority, vexing the tongue-tied diplomat by running verbal circles around him in conversation.

Renée's scaling down of penile presumption, as well as her incisive observations on the "phallacy" of male size and privilege, drives the wedge ever more deeply between bodily penis and symbolic phallus.[36] If the silent *e* that marks the difference in their shared name is that letter whose responsibility is to both signify and stabilize a relationship of gender, the silent "e" also accounts for a certain unavoidable symbolic *e*-masculation that Gallimard undergoes at the hands of Renée. In this particular world, Gallimard clearly lacks the *e*. As a consequence, the diplomat, in all his encounters with his female double, cannot avoid confrontation with—he can no longer render invisible—his heterosexual failures. On the contrary, the diplomat's relationship with Renée comes to epitomize all his interactions with the white women of the drama: castration and lack return to sit squarely on the shoulders of the white male.

A Homosexual and a Fetishist: Rice Queens and Yellow Fever

How might we reconcile Gallimard's curious attraction to the paternal legacy but not to white women and heterosexuality?[37] Can the fetish serve to deny male homosexuality rather than female castration? Can the fetishist be a homosexual?

On the face of it, these questions might seem rather untenable, since Freud claims that it is precisely the fetish that saves the little boy "from becoming a homosexual, by endowing women with the characteristic which makes them tolerable as sexual objects."[38] Yet the distinct homosexual and fetishistic pathways by which Freud leads the boy out of the horror of female castration are not so straight as never to cross. If the male fetishist creates a penis substitute and projects it onto the body of the female to make her an acceptable sexual object, this projection is entirely necessary, we learn, for the very reason that the boy holds an incredible narcissistic investment in the corporeal integrity of his male organ: "No, that [female castration] could be true: for if a woman had been castrated, then his own possession of a penis was in danger; and against that there rose in rebellion the portion of his narcissism which Nature has, as a precaution, attached to that particular organ."[39]

And here Freud implies that the heterosexual man is no more, no less, a (displaced) narcissist who can only love those objects that remind him of himself, can love only those objects endowed with a penis, with the corporeal outline of his own bodily ego. According to this logic of similitude and false equivalence, the female body becomes a substitute for the male body as heterosexuality becomes a substitute for homosexuality. As such, the homosexual—traditionally excluded from Freud's cast of anaclitic love objects—would nevertheless be the one love object holding the greatest psychic cache for the heterosexual man. Not only does the homosexual man reassuringly and faithfully mirror his body back to the heterosexual man; furthermore, the homosexual man also has a putative narcissism that would be a potent reminder of the renounced libidinal territory the heterosexual man relinquished in his departure from narcissistic to anaclitic (heterosexual) love.[40] In this scenario, the simultaneous masculine (dis)avowal of homosexuality structures the very condition of possibility by means of which conventional white masculinity is allowed to emerge.

How might this model of fetishism and homosexuality intersect with Gallimard's racial castration of the Asian male? How might the disavowed Asian male penis that Gallimard refuses to recognize on Song's body serve as a displaced representative of a tabooed homosexual and racial desire? The psychic configuration of "reverse fetishism" in

M. Butterfly suggests that Gallimard's denial of Song's penis works not merely to shore up a heterosexual relationship between white man and woman; it also covers up an abjected homosexual desire for the Asian male body. In this sense, we might describe this scenario as Gallimard's "passing" between an acceptable white male heterosexuality and an unacceptable white male homosexuality. How might the diplomat's refusal to see the Asian penis before him pass off a prohibited homosexual desire for that masculine body as a normative heterosexuality in the face of whiteness?

As discussed earlier, the cruel white man and the submissive Oriental lotus blossom mark a narrative of imperial knowledge that is assiduously cultivated and rescripted by the colonial order. Yet this phantasmatic—deployed from Puccini to Ambassador Toulon—as well as the diplomat's numerous anatomical failures with white women come ultimately to qualify Gallimard's tenuous position (and finally his life) within the colonial matrix of white heterosexual power. If the *Madama Butterfly* phantasmatic occupies the acceptable side of a colonialist fantasy, the conscious side of authorized desire, how might we describe the unacceptable underside of this fantasy, the unconscious denial of a tabooed desire? To answer these questions, we might turn to Hwang's striking afterword to the play, in which he offers a potential explanation for the diplomat's state of divided belief, one unnamed in the drama proper:

> Gay friends have told me of a derogatory term used in their community: "Rice Queen"—a gay Caucasian man primarily attracted to Asians. In these relationships, the Asian virtually always plays the role of the "woman"; the Rice Queen, culturally and sexually, is the "man." This pattern of relationships had become so codified that, until recently, it was considered unnatural for gay Asians to date one another. Such men would be taunted with a phrase which implied they were lesbians.
>
> Similarly, heterosexual Asians have long been aware of "Yellow Fever"—Caucasian men with a fetish for exotic Oriental women. I have often heard it said that "Oriental women make the best wives." (Rarely is this heard from the mouths of Asian men, incidentally.) This mythology is exploited by the Oriental mail-order bride trade which has flourished over the past decade. American men can now send away for catalogues of "obedient, domesticated" Asian women looking for husbands. (98)

According to Hwang, the concepts of Yellow Fever and Rice Queens are constructed along congruent lines of heterosexual and homosexual submission—the conscious and acceptable as well as the unconscious and abject sides of a colonialist fantasy. The concept of Yellow Fever exists squarely within the approved norms and acceptable knowledges of a conventional colonial order, working to buttress white male heterosexuality through the possession and exploitation of the native brown woman.

Conversely, the suppressed equivalent of this phenomenon is the homosexual Rice Queen fantasy. This Rice Queen fantasy—entailing attachment to and desire for the Asian male body—exists squarely within the tabooed regions of symbolic prohibitions against homosexuality and nonwhiteness. Its emergence into the domain of visibility would thus shed light on the abject underside of the symbolic order, an order whose stability is contingent upon not only the disavowal but also the violent suppression of homosexuality and nonwhiteness. In this regard, we might view Gallimard's psychic makeover and denial of Song's penis as serving a dual purpose. Gallimard's castration of the male opera singer could function as both an attempt to buttress his flagging white masculinity and an effort to remake the unacceptable Asian male body into an acceptable Asian female form for colonial consumption, enjoyment, and privilege.

This double-sided fantasy explains how the white diplomat's failures with white women might be interpreted through both a heterosexual and a homosexual valence. I would suggest, finally, that we must read Gallimard's state of divided belief through both of these possibilities: a failed heterosexuality in the face of whiteness and an occluded fantasy of homosexual desire. The former serves as a psychic mechanism through which the symbolic norms of heterosexuality and whiteness are shored up and consolidated in Gallimard's colonial world; the latter serves as a psychic mechanism through which symbolic prohibitions against homosexuality and nonwhiteness are suspended and called into question.

In which fantasy—the *Madama Butterfly* or the Rice Queen phantasmatic—does Gallimard hold the most faith? Is the diplomat finally heterosexual or homosexual? This question may ultimately be unanswerable, for in a larger sense Gallimard's putative ignorance concerning Song's anatomical sex suggests a fundamental equivocation—as well as the fluidity of sexual identification and desire—that structures the symbolic order itself. It suggests the ultimate unknowability and therefore the unreliability of sex and sexual practice as indicators of a psychic truth or an unwavering sexual disposition. In slightly different terms, Gallimard's psychic equivocations over Song's anatomy concede the inevitable failure of symbolic norms and prohibitions to command faithful versions of heterosexuality and whiteness that they cannot ultimately produce, enforce, or guarantee.[41]

Nevertheless, if the very conception of our bodily ego and borders of the self come to be informed by a threat of symbolic and material punishment—a threat of pain, a threat of bodily disintegration, and a threatened loss of social identity—it may be that Gallimard's ostensible obeisance to a conscious *Madama Butterfly* fantasy serves as a mechanism of self-preservation and advanced self-punishment, the compensatory result of an unconscious disavowal of a desired Rice Queen phantasmatic. Indeed, Butler writes, the symbolic order marshals an incredible force of coercion: "When the threat of punishment wielded by that prohibition [against homosexuality and nonwhiteness] is too great, it may be that we desire someone who will keep us from ever seeing the desire for which we are punishable, and in attaching ourselves to that person, it may be that we effectively punish ourselves in advance and, indeed, generate desire in and through and for that self-punishment" (*Bodies*, 100). Should we read Gallimard's wavering allegiance to symbolic norms of heterosexuality and whiteness as a rebellion against or as a submission to this advance self-punishment?

Gallimard's passing between an acceptable white male heterosexuality and a tabooed white male homosexuality brings with it not only psychic relief but concrete material rewards. The diplomat's passing—whether consciously or finally unconsciously achieved—is reinforced by a corresponding framework of economic and political benefits. As Earl Jackson Jr. observes, gay white males occupy "a peculiar position in a heterosexist society in that, as men (if they are not 'out'), they potentially have full access to the very power mechanisms that repress them and their fellow 'outsiders,' who cannot 'pass,' white women and people of color of any sexual orientation." [42] The political, economic, and cultural stakes are high for the passing gay white male: full access to the world of colonial privilege and rewards. In light of these considerable material advantages, could Gallimard's putative ignorance be seen as conscious bad faith? Could Gallimard's anatomical blunder be seen as a consciously self-denying homosexuality encouraged by the likes of Toulon and the pontificating judge?

This question—yet another version of "Did Monsieur Gallimard know you were a man?"—may not be answerable. However, unconscious self-deception and conscious bad faith often have similar results in the social context of the real world. The material rewards of Gallimard's passing as a heterosexual conqueror in Toulon's colonial regime are great—promotion and adulation by others—whereas the consequences of Song's disrobing and Gallimard's exposure as a homosexual lead to imprisonment, ignominy, and death. Hence, questions of the conscious intent to pass must be considered, for venal complicity in a system of colonial privilege enjoyed by gay white men who do consciously pass is a phenomenon all too familiar in Hwang's context of colonial, cold war China as well as in our contemporary Western context.[43]

If, as I have argued throughout this chapter, the power of symbolic norms of heterosexuality and whiteness functions largely through the tacit veiling of their collusionary ideals, then rendering visible by naming the invisible workings of a compulsory system of both heterosexuality and whiteness is an imperative project. Gallimard's passing and his slippage from normative ideals of white masculinity can be used to provide a model through which we may contest and dislodge the social structures that seem to guarantee an immutable and universal position of privilege to the normative white male subject. To this effect, I conclude with a final interpretation of fetishism and the failure of heterosexuality and whiteness. I conclude, that is, with the failure of the fetishizing Ambassador Toulon, the most strongly coded "sufficient" white male subject of the drama, to prevent even himself from falling into the abjected domain of homosexual desire.

The Confidence of the Thing

We come to learn in Freud's essay "Fetishism" that the struggle that impels divided belief and calls for the psychic mechanism of the fetish is not merely the sight of female "castration" but the truly threatening proportions that this visual castration takes when coupled with the threatening prohibitions of the father. In this respect, what the little boy struggles against in "Fetishism" is the father himself and the ambivalent attitudes of both hatred and love that his paternal authority elicits.

My observations on the father-son drama that underpins fetishism are supported in the Freudian text by an interesting story of denial, which I would describe as the urtext of castration, that of two young boys who disavow the death of their father. Describing one of the youngsters, who "oscillated in every situation in life between two assumptions" of divided belief, Freud observes, "the one, that his father was still alive and was hindering his activities; the other, opposite one, that he was entitled to regard himself as his father's successor."[44] The boy's state of split knowledge thus suggests that the assumption of the paternal position is ultimately an ambivalent process that is never complete. To borrow loosely from the logic of fetishism: the boy can and cannot be his father.

If the purpose of fetishism is to normalize a relationship between a (white) man and woman, then this psychic mechanism serves to encourage and facilitate the assumption of the father's place, Freud suggests, specifically through the axis of sexuality, by offering the boy a pathway into heterosexual desire. In other words, fetishism, by (re)making the female body an acceptable locale for his libidinal investments, encourages the boy to identify with the heterosexual position of the father while denying any residual homosexual desire that he may have for him. This psychic process, as we have observed, occurs only by (re)configuring the female body in the guise of the male—by neutralizing the "horror" of her sexual difference and lack. And in this regard, we witness in fetishism a rather overt attempt on the part of the little boy to write out a desire for the father, which is nevertheless curiously preserved in the male form that the female body must invariably assume. Consequently, the social order—its system of compulsory heterosexuality—is maintained by a tenuous line between heterosexual identification and a constant promise of resexualized homosexual desire. Here we must remember that the "pangs of conscience" resulting from the little boy's identification with the father through the sublimation of his homosexual desire are, as Judith Butler points out, "nothing other than the displaced satisfactions of homosexual desire" (*Bodies*, 277). These pangs, whose role lies in keeping the boy from acknowledging a prohibited desire for his father, are in no way secure, for they are the displaced result of a psychical conservation of homosexual desire and not an obliteration of it.

In my reading of *M. Butterfly*, I have focused attention on Gallimard as a hyperbolically marginal male figure occupying the conventional borders of white masculinity. The diplomat's shaky relationship with paternal authority is, however, not an anomalous psychic position but one that all white men come to embody, including Ambassador Toulon himself, the most strongly coded father figure in the drama. In highlighting the phallic failures of white heterosexual masculinity in general, Hwang thus qualifies its universalizing pretensions. Let us return one last time to this dynamic father-son duo. Promoting Gallimard to vice consul, Toulon offers a few words of advice to his new protégé in training:

> TOULON: Humility won't be part of the job. You're going to coordinate the revamped intelligence division. Want to know a secret? A year ago, you would've been out. But the past few months, I don't know how it happened, you've become this new aggressive confident . . . thing. And they also tell me you get along with the Chinese. So I think you're a lucky man, Gallimard. Congratulations.
>
> *They shake hands. Toulon exits. Party noises out. Gallimard stumbles across a darkened stage.*

GALLIMARD: Vice-consul? Impossible! As I stumbled out of the party, I saw it written across the sky: There is no God. Or, no—say that there is a God. But that God . . . understands. Of course! God who creates Eve to serve Adam, who blesses Solomon with his harem but ties Jezebel to a burning bed—that God is a man. And he understands! At age thirty-nine, I was suddenly initiated into the way of the world. (37–38)

Embracing the psychic contract of Toulon's old-boy network, Gallimard comes to realize that his emotional battering of the Oriental diva has been swiftly and richly rewarded. Indeed, Gallimard would be—as Toulon suggests—"out" were it not for his racial buttress, his ability to "get along with the Chinese." The silence of whiteness—the race that need not speak its name—thus ensures that Gallimard need not speak his (homo)sexuality. At age thirty-nine, Gallimard's interpellation into a colonial realm of heterosexual and white privilege is rather late. He "matures" only under the tutelage of Toulon, who rewards the late bloomer with an unexpected promotion.

In his enthusiastic response to Toulon, Gallimard unwittingly begins to mime the ambassador's lessons through an equivocating turn to biblical law: "There is no God. Or, no—say that there is a God. But that God . . . understands. Of course! God who creates Eve to serve Adam . . . that God is a man." The diplomat suggests, through biblical references to Adam and Eve, that his promotion to vice-consul signals divine acceptance of the lotus blossom fantasy. Yet, although the rhetoric of the language of Genesis is meant to lend an eternal vision to Gallimard's symbolic revelations, the fact that this knowledge is "written across the sky" produces a contradictory feeling of transience. The truths of this religious law are written in air, and the urgency of Gallimard's newfound confidence in normative white masculinity has no solid foundation.

Are we back in the territory of fetishism? We must note that Toulon and Gallimard's dialogue is firmly embedded in the logic of divided belief, the willful splitting of heterosexual identification from homosexual desire. Invoking yet again the open secret and knowledge of colonial presumption—the possession of the Oriental lotus blossom—Toulon attempts to forestall any psychic equivocation on the part of Gallimard by installing him in a psychic network of heterosexuality and whiteness through his material promotion to vice consul. Pay attention to the ambassador's words, however. The diplomat's assumption of a place within the paternal legacy is dependent upon a "revamped intelligence division." As dictated by Toulon, this division of intelligence—Gallimard's knowing and not knowing (of Song's penis, of there truly being a sexist

God)—is one that ultimately becomes emblematic of an unstable white male heterosexuality *tout court*.

As such, fetishism and divided belief become the privileged psychic linchpin for the maintenance of white male colonial subjectivity as the universal norm. In this regard, we must note that the figure of the aggressive woman—Eve and Jezebel—explicitly invoked as the heterosexual buttress of the white male subject is finally overshadowed by an occluded homosexual desire. In Toulon's congratulatory words to the new vice-consul, the ambassador invariably turns Gallimard into a fetishized object, resexualizing the borders of a prohibited homosexual desire. "You've *become* this new aggressive confident . . . *thing*" (my emphasis), he tells Gallimard. What is the all-powerful thing that Toulon euphemistically describes but the delegated symbol of male privilege and abuse—the anatomical penis as symbolic phallus? How might we interpret Toulon's conflation of penis and phallus? And what does it mean that Gallimard has "become this new aggressive confident . . . thing" for Toulon—has become, in effect, the phallus for the ambassador?

Mark Chiang suggests that in becoming the phallus "Gallimard no longer occupies the position of the man, who is possessor of the phallus; he occupies the position of the woman, whose only hope is to be the phallus. . . . Masculinity in this reading would seem to be just as much a fetish, just as much the object of fetishization, as femininity. If Gallimard accedes to the plenitude of heterosexual masculinity, it is by making himself over into the phallus, by becoming a fetish for Ambassador Toulon."[45] If, as Lacan argues in "The Signification of the Phallus," the male must have the phallus and the female must be the phallus, then no longer can white masculinity lay claim to having the phallus in *M. Butterfly* once Gallimard has become this privileged signifier.[46] If the male Gallimard can become—is made to be—the phallus for Toulon, then masculinity, as Chiang points out, is apparently "just as much a fetish, just as much the object of fetishization, as femininity." The male body itself is (re)made to function for Toulon as the locus of libidinal investment and homosexual desire.[47] Gallimard's bodily frame comes to mark the conceptual limits of the ambassador's (hetero)sexual desire. As such, no longer is a female body—or even an Asian male dressed up as a female—required to be the phallus for the white male. Instead, Gallimard can be the phallus for Toulon, a homosexual relay of a white male object for a white male subject. Here, homosociality and its exchange of women gives way to a libidinal economy that no longer, for the moment, requires their presence. Undoubtedly, we have returned to the narcissistic psychic terrain in which the normative white male subject sees only himself everywhere he looks.

Toulon's brief discourse on Gallimard as a thing speaks not only to the contradiction of a Lacanian binary—the having of the phallus on the part of the male and the being of the phallus on the part of the female—but also to the very collapse of the having/being distinction that legitimates normative white male heterosexuality as the universal norm of the social order. In other words, if one can only have the phallus as a male, Gallimard's falling out of this naturalized framework suggests that the logic of a compulsory heterosexual matrix requiring that one can either have or be the phallus is beset by a fundamental contradiction, an irreconcilable state of anxiety over having and being the phallus that can never be fully surmounted or strictly separated. The French ambassador's configuration of Gallimard as the phallus thus comes to illustrate a nagging yet entirely normative equivocation at the heart of conventional white masculinity: a having that can never be fully had and a being that can never fully be.

Ultimately, as *M. Butterfly* brilliantly illustrates, borders between heterosexual identification and homosexual desire, between white and nonwhite identity, are hardly clear-cut; they are unable to function in isolation. This brief exchange between the ambassador and the diplomat renders visible the insistent partitioning of heterosexual identification from homosexual desire that underwrites normative white male subjectivity. Furthermore, this masking of homosexual desire also involves the masking of whiteness as an invisible racial category. The lotus blossom fantasy—Toulon's open "secret," which underpins all the ambassador's exchanges with Gallimard—attests to conventional white male subjectivity's resolute dependence on the maintenance of both a hegemonic whiteness and an occluded racial boundary. And it is this complex crossing of (homo)sexual and racial difference, exposed in Gallimard's donning of whiteface, that not only marks the extravagant failure of his *Madama Butterfly* phantasmatic but insists on a sustained investigation of racial difference in conventional psychoanalytic paradigms of sexual difference such as fetishism.

In the final analysis, Gallimard's application of a thick layer of white makeup to his face—his colonization and assumption of the "other"'s place—must be read not merely as an attempt to deflect the explicit homosexual implications of Song's penile unveiling but as the unveiling of whiteness as a fetishistic application itself, a mask. This relativizing of whiteness as a universal racial category acknowledges the constructedness of both sexual and racial categories. It stresses the need to enlarge our critical focus in Asian American, ethnic, feminist, gender, and queer studies by considering—by naming—heterosexuality and whiteness at one and the same time as they work in tandem to secure the symbolic ideals of colonial authority. In applying this white mask to his face, Gallimard's actions acknowledge that one can be neither heterosexual nor white, that symbolic ideals of colonial rule demanding compliance to universal notions of heterosexuality and whiteness can only be approximated—that they are ultimately unfulfilled and unfulfillable.

In *M. Butterfly*, the possession of the lotus blossom fantasy exacts an expensive toll on Gallimard, for the fetishistic costs of arresting the trauma of homosexual and racial difference at the site of the Asian male body require a definitive rift in the diplomat's ego, "which never heals but which increases as time goes on."[48] It is the concerted focus on the attendant sexual and racial crossings of this rift that turns the analytic lens of Asian American studies and psychoanalytic theory onto heterosexuality and whiteness as universalizing categories for deconstruction in a new cultural politics—and play—of differences.

FOUR

Male Hysteria — Real and Imagined — in

Eat a Bowl of Tea and *Pangs of Love*

All symptoms, after all, are states of conviction.

ADAM PHILLIPS, "Keep It Moving"

What is the relationship between assimilation and illness, between as-similation and hysteria? Much of Asian American literature is popu-lated with hysterical female bodies.[1] For instance, the narrator of Maxine Hong Kingston's *The Woman Warrior: Memoirs of a Girlhood among Ghosts* falls mysteriously ill after torturing a fellow Chinese American classmate for what she most abhors in herself: unwavering and unrelent-ing silence. "The world is sometimes just, and I spent the next eighteen months sick in bed with a mysterious illness," the narrator recounts. "There was no pain and no symptoms, though the middle line in my left palm broke in two. Instead of starting junior high school, I lived like the Victorian recluses I read about."[2] Unable to trace the etiology of her disease, Kingston's narrator postpones for a year and a half her entry into junior high school. Not unlike the numerous female hyster-ics who populate the frigid landscapes of popular Victorian novels, she withdraws entirely from the public sphere and the normal social activi-ties that characterize typical girlhood adolescence. This retreat from the public space of the classroom — perhaps the most crucial site of child-hood integration into national ideals of proper citizenry — does not prove to be a psychic burden for Kingston's narrator. On the contrary, it pro-vides her with unequivocal psychic relief: "I saw no one but my family, who took good care of me. I could have no visitors, no other relatives, no villagers. My bed was against the west window, and I watched the seasons change the peach tree. I had a bell to ring for help. I used a bedpan. It was the best year and half of my life. Nothing happened" (182).

Nothing happened. Why is it that, for Kingston's Asian American narrator, social stasis equals psychic stability and health—the best year and a half of her young life? What does it mean that in *The Woman Warrior* hysteria's cure lies in total withdrawal from the public sphere rather than steadfast integration into it? Does hysteria result from the narrator's individual yet thwarted attempts to "fit in" socially? Or does hysteria function, in fact, as a larger social symptom of the torturous psychic constraints and sobering material realities under which Asian Americans—female as well as male—are assimilated into the public domain? For Asian Americans, are *assimilation* and *psychic health* antipathetic terms?

In light of this discussion, it is not surprising to note that much of Asian American literature is also populated with male hysterics. Yet to describe the protagonists in Louis Chu's *Eat a Bowl of Tea* and David Wong Louie's collection of short stories, *Pangs of Love*, as male hysterics is finally both an easy and a difficult task.[3] It is easy because Chu's Ben Loy as well as many of Louie's Chinese American male characters exhibit symptoms of hysteria—mysterious symptoms all relating to sexual impotence and resulting in complicated withdrawals from the social realm. It is difficult because Western medical, juridical, and philosophical discourses have long associated the "disease" of hysteria exclusively with the female body.[4] Yet my brief discussion of *The Woman Warrior* positions hysteria in relation to questions of not only sexual but racial difference, to issues of Asian American integration and assimilation into the public sphere. In this particular context, what would it mean to describe Chu's and Louie's Chinese American characters as male hysterics?

It is important to remember that Chu's and Louie's novels—which were published in 1961 and 1991, respectively—engage quite different moments in Asian American history and culture. Chu's Ben Loy circulates in a post–World War II Chinatown "bachelor community" in which vestiges of legalized exclusion, the effects of racial segregation, and stereotypes of Asian Americans as the unassimilable yellow peril continue to dominate. Chu's early 1950s New York is a reflection of a long legacy of American anti-Asian immigration and antimiscegenation laws that configure the immigrant inhabitants of Chinatown as noncitizen aliens. This legislated exclusion from equal membership in the nation accounts for the production of Chinatown as a bachelor community— predominately male and with a long history of distorted gender relations. In this regard, the nullification of the National Origins Law by the

Magnuson Act of 1943, which allowed the enfranchisement of Chinese immigrants as citizens, as well as the enactment of the War Brides Act in 1945 (emended in 1947) which allowed the reunification of Chinese wives and children with husbands and fathers who had served in the U.S. military, mark the vexed transition of a marginalized and segregated racial community on the verge of biological extinction to its promised renewal as a site of familial and cultural reproduction.[5] From this vantage, *Eat a Bowl of Tea* might be described as charting the problematic transformation and promised assimilation of Chinatown and Chinese Americans into the larger national polity.

In contrast to Chu's *Eat a Bowl of Tea*, Louie's *Pangs of Love* depicts the post-1965 urban landscape of what Gayatri Chakravorty Spivak and others have termed the "new immigrant."[6] Louie's 1980s multicultural world is one in which legally sanctioned racial exclusion and segregation are in theory no longer ascendant. The passing of the McCarran-Walter Act of 1952, which relaxed immigration quotas as an expression of anti-communist cold war policy, and the Immigration and Nationality Act of 1965, which radically expanded quotas for Asian immigrants through its revised preferences, are commonly seen as legal culminations that marked the reversal of anti-Asian exclusion, a reversal inaugurated by the Magnuson Act in 1943. This period of national reversal and the liberalization of immigration policy between 1943 and 1965 describes what Lisa Lowe terms the legal and historical transformation of "Asian *alien* into Asian American *citizen*" (*Immigrant Acts*, 10). Indeed, unlike Chu's segregated Chinatown bachelors, the Chinese American men populating Louie's short stories are overwhelmingly hyperassimilated "model minorities," living in cities and upscale suburbs under the putative banner of integration and social acceptance. Moreover, unlike most of *Eat a Bowl of Tea*'s Chinese American male characters, who are exploited, low-wage laborers in the laundry, restaurant, and other service-sector industries, the characters in *Pangs of Love* are highly paid professionals, not only the objects but also the subjects of an expansive global capitalism. In this respect, Louie's Chinese American men are representational testaments to the historical displacement of the yellow peril stereotype—which dominated the representation and racialization of Asian American male subjectivity prior to World War II—by the contemporary "model minority" myth—the hyperassimilated national figure of racial success and harmony. It is important to note that this success and harmony are often used in exceptionalist national rhetoric to validate the notion (instituted by the juridical turn in the 1954 *Brown v. Board of Education* Supreme Court decision) that the U.S. nation-state is a color-blind society.

Lowe points out that this transformation of Asian alien into Asian American citizen "institutionalizes the disavowal of the history of racialized labor exploitation and disenfranchisement through the promise of freedom in the political sphere. Yet the historical and continued racialization of the Asian American, as citizen, exacerbates the contradictions of the national project that promises the resolution of material inequalities through the political domain of equal representation" (*Immigrant Acts*, 10). How does this shift in the state's organization and interpretation of Asian immigrants from unassimilable to assimilated expose the inadequacy of state institutions to deliver on the promise of freedom and equal representation? In this particular context, what does it mean for male hysteria to bridge two distinct periods of Asian American immigration history, racialization processes, and representational politics? How might Louie's male hysterics qualify the teleological narrative of political equity? How might male hysteria expose the contemporary administration of Asian Americans—figured now as model minorities and exemplary citizens—as the continuing genealogy and disavowed trace of an institutionalized history of Asian American exploitation and exclusion? What, in other words, does Asian American male hysteria symptomize socially and politically?

This chapter begins with a short theoretical account of the genealogy of hysteria. It considers hysteria's gendered origins in the female body as well as its psychoanalytic evolution through the category of the unconscious. Through an account of hysteria as what Slavoj Žižek terms the "testimony of a failed interpellation,"[7] I analyze *Eat a Bowl of Tea* and *Pangs of Love* in order to develop a critical theory of male hysteria—of Asian American racial hysteria—attendant to past and contemporary processes of Asian American immigration, assimilation, and racialization as well as national mechanisms of historical disavowal and exclusion.

The Wandering Womb

What does a Woman Want?
SIGMUND FREUD, Letter to Marie Bonaparte

Dating from 1900 B.C., the oldest surviving Egyptian medical papyrus attributes hysteria to improper migrations of the female womb.[8] In the Greek tradition, Hippocrates not only linked hysteria to the "wandering womb" but also to "abnormal" sexual activities. Lacking appropriate moisture, the uterus—described by Plato in the *Timaeus* as an independent animal longing to procreate—begins to shift restlessly around the female body, causing a host of hysterical symptoms: shortness of breath, fainting, vomiting, loss of voice, headaches, and convulsions. The prescribed remedies for the hysteric's wandering womb and its reproductive urges are marriage, (hetero)sexual intercourse, pregnancy, and maternity. From medieval times until the nineteenth century, definitions of hysteria continued to evolve—from supernatural interpretations relating to witchcraft and heresy to notions of the disease as an imbalance of humors and sympathies to the possibilities of a mental origin for the illness. Through all these various historical interpretations, however, one thing endured. The classic Egyptian and Greek "diagnosis of female sexual disturbance, and a cure by submission to the yoke of patriarchy (the reproduction of mothering)," Charles Bernheimer notes, "remained basic to the medical concept of hysteria" (3). Gerard Wajeman suggests that "hysteria clings to woman."[9] This enduring historical connection, as critics are quick to point out, can be immediately detected in the etymology of the term. The word *hysteria* derives from the Greek root *hystera*, meaning "uterus."

In the late nineteenth century—often considered the golden age of hysteria—both Freud and Jean-Martin Charcot (the notorious French physician whose spectacular seminars on hysteria at the Salpetrière Freud attended) were among the first medical authorities to contend that hysteria was not a disease exclusively afflicting women.[10] Charcot describes more than sixty male patients in his case histories on hysteria.[11] And in "Observation of a Severe Case of Hemi-Anaesthesia in a Hysterical Male" (1886), Freud responds to the challenge of his teacher Hofrat Professor Meynert to present before the Vienna Society of Medicine a convincing case of male hysteria. "Before beginning my demonstration," Freud writes, "I will merely remark that I am far from thinking that what I am showing you is a rare or peculiar case. On the contrary, I regard it as a very ordinary case of frequent occurrence, though one which may often be overlooked."[12] What allowed for this shift in historical and theoretical perspective—hysteria's encompassing of not just female but also male bodies?

It was Freud's "discovery" of the unconscious that provided the theoretical leverage that allowed him to speculate on the possibility of male hysteria. Indeed, as many psychoanalytic critics note, Freud developed his theory of the unconscious largely in relation to his studies on hysteria and his subsequent investigations of its relation to the dreamwork. Jacques Lacan points out that "Freud's first interest was in hysteria. He spent a lot of time listening, and while he was listening, there resulted something paradoxical, . . . a *reading*. It was while listening to hysterics that he *read* that there was an unconscious."[13] By contending that the hysterical symptom arose not from organic disturbances of the wandering womb but from repressed psychic traumas in the unconscious, Freud's psychoanalytic account of the disease divested it for the first time from its privileged connection to the female body. That is, it separated hysteria from any absolute relation to the anatomical distinction between the sexes.

Freud's account of hysteria allows us to extract the disease from the realm of sexual stigma and moral degeneracy by defining it not as an organic failure of the female body but as a psychic effect of something that we are all liable to do: forget the past. "Hysterics suffer mainly from reminiscences," we are told in *Studies on Hysteria*.[14] Their suffering is due to a selective blockage of traumatic memories (most notably memories of sexual seduction), which have been repressed into the unconscious.[15] Hysteria, Freud maintains, is the result of "somatic conversion." This is a process through which the unconscious speaks these traumatic memories through their transformation into physical symptoms.[16] It is because language fails the hysteric—fails, that is, to give adequate expression to these reminiscences—that the body must speak instead for the unconscious. From a slightly different perspective, we might say that the hysteric always remembers in a displaced manner. For the hysteric, traumatic memories can never be confronted head on. Rather, they are transformed into corporeal symptoms so that the body becomes the discursive field upon which unconscious traumas find their displaced expression.

Jacqueline Rose reminds us that "Freud's work on hysteria started precisely with a rejection of any simple mapping of the symptom onto the body (Charcot's hysterogenic zones). By so doing he made of hysteria a language (made it speak) but one whose relation to the body was decentered, since if the body spoke it was precisely because there was something called the unconscious that could not."[17] If the hysterical symptom speaks through the body, this speaking occurs only indirectly through a network of denatured signifiers no longer attached to the body in any immediate one-to-one relationship. Freud's studies on hysteria thus depart from predominant theoretical accounts of his predecessors, who insisted upon a direct correspondence between hysteria—the wandering womb—and its corporeal symptoms—aphasia, coughing, fainting, convulsions, paresis, and so on. Unlike earlier uterine theories of the disease, Freud's notion of the unconscious introduced for the first time an insistently psychic basis for the disease. His psychoanalytic account of hysteria proffers the unconscious as a type of third-term mediator between the psychic root of the symptom (the traumatic memory) and its corporeal expression (the hysterical sign). Through the category of the unconscious, the hysterical symptom and the corporeal body are thus triangulated and split.

Freud's psychoanalytic account of hysteria thus offers us an important critical intervention in terms of the maintenance of sexual difference. By opening up a theoretical space in which to resist direct biological mapping of the hysterical symptom onto the corporeal body, Freud allows us to understand that hysteria need not be restricted to the female body. In short, Freud's movement away from any exclusive correspondence between the wandering womb and the hysterical symptom provides a way for us to imagine an account of male hysteria. Since the hysterical symptom is the result of a psychical and not an organic disturbance (of the womb), it follows that these denatured signifiers could attach themselves to either female or male bodies. Simply put, the fact that everyone possesses an unconscious means that anyone can exhibit hysteria. Traumatic memories can potentially manifest themselves in *any* body, a somatic rendering of hysterical symptoms unrestricted by anatomical sex.

Not only did many of his early case histories explore the category of male hysteria, but Freud came to diagnose himself, and his brother, as male hysterics.[18] Lacan notes that Freud's initial investigation of hysteria—from which the field of psychoanalysis later emerged—involved a startling self-implication: Freud "could not avoid participating in what the hysteric was telling him"—he felt affected by it. "It is because he hears and feels the woman's suffering within himself," Shoshana Felman adds, "because he finds the feminine complaint inscribed in his own body," that Freud is moved toward self-reflection and an exploration of the relationship between hysteria and male subjectivity (*What Does a Woman Want?*, 101). Despite the fact that Freud originally pursued a theory of male hysteria, in the end he abandoned the project, refusing to develop any further a theoretical account of hysteria across lines of sexual difference, ultimately reconnecting the disease to the female body. In this way, Daniel Boyarin and others have noted, Freud displaces male hysteria from the traumatized (Jewish) male body to reconfigure the disease once again as largely descriptive of a (deracinated) female condition.[19] Lacan writes that "everything in the resulting rules through which [Freud] established the practice of psychoanalysis is designed to counteract this consequence [of self-implication], to conduct things in such a way as to avoid being affected" (*Kanzer Seminar*, 101). Why is this so? Why does the genealogy of hysteria as pathological female subjectivity—as the uncontrollable wandering womb—continue to endure? What exactly does hysteria imply socially and politically about male subjectivity?

The social meanings of hysteria as a discourse of protest have been widely deliberated by feminist critics. For instance, in their dialogue concerning Freud's most famous case history, recorded in "Dora: Fragment of an Analysis of a Case of Hysteria" (1905), Hélène Cixous and Catherine Clément advocate two widely divergent points of view.[20] In "The Untenable," Cixous and Clément debate hysteria's effects on the dominant social order. Is Dora, they ask, the heroine against or the victim of the oppressive patriarchal demands that are exacted upon her by a Victorian bourgeois familial structure?

Both Cixous and Clément agree that Dora's hysteria is the product of a complaint—a complaint against patriarchy, a complaint against what Lévi-Strauss describes as "elementary structures of kinship" and what Gayle Rubin later calls "traffic in women." Objecting to a male-dominated Viennese society that underwrote the systematic and blatant exchange of women between men, Dora's hysterical condition is the effect of a refusal to be used. Dora (whose real name was Ida Bauer) cannot accept being exploited by her father (Philip Bauer), who attempts to hand her over, as an "object of barter," to his admired friend, Herr K, in exchange for Herr K's wife. Adding insult to injury, Philip Bauer drags Dora to Freud's doorstep with the implicit mandate that the doctor reconcile his hysterical daughter to her unsavory fate.

In his introduction to Freud's case history, Philip Rieff notes that Dora wants nothing to do with this bargain: "The sick daughter has a sick father, who has a sick mistress, who has a sick husband, who proposes himself to the sick daughter as her lover. Dora does not want to hold hands in this charmless circle—although Freud does, at one point, indicate that she should."[21] Dora's hysteria is thus generated as an unconscious protest against the social pressure to accept her place within this circle and along with it the institutionalized abuse of women. In this regard, Dora's hysteria might be seen not as an aberrant but as an entirely emblematic reaction to a patriarchal society that renders the female condition impossible and "proper" female social responsibility odious.[22] We are given, then, in this notion of hysteria as social protest a compelling political reason to retain *hysteria* as a term of critical analysis. As a mode of political resistance, hysteria signals the refusal of a female subject to occupy her proper place within a patriarchal society, her refusal to submit to dominant modes of identification, and her refusal to comply with conventional mores—a social, not an anatomical, wandering from one's culturally assigned position.[23]

While Cixous and Clément both interpret hysteria as a reaction-formation to the patriarchal exploitation of women, they strongly disagree about the ultimate social effects of this protest. Does hysteria contest or conserve the dominant order of things? Do we regard Dora as a heroine or victim of this system? Cixous reads Dora's hysteria—her desire to get off this "hideous merry-go-round" (278) of illness and infidelity—as politically redeeming. Noting that Dora "sees women massacred to make room for her [and] knows that she will have her turn at being massacred" (285), Cixous interprets Dora as heroine and hysteria as not only contesting but finally exploding the social order. "The girl has understood," insists Cixous.

> Dora seemed to me to be the one who resists the system, the one who cannot stand that the family and society are founded on the body of women, on bodies despised, rejected, bodies that are humiliating once they are used. And this girl—like all hysterics, deprived of the possibility of saying directly what she perceived, of speaking face-to-face or on the telephone as father B. or father K. or Freud, et cetera do—still had the strength to make it known. It is the nuclear example of women's power to protest. It happened in 1899; it happens today wherever women have not been able to speak differently from Dora, but have spoken so effectively that it bursts the family into pieces. . . . Dora broke something. (285, 288)

Deprived of the ability to protest directly, Dora nevertheless speaks through her unconscious, through her hysterical symptoms. For Cixous, then, hysteria represents an effective "language" of female resistance in a social order that renders direct expression nearly impossible for women. An expression of women's power to protest, Dora's hysteria not only "bursts the family into pieces" but finally breaks something. It breaks, Cixous maintains, the rigid structure of the familial order.

In contrast to Cixous, Clément cannot view the hysterical condition through such a sanguine lens. While hysteria might temporarily disrupt the social order, Clément concedes, it is finally politically ineffectual not only because its language is an imaginary one in excess of symbolic expression but because it cannot permanently change the enduring patriarchal imperatives of the social order. Hysteria, Clément argues, "mimics, it metaphorizes destruction, but the family reconstitutes itself around it. As when you throw a stone in water, the water ripples but becomes smooth again. . . . That doesn't change the structures, however. On the contrary, it makes them comfortable. . . . [I]t introduces dissension, but it doesn't explode anything at all; it doesn't disperse the bourgeois family, which also exists only through its dissension, which holds together only in the possibility or the reality of its own disturbance, always reclosable, always reclosed" (286, 287). Unlike Cixous, Clément reads Dora's hysteria as finally contained, containable, within the closed cell of the bourgeois family. While hysteria may introduce dissension into this social structure, it does not break the family unit, which quickly reconstitutes itself around Dora's maladies. This dispersion allows Dora's protest to be registered, but ultimately this protest is naturalized. "Dora broke something," Cixous insists. "I don't think so," Clément concludes. "A heroine for Cixous," Jane Gallop observes, "Dora is only a victim for Clément." [24]

Ultimately, I would like to suggest, it is neither possible nor useful to read hysteria as a psychic or a political state of either/or—as only a negative sign of an oppressed normative feminine condition or as only a positive sign of the rejection of femininity's social constraints. The role of the hysteric, Gallop argues, is decidedly ambiguous (202). Hysteria contests the social order, but this contestation can be contained, co-opted, and commodified. The hysterical symptom is, as Adam Phillips suggests, a state of conviction—one that is decidedly double edged. On one hand, this state of conviction is a social positioning in which the hysteric finds herself trapped and enclosed (as an object) by patriarchal norms and ideals. On the other hand, this state of conviction is also a psychic condition by means of which the hysteric stringently resists that social positioning (as a subject) through a set of alternate personal beliefs. Rather than trying to determine once and for all whether the hysterical condition ultimately contests or conserves the dominant order of things, I would like to focus on hysteria's double-edged status—on its ambiguity and the productive potential of this ambiguity.

In the final analysis, we might say that hysteria marks a tear in the patriarchal order. The hysterical condition, if nothing else, indicates the failure of the social order to produce successfully those it seeks to name and to regulate successfully those it seeks to deny. "In the last resort," Slavoj Žižek asks, "what is hysteria if not precisely the effect and testimony of a failed interpellation; what is the hysterical question if not an articulation of the incapacity of the subject to fulfill the symbolic mandate?" (113). Refusing—or unable—to occupy her proper social position, the hysteric points to interpellation's failure. As Louis Althusser puts it, the hail hits its target only 90 percent of the time: "One individual (nine times out of ten it is the right one) turns round." [25] In this regard, hysteria's ambiguity functions as an emphatic testimony against symbolic mandates that seek to prescribe how women like Dora must live out their traditional roles as wives, mothers, or daughters. In other words, the ambiguity of the hysterical condition, neither inherently radical nor inherently conservative, nevertheless marks a particular historical instance in which symbolic mandates cannot produce or achieve their intended effects. The hysterical condition calls attention to the social order's failure to discipline, regulate, coerce, or finally socialize its others into their proper social places. Is it any surprise that the female hysterics populating Freud's couch are highly intelligent, active, and ambitious women who eschew the passive domesticity allotted to them by their fathers, husbands, and brothers?

Indeed, from this particular angle, hysteria's ambiguous double-edged status might not only be described as the symbolic's failure to socialize its repressed others; it might also be said to mark the emergence of the repressed histories of these others. In *For They Know Not What They Do*, Žižek elaborates upon his assertion of hysteria as a "failed interpellation," focusing on the role of history as it intersects this failure. Hysteria, he contends, is "the subject's way of resisting the prevailing, historically specified forms of interpellation or symbolic identification."[26] "History," as Cixous points out, "is always in several places at once, there are always several histories underway" (293). Indeed, Freud himself observed during his Clark lectures in the United States that hysteria "might perhaps be best understood as analogous to a kind of overinvolvement in history."[27] In this regard, hysteria serves to exhume the disavowed, alternate, and buried stories of its sufferers.

Male Hysteria, or What Do They Want?

By reading hysteria as marking a failed interpellation into the normative ideals, official histories, and symbolic positions of the social order, we come to understand the scandalous implications of hysteria for male subjectivity. In a patriarchal world, the presence of the male hysteric would paradoxically imply the refusal of that male subject to occupy a symbolic position that prizes his social role above those of all others. That Freud could not finally imagine male hysteria as an operative term under these conditions comes, then, as no real surprise. The presence of male hysteria calls attention to a flaw in the logic of patriarchal assumption that Freud, as well as the Victorian society in which he lived, attempted to describe, uphold, and produce. To be a male hysteric, as Paul Smith points out, is to have reneged upon the paternal responsibilities of the Oedipal contract, "to have abandoned to some degree the here and now—or, in short, to have failed to live up to the demands of the Oedipalized world. And this is not what 'men' are assumed to do. The Oedipus divides those of us who are assumed to obey—and to be able to obey—the law from those who are assumed to be unable. In this sense the Oedipus entails the demand that men forget a past in favor of access to the law."[28] In the patriarchal community of fin de siècle Vienna, the male subject is encouraged to relinquish any hysterical reminiscences of the past in favor of what is promised to be a glorious future: unimpeded access to paternal privilege. The presence of the male hysteric in Freud's Oedipalized world would signal, then, the breakdown of conventional masculine identifications and desires, the failed delivery of a glorious future, and the problematic blockage of patriarchal assumption. This return of disavowed histories implies not only the subversion of patriarchal laws but also the erosion of patrilineal transmission from fathers to sons. Ultimately, it marks the very uncoding of men as men. As Smith neatly summarizes it, the male hysteric "is what always exceeds the phallic stakes, jumps off."[29]

Indeed, when male hysteria does make an appearance at the turn of the nineteenth century it appears as a psychic condition that attaches itself to male subjects insistently marked by particular class deficiencies. That is, the male hysterics about whom Charcot and Freud write are largely lower-class male laborers traumatized by "railroad spine and brain" (hysterical paralysis)—by the ravages of industrialization. Lynne Kirby observes that, in adapting a notion of male hysteria to a dominant female model, Charcot was at a loss to explain this astonishing appearance of hysterical symptoms in virile working-class men since it was generally assumed that hysteria should be found among the "effeminate" men of the upper classes—homosexuals—and not among the strong and vigorous proletariat (123). What emerged ultimately from this fin de siècle portrait of male hysteria was the contradictory conclusion that, while the most frequent cases of female hysteria were to be found in the upper classes, the precise opposite applied in the case of men. Male hysteria was most common among the working classes.[30]

Although Charcot and Freud did not analyze the social implications of this class divergence, I would like to do so. In assigning the hysterical diagnoses to lower-class railroad workers and industrial laborers performing manual jobs in a rapidly industrializing European society, hysteria served to mark off and produce particular male bodies as ill and diseased specifically through the axis of class differences. "In a kind of mirror image of otherness," Kirby concludes, "one can see that cultural displacement as massive as nineteenth-century mechanization and urbanization—railway-assisted—made of its traumatized victims something like female hysterics. In other words, it emasculated men, even if only, for some, those of a certain class. Women, proletarian men, and marginals thus bore the brunt of the shocks of modernity" (124). Objects of labor, these lower-class workers are marked off and socially unmanned, clearly separated from those men of the bourgeois and upper-classes who are subjects of capital and consequently, as it were, owners of their labor.

In this vein, hysteria not only testifies to a failed social interpellation but it also speaks to the production of subjects marked by particular deprivileged social positions. In other words, it speaks to the production of a class of male subjects who are excluded by and large from symbolic privileges because of their class.[31] In this expanded capacity, male hysteria also comes to mark off as well as create powerless bodies—both female and male—defined against the universal (white, middle-class, heterosexual) normative male subject. Daniel Boyarin suggests, insofar as "gender is a set of cultural expectations and performances, usually but not determinately mapped onto the 'anatomical differences between the sexes,' it becomes impossible to assume constant genderings in cross-cultural comparison. If being gendered 'male' in our culture is having power and speech—phallus and logos—the silenced and powerless subject is female, whatever her anatomical construction" (118). As such, this model of male hysteria—significantly crosshatched by class issues— provides us with one critical way to discuss the Asian American male subject as economically marked through the exploitation and disenfranchisement of his labor. How might we expand our present discussion of male hysteria and class dynamics to better account for problems of racial difference? What does a woman want? What do they—as it is often asked of people of color—want?[32] What does the hysterical Asian American male want? Configuring race through the question of hysteria—considering the "native" question by means of the "woman" question, as it were—raises an intersectional question that Ben Loy's hysteria in *Eat a Bowl of Tea* begins to address.

Bachelor Society, Geographical Impotence, Biological Extinction: Eat a Bowl of Tea

> The mother, once her role is fulfilled, is through. As the
> Germans say: "Der Mohr hat sein Pflicht getan, er kann gehen."
> The Moor has done his job, out with him. Now he can go. That is
> Othello in "The Moor of Venice." You can replace "the Moor"
> with the mother. She is done making kids, so she is made
> secondary in the story.
> HÉLÈNE CIXOUS, "The Untenable"

Like Shakespeare's Othello, "The Moor of Venice," Louis Chu's Ben Loy Wang puts his body on the line as a soldier—not for the security of Venice but for the sake of the U.S. nation-state. Surprisingly, however,

Ben Loy's sacrifice to the U.S. military body as a stalwart protector of American democracy does not lead to his unimpeded integration and assimilation into the mainstream American social body. Instead, like Othello, forever "of" but never from Venice, Ben Loy's transformation from Chinese alien into American citizen after the 1943 congressional lifting of the ban on Chinese immigration and naturalization remains questionable and secondary to his adopted country.

Eat a Bowl of Tea charts the tenuous transition of a dying Chinatown from a bachelor society to its promised rebirth as a site of familial and cultural reproduction. An ex-soldier of World War II, Ben Loy is permitted, through the War Brides Act of 1945, to bring his wife, Mei Oi, from China to reside with him in the United States. After over half a century of exclusion acts directed against the Chinese (1882–1943), anti-miscegenation laws enacted against this community, and the juridical barring of Chinese wives from entering the United States, the Wang couple is given the incredible opportunity to start a family.[33] In doing so, they are not just given the chance to create a new generation of Chinese Americans for a racialized community on the verge of biological extinction. They are also given the chance precisely through this renewal and reproduction of the nuclear family for of a type of unprecedented inclusion and integration into the U.S. nation-state hitherto impossible for any Asian American ethnic group. In Chu's novel, the drama of reproducing the nuclear family comes to be the sine qua non of Chinese American assimilation into national body. However, this renewal and reproduction, this integration into the U.S. nation-state precisely through the very question of renewal and reproduction, proves vexed.

Ben Loy is impotent, and his malady is a spatial impotence—a selective geographical failing—that must finally be recognized as a form of male hysteria. Ben Loy's inability to "get it up" for Mei Oi is confined only to the spatial boundaries of New York's Chinatown. Inside this segregated community, Ben Loy cannot perform. Outside its segregated borders, he can. Put another way, Ben Loy can only regain his potency when he leaves the historical and spatial framework of emasculation that is New York's—indeed—America's, Chinatown. But can he ever really leave? As a Chinese American immigrant striving to assimilate into the mainstream community, Ben Loy is impotent in the United States but not in China. Within the boundaries of the U.S. nation-state, he can temporarily assert his masculinity but only while on vacation, ironically, in the nation's capital, and only while hundreds of miles away from his feminized position as a Chinatown waiter. Within his everyday racialized community, Ben Loy cannot muster such assertion. This selective geographical impotence speaks to a hysterical root at the base of his flaccid condition. In such a light, Ben Loy's impotence cannot be characterized as the result of an organic ailment. On the contrary, it must be described as an unconscious effect of his limited social role within the segregated borders of Chinatown as well as his limited access to the larger space of the U.S. nation-state.³⁴

In *Eat a Bowl of Tea*, racial difference drives Ben Loy's sexual symptoms. As such, it might be said that his hysterical impotence marks an unconscious protest against past exclusions and economic exploitations suffered by Chinese male immigrants in America. That is, his hysterical symptoms reprise a long-repressed history of institutionalized racism and disenfranchisement that subordinated the Chinese male immigrant as alien and thus excludable, while configuring him as socially emasculated and powerless. This history of social impotence manifests itself in Ben Loy's hysterical impotence. Politically, economically, and culturally weak, and firmly enclosed within the segregated borders of Chinatown, he is also physically and psychically deficient in this space. As the U.S. nation-state transforms its Asian aliens into American citizens, Lowe argues, it must necessarily disavow and misremember its history of institutionalized exclusion. Ben Loy's male hysteria might thus be said to contest this misremembering by marking an alternate and "other" history of racialized trauma. In this regard, Ben Loy's male hysteria does not indicate, as Žižek puts it, "the incapacity of the subject to fulfill the symbolic mandate" or even his refusal to occupy a symbolic position within nationals ideals of a proper masculine citizenry. Rather, Ben Loy's male hysteria might be said to testify to the Asian immigrant's long history of emphatic exclusion from these national ideals. From another angle, then, Ben Loy's condition might be characterized as a type of Asian American racial hysteria. That is, to speak about Asian American male subjectivity and hysteria is at once to be speaking about racial hysteria. For Ben Loy, male hysteria and racial hysteria are constitutive and intersecting discourses that mark his symbolic disenfranchisement from the normative national ideals of white masculinity.

Ultimately, Ben Loy's hysterical impotence contravenes a dominant version of U.S. national history that denies a legacy of institutionalized racism and uneven processes of immigration, assimilation, and racialization even as it constitutes the nation-state as a political sphere of abstract equality and an economic bastion of equal opportunity. Moreover, in preventing him from siring the needed paternal offspring for the renewal of a dying bachelor society, Ben Loy's male hysteria marks an unconscious conviction against present social conditions that suspend his integration into mainstream society. For instance, almost the entire narrative plot of *Eat a Bowl of Tea* takes place within the confines of New York's Chinatown, in a Chinese restaurant in Stanton, in a Chinese laundry in Newark, and in China itself. In Chu's novel, the juridical lifting of exclusion does not translate into either the spatial desegregation of this ethnic ghetto or greater access to the public sphere of America. It neither translates into greater personal freedom nor offers increased economic independence to Ben Loy. Indeed, the entire social world of *Eat a Bowl of Tea*, subtitled "A Novel of New York's Chinatown," occurs within a deeply segregated space that, in its remarkable isolation from the public world outside its borders, seems to implode upon itself. Alteration of the law does not guarantee a concomitant shift in the social practices against—or the dominant perceptions of—the Chinese male immigrant in realms outside the juridical. Put simply, changes in immigration law do not necessarily translate into a concomitant easing of alternate forms of everyday exclusion and disenfranchisement, material or psychic, which continue to endure.

Ben Loy's hysterical failure jeopardizes the renewal of the dying Chinatown bachelor society as it symptomizes the enduring problem of immigration, assimilation, and racialization for Chinese immigrants, their continued distance from the abstract national body and ideals of fully enfranchised citizenship. If the fulfillment of the patriarchal mandate depends upon the heterosexual logic of reproduction and the siring of male heirs, Ben Loy's impotence locates him firmly outside this paternal logic. In this regard, male hysteria in Chu's novel also symbolizes the continued exclusion of Chinatown from traditional structures of patriarchal assumption. The specter of extinction continues to loom large, as Ben Loy is unable to assume a proper masculine role in either the mainstream public sphere or his own minority community. Consequently, his hysteria ultimately exposes the crisis of assimilation as a type of double jeopardy. For Ben Loy, Asian American racial hysteria marks assimilation as the physical and psychic coping with incommensurability on two fronts: both the mainstream and minority worlds. This social crisis—on the side of "Asian" and on the side of "American"—is one somatized by Ben Loy as a hysterical response. For Chu's male protagonist, assimilation and dis-ease proceed hand in hand.

Looking for My Penis

Ultimately, Ben Loy's crisis of assimilation is assumed by Chu's female characters as well. This crisis of assimilation disrupts traditional (hetero)sexual relations between the sexes, lending a racialized valence to

Freud's provocative assertion that for men and women "love is a phase apart." [35]

Not surprisingly, the history of the bachelor society in America is one of nonnormative gender relations. The socially disempowered bachelors who populated New York's Chinatown are symbolized in *Eat a Bowl of Tea* as feminized subjects through their incessant gossip and idle lingering. Indeed, almost all significant news in Chinatown is passed by word of mouth: "In a homogeneous community like Chinatown, people spent most of their free time in the shops, sipping tea or coffee, just talking with their friends. Each had his own favorite spot. The coffee shop. The corner candy store. The barber shop. The steps in front of the Chinese school" (113). Gossip—an improper mode of social discourse typically associated with women not men—is contrasted to yet another, more important, gender reversal: the alignment of the proper agency of the letter of the law with women. It is female rather than male bodies that inaugurate narrative action in Chu's novel through their appeal to the letter of the law. Hence, we might read Asian American male hysteria as also indexing this reversal of traditional gender roles.

We must remember that it is Lau Shee, Ben Loy's mother in China, who sets the plot of *Eat a Bowl of Tea* in motion through an admonishing letter written to her husband, Wah Gay:

> Dearly beloved husband . . . as if I'm talking to you face to face. More than twenty springs have passed since you left the village. Those who go overseas tend to forget home and remain abroad forever. I hope my husband is not one of those. Ben Loy is now a man. It is your responsibility to see that he comes home and makes himself a family. Many veterans are now returning to Sunwei to take a bride. (23–24)

Lau Shee's missive is a nagging reminder of what must be done—the arrangement of Ben Loy's marriage—and only with this letter in hand is Wah Gay finally spurred into compliance. Lau Shee's letter keeps Wah Gay sleepless at night. He rereads its requests—its hope for the renewal of family—as he ponders the abnegation of his proper masculine responsibilities not only to his son but to his wife: "He was all alone now. Each time he had received a letter from his wife he began to relive the past. He knew it was not right to let the old woman stay in the village by herself. He often wondered, during lonely moments, if perhaps someday he and Lau Shee would have a joyous reunion" (24). Hysterics, Freud tells us, suffer mainly from reminiscences. And as Wah Gay relives the past the burden of unlived symbolic promise fills him with longing. Unlike in the world of Freud's Dora, in Chu's realm of overseas bachelors it is the forward-looking wives in China, instead of their nostalgic husbands in America, who assume paternal responsibility for the future, as well as the future exchange, of their children.

The breakdown of the patriarchal assumption for the Chinese immigrant male is evident in the symbolic reversal represented by Lau Shee's letter, as it is equally foreshadowed by the circumstances of Ben Loy's arrival in China to take a wife. In Sunwei, the Chinese immigrant male body is figured as a site of social crisis by the female matchmakers enlisted to broker Ben Loy and Mei Oi's conjugal union. From the outset, the matchmaker hired by Jung Shee, Mei Oi's mother, voices a series of doubts about Ben Loy's potency. The matchmaker's misgivings serve not only to reprise historical conceptions of an attenuated Chinese male subjectivity in America but to foreshadow Ben Loy's subsequent impotence with his bride. These apprehensions represent an enduring historical legacy of Chinese American male subjectivity as a masculinity constrained by limited means. Importantly, in *Eat a Bowl of Tea* these social perceptions are internalized by the women. Indeed, it might be said that the social and material emasculation of the Chinese immigrant man in America gains its ideological hold and a most potent psychic efficacy through this internalization on the part of their intended partners. Looking for Ben Loy's penis—to borrow a phrase from Richard Fung—comes to be displaced downward onto the suspect terrain of the young soldier's "artificial" legs (figs. 10–12):[36]

> The following day Jung Shee's matchmaker showed up at the *gimshunhock's* house about noon, excited and out of breath. "The girl's mother said everybody is saying that [Chinese] American soldiers returning to China all have artificial limbs," she announced heatedly. "They are either lepers or are with unnatural legs." She paused to catch her breath, adding that a woman of her age grew breathless from all that walking from Mei Oi's village on such a chilly day. "I told them all this talk about artificial legs and diseases is rumor. You know how people talk. But Mei Oi's mother . . ."
>
> "You go back and tell her my Ben Loy is a healthy boy with two good hands and legs," Lau Shee shouted, pointing to her son.
>
> "She asked me to be sure and take a look at Mr. Wang's legs," said the matchmaker uncertainly.
>
> "You will do no such thing!" screamed Lau Shee.
>
> Before his mother could stop it, Ben Loy quickly pulled both his trouser legs up above the knees. "Here, look. Take a good look," he laughed.
>
> The old matchmaker sprung her neck out like a chicken picking

at grains in the open courtyard, and sniffed at Ben Loy's exposed leg. The *gimshunhock* raised his hand and slapped hard at the calf: "See? Flesh and blood."

"Heh heh heh, that's what I've told them right along," remarked the matchmaker dryly and left. (53–54)

Like the female hysteric whose body animates a discussion among the members of her male audience, Ben Loy's exposed body is presented as an object of social discourse. This is an important reversal of the typical Freudian scenario in which a conversation between two men is triangulated across the body of a woman. Here, Chu presents us with a reversal of gender roles as the Chinese American male body is placed in a feminized frame by two women—rendered an object of scrutiny and a locus of doubt. In a reprisal and reversal of the logic of female hysteria, Ben Loy's male body comes to be placed through the axis of racial difference in a discourse of national disease and social pathology: "[Chinese] American soldiers returning to China all have artificial limbs. . . . They are either lepers or are with unnatural legs." Here, the racialized, wounded male body is also constituted as the carrier of disease. This discourse of racial contamination thus opens upon the terrain of the social leprosy that is Ben Loy's legacy in America.

Throughout *Eat a Bowl of Tea*, the materiality and material inadequacy of Ben Loy's male body emerge in the field of the visible with a notable vengeance. We might characterize this materialization and visualization as marking a return of the repressed. Importantly, this is a return of the Chinese American male body not only from a narrative process that traditionally configures the normative (white) male body (as was discussed in chapter three) as absent and transcendent but also a turning away of the Chinese American soldier from discourses of abstract equivalence. In other words, it is typically believed that the nation's military body is governed by the fundamental logic of abstract equivalence—that every soldier is the same. However, the matchmaker's sustained attention to the figure of the Chinese American soldier as a carrier of disease exposes particularisms of race and racialization that render notions of universalism particularly tenuous. This attention to the universalism of the military body is highlighted in Wayne Wang's film version of this particular scene in *Eat a Bowl of Tea* through the matchmaker's insistence that Ben Loy don his soldier's uniform.[37]

While the purpose of the uniform is to naturalize the incommensurabilities of socially marked bodies, the materiality of certain socially marked bodies returns to insist on their particular differences. For instance, once Shakespeare's Othello has done his job defending Venice's

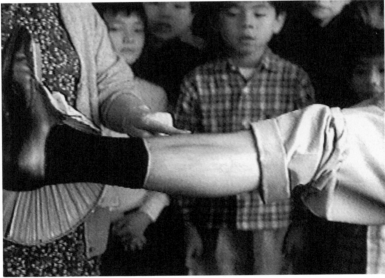

Figures 10–12 Looking for my penis: Ng Yuen Yee and Russell Wong in Wayne Wang's *Eat a Bowl of Tea* (Columbia Pictures)

borders, he must be expelled, rendered secondary, as Cixous puts it.[38] By successfully defending the borders of Venice, Othello falsely believes that he has earned the right to a place in its society through his conjugal union with Desdemona, the daughter of the Venetian senator, Braban-tio. However, Othello is firmly excluded from participating in this type of symbolic exchange—an exchange that would mark him as a mem-ber of Venetian society. As the definite article comes to mark Othello's name—his exemplary and singular status—it also excludes his entry into the larger body politic. In this respect, Iago's unrelenting persecu-tion of "the Moor of Venice" might be understood as the continual expo-sure of myths of abstract equivalence, the continual betrayal of dreams of universalism and assimilation.

We might think of Ben Loy's service to the U.S. military in a simi-lar vein. While his successful military tour grants him putative access to the legal rights and privileges of national membership, his hysteri-cal impotence qualifies this dream of inclusion and integration for the Chinese American soldier. In *Tangled Memories*, Marita Sturken writes that the bodies of surviving Vietnam veterans "resist the closure of his-tory." Indeed, she argues, "history operates more efficiently when its agents are no longer alive. These veteran bodies, dressed in fatigues, scarred and disabled, contaminated by toxins, refuse to let certain narratives of completion stand. Memories of war have been deeply encoded in these bodies, marked literally and figuratively in their flesh."[39] Sturken's analysis of the soldier's body from the Vietnam War calls attention to a physically scarred body whose visible wounds resist the closure of national history by encoding its violence. Ben Loy's predicament expands Sturken's critique by suggesting that the wounded veteran's body can also be a psychically scarred one. That is, although Ben Loy's bodily integrity seems intact, his hysterical impotence, similar to a physically scarred body, qualifies his full membership in the nation-state as it simultaneously resists the closure of national history.

Ben Loy's internal, psychic wound recalls Victor Burgin's compelling notion of "internal exile." In "Paranoiac Spaces," Burgin writes that "institutionalized racism may ensure that racial minorities live in a condition of internal exile within the nation in which they are citizens—an exile that, if it is not legal, cannot be named."[40] Internal exile cannot be recognized by the law, for it exists outside the law's proper jurisdiction, rendering its sufferers—and even its citizens—invisible and illegitimate. Writing about John Okada's novel *No-No Boy*, Sanda Mayzaw Lwin notes that internal exile is a condition unrecognizable within the realm of legal discourse: "The term 'internal exile' is inadequate to describe the condition that is its referent—it is a contradiction in terms suggesting simultaneously a sense of deepest interiority and organic physicality (internal) as well as banishment and expulsion by the state (exile)" (132). "Internal exile" may thus begin to describe Ben Loy's hysterical impotence as a wounded condition that, in its interiority, exists outside the proper realm of the law yet at the same time signifies a state of alienation that may be described as one of the law's debilitating effects. As such, for Ben Loy, as for Burgin, exile is not just about physical displacement from the borders of the nation but also about psychical displacement. Indeed, Ben Loy's male hysteria suggests that the inward displacement of exile functions to authorize the law's refusal to recognize racism in its other manifest and more subtle forms. How does Ben Loy excavate himself from this condition of "internal exile"?

Assimilation in the Age of Hysteria

Chu suggests that if "internal exile" renders Ben Loy as well as his hysterical condition illegitimate, then the answer to this impasse must also involve illegitimate solutions. Upon their return to New York, Ben Loy and Mei Oi face the tremendous task of reviving the paternal legacy for the dying Chinatown bachelor society: the biological repopulation of its inhabitants. Paralyzed by the weight of this historical burden and rendered immobile by the representational history of Asian masculinity in America, Ben Loy's hysterical condition reaches its narrative apotheosis: all conjugal relations with his spouse come to a grinding halt. The "no can do" Ben Loy thus becomes the Chinese bachelor society's abject object of discussion. Mortifying news of his impotence is passed from elder to elder through an informal network of gossip.

Chu's resolution to Ben Loy's hysterical condition is rather stunning. Significantly, it is heterosexual female desire that is left with the responsibility not only of restoring Ben Loy's flaccid masculinity but of finally rescuing Chinese America from extinction. That is, if Ben Loy's male hysteria marks a disavowed history that places him outside structures of traditional patriarchal privilege—eccentric to the position of male subject of desire and exterior to the imperatives of reproductive heterosexuality—then this position must ultimately be ceded to the Chinese American female, reclaimed by Mei Oi. Mei Oi's affair with Ah Song—and her ultimate conception of a male heir through a series of illegitimate encounters with this notorious Chinatown seducer—initially comes about through the scandalous transformation of the Chinese American female into a subject of desire.

If Ben Loy's male hysteria comes to be "cured," if Chinese America is allowed to live and continue, it is only because of this illegitimate detour through female desire, this writing in of female desire not fully accountable to the law. Illegitimacy breeds illegitimacy as Mei Oi confronts her interdicted desire for Ah Song: "The mere reference to the word *lover* made her shudder. She had never dreamed that she would ever apply the term *lover* to herself. Right or wrong, justified or not, she was only human in wanting to be a woman. In Chinese weekly magazines, as well as in the newspapers, she had frequently come across the word *lover*, spread out across the pages in large letters. These stories had seemed so distant and out of reach" (172; Chu's emphasis). Ultimately, female desire breeds a type of female agency as a strongly coded, desiring "I" unexpectedly emerges from Mei Oi's encounters with Song. For Mei Oi, "lover," once an unfamiliar concept associated with the distant scandals of magazines and newspapers, allows her to assume the symbolic position of desiring subject—a position typically reserved for men in a patriarchal society. Indeed, it is Mei Oi's very name, "beautiful love," that catalyzes this emergence of female agency. Mei Oi first uses this "I" to address her desire for Song, but finally she redirects her "improper" desires to her husband. On the last page of Chu's novel, Mei Oi tells Ben Loy: "I *love* you so very much" (250; emphasis added).

While Mei Oi's scandalous actions are condemned by the patriarchs of Chinatown, the birth of her son is also what allows this dying bachelor society not only to live on in a displaced manner but to reclaim female desire and reinsert it back in line with patriarchal imperatives. Indeed, the classic prescription for hysteria's cure—marriage, heterosexual intercourse, pregnancy, and maternity—is a quotidian narrative fulfilled by Mei Oi. These men do not live along the strict Confucian lines of established hierarchies so often cited by them but in an illegitimate form. Chu suggests that this moment of illegitimacy—of the emergence of the female agent of desire—is the very historical and social condition through which an illegitimate Chinese community in America can survive.

In "Secular Criticism," Edward Said delineates the evolution of community relationships under siege. Writing about the opposition of filiation (biological reproduction) to affiliation (cultural reproduction), Said asks "if biological reproduction is either too difficult or too unpleasant, is there some other way by which men and women can create social bonds between each other that would substitute for those ties that connect members of the same family across generations?"[41] While for Said, this dynamic of filiation and affiliation represents the exemplary condition of modernity's displacements, it is important to contest the heterosexist assumptions of this model. That is, does affiliation always function as a substitute for a failed filiation and primal heterosexuality? Is affiliation always compensatory to filiation? Can we imagine a model of productive affiliation that bypasses the insistent hierarchy that configures biology as always trumping culture? (These possible affiliations are explored in the epilogue.)

In the context of *Eat a Bowl of Tea*, however, affiliation is strongly configured as compensatory to filiation. Mei Oi's illegitimate desire emerges as a response to the historical conditions in the United States that make biological reproduction nearly impossible for the Chinese male immigrant. The birth of her "love child" and male heir is what finally cures Ben Loy's hysterical predicament. Her husband's ultimate acceptance of Mei Oi and Ah Song's illegitimate son as his own speaks to the forced turn from filiation to affiliation. Indeed, it reprises the long unofficial history of "paper sons," who exist at the heart of an illegitimate patriarchal Chinese enterprise in America. As such, Mei Oi and Ah Song's love child is only the latest installment in a model of assaulted patrilineal assumption based not on blood but on culture.

This model of cultural transmission, Sau-ling Cynthia Wong writes, ultimately provided the emerging Asian American studies movement with a novel way of recuperating a workable notion of survival:

Though immigration laws changed in 1965, the Asian American movement took place at a time when the effects of the new legislation were just beginning to be felt, and the aftermath of Exclusion was still very visible in Chinatowns and Manilatowns. As Frank Chin's short story "The Only Real Day" shows, if biological reproduction is impossible for Chan, the old waiter from the Exclusion era, his only hope for cultural transmission lies in revising the descent-based notion of the Chinese family to include a biologically unrelated male child, the American-born, English-speaking Dirigible. It is, in part, the predicament of males like Dirigible that calls for the cultural tenets informing the *Aiiieeeee!* Introduction: since genetic patrilineality is unfeasible, culture must be dissociated from blood, and the concept of an ever-evolving Asian American culture unencumbered by expectations of "authenticity"—whether of pedigree or of cultural practices—must be allowed to flourish.[42]

Yet, as Wong notes, this affiliation is an implicitly gendered act. Indeed, the *Aiiieeeee!* school's unspoken goal, I would argue, is to recuperate a legacy of patriarchal assumption—one mired in a heterosexist framework that privileges masculine traceability as a prerequisite, even if in an eroded form. Is Mei Oi's phantasmatic "love child" ultimately accepted by the Chinatown bachelor society because he is a male and not a female heir, the carrier of a bloodline? Thus, the seemingly "antiessentialist" cultural enterprise of 1960s Asian America is, Wong concludes, "at heart, a means to recuperate essentialism in some disguised or attenuated form: a compromise with the realities of the threatened patriline for which *traceability* is a prerequisite. A filiative impulse lurks beneath the persuasive general logic of affiliative theory" ("Chinese/Asian American Men," 189; Wong's emphasis). In the final analysis, if the male hysteric in Chu's novel must relinquish his position of desire for the articulation of a female subject "I," this is a tolerated and temporary compromise finally meant to reinsert the Chinese immigrant male into a renewed patriarchal framework. The articulation of female desire in *Eat a Bowl of Tea* may reconfigure the traditional relations between the sexes, but it also finally cures Ben Loy of his male hysteria by salvaging the Chinese phallus in America in an affiliated and attenuated form.[43]

Eat a Bowl of Tea concludes with Ben Loy and Mei Oi's exile to San Francisco. In his introduction to the 1979 edition of Chu's novel, Jeffrey Chan writes that

there is no question in Chu's narrative about what determines the paternity of the child Mei Oi bears, as if illegitimate beginnings lend strength and continuity to a new generation of Chinese-Americans. In a bachelor society women are scarce, and having children, a family, is difficult. So it is culture, the social environment of a dying generation, that determines paternity in this situation. Further, it is no coincidence that Chu sends Ben Loy and Mei Oi to San Francisco for Ben Loy to reclaim his virility, his paternity, and his wife. His return to San Francisco to make himself anew is not the response of a sojourner. He is a Chinese-American remaking a covenant with Gum Sahn, what the first generation called America, the Golden Mountain. He returns to the city where Chinese-America first began.[44]

If the historical conditions giving rise to male hysteria in Eat a Bowl of Tea call for unorthodox solutions—the emergence of female desire—this swerve into the illegitimate is finally temporary. Culture, I would emphasize, always determines paternity, and Chan reads the end of Chu's novel, the couple's return to San Francisco, as not only the promised rebirth of Chinese American culture but also the simultaneous reclaiming of male virility, male paternity, and a traditional masculinist relation between the sexes. However, is this reuniting of Chinese America with heterosexist assumptions of paternal descent—this renewal of the Chinese American male legacy—premature, a fantasy of projected wholeness, a false image?

Describing Ben Loy and Mei Oi's conjugal union on the final page of Eat a Bowl of Tea, Chu writes: "For this hour, all creation existed solely for them. Their bed was the universe, the stars, the sun, the moon, the air, heaven and earth. The room was incandescent . . ." (250). Chu's ellipses suggest an indeterminacy to this image of suggested completion. Indeed, the renewal of Chinese American male heterosexual potency is maintained only "for this hour" and only through the couple's total withdrawal from the domain of the social, of culture. While their sexual union effaces all borders, spatial and psychological, this cosmic state is not only romantic convention but also contrived. It suggests that Ben Loy and Mei Oi can only come together by suspending themselves from the social world and the Chinatown culture of their fathers. In other words, it is not their perfect union that creates this cosmic universe; it is their isolation in this cosmic universe that facilitates their perfect union.

Chu's phantasmatic ending to Eat a Bowl of Tea suggests that Chan's sanguine heralding of normative heterosexual masculinity's rebirth might be premature. The hope for masculine renewal and integration comes only through continual exile (in San Francisco) and displacement (into a cosmic universe). Is the hope for male hysteria's cure—the hope for the couple's racial assimilation into America—only possible through this detachment and alienation? Set in the multicultural age of Asian American citizenship and equal opportunity, David Wong Louie's *Pangs of Love* provides a site of investigation.

Model Minorities, Multiculturalism, Postmodern Chinatowns: Pangs of Love

> I had a conversation with the show's producer. He said my
> story was too complex. He wanted me to simplify it. He advised
> me that if I wanted listeners' sympathy I should consider dropping
> the "Chinese stuff." Before I listened to another word, I told him
> that I hoped one day he'd be lonesome and heartbroken in
> the back roads of China, thousands of miles from Western
> ears, and the nearest ones carved from stone.
> DAVID WONG LOUIE, "Birthday"

Ben Loy's male hysteria marks the tenuous transition of Chinese alien into American citizen during an era of late 1940s triumphant American exceptionalism. The world of *Eat a Bowl of Tea* is a segregated Chinatown, absolute in its isolation from the mainstream public sphere. In contrast, David Wong Louie's dark collection of short stories, *Pangs of Love,* depicts a multicultural 1980s world of Asian American "model minorities" in the age of assimilation and citizenship.[45] The Chinese American men we encounter in *Pangs of Love* have a type of mobility and access to the public sphere unimaginable in the era of *Eat a Bowl of Tea.* These short stories—set in cities, upscale suburbs, and the beaches of Long Island—depict an ostensibly desegregated and integrated Asian America through the proliferation and hybridity of their multiple locations.[46] Set after the 1943–65 liberalization of immigration laws, after the 1954 *Brown v. Board of Education* decision "dismantling" legalized segregation, after the civil rights and ethnic power movements, and after the advent of Stonewall and second-wave feminism, the world of Louie's short stories cannot be more different from the gritty post–World War II Chinatown ghetto of Chu's novel.

It is also crucial to note that Louie's Chinese American males are no longer subject to the parricidal immigration laws that threaten the biological existence of Chu's bachelor society. Indeed, since the passing of the 1965 Immigration and Nationality Act, Asian America has been renewed not only through biological reproduction but through the widespread arrival of "new Asian immigrants," the post-1965 wave of Asians from East Asia, Southeast Asia, and South Asia that has shifted the demographics of Asian America from predominantly native-born to a present majority of first-generation arrivals. Louie's male characters are not traditional Chinatown cooks, waiters, or laundrymen. They are no longer just the objects but also the subjects of capitalism, a professional class of commercial artists, cafe owners, corporate chemists, and designers of home video games—model minorities with economic mobility. As Sau-ling Cynthia Wong observes, these men "know their way around the America of the Reagan-Bush era, use its products, speak its lingo; they drive expertly and not only sleep with white women but break up with them with regularity" ("Chinese/Asian American Men," 182). Existing in a world in which legislative injunctions against their immigration, naturalization, reproduction, miscegenation, and economic livelihood have been putatively eliminated, they can exist and reproduce, politically, economically, and culturally, without fear. One starts with the distinct impression that the Chinese American men populating Louie's collection should be exempt from paternal anxieties over emasculation. Yet male hysteria exists everywhere in *Pangs of Love*.

Unlike *Eat a Bowl of Tea*, in which male hysteria is isolated in one pathologized body, male hysteria in *Pangs of Love* is dispersed across bodies, spaces, and even objects. Throughout Louie's short stories, this dispersion acquires a distinct vocabulary. For example, one cannot help but notice in the titles of the stories a network of hysterical possibilities: "Displacement," "Pangs of Love," "Love on the Rocks," "Disturbing the Universe," "One Man's Hysteria—Real and Imagined—in the Twentieth Century." Like Ben Loy, Louie's Chinese American men—their Asianness often mentioned or implied only in passing—are wracked with hysterical impotence. This condition not only insists upon a critique of the Asian American model minority myth in the age of multiculturalism, assimilation, and citizenship as the site for the continuing and disavowed legacy of racist exclusion against Asians; it also insists upon an analysis of the social conditions that continue to generate failures—real and imagined—of a thwarted patriarchal assumptions everywhere in *Pangs of Love*'s postmodern world. What might we say about male hysteria—real and imagined—in Louie's late twentieth century?

Hysterical Bodies

Manini Samarth observes that each story in *Pangs of Love* "seems a gesture toward or a relinquishing of a relationship."[47] Samarth provides a crucial starting point for our analysis. Unlike the hysterical impotence that is literally somatized on Ben Loy's corporeal body, the hysterical impotence plaguing the Chinese American male body in Louie's world takes on a more diffuse and abstract pattern of disconnection and relinquishment across a series of bodies. As such, it calls continual attention to hysteria not as individual pathology but as social dis-ease, a group malaise, even a lifestyle. *Pangs of Love* marks this condition of male hysteria through the insistent failure of (hetero)sexual miscegenation between the sexes: the Chinese American man's inability to sustain a lasting relationship with a white woman. The cause of this failure of sexual relations—the impossibility of sexuality itself—is not organic but decidedly psychic.

In "Bottles of Beaujolais," for instance, the narrator, a Chinese waiter in a Japanese sushi restaurant, unable to express his desire to Luna, the chain-smoking white female financial analyst, slices his hand in order to create for her a bottle of French Beaujolais from Japanese sake. This image of bodily mutilation might be thought of as a hysterical symptom of failed miscegenation in the age of diversity. The promise of miscegenation and desegregation has only repellent effects. Like curdled milk, the blood coagulates "into a cinnamon crust, sealing the sake underneath" (52). In "Love on the Rocks," Buddy Lam's hysterical impotence also has maudlin and gruesome results. When his marriage to his white Vassar-educated wife Cookie fails, Buddy murders her and puts her corpse on ice. Every evening Buddy makes a trip to the local supermarket, repacking Cookie's frozen body with a new supply of "rocks" as he carries on an internalized conversation with her. In this solipsistic manner, Buddy continues to conduct what necessarily should be an intersubjective marital affair in its displaced intrapsychic form. In the eponymous title story of the collection, "Pangs of Love," the male narrator also broods upon his history of failed sexual relationships with white women. He tells us, for instance, about the impotence he experiences with his former girlfriend, Amanda. He admits to bolstering his flaccid masculinity with a chemical aphrodisiac created in his laboratory—Musk 838/Lot no. 19144375941–3e—meant to "jump start" his sexual relations with her.

Throughout these stories, Louie's Chinese American men are hysterically impotent with white women, and this impotence compromises the notion of Asian American assimilation through the specific access of promised integration and miscegenation. This hysterical impotence emphatically precludes the siring of heirs while exempting yet again these Chinese American citizens from a proper place in the line of patrilineal assumption and national inheritance. There is, practically speaking, not one male heir in Louie's entire collection. And the one who does exist, in "One Man's Hysteria—Real and Imagined—in the Twentieth Century," exists only in the narrator Stephen's imagination. A fiction writer, Stephen names his male heir Todd—a name tracing its roots to the German for "dead"—pointing to a type of hysterical stillbirth worthy of Breuer's "Fräulein Anna O." Stephen's white girlfriend scoffs at this idea of progeny: "I know nothing about [multiple orgasms] from first-hand experience. I haven't been privileged to such delirium. But my memory is good. I remember our first time. Your pal down there be-tween your legs took the night off" (147). In the age of equal opportu-nity, the male characters in *Pangs of Love* are no longer segregated in the ethnic ghettos of Chinatown. Nevertheless, they continue to experi-ence a type of emotional segregation from whiteness. Indeed, this seg-regation from whiteness comes to permeate—to be desegregated into—the entire spatial world of *Pangs of Love*. I turn to Louie's opening story, "Birthday," to investigate this dispersion of hysteria into space.

Hysterical Space

In "Birthday," issues of the law and patriarchal assumption emerge with a vengeance. The story begins with sustained attention to the spatial boundaries of house and home. "Birthday" opens with a white man out-side the narrator's door, an ostensible trespasser who pounds away with a physical force that threatens to dissolve the borders separating them. The narrator, Wallace Wong, tells us: "There's a man outside the door. He pounds away at it with his fists, and that whole side of the room shakes. He can pound until the house falls. I don't care, it's his house; he can do with it what he pleases" (3). What initially seems to be an image of trespass and violation, however, immediately reverses itself. We come to understand that, despite being locked "outside the door," the white man is not trespassing. It is the Chinese American narrator, in fact, who has barricaded himself inside the white man's house. "Birthday" and *Pangs of Love* thus begin with an image of the Chinese American male narra-tor's occupation of an illegitimate space in which he does not belong. This image of trespass proves to be a type of urtext for reading Louie's collection. Throughout, Chinese American male characters find them-selves in houses and homes to which they have no claim, and this inde-terminate locationality is ultimately related to a racialized male hysteria.

"I came to see the boy," Wallace Wong explains to us in the third para-graph of "Birthday." He goes on to elaborate: "It's true I have no rights except those that come with love. And if I paid attention to what the court says, I wouldn't be here. The court says the boy belongs to the man, the boy's father. This has been hard to take. After all, the boy calls us both by our first names, and as far as I'm concerned that means we're equals" (3). Jilted by Frank's ex-wife, Sylvie, Wallace demands access to Frank and Sylvie's son, Welby. Yet, as Wallace points out, under the eyes of the law he has no legal recourse to the white son.

Wallace insists that Welby recognize not only the name of the white father but also of the yellow father: the "boy calls us both by our first names, and as far as I'm concerned that means we're equals." However, in the juridical realm it is not the given name but the patronym that is at stake, and the court has already ruled that Wallace has no recourse to this paternal privilege. Wallace also emphatically states that his right to the white son (with whom he fantasizes "an afternoon of baseball—sunshine, pop, [and] hotdogs") comes through "love," a category of affect patently unrecognizable to the law.

The law does not—cannot—acknowledge the emotional valence that binds Wallace, Sylvie, and Welby together: "The boy's mother is gone from the picture. . . . Losing the boy almost killed her. All those days in court for nothing. What did that black robe know about the weave of our three hearts? The man won custody. Perhaps he bribed the judge; it's happened before" (4). The "black robe's"—the law's—decision to grant custody to the biological father thus dissolves the new multicultural family created by Wallace, Sylvie, and Welby's bonds of love. Here is an example of an emotional affiliation that produces the possibility of a new formation of family and community not compensatory to a heterosexist notion of filiation. Fatherhood, Wallace reveals to us, is always a leap of faith. Not surprisingly, this is a philosophy and new social formation that the court refuses to recognize or validate.

Indeed, the fact that the law sides with the white biological father —who perhaps bribed the judge—suggests that the law is undeniably biased (linking fatherhood to biology, heterosexuality, and whiteness) and potentially venal. Even more, in its refusal to recognize the affect that it cruelly dissolves, the law forces the Chinese American male into a type of permanent and suspended internal exile. "Birthday" suggests that internal exile may be the very normative psychic condition under which the Asian American male model minority continues to be racialized and excluded in the age of multiculturalism. Wallace Wong tells us that by being in Frank's house he is violating the court's order dictating that he not be there. As such, Wallace literally finds himself inside the space from which he has been exiled. Being *inside* this interdicted space, he thus literally embodies the notion of internal exile. A psychic condition, internal exile becomes thoroughly spatialized. The male hysteric and his space are one. Space assumes the status of hysterical space.

In a contemporary social context that insists upon the practice of a "color-blind" society—constituting those minorities who expose structures of race and racism as being pathologically attached to their victimhood—internal exile assumes a status of paramount and paradigmatic significance. In *Eat a Bowl of Tea,* male hysteria is indexed to a specific location—the segregated space of Chinatown. It is only in Chinatown that Ben Loy is impotent. However, in the age of desegregation—the age of postmodern Chinatowns—this geographical specificity has become abstracted. It has disappeared and been dispersed into its scattered fragments. Male hysteria has migrated everywhere, making it particularly hard to locate and label. It has moved into every space, internalized and externalized, so that space itself becomes a hysterical symptom, as Raymond Williams describes, a generalized structure of feeling. Wallace's internal exile—his alienation from house, home, family, and love—may thus begin to account for the hysterical impotence permeating all the Chinese American male subjectivities in their various spaces everywhere. This internal exile and hysterical impotence are not only the result of the law's debilitating effects but are categorically unrecognized by either the law or a mainstream society attached to its notions of abstract equality.

In a fit of desperation, Wallace calls a radio psychologist. Banned even from the air (!), Wallace instead talks to the radio show's producer, who, like Frank the moviemaker, sanitizes Wallace's claims to difference, rendering them invisible:

> I had a conversation with the show's producer. He said my story was too complex. He wanted me to simplify it. He advised me that if I wanted listeners' sympathy I should consider dropping the "Chinese stuff." Before I listened to another word, I told him that I hoped one day he'd be lonesome and heartbroken in the back roads of China, thousands of miles from Western ears, and the nearest ones carved from stone. (9)

In a "color-blind" multicultural society, color can never be seen—only aestheticized and commodified—even when it is staring you in the face. The official color-blind society inaugurated by *Brown v. Board of Education* and heralded by the Reagan-Bush era of diversity management is especially insidious in its exploitation of a universalism blind to the particularisms that it ruthlessly produces and manages. This management is especially problematic when thought of in these specific terms: abstract equality exists everywhere; the Asian American model minority is a triumphant example of the abstract equivalence of all American citizens; equal opportunity is available to all; those who suffer can only blame themselves. This type of universalism is particularly dangerous for the ways in which it is often used to divide different racialized groups in the United States. The model minority myth, for example, is frequently cited as a rejoinder to the assertion of this nation's systemic institutionalized economic failure of African Americans and Latinos. Indeed, Louie ends "Birthday" with the image of a birthday cake whose frosting entails the mixing of "the chocolate with the sugar and the yolks" (17). This problematic mixing of a "melting pot" of black, white, and yellow is one of the fundamental issues that undergirds questions of social justice in the age of corporatized multiculturalism.

Male hysteria in Louie's short stories exposes a virulent universalism that is blind to continuing and uneven processes of race, gender, and class formation. Thus, even though Stephen the narrator in "One Man's Hysteria—Real and Imagined—in the Twentieth Century," exhibits a breathtaking fluency in the Western canon—believing that committing European metaphysical poetry to heart will save the world in the event of nuclear holocaust—anxieties of "real and imagined" assimilation and extinction continue to plague him. This is an absolute internal exile that exposes a virulent discourse of universalism that contradicts a national project of abstract equivalance and equal representation. This debilitating psychical conflict—which I have described elsewhere as a type of racial melancholia of ungrieved and ungrievable losses—must be recognized and confronted.⁴⁸

In his analysis of the model minority myth in the late 1970s, Bob H. Suzuki rings such a warning bell. He notes how the model minority stereotype has resignified dominant perceptions of Asian Americans from yellow peril to assimilated mascot in the span of a few short decades.⁴⁹ He notes that the assimilation of the model minority into mainstream society remains dubious—especially given the high costs of this transformation. The myth exacts an expensive psychological toll—what I have been calling internal exile—that is ignored and unrecognized by mainstream society:

> Asian Americans have argued that the high psychological cost paid by middle-class Asian Americans for this apparent "success" has far outweighed the socioeconomic benefits.
>
> According to this point of view, over-anxious attempts by Asian Americans to gain acceptance have stripped them of their dignity and have caused many of them to suffer from severe psychological disorders characterized by lack of confidence, low self-esteem, excessive conformity and alienation. Thus, far from having succeeded in American society, the argument goes, Asian Americans continue to be victims of white racism, albeit insidiously subtle in form. (25)

It is the "insidiously subtle" forms of internal exile that must be recognized in the age of multiculturalism and Asian American citizenship. Because male hysteria cannot be indexed to a specific space anymore, the potential that it will go unrecognized is all the greater. The material effects of these erasures and violences are great. For example, as I indicated earlier, Wallace, Sylvie, and Welby's affective and affiliative bonds constitute a new multicultural formation of historical "make-do" families from the era of exclusion—such as that of Ben Loy at the close of *Eat a Bowl of Tea*. Wallace's new family is based not on the concept of a fraught and recuperated filiation but on an affiliation potentially outside the framework of compensation and loss. However, Louie's contemporary version of this make-do family proves to be even more tenuous in its precarious existence than its historical predecessor was. In "Birthday" the family of affiliation is dissolved by a triumphant return to a model of filiation and biologism, a model inscribed by universalizing whiteness and heterosexuality. This is a model that, in our contemporary moment, is still the predominant rule.

Hysterical Furniture

I would like to end this chapter with a brief discussion of the eponymous title story of Louie's collection, *Pangs of Love*. Pang, the narrator's family name, also describes the psychic stab of pain that underwrites the hysterical conflict between racial and sexual identity of Chinese American male subjectivity. In "Pangs of Love" this hysterical conflict assumes the form of the Chinese American narrator's brother, Bagel, a homosexual living with three gay white men and two cats, all of whom share a beach house on Long Island. Bagel's Chinese American male subjectivity–his new form of affiliation, which bypasses the demands of biological reproduction vocalized by his mother, Mrs. Pang—is constituted by Louie as an especially problematic type of (new) Chinese American male subjectivity. That is, for Bagel the possibilities of a new model of affiliation prove entirely antipathetic to his racial identity. The narrator describes Bagel's house in the following manner:

> Bagel's house is white. Even the oak floors have been bleached white. A stranger in a white turtleneck and white pleated trousers opens the door. He's very blond, with dazzling teeth and a jawline that's an archeologist's dream. "Well, look who's here," he says, "the brother, et al." We shake hands, and he says his name's Nino. Nino leads us to the sun-washed living room and introduces us to Mack, who's sprawled out over a couch with the *Times*. My mother

whispers that she'd warned my brother against buying a white couch because it wouldn't "withstand the dirt," but she's surprised at how clean it looks. (88)

In this dazzlingly white environment, Nino's blond hair and dream jawline seem to be an intrinsic extension of his (racialized) surroundings. But Bagel's position within this white space is vexed. The Chinese American brother's attempts to affiliate with this queer world prove to be at the cost of a split subjectivity that denies his racial differences even while it continually exposes it. Unlike the other three men of the house, who are all dressed in white, Bagel is sartorially mottled, "decked out in hound's-tooth slacks, tight turquoise tennis shirt, and black-and-white saddle shoes" (89). Bagel's body literally stands out in this whitewashed environment. His mimicry of its aesthetic ideals—"Bagel's got bulk. He pumps iron. I feel as if I'm holding a steer" (89), the narrator tells us—is condemned to failure.

In "Of Mimicry and Man: The Ambivalence of Colonial Discourse," Homi Bhabha describes the ways in which a colonial regime impels the colonized subject to mimic Western ideals of whiteness. At the same time, this mimicry is also condemned to defeat. Bhabha writes, "Colonial mimicry is the desire for a reformed, recognizable Other, as *a subject of a difference that is almost the same, but not quite.* Which is to say, that the discourse of mimicry is constructed around an *ambivalence;* in order to be effective, mimicry must continually reproduce its slippage, its excess, its difference. . . . *Almost the same but not white.*" [50] Bhabha has located and labeled the social imperative to assimilate as the colonial structure of mimicry. He marks not only this social imperative but also its inevitable, built-in failure. This doubling of difference that is almost the same, but not quite, almost the same but not white, results in ambivalence, which comes to define the failure of mimicry.

Bagel's attempts to align himself with a new queer family and home—his pumped-up muscles and off-color clothes—give way to a psychic ambivalence that might ideally be described through the dynamics of mimicry. This is a queer affiliation, which demands the imitation of whiteness but ultimately finds this imitation intolerable. When Mrs. Pang, for example, drips soy sauce onto the off-white armchair in which she has chosen to sit, all the men of the house become hysterical. Unable to face this intrusion of brownness into their white world, they close ranks to become one coherent body in force: "Within seconds, Nino, Mack, Jamie, and Bagel converge on the stains with sponges, Palmolive dishwashing detergent, paper towels, and a pot of water. An eight-armed upholstery patrol" (89). In the space of the Long Island beach house, the furniture itself comes to manifest the hysterical symptoms of a thwarted assimilation. This hysterical symptom is ultimately referenced back to Bagel. Nino's ironic comment—"God, Billy . . . you always look so pulled together" (89)—calls attention to mimicry's built-in failure, its refusal of assimilation. In scrubbing out the brownness that stains the off-white armchair, Bagel becomes the agent of his own self-exclusion. Indeed, mimicry might be said to underwrite the process of racial hysteria and internal exile that comes to form and define Bagel's subjectivity. In the era of postmodern Chinatowns, the malady of mimicry might be characterized as the dispersed form of the illness of assimilation.

While the figure of the homosexual is insistently figured in a homophobic society as the end of civilization, the end of culture, the end of race, and the end of history, I would like to resist any reading suggesting that Bagel's homosexuality is the dead end of Chinese American racial and cultural integrity, especially given the long and complex history of immigration exclusion and bars to citizenship against this immigrant group. Instead, I would insist on reading Bagel's domestic predicament as proffering a new form of community directly addressing the ravaged material history of racial exclusion and sexual disenfranchisement overshadowing Chinese American male subjectivity in the age of multiculturalism. If the end of the twentieth century has brought upon us the exhilarating possibility of queer affiliations neither compensatory nor adjunct to the reign of a biologistic heterosexuality and whiteness, we must develop forms of affiliation that are scrupulously attendant to sexual as well as racial differences. (These new possibilities for "home" are the topic of the next chapter on queerness and diaspora.) In Bagel's queerness, might we find the recuperated form of Freud's banished figures of the primitive and the homosexual?

"Pangs of Love" ends with an impossibly sweetened image of bitterness that aptly symbolizes the dangerous politesse of a multicultural age. Attempting to smooth over the racial and (homo)sexual tensions underpinning their Long Island gathering, the narrator passes out yet another chemical concoction to the unsuspecting guests:

> I say nothing. I pull out from my pocket gold-foil packets the size and shape of condoms. Inside each is a tablet developed at the lab. You dissolve it in your mouth, and it will disguise the sourness of whatever you drink or eat. I pass them to everyone at the table.
>
> They won't know what has happened. They will laugh, delighted by the tricks of their tongues. But soon the old bitterness in our mouths will be forgotten, and from this moment on, our words will come out sweet. (98)

These sweet words are the rhetoric of juridical equality and justice. They are condoms for the mouth, covering a suppressed bitterness that might well characterize the politics of difference into the twenty-first century. In the thirty years spanned by the publications of *Eat a Bowl of Tea* and *Pangs of Love*, Asian Americans have occupied one of the most charged sites of national anxiety and the idealization of assimilation. In the span of three short decades, that is, Asian Americans have moved from yellow peril to model minorities. As a dis-ease indexing national fears of immigration, assimilation, and racialization, male hysteria serves as a psychic link between these two historical periods, the era of the Asian alien and the era of Asian American citizenship. The enduring presence of male hysteria suggests that anxiety and idealization—yellow peril and model minority—are not opposite phenomena; indeed, they exist on the same material and psychic continuum. Together Chu and Louie's attention to male hysteria qualifies the teleological narrative of American positivism. Ultimately, the multicultural age of Asian American citizenship and the society of the color-blind do not represent a state of greater advancement or an advanced condition of moral progress. Asian American male hysteria calls attention to these universalisms and incommensurabilities. It calls for the continual investigation of assimilation and illness, not for their individual pathological bases but for their social and political etiologies.

EPILOGUE

Out Here and Over There: Queerness and

Diaspora in Asian American Studies

Impossible Arrivals

As we have witnessed in the works of Kingston, Chin, Kaneko, Hwang, Chu, and Louie issues of home for Asian Americans are particularly vexed. Historically configured as either unassimilable aliens or perversely assimilated and thus "whiter than white" (the sojourner/yellow peril thesis versus the model minority myth), Asian Americans have at best a dubious claim to citizenship and a place within the U.S. nation-state.[1] A sense of membership within the larger national collective has traditionally followed the political, economic, and cultural incorporation of a Western European ethnic group under the banner of immigration and assimilation as well as through the spatial metaphorics of the United States as a point of arrival and melting pot. However, recent debates in Asian American studies about diaspora—its focus on point of departure and displacement from origin—insist that we (re)think the problematics of home in this field.[2] Suspended between departure and arrival, Asian Americans remain permanently disenfranchised from home, relegated to a nostalgic sense of its loss or to an optative sense of its unattainability.

Approaching this problem of home from a spatial angle, we might reasonably wonder: where, after all, is Asian America? Can Asian America finally be located, designated, or pinned down? A quasi-geographical term that gained popularity in the 1970s, *Asian America* is being invoked with increasing frequency today.[3] A siteless locale with no territorial sovereignty, the term *Asian America* underwrites, as Sau-ling Cynthia Wong suggests, "a yearning for the kind of containing boundaries and contained site enjoyed by the dominant society, a nation-state" —a home.[4] To refigure this particular spatial dynamic in relation to Oscar V. Campomanes's suggestive claims about Filipino American literatures, Asian American identity might well be considered more in conjunction with a discourse of exile and emergence than with one of immigration and settlement.⁵ In this manner, considering diaspora in Asian American studies works to undermine and dislodge any smooth alignment of home and nation-state. Moreover, the popular presumption in both Asian American and American studies that our intrinsic fields of inquiry are necessarily grounded in one location—the domestic space of the United States—would merit reconsideration through the lens of a more spatially—that is, diasporically—encompassing theoretical framing.

Thinking for a moment outside the traditional borders of Asian American studies, for those of us also invested in the field of queer studies questions of home prove equally problematic. The often literal ejection of queers from their homes—coupled with their marginalization by pervasive structures of normative heterosexuality—attests to similar dilemmas that emerge around this issue. Traumatic displacement from a lost heterosexual "origin," questions of political membership, and the impossibilities of full social recognition dog the queer subject in a mainstream society impelled by the presumptions of compulsory heterosexuality. In this particular ordering of the social sphere, to "come out" is precisely and finally never to *be* "out"—a never-ending process of constrained avowal, a perpetually deferred state of achievement, an uninhabitable domain. Suspended between an "in" and "out" of the closet—between origin and destination and private and public space—queer entitlements to home and nation-state remain doubtful as well.⁶

How might we think about queer notions of home in this particular context of impossible arrivals? To take one example, let us turn to Jennie Livingston's *Paris Is Burning*.⁷ A 1991 film documenting the everynight lives of a group of Harlem drag queens, *Paris Is Burning* chronicles a series of elaborate voguing contests and drag balls in which participants contend with one another under the sponsorship of their "houses" and "house mothers" (The House of Xtravaganza, The House of Ninja, etc.). That Livingston's film obsessively rescripts the topic of house and the subject of kinship in its narrative and thematic content suggests that anxieties about loss of home remain psychically central to queer (as well as racialized) cultural projects and social agendas.⁸ Moreover, the political monikers of activist groups such as Queer Nation, which tenaciously locate questions of membership within a larger national collectivity, propose that home as a regulating principle might, on reflection, constitute one of queer activism's organizing conditions of possibility.⁹ In its alignment with the nation-state, home becomes the site of validation, the privileged location for the benefits of citizenship, the central place of belonging.

While *Paris Is Burning* and Queer Nation might offer potential ways to disturb traditional understandings of membership in the U.S. nation-state, their multiple invocations of home nonetheless suggest that queers, like Asian Americans, harbor yearnings for the kind of contained boundaries enjoyed by mainstream society. Hence, despite frequent and trenchant queer dismissals of home and its discontents, it would be a mistake to underestimate enduring queer affiliations with this concept. The solution, of course, is neither to reinforce nor to reify the hegemonic regimes of heterosexuality and whiteness that facilitate unimpeded access to home, citizenship, and membership in a social community. Indeed, to repeat my assertion throughout *Racial Castration,* the goal is to contest the inevitability of these normative structures while deconstructing their mechanisms of exclusion.

Taken together, these numerous problems of home urge us to consider the intersection of queerness and diaspora—the implications of their various crossings—in Asian American studies. How might we theorize queerness and diaspora against a historical legacy that has unrelentingly configured Asian Americans as exterior or pathological to the U.S. nation-state? How might queerness and diaspora provide a critical methodology for a more adequate understanding of Asian American racial and sexual formation as shaped in the space between the domestic and the diasporic? What enduring roles do nations and nationalism play in the delineation of such a critical project? This closing chapter is a speculative treatise on one critical direction in which Asian American studies might productively move in relation to both diasporic studies and queer theory. In particular it attempts to rethink questions of kinship and new affiliations.

This chapter is speculative in part because the pairing of queerness with diaspora demands a rather dramatic critical turn against the conventional ways in which diaspora has been philosophically configured to the exclusion of queer networks. Tracing its genealogy to the book of Deuteronomy, *diaspora* is both a verb—meaning "to disperse" or "to sow"—and a proper noun referring to the scattering of the Jews. According to the *Oxford English Dictionary, diaspora,* an ancient term in Hebrew and Greek, appeared rather recently in English usage (1876). Khachig Tölölyan notes in the 1991 introduction to the inaugural issue of *Diaspora: A Journal of Transnational Studies* that we "use 'diaspora' provisionally to indicate our belief that the term that once described Jewish, Greek, and Armenian dispersion now shares meaning with a larger semantic domain that includes words like immigrant, expatriate, refugee, guest-worker, exile community, overseas community, ethnic community. This is the vocabulary of transnationalism, and any of its terms can usefully be considered under more than one of its rubrics."[10] It is important to point out that, in Tölölyan's explication of the term, the political implications of *diaspora* both in its traditional and its contemporary usages are inherently unstable with regard to the nation-state. That is, diasporas can be sites of political resistance to the nation-state. However, they can function as unusually conservative sites of nationalism as well. Put otherwise, while diasporic communities are sometimes the paradigmatic other of the nation-state, they are at other times, Tölölyan contends, "its ally, lobby or even, as in the case of Israel, its precursor. . . . Diasporas are sometimes the source of ideological, financial, and political support for national movements that aim at a renewal of the homeland (Sun Yat Sen, Yasser Arafat)" (5). Hence, it is crucial to remember that diasporas are not invariably oppositional to the entity of the nation-state. Their political functions are not so predetermined.

In this regard, how has sexuality traditionally functioned in conceptions of diaspora? Jee Yeun Lee notes that in reifying the category of the nation-state diasporas often "rely on heterosexist conceptions of kinship and lineage to define community. As a concept, diaspora may be even more prone to myths of reproductive heritage than the nation, whose boundaries can at least be tracked geographically. But if a people is spread over various lands, according to this line of thought, how else can you tell if someone belongs to the diaspora than through a family tree?"[11] Lee flags the heterosexist practices of conservative diasporas that rely on community organization through strict lines of filiation and kinship. How might we rethink the underlying political assumptions of a diaspora organized in this manner—organized, that is, around the conservation of racial and ethnic dispersion? What could thinking about a diaspora largely ordered through the lens of sexuality—through a focus on queerness—possibly offer us in Asian American as well as queer studies? If diasporas are not inherently sites of political resistance—as queer is not always an oppositional or radical state of being—what might the unorthodox pairing of queerness and diaspora politically yield?[12] How might a queer diaspora provide new methods of contesting traditional kinship structures, of reorganizing communities based not on filiation and biology but on affiliation and the assumption of a common set of social practices or political commitments such as economic and social justice? What new forms of community could emerge from a diasporic and queer challenge to the linking of home and the nation-state?

In approaching diaspora and queerness through this particular set of issues, I hope to create a productive dialogue between Asian American and queer studies. I hope, that is, to bring together two disciplines that have remained traditionally unconnected through specific attention to a diaspora focused on sexuality. In considering the material and theoretical intersections of queer diasporas for Asian Americans, this chapter also engages contemporary debates on the internationalizing of American studies. Investigating American studies in physical sites outside the immediate borders of the United States and in theoretical sites with which it is typically not associated offers new understandings for the current hateful and conservative national backlash against people of color and queers. It would be a mistake to align in too analogous a manner the political agendas and intellectual concerns of Asian American, American, queer, and diasporic studies. However, it does seem clear from the above discussion of home that we must undertake a serious examination of how social relations within our domestic borders inflect, and in turn are inflected by, the diasporic, by framings of transnational capital, immigration, and labor. I offer the following speculations on queerness and diaspora in Asian American studies with the hope of yielding some new methods of thinking about how this rapidly expanding field provides unexplored theoretical paradigms for a crucial evaluation of American identity, home, and nation-state in an age of globalized sexual and racial formations.

Heterosexuality and the Domestic

In order to trace the increasingly important relationship between queerness and diaspora in Asian American studies in the late 1990s, it is useful first to consider a brief history of the Asian American studies movement as it originally formed around the domestic imperative of claiming the U.S. nation-state.[13] In the shadow of 1950s and 1960s civil rights struggles, the emerging Asian American studies movement focused much of its political energy and theoretical attention on domestically based race relations within the geographical boundaries of the U.S. nation-state. Modeled on the cultural nationalism of the Black Power movement, the Yellow Power movement during this period largely endorsed a political platform of identity-based politics, racial separatism, and a Marxist-inspired class critique of American capitalism. The Asian American cultural nationalist project, perhaps best exemplified in the academy by Frank Chin's *Aiiieeeee!* group, centered its attentions on local Asian American communities as sites of resistance for the mobilizing of political action, the building of alternative economic institutions, and the creation of an oppositional nativist culture.[14]

In the 1975 prefatory manifesto to their now-classic collection of

Asian American writings, *Aiiieeeee! An Anthology of Asian-American Writers,* the editors contend that "legislative racism and euphemized white racist love" have consigned Asian Americans to a state of "self-contempt, self-rejection, and disintegration."[15] A remedy, the *Aiiieeeee!* group insists, demands the assertion of an Asian American identity with its own unique political as well as recognizable cultural parameters. Rejecting the dominant either/or conception of Asian American identity as forever divided—split between the Asian and the American and between Asia and America—the editors insist on claiming the domestic sphere as their own. Hence, they link entitlement to the public sphere of the nation-state with the private prerogatives of home.[16] Seizing upon their self-definition of *Asian American,* they emphatically state that the

> myth of being either/or and the equally goofy concept of the dual personality haunted our lobes while our rejection by both Asia and white America proved we were neither one nor the other. Nor were we half and half or more one than the other. Neither Asian culture nor American culture was equipped to define us except in the most superficial terms. However, American culture, equipped to deny us the legitimacy of our uniqueness as American minorities, did so, and in the process contributed to the effect of stunting self-contempt on the development and expression of our sensibility that in turn has contributed to a mass rejection of Chinese and Japanese America by Chinese- and Japanese-Americans.[17]

In delineating an integrally and a psychically "whole" Asian American subject against this model of either/or split subjectivity, cultural nationalism's political project was centered squarely on Asian American claims to the space of the U.S. nation-state as enfranchised citizen-subjects.

The *Aiiieeeee!* model worked to configure Asian Americans as a racialized minority group with inviolable political needs, economic concerns, and cultural contours.[18] Rejecting the mainstream stereotype of Asian Americans as anomalous ethnic novelties ill fitted to the general sociopolitical landscape of the U.S. nation-state, cultural nationalism's energies focused on not merely defining but prescribing who a recognizable and recognizably legitimate Asian American racial subject should ideally be: male, heterosexual, working class, American born, and English speaking. Noting that it "is an article of white liberal American faith today that Chinese men, at their best, are effeminate closet queens like Charlie Chan and, at their worst, are homosexual menaces like Fu Manchu,"[19] the *Aiiieeeee!* group envisioned the prototypical Asian American male as a grassroots activist who would counter dominant mainstream stereotypes of the passive Asian American male sissy, "devoid of manhood," through his consciously oppositional voice, his militant attitude, and his resistance to bourgeois social convention.[20] As we have witnessed in each chapter of this book, feminization is a crucial issue that plagued Asian American male subjectivity throughout the nineteenth and twentieth centuries. It is fair to say, however, that with the publication of *Aiiieeeee!*, feminization—and resistance to feminization—became one of Asian American studies' motivating and central debates.

Past as well as present Asian American feminist and queer commentators have rightly noted the *Aiiieeeee!* group's problematic assumptions of a narrowly defined concept of Asian American male identity.[21] These critics observe that by staking their cultural nationalist project on such an inflexible and strict notion of identity—on the recuperation of a strident Asian American masculinity and a "pure," heroic, Asian martial tradition—the *Aiiieeeee!* group reinscribes a dominant system of compulsory heterosexuality with all its attendant misogyny and homophobia. Paradoxically, then, cultural nationalist tenets mirrored the mainstream heterosexist and racist structures by which stereotypical conceptions of Asian American men as "efficient housewives"—as effeminate, illegitimate, and divided—were produced in the first instance.[22]

This critique of cultural nationalism is by now not only well known but well rehearsed. In criticizing the *Aiiieeeee!* group's reliance on this narrow definition of Asian American identity, however, Asian American cultural commentators have failed to remark upon the specific connection between the *Aiiieeeee!* group's focus on the domestic and their focus on the heterosexual. That is, they have failed to remark upon the *Aiiieeeee!* group's implicit linking of cultural nationalism's claims on the domestic space of the nation-state as a naturalized function of compulsory heterosexuality. In this instance, the paradoxical double meaning of *domestic* as both the public space of the masculine (nation-state) and the private realm of the feminine (home) is brought into relief and contradiction, the forced reconciliation of their crossing contingent on the strict repression and disciplining of the latter to the former. Put otherwise, a public Asian American male identity is purchased through the emphatic possession of and control over a popularly devalued private realm, constituted here as both the feminine and the homosexual.

This coupling of the cultural nationalist project with the heterosexual is neither intrinsic nor predetermined.[23] Thus, we must be careful not only to critique vigorously the patriarchal complicities of the Asian American cultural nationalist project but also to consider how this disciplining of the domestic, the forced repression of feminine and homosexual to masculine, and of the home to the nation-state, is a formation in need of queering. How does Asian American cultural nationalism's claiming of the domestic through the heterosexual preempt a more comprehensive investigation of an Asian American male identity undercut by anxieties of feminization as well as a political platform informed by issues of queerness and diaspora? If the elevation of the domestic and the heterosexual in Asian American cultural nationalism has worked to disavow and preclude a discussion of the queer and the diasporic from the inception of the Yellow Power movement's political and intellectual genealogy, how might we rethink the historical effects of the Asian American movement's (heterosexual) desire for the domestic? How might we invoke a queer and diasporic assumption of the domestic to denaturalize claims on the nation-state and home as inevitable functions of the heterosexual?[24]

Return of the Repressed: Risking the Asian(-)American Hyphen

The relative success of Asian American cultural nationalism's (heterosexual) desire for the domestic might perhaps be best examined in light of the continuing debates on the Asian American as a hyphenated identity: *Asian American* versus *Asian-American*. As I understand the argument, attempts to excise the hyphen from this term reflect on a grammatical level cultural nationalism's desire to eschew the notion of a split subjectivity while claiming the uniqueness of Asian American identity as "whole" and wholly viable within the space of the nation-state. Hence, the elimination of the hyphen from this term claims not only psychic but also spatial entitlement to Asian American membership within the larger U.S. national collective. If diasporic tenets suggest a suspension between departure and arrival, between origin and destination, for the Asian American subject—the sustaining of a spatial hyphen—then cultural nationalism's desire to claim the space of the domestic as our own relies upon the definitive excision of this marker.

The hyphen debate remains interesting for several reasons. The frequency with which the repressed hyphen returns to mark the term *Asian(-)American* with randomness clearly suggests that Asian American claims to the domestic space of the nation-state as home and as citizen-subjects are far from resolved.[25] The difficulty of banishing the hyphen from this term functions, then, as a (grammatical) symptom vitiating Asian American claims to membership in the U.S. nation-state. Moreover, the slippage of *Asian* and *American* calls to our attention the tenuous coupling of *nation* and *state* itself, whose own hyphenated stability is secured, among other ways, through the sustaining ambiguity of *Asian(-)American* as a hyphenated and thus foreign, exotic, and excludable identity.[26] The arbitrariness with which the hyphen continues to re-appear thus underscores the conceptual and political limits of cultural nationalism's (heterosexual) desire for the domestic—to challenge effectively enduring historical configurations of Asian Americans as aliens, exterior to the nation-state and divided between "over here" and "over there."[27] If the continual return of the repressed hyphen marks the impossibility of cultural nationalism's naturalizing turn to the domestic and heterosexual—functioning as the enduring symptom of the vicissitudes of this turn—then might we begin to reevaluate the efficaciousness of cultural nationalism's domestic and heterosexual project against alternative theoretical models and political strategies?

Can the hyphen in *Asian(-)American* only ever be a grammatical effect of mainstream prejudice and exclusion? Does the orthographic excision of the hyphen laminate, to borrow from Barthes's theoretical vocabulary on the photograph, Asian with American identity in ways that obviate more careful analyses of the double consciousness thrust upon Asian American psyches by mainstream society? Might we begin to reconsider the hyphen not just as a grammatical marker of Asian American disenfranchisement from the sphere of the domestic (in both its private as and public manifestations) but as a necessary risk for a more sufficient analysis of old and new forms of Asian American racial and sexual formations? Might risking the hyphen yield a theoretical model beyond the domestic and the heterosexual as the presumptive limits of an efficacious Asian American political project? Do historical reasons and current political uses call for hyperbolization, and not the removal, of the hyphen to create spaces for future (re)articulations of Asian American identities?

It seems to me that one possible effect of risking the hyphen would be to force Asian American studies beyond the borders of the domestic—to confront the status of *Asian* in the term *Asian American*.[28] It is wise to remember that the very genesis of Asian American studies was, as Sucheta Mazumdar points out, international from its inception.[29] In configuring a political platform around the domestic, Asian American cultural nationalism relied heavily on the political lessons of Vietnam War protests, Maoist movements in China, and other actions in the Third World. Sau-ling Cynthia Wong notes that in the early days of the movement "transnational concerns had a way of looping back to the domestic once political lessons had been extracted," the linkage between the domestic and the international being "more in the nature of inspiration and analogy, with 'foreign' spheres of struggle lending strength and legitimacy to the American minority political enterprise."[30]

We need to be critical of the ways in which this looping back effaces a certain historical legacy of the international in the Asian American studies movement—a repression mimed by the desire to banish the hyphen in *Asian(-)American*. This banishment leads to an arrested notion of Asian American identity while simultaneously closing off alternative possibilities for political resistance, coalition, and organization across not only multiple locations but multiple constituencies. For example, new Asian American immigration—that is, post-1965 Asian immigrant subjects and post-1965 Asian immigrant communities in the United States—continues to disrupt the traditional disciplinary boundaries of Asian American studies (as well as disciplinary paradigms underwriting American studies and Asian area studies). New post-1965 immigration from Vietnam, South Korea, and the Philippines cannot be understood, for instance, outside of U.S. neoimperialist interventions and colonialism in these regions—the disciplining and ordering of Asian American identities that begin "over there" rather than "over here" within the domestic borders of the United States.[31] As such, any serious understanding of Asian American racial formation must be considered in relation to a comparative and internationalist model of subject formation and subjection beyond the real and imaginary borders of the U.S. nation-state.

To risk the hyphen in this instance is to recognize the interpenetrations between the diasporic and the domestic in the historical and contemporary genesis of *Asian(-)American* as a political identity and an oppositional social movement. To recognize these interpenetrations is not only to reevaluate the genealogies of past Asian immigrant settlement but also to recognize contemporary shifts in Asian American demographics as the present index of U.S. nationalism and nationalist legacies in a global framework. From a slightly different angle, if the period from 1850 to World War II, as Lisa Lowe contends, configures Asian immigration to the United States as a site for the eruptions and resolutions of contradictions between the national economy and the political state, the period since World War II represents Asian immigration as the locus of contradictions between the nation-state and the global economy.[32]

In a contemporary context, the current demand for the use of the hyphen remains significant when one considers the political landscape of the 1990s as one that was increasingly influenced by the shifting transnational flows of global capital, immigration, and labor. In the thirty-plus years since the passage of the 1965 Immigration and Nationality Act, the demographic landscape of U.S. immigration has been completely transformed, with Asians, Central Americans, Mexicans, and Caribbeans constituting 80 percent of all migration to the United States.[33] Today, the resulting shift in Asian American identity from an American-born to a majority-foreign-born model (from not only East Asia but also Southeast and South Asia) calls attention to an emerging group of Asian Americans whose ongoing political, economic, and cultural ties to and dependency upon the Pacific have produced unprecedented Asian American identities. For instance, a new transnational vocabulary has arisen with regard to contemporary familial as well as group configurations in these multiple spaces: satellite people, parachute kids, reverse settlers, and flexible citizenship, to name but a few.[34] These contemporary phenomena underscore the diasporic within the domestic, calling attention to the ways in which global flows of capital not only give rise to new Asian American identities but also reinforce, renew, and recreate the historical disenfranchising of Asian Americans from the U.S. nation-state in ways we have yet to analyze.[35] Taken together, these historical conditions and contemporary phenomena underwrite a reemergence of the hyphen in *Asian(-)American* through the (re)articulation of Asian American racial formation throughout various global sites and locales.

In delineating a contemporary Asian(-)American political project around the hyphen and globalization, however, we must remember that arguments characterizing the nation-state as losing significance in diasporic formations fail to recognize the absolute need of global capital to exert its demands within the concrete, localized space of the nation-state. Global capital, Saskia Sassen reminds us, exerts its demands through effective claims on nation-states to guarantee its economic rights within both a global and a domestic context.[36] As such, Sassen's caveat urges us to think not only of U.S. racisms as they travel through an international arena but also of the global effects of racial formation as they manifest themselves within the local space of the United States.[37] How, for instance, might we analyze the current massive attack on civil rights in the United States for immigrants, people of color, and gays and lesbians as an effect of globalization? What are the possible new meanings of *race* as it crosses various national borders and locales? In configuring my concerns in this way, I am not arguing for a diasporic viewpoint that subsumes the domestic. Rather, I am arguing for a vigilant examination of the diasporic in contemporary analyses of Asian American racial formation and oppositional politics. I am advocating a recognition that the diasporic and the domestic were intertwined from the start.

Given the historical internationalism of Asian American identities and Asian American studies, and given the contemporary flows of global capital, immigration, and labor, might we risk the hyphen in Asian(-) American studies in order to focus attention on the international as a strategy that can help us claim membership in the national? Might we (re)claim and not dismiss the hyphen for its political potential and its oppositional possibilities? Lowe reminds us in "Heterogeneity, Hybridity, Multiplicity: Asian American Differences" that the 1990s marked a historical moment in the field of Asian American studies in which we could and had to reconsider notions of Asian American identity not only in terms of similarity and unity but in relation to particularity and difference as the necessary basis for continual, renewed, and efficacious political action.[38] Indeed, what might a hyperbolization of the hyphen offer in terms of calling attention to new and uneven political practices in various sites and locales and across various identities and sexualities claiming the label Asian(-)American? How might this hyperbolization of the hyphen in Asian(-)American supplement cultural nationalism's political focus on the domestic and the heterosexual with an explicit consideration—a histrionics even—of the diasporic and the queer?

Queerness and Diaspora in Asian American Studies

To consider the hyphen in Asian American studies requires the investigation of diaspora as a function of queerness. This is queerness not only in the sense of sexual identity and sexual practices; it is also queerness in the sense of a critical methodology for evaluating Asian American racial formation across multiple axes of difference as well as in numerous local and global manifestations. How does queerness as a critical methodology provide a theoretical vantage point for thinking out past, present, and future Asian American political, economic, and cultural practices?

I want to approach these questions by juxtaposing two articles from recent issues of *Amerasia Journal*.[39] In the first volume, a special issue on lesbian, gay, and bisexual topics entitled "Dimensions of Desire: Other Asian and Pacific American Sexualities: Gay, Lesbian and Bisexual Identities and Orientation," Dana Y. Takagi notes in her lead article the potential of gay and lesbian sexual identities to dislodge the ossified masculinist notions of cultural nationalism. She eloquently argues for the need to recognize different sexual identities that also lay claim to the label *Asian American*. By doing so, Takagi insists, we can begin to rethink and reevaluate "notions of identity that have been used, for the most part, unproblematically and uncritically in Asian American studies" since its inception in the early 1970s around the tenets of cultural nationalism. She suggests that we ought to be talking seriously about the junctions of "gay and lesbian sexuality and Asian American Studies" because of the continued "theoretical trouble we encounter in our attempts to situate and think about sexual identity and racial identity" together.[40]

Takagi invokes gay and lesbian sexuality (she does not use the term *queer*) in the sense of sexual identity and practices that gain their meaning through the polarization of an oppositional heterosexuality and homosexuality.[41] To the extent that Asian American cultural nationalism was dependent on an unexamined notion of the "ideal" subject as male and heterosexual, the introduction of gay and lesbian sexuality into Asian American studies challenges this outdated conception of the "proper" Asian American subject by reconsidering racial formation through the lens of sexual multiplicity. However, in gesturing toward the possibility of a dynamic relationship between racial and sexual difference, Takagi's essay also points us in the useful direction of thinking about a potential (albeit unrealized) political project of queerness in Asian American studies neither restricted to nor exhausted by sexual identity and practices. How might we consider queerness as a critical methodology that intersects Asian American identity formation across multiple axes of difference and in highly dynamic ways?

Let me return for a moment to a passage from Lowe's *Immigrant Acts* discussed in the introduction to this volume. In this passage, Lowe notes the ways in which immigration exclusion laws and bars to citizenship not only racialized but also gendered the Asian American subject. "Racialization along the legal axis of definitions of citizenship," Lowe writes, "has also ascribed 'gender' to the Asian American subject. Up until 1870, American citizenship was granted exclusively to white male persons; in 1870, men of African descent could become naturalized, but the bar to citizenship remained for Asian men until the repeal acts of 1943–1952. Whereas the 'masculinity' of the citizen was first inseparable from his 'whiteness,' as the state extended citizenship to nonwhite male persons, it formally designated these subjects as 'male,' as well" (11). Lowe analyzes the ways in which social definitions of maleness are inextricably bound to hegemonic conceptions of whiteness. As such, she provides a provocative model for thinking about Asian American sexual and racial formation not as separate processes of identity formation. Sexuality and race cannot be restricted in singular isolation. To the contrary, they come into existence in and through a dialectical relationship with one another.

Lowe's model thus provides a theoretical grounding that can focus our attention on the dynamic relationship between sexuality and gender formation as they frame and are framed by Asian American racialization processes. The model provides a way for scholars in Asian American studies to consider queerness as a critical methodology based not only on content but on style and form. Thinking about queerness in this way highlights the need for those of us in Asian American studies to understand that legal and cultural discourses on "deviant" sexuality affect not merely those contemporary Asian American subjects who readily self-identify as gay or lesbian (a strict form of identity politics); rather, queerness comes to describe, affect, and encompass a much larger Asian American constituency—whatever their sexual identities or practices—whose historically disavowed status as U.S. citizen-subject under punitive immigration and exclusion laws renders them "queer" as such.

I am sketching a conception of queerness in Asian American studies that exceeds the question of sexuality as a narrowly defined or singular category by considering the ways in which other critical and intersecting axes of difference give legibility to our social identities. From a slightly different angle, I am focusing on a politics of queerness that can function for Asian American studies as a wide method of racial critique, considering at once a network of social difference and political concerns as it dynamically underpins the formation of Asian American subjectivity. This focus on queerness, like our focus on the question of psychoanalysis, implicitly demands the investigation of Asian American racial formation through broad social categories and epistemologies, including (but not limited to) questions of sexuality and sexual identification.

Let me turn now to my second example from *Amerasia Journal* in order to consider how this expanded notion of queerness as a critical methodology for the examination of Asian American subject formation works in conjunction with diaspora in multiple global and local sites. In a special issue "Thinking Theory in Asian American Studies," published on the discipline's twenty-fifth anniversary in the academy, Takagi and Michael Omi (in their roles as guest coeditors) note in their introduction that the

> waning of radical political movements in the 1980s had attendant effects on theory and politics within Asian American Studies. We feel that the absence of a sustained and coherent radical theory of social transformation led to a retreat to more mainstream, discipline-based paradigmatic orientations. Contributing to this trend was the increasing "professionalization" of the field in academic settings, the demands of tenure and promotion for faculty members, and the entrance of newcomers to the field trained in specific disciplines who had not participated in the new social movements of the previous decades. The result of this has been the contraction of space for dialogue across the disciplines—one which could have critically interrogated disciplinary boundaries and fostered cross-disciplinary perspectives.[42]

How does this passage relate to Takagi's earlier claims for Asian American gays and lesbians as well as to my earlier remarks on queerness as a methodology not only attendant to content but to form and style? How might we evaluate Takagi and Omi's observations on the "waning of radical political movements" in Asian American studies in the 1980s against the emergence of queer activism and the AIDS movement during this same historical period?

That two Asian American critics as perceptive as Takagi and Omi fail to consider the historical contributions of Asian Americans to queer activism and the AIDS movement is indicative of the difficulties we still face in Asian American studies systematically to integrate not only issues of (homo)sexuality but issues of queerness into our critical vocabulary and theoretical discussions. This difficulty, I would also note, results from an intransigent failure on the part of mainstream gay and lesbian scholarship to consider queerness in the broader context I have sketched. In its consistent elision of race as a conceptual category for analysis, mainstream gay and lesbian scholarship fails to embrace queerness as a critical methodology for the understanding of sexual identity as it is dynamically formed in and through racial epistemologies. This integration is a crucial project given the alarming ways in which mainstream gay and lesbian political organizations have shaped, for example, current political claims and debates such as gay marriage as issues of civil and equal rights. This shaping, of course, is in opposition to the scaling back and massive attacks on affirmative action for people of color as special rights.) [43]

Takagi and Omi are certainly correct in their suggestion that the 1980s marked a demonstrable shift in Asian American political activism and the Asian American studies movement. Unquestionably, the apotheosis of global capital under the Reagan and Thatcher administrations, the collapse of communism in the Soviet Union and Eastern Europe, and the dismantling of prolabor movements and unions led to a concomitant shift in Asian American studies away from a traditional class-based critique of race. [44] Yet this shift, I would emphasize, might also be thought of as a displacement of progressive Asian American politics — and sustained class-based analyses of racial formation — into new realms of struggle rather than the disappearance or waning of radical political movements. This is not to say that issues of class should no longer be vigilantly pursued in their new global and local configurations but that our interrogation of Asian American racial formation must also be mediated by analyses of other forms of domination.

Globalization has shifted current frameworks of resistance. Therefore, we in Asian American studies cannot ignore the rise of queer activism (as well as critical debates on multiculturalism and cultural studies) in the 1980s as a visible and oppositional political movement.[45] If the global restructuring of capital in the 1980s dismantled a traditional class-based critique of race as the foundation for "radical political movements" in Asian American studies, we must consider how this attack on the field of progressive politics relates to the rise of queer activism and its critique of subject formation as a viable strategic alternative to a transformative Asian American political platform.[46] How does queer studies' critique of the subject come to function as a displaced marker for more traditional class-based analyses of race in Asian American studies?

To the extent that Takagi recognizes (in "Maiden Voyage") the dislodging of Asian American identity from its cultural nationalist moorings as a function of "gay and lesbian" sexualities, she offers a way for us to reconsider Asian American subjectivity in more capacious ways. Indeed, the now familiar critique of the subject of Asian American cultural nationalism as equating political efficacy not with particularity and difference but with similarity and unity as the basis for social action traces much of its theoretical roots to work done in queer (as well as feminist) activism and cultural studies during this time. Queerness, then, can help us to articulate how Asian American sexual, racial, and class formations come into existence in relation to one another. To the extent, however, that Takagi and Omi (in "Thinking Theory") overlook queer activism's ascendant role in oppositional politics in the 1980s, they miss the opportunity to understand queerness as it intersects with Asian American studies—queerness as a critical methodology that promises to open up a much broader set of Asian American identities as well as a more extensive set of Asian American concerns and locations.

How does Asian American queerness function not just in terms of identities but in terms of locations? If global restructuring of capital in the 1980s worked to clear the discursive field of oppositional class politics for a queer critique of the subject as one of progressive politics's new sites, then we must recognize and evaluate this displacement. This is a contemporary displacement, I reiterate, that emphasizes sexuality and globalization—queerness and diaspora—in Asian American studies. If earlier Asian American cultural nationalist projects were built on the political strategy of claiming home and nation-state through the domestic and the heterosexual, a new political project of thinking about this concept in Asian American studies today would seem to center around queerness and diaspora—its rethinking of home and nation-state across multiple identity formations and numerous locations "out here" and "over there." In the beginning of the new millennium, queerness and diaspora should be used not only to reevaluate the past but to orient the future development of Asian American political projects and strategies whose claims on a politics of social transformation can be acknowledged as such. This moment should be marked by a definitive shift away from a politics of cultural nationalism to a politics of transnational culturalism.

How might these various theoretical speculations on queerness and diaspora in Asian American studies appear in a material context? What might a queer Asian American in a globalized frame look like? I end this chapter and book with two brief analyses: Ang Lee's 1993 film, *The Wedding Banquet*, and R. Zamora Linmark's 1995 novella, *Rolling the R's*.[47] Ang's transnational film provides us with one model for thinking about the possibilities—and ultimate limitations—of an emergent queer and diasporic Asian American male identity. Through its emphatic turn to the global, Linmark's queer novella provides us with promising new methods for contesting a domestic image-repertoire that has continually limited and constrained representations of Asian American masculinity.

Out Here and Over There:
The Wedding Banquet *and* Rolling the R's

At first glance Gao Wai-Tung (played by Winston Chao) in Ang Lee's *The Wedding Banquet* provides what might be considered to be an unprecedented representation of Asian American male identity within the domestic sphere of the U.S. nation-state. Considering the immigrant's queer and diasporic status with regard to his domestic situation in the urban metropole of New York City yields a rather startling picture that diverges from mainstream stereotypes of Asian American men as well as dominant portrayals of them in the popular gay press and media.[48]

Reviewing the film upon its release in 1993, I noted that *The Wedding Banquet* was the first wide-release motion picture in this country that significantly reconfigured the dominant Rice Queen dynamic so prevalent in the mainstream gay community. This stereotype, explored in chapter three's discussion of *M. Butterfly*, relies upon the racist coupling of passive gay Asian (American) men—the continuous recirculation of Puccini's *Madama Butterfly* fantasy—with objectionable Rice Queens— white men attracted to gay Asian (American) men through their orientalized fantasies of submissive "bottoms."[49] That *The Wedding Banquet* significantly revises this Rice Queen dynamic, depicting a successful, savvy, and handsome Asian male who is not in a relationship of economic dependence with a homely white man twice his age, marks a laudable departure from the pervasive stereotype of the white daddy and the Asian houseboy endemic to mainstream gay culture. In my mind, Lee's innovative portrayal inaugurates a potential (though ultimately unfulfilled) shift of a stereotypical Asian American gay male image away from normative domestic representations toward a queer and diasporic formation. It is this detour through queerness, coupled with this turn toward the global, that takes us someplace new in terms of the dominant domestic image-repertoire. *The Wedding Banquet* challenges traditional stereotypes of Asian American men by instituting a new set of potentially enabling representations.

In light of our discussion about the vexed claims of both Asian Americans and queers on home and the nation-state, Wai-Tung's portrayal in *The Wedding Banquet* is notable for the fact that he is enfranchised as a U.S. citizen. Given the long national history of Chinese exclusion and barriers to U.S. citizenship, Lee's rendering of Wai-Tung as citizen verges on — indeed, becomes dependent upon — the queer. Through his ability to claim the domestic space of the U.S. nation-state as a legitimate home — and through his ability to be legally recognized in his claims — queerness and diaspora emerge in Lee's film as a new and privileged form of Asian American male subjectivity. Earlier I asked what a diaspora organized in terms of sexuality, and not just racial or ethnic dispersion, might offer. This expansion of citizenship and legal claims through the combination of queerness and diaspora is one potential yield. Furthermore, it is important to note that not only is Wai-Tung enfranchised as a U.S. citizen, it is through his diasporic queerness that Wei-Wei (played by May Chin) obtains her coveted green card and her own legal status — a reframing of Asian American identity outside of traditional heterosexual and white domestic familial configurations. This reconfiguration and reworking of kinship lines is another unexpected material consequence of queerness and diaspora's unpredictable combination. It is another way in which Lee's attention to a queer diaspora expands the conventional image-repertoire by reworking its representations through a challenge to its traditional exclusions.

Nevertheless, we must remember, it is also precisely because of the conflicted affiliations that constitute Wai-Tung's queer and diasporic positioning that he is impelled to accept a staged heterosexual marriage to Wei-Wei. Under the constant goading of his heir-demanding parents (played by Lung Sihung and Gua Ah-la), who still reside in Taiwan, Wai-Tung finally acquiesces to the fake marriage and tax break orchestrated by his white lover Simon (played by Mitchell Lichtenstein). Ultimately, the creation of a queer diaspora and a new multicultural queer family (figs. 13 and 14) organized by and around this new type of Asian American male subjectivity are qualified by the demands of enduring heterosexual filiative imperatives. In this manner, *The Wedding Banquet* might better be thought of less as a film that inaugurates a successful queer

Figures 13 and 14 For better or for worse; for richer or for poorer: Mitchell Lichtenstein, Winston Chao, and May Chin in Ang Lee's *The Wedding Banquet* (Samuel Goldwyn Co.)

and diasporic Asian American male subjectivity than as one that is set in motion by the very question of queerness and diaspora. Queerness and diaspora function as signs for the very confusion of Asian American identity that Lee's film strives to institute, investigate, and resolve.

Might we think of this rather unprecedented portrayal of Wai-Tung in the realm of the domestic space of the nation-state as one only purchased in the global arena of liberal capitalism through the rescripting of a quotidian patriarchal narrative? In a compelling reading of *The Wedding Banquet*, Mark Chiang considers the diasporic representations of the film in light of its domestic dimensions, noting that the film's resolution "depends most intently upon the disciplining of Wei-Wei as the figure of resistance, so that it is only Wai-Tung's impregnation of her, which turns out to be the mechanism of his control over her, that allows the ending to take place in a configuration that resolves the conflicts between the men. The consolidation of a transnational patriarchy of capital is fundamentally dependent upon the subordination of women and labor, and women and labor are conflated in the film, so that woman becomes the very sign of labor."[50] Wai-Tung's position as enfranchised citizen of the U.S. nation-state (and a subject of capital) is made possible only through his subordination of the diasporic Third World woman (as an object of capital). Emancipation for Wei-Wei — her escape from the global underclass of undocumented workers and migrant laborers — comes up against emancipation for Wai-Tung, whose fulfillment of his Chinese father's paternal mandate demands her acquiescence to keep and not abort their (male) child.[51]

This purchase of queer Asian American citizenship is brokered on the level of the global, enabled only through Wai-Tung's complicit relationship with the transnational management of capital, resources, and labor.[52] This management of capital thus qualifies the potential of a progressive queer and diasporic political project for social transformation. After all, only by gaining control over Wei-Wei's material (Wai-Tung is her slumlord and thereby controls her claims on home) and reproductive labor is Wai-Tung able to secure his own claims within the borders of the U.S. nation-state as a legitimate home. As such, queer and feminist discourses are also at odds when considered against the domestic and the diasporic dimensions of *The Wedding Banquet*. Wai-Tung's (potential) queerness comes to organize a host of conflicting differences — sexual, gender, race, class, and space — shutting down the position of the Third World woman through its expansion into both local and global capitalist arenas.

Like the earlier Asian American cultural nationalist project, Wai-

Tung's access to the domestic space of a public U.S. nation-state finally depends upon queer control over and possession of a devalued feminine realm—Wei-Wei's home, privacy, body, labor, and child. Hence, we might describe queer diaspora in *The Wedding Banquet* as a formation that rescripts a domestic patriarchal narrative of home and nation-state, of private and public, on a global scale. To think about the queer and diasporic formation of Asian American male subjectivity in *The Wedding Banquet* is to understand that the domestic tranquility that marks the end of the film has been purchased at a high price, one borne by the figure of the Third World woman. This is a model of queer and diasporic Asian American subjectivity that, as Sau-ling Cynthia Wong suggests, might be far more useful if critiqued as "*modes* rather than *phases*" of identity, a cleaving of queerness and diaspora that cannot be "lauded as a culmination" over the domestic or feminine, "a stage more advanced or more capacious."[53]

Ultimately, *The Wedding Banquet* provides a qualified model of a progressive queer and diasporic Asian American male subjectivity; queerness and diaspora in Lee's film do not constitute any inherent challenge to local and global status quos. *The Wedding Banquet* provides a new model for thinking about the numerous pitfalls of queerness and diaspora as an integral mode of Asian American domestic claims to home and nation-state at the turn of this past century. At the same time, this model requires vigilant critical scrutiny for the enabling positions as well as the disabling violences it effects. It is a tortured model that recontextualizes our very notions of Asian American citizenship in both the larger global arena and the domestic realm of a liberal, capitalist, U.S. nation-state, which today is rapidly and urgently (re)consolidating itself as the preeminent and unforgiving bastion of economic freedom, straightness, and whiteness.

I would like to end this chapter and *Racial Castration* with a brief analysis of R. Zamora Linmark's *Rolling the R's*, a remarkable novella chronicling the travails of a group of pan-Asian and Pacific immigrant adolescents and teenagers in Honolulu's downscale Kalihi district. Like *The Wedding Banquet, Rolling the R's* brings together queerness and diaspora in innovative, destabilizing, and compelling ways that contest the dominant representations comprising the domestic image-repertoire. Through its multilayered assault of cultural, linguistic, and narrative hybridity, *Rolling the R's* ultimately exposes the uneven production of abstract nationalist subjects through the management and erasure of a host of disavowed social identities and differences. *Rolling the R's* shatters the popular myth of Hawai'i as an island paradise and vacation resort free of racial tension and ethnic strife. It presents the reader with competing native, local, and mainland nationalisms and an ugly colonial history of U.S. political domination, economic exploitation, and cultural hegemony. Set in the manic disco era of the 1970s, Linmark's novella accomplishes this shattering not only through its insistent attention to Hawai'i's colonial status in relation to the U.S. mainland but through its incisive critique and reimagining of the intransigent Asian American and Pacific Islander ethnic hierarchies that organize and divide the island's immigrant inhabitants. (This is a social hierarchy with established East Asian Japanese and Chinese at the top and new immigrant Filipinos, Vietnamese, and Pacific Islanders at the bottom).

It is crucial to point out that the possibility of surmounting the various internal and external, intersecting and conflicting streams of Asian American social discord that animate *Rolling the R's* is mobilized precisely through a diasporic immigrant subjectivity organized by queerness. That is, while the disparate ethnic affiliations of the immigrant adolescents who populate Linmark's novella threaten to divide further their tenuous loyalties, it is precisely sexuality—an obsessive queer sexuality that permeates *Rolling the R's* from beginning to end—that binds them together as a social group with a common sense of purpose and esprit de corps. In this regard, the coalitional possibilities of "Asian American" as a viable or even workable group identity are engaged, renewed, and rendered efficacious by this detour through queerness. Indeed, while a recurring queerness orders Linmark's novella, it functions not just in the register of sexuality but as an organizing topos that affirms rather than effaces a host of alternate differences. As a consequence, constitutive differentials of nationality, sexuality, race, and class are rendered heterogeneous, creating complex and shifting rather than singular and static social histories of individual development.

The very narrative form that *Rolling the R's* assumes—with its hybrid episodes of letters, dream sequences, streams of consciousness, poems, book reports, dramatic monologues, scripts, progress reports, vocabulary lessons, and songs—might be characterized not only as miming this heterogeneity but as being distinctly queer. In Linmark's text, queerness gains its very meaning and discursive consistency as a critical terrain on which overlapping histories of sexuality, experiences of racialization and gendering, narratives of immigrant trauma and displacement, and strategies of class oppression and resistance are mobilized. Linmark's queer immigrant narratives, Chandan Reddy notes, "refuse to either hierarchize historical differentials or provide totalizing viewpoints. If one were to discuss an immigrant narrative of formation, for example, identifying as a 'queer' immigrant rather than an American immigrant powerfully deflects identification with the U.S. . . . The cultural formation of 'queer Asians' establishes 'queer' as the subjective site that registers Asian immigrant displacement, immigrant racialization, and the continuing force of the historicity of homeland for the racial immigrant. . . . These 'queer' narratives explore the uneven determinations of multiple histories 'piled up,' 'over-ripe,' and 'decaying' within their narrative space." [54]

Rather than demanding the abnegation of homeland or the sublation of it—of Asian—into standard American narratives of immigration, assimilation, and settlement, the queer diaspora that organizes the six male and female stars of Linmark's novella—Edgar Ramirez, Vicente de los Reyes, Mai-Lan Phan, Florante Sanchez, Loata Faalele, Katherine Katrina-Trina Cruz—offers something patently different. That is, it emphatically substitutes a queer affiliation that preserves individual histories of development for a more conventional notion of diaspora ordered by racial filiation and abstract narratives of group identity. This type of queer affiliation allows us a particular insight into debates on minoritarian identity politics. It allows an understanding of queerness as a form of social and political organization that proffers the provisional identity of a name. This is a name under which progressive politics can be strategized and rallied, one not predicated on the suppression but rather on the engagement of racial, gender, class, and national differentials for its social efficacy and effectiveness. In our contemporary moment, this is what a diaspora organized around queerness potentially offers.

In *Rolling the R's,* Linmark brokers this queer insight and affiliation across a number of youthful age groups, thus establishing a historical legacy and an emotional inheritance not just horizontally but vertically shared across generations. He writes about Orlando Domingo, a senior at Farrington High School, whose fierce overidentification with Farrah Fawcett of the television series *Charlie's Angels* causes him to insist that others call him "Farrah . . . as in Far-Out Farrah, or Faraway Farrah" (23). Orlando spends copious amounts of time styling his locks into "the million-dollar mane coveted by Farrah wanna-be's" (24). This Farrah Flip is accessorized with "a fire-engine red polyester long-sleeved shirt tied around his 24" waist, yellow bell-bottoms, and Famolare platforms. His face is painted, courtesy of Helena Rubinstein's The Paris Boutique Kit, which includes lipstick and nail lacquer, and Aziza's Shadow Boutique. Twelve shimmering eye colors for every occasion" (24).

Orlando's over-identification—indeed, his intense sexual and racial cross-identifications—with Farrah Fawcett arouses extreme consternation on the part of agitated Farrington High School authorities. The football coaches, Mr. Akana and Mr. Ching, as well as the principal, Mr. Shim, are especially disgruntled. Unable to normalize Orlando as an abstract citizen-subject of that particular educational institution, Principal Shim considers more drastic measures:

> Leaning back in his vinyl chair, Principal Shim considers the possibility of expelling or suspending Orlando on the grounds that he is endangering the mental health of other students, especially the athletes. But he can't. Not after he examines Orlando's file:
>
> Born in Cebu in 1962; Immigrated to Hawai'i at the age of ten; Lives with mother in Lower Kalihi; Father: Deceased; Speaks and writes English, Spanish, Cebuano, and Tagalog; Top of the Dean's List; Current GPA: 4.0; This year's Valedictorian; SAT scores totaling 1500 out of 1600; Voted Most Industrious and Most Likely To Succeed four years in a row; Competed and won accolades in Speech and Math Leagues, High School Select Band, Science Fairs, and Mock Trials; Current President of Keywanettes, National Honor Society, and the Student Body Government; Plans to attend Brown University in the fall and eventually take up Law.
>
> Principal Shim closes the file and throws it on his desk.
>
> "I can't expel him. Maybe suspension." He squirms at the thought of Orlando turning the tables and charging him, Mr. Akana, Mr. Ching, and the Department of Education with discrimination against a Filipino faggot whose only desire is to be Farrah from Farrington, as in Farrah, the Kalihi Angel. (25)

Orlando's school file reads like a précis of a model minority's stunning achievement of the American dream. It illustrates a consistent history of superior academic accomplishments in face of material deprivation and in the absence of a traditional nuclear family structure. Orlando's file indicates as well a type of well-roundedness (outside of the math and sciences) not typically associated with the model minority subject, especially a recent Asian immigrant. Linmark is not content, however, to let his resignifying project of this queer immigrant rest there. Indeed, Linmark extends this project to its imaginable limits by bringing together the model minority myth with the image of the flaming Filipino faggot.

Orlando's outrageous physical comportment as a Farrah Flip, coupled with his academic achievements as a model minority, forces two disparate and stereotypical images into conceptual overload. This improbable bringing together of the model minority myth with a flagrant and flaming queer sexuality, as well as the stitching together of a racialized diasporic immigrant identity with dominant images of the (white) drag queen, mark a novel combination of queerness and diaspora that challenges, resists, and ultimately explodes the dominant representations and expectations that crowd our domestic image-repertoire.

Orlando's Farrah Flip marks both his queerness and his racialization as a diasporic Filipino. This crossing of queerness and diaspora disturbs many of his less than generous high school authorities and peers, all of whom emphatically conclude that Orlando has "flipped-out." Nevertheless, Orlando's outrageous and unwavering composure—accompanied by his unimpeachable academic achievements, his stellar social accomplishments, and his stalwart political resistance to conventional norms and ideals—also serves as a point of exuberant identification, of unmitigated inspiration, for the younger generation of queer diasporic children that populates *Rolling the R's*. Unlike the constrained and painful queer childhood that overshadows Kaneko's young Japanese American boys during wartime internment, for instance, this is a queer childhood marked by psychic strength and material resistance to the demands of the law and the demands of others—a flipping of traditional representations and expectations. It is Linmark's remarkable detour through queerness and diaspora that allows this explosion and reworking of stereotypical images and categories, this wonderfully deranged and transformative bildungsroman. It is this turning to queerness and diaspora that provides us with a new set of images for a different type of Asian American male subjectivity in the twenty-first century.

NOTES

INTRODUCTION

1 David Henry Hwang, *M. Butterfly* (New York: Plume, 1989), 83.

2 Jeffery Paul Chan, Frank Chin, Lawson Fusao Inada, and Shawn Wong, eds., *The Big Aiiieeeee! An Anthology of Chinese American and Japanese American Literature* (New York: Meridian, 1991), xiii.

3 Richard Fung, "Looking for My Penis: The Eroticized Asian in Gay Porn Video," in *How Do I Look?* ed. Bad Object Choices (Seattle: Bay Press, 1991), 153.

4 Sigmund Freud, "Fetishism," in *The Standard Edition of the Complete Psychological Works of Sigmund Freud*, ed. James Strachey (London: Hogarth, 1955), 21:152–57.

5 In the juridical realm, the Gentleman's Agreement (Act of 2 March 1907, chap. 2534, §3, 34 Stat. 1228) between the United States and Japan worked toward this type of racial specificity. The Japanese, agreeing to curtail emigration from Japan, were exempted from U.S. laws barring Asian immigration.

6 In recent years, several well-known psychoanalytic feminist and queer scholars have written books with individual chapters or sections exploring psychoanalysis and racial difference. See, for example, Mary Ann Doane, *Femme Fatales: Feminism, Film Theory, Psychoanalysis* (New York: Routledge, 1991); Judith Butler, *Bodies That Matter: On the Discursive Limits of "Sex"* (New York: Routledge, 1993); Diana Fuss, *Identification Papers* (New York: Routledge, 1995); Kaja Silverman, *The Threshold of the Visible World* (New York: Routledge, 1996); and Ann Pellegrini, *Performance Anxieties: Staging Psychoanalysis, Staging Race* (New York: Routledge, 1997). More recently, several African American feminist scholars have produced notable book-length examinations of black novels through the lens of psychoanalysis. See Saidiya V. Hartman, *Scenes of Subjection: Terror, Slavery, and Self-Making in Nineteenth-Century America* (New York: Oxford University Press, 1997); and Claudia Tate, *Psychoanalysis and Black Novels: Desire and the Protocols of Race* (New York: Oxford University Press, 1998). In the fields of Latino and performance studies, see José Esteban Muñoz, *Disidentifications: Queers of Color and the Performance of Politics* (Minneapolis: University of Minnesota Press, 1999). See also recent anthologies such as Elizabeth Abel, Barbara Chris-

tian, and Helene Moglen, eds., *Female Subjects in Black and White: Race, Psychoanalysis, Feminism* (Berkeley: University of California Press, 1997); and Christopher Lane, ed., *The Psychoanalysis of Race* (New York: Columbia University Press, 1998).

7 Norma Alarcón, "The Theoretical Subject(s) of *This Bridge Called My Back* and Anglo-American Feminism," in *Making Face, Making Soul: Haciendo Caras*, ed. Gloria Anzaldúa (San Francisco: Aunt Lute, 1990), 356–69.

8 Sigmund Freud, *Totem and Taboo: Some Points of Agreement between the Mental Life of Savages and Neurotics*, in Freud, *Standard Edition*, 13:1.

9 David Kazanjian, "Notarizing Knowledge: Paranoia and Civility in Freud and Lacan," *Qui Parle* 7.1 (fall-winter 1993): 103. Much of my argument on the crossing of the figures of the primitive and the homosexual is indebted to Kazanjian's article as well as his personal discussions of this problem with me. I would like to thank him for this critical dialogue.

10 Sigmund Freud, "On Narcissism: An Introduction," in Freud, *Standard Edition*, 14:75.

11 See Judith Butler, *The Psychic Life of Power: Theories in Subjection* (Stanford: Stanford University Press, 1997), 132–66, for an elaboration of how a hierarchy of gender and a system of compulsory heterosexuality are melancholically formed through a doubly disavowed repudiation of never having loved the father and never having lost him.

12 See Daniel Boyarin, "Freud's Baby, Fliess's Maybe: Homophobia, Anti-Semitism, and the Invention of Oedipus," *GLQ: A Journal of Lesbian and Gay Studies* 2.1–2 (winter-spring 1995): 115–47; Jonathan Geller, " 'A Glance on the Nose': Freud's Inscription of Jewish Difference," *American Imago* 49 (1992): 427–44; Sander Gilman, *The Jew's Body* (New York: Routledge, 1991); and Ann Pellegrini, *Performance Anxieties*. All of these works argue that Freud enacts a similar displacement of racial difference into the realm of sexual difference in his theories on hysteria. These critics maintain that Freud displaces hysterical symptoms from the marked Jewish male body to the deracinated female body. This displacement symptomatizes the psychic and material burdens of Jewish racial otherness for Freud, a displaced racial otherness made legible in the arena of sexual difference. In making hysteria a mark of female sexual difference, Freud seeks to make possible the Jewish male's claims on normative masculinity and a Christianized whiteness. Chapter four of this book explores this problematic. We might also note that Freud, as Mary Ann Doane points out in *Femmes Fatales,* uses the term *dark continent* to describe female sexuality as "an unexplored territory, an enigmatic, unknowable place concealed from the theoretical gaze and hence the epistemological power of the psychoanalyst" (209). Here, the "dark origins" of the primitive converge with female sexuality as the dark continent and a marker for a displaced racial otherness.

13 Turning to issues of sexuality in Asian American racial formation is especially important. Questions of sexuality must be considered in relation to the waning of class-based critiques of race, which have been challenged

and eroded in the age of globalization. See, for instance, Victor Burgin, *In/Different Spaces: Place and Memory in Visual Culture* (Berkeley: University of California Press, 1996): "The enormous wealth accumulating in the newly 'global' economy, however, has yet to 'trickle down' to the unemployed, the deranged, and the diseased who accumulate not only at its spatial margins but also at its centers—on the streets of the world's richest cities. However, although the economic gap between wealthy and poor has increased in this last quarter of a century, the rights most conspicuously claimed today are more likely to be the civil rights of a social minority than the material rights of a broader economic class. Toward the close of the twentieth century, various forms of 'identity politics' have largely superseded the economic-class politics that was the privileged form of social contestation at the beginning of the century" (193). I will return to this issue of sexuality and race, as well as class and globalization, in the epilogue of this book, where I discuss queerness and diaspora in a transnational age.

14 See also the introduction to David L. Eng and Alice Y. Hom, eds., *Q & A: Queer in Asian America* (Philadelphia: Temple University Press, 1998), 1–21.

15 See, for example, the feminist literary criticism in Elaine H. Kim, *Asian American Literature: An Introduction to the Writings and Their Social Context* (Philadelphia: Temple University Press, 1982); Sau-ling Cynthia Wong, *Reading Asian American Literature: From Necessity to Extravagance* (Princeton: Princeton University Press, 1993); King-Kok Cheung, *Articulate Silences: Hisaye Yamamoto, Maxine Hong Kingston, Joy Kogawa* (Ithaca: Cornell University Press, 1993); Lisa Lowe, *Immigrant Acts: On Asian American Cultural Politics* (Durham: Duke University Press, 1996); and Traise Yamamoto, *Masking Selves, Making Subjects: Japanese American Women, Identity, and the Body* (Berkeley: University of California Press, 1999). More recently, David Leiwei Li, in his *Imagining the Nation: Asian American Literature and Cultural Consent* (Stanford: Stanford University Press, 1998), and David Palumbo-Liu, in his *Asian/American: Historical Crossings of a Racial Frontier* (Stanford: Stanford University Press, 1999), have provided critical studies that focus in part on issues of masculinity.

16 King-Kok Cheung, "The Woman Warrior versus The Chinaman Pacific: Must a Chinese American Critic Choose between Feminism and Heroism?" in *Conflicts in Feminism*, eds. Marianne Hirsch and Evelyn Fox Keller (New York: Routledge, 1990), 244.

17 For an elaboration of this women's studies/gender versus queer studies/sexuality distinction, see Judith Butler, "Against Proper Objects," *differences: A Journal of Feminist Cultural Studies* 6.2–3 (summer-fall 1994): 1–26.

18 Mae Ngai notes that the 1790 naturalization act granted all "free white persons" (not just, as Lowe writes, white male persons) the right to claim citizenship. It was not until after the Civil War, with the passage of the Thirteenth, Fourteenth, and Fifteenth Amendments to the Constitution, that the naturalization statute was enlarged to include free men of African nativity or descent in 1870. In language, the 1790 statute is technically gen-

der neutral. As such, definitions of citizenship would also by logical extension be so. Nevertheless, as women continued to be barred from fundamental rights of U.S. citizenship such as voting until 1920, with the passing of
the Nineteenth Amendment, Lowe's larger contention that in this historical
period, "as the state extended citizenship to nonwhite male persons, it formally designated these subjects as 'male,' as well" seems justified. I would
like to thank Mae Ngai for discussing this issue with me.

19 See Victor G. Nee and Brett de Bary Nee, *Longtime Californ': A Documentary Study of an American Chinatown* (Stanford: Stanford University Press,
1972), which documents the range of professions undertaken by Chinese
male immigrants in San Francisco's Chinatown.

20 For critical studies of these stereotypes in the popular and mass media,
see James S. Moy, *Marginal Sites: Staging the Chinese in America* (Iowa City:
University of Iowa Press, 1993); Darrell Hamamoto, *Monitored Peril: Asian
Americans and the Politics of TV Representation* (Minneapolis: University of
Minnesota Press, 1994); and Robert G. Lee, *Orientals: Asian Americans in
Popular Culture* (Philadelphia: Temple University Press, 1999).

21 Page Act, Act of 18 February 1875, chap. 80, 18 Stat. 318. See also Sucheng
Chan, ed., *Entry Denied: Exclusion and the Chinese Community in America,
1882–1943* (Philadelphia: Temple University Press, 1991); and Bill Ong Hing,
Making and Remaking Asian America through Immigration Policy, 1850–1990
(Stanford: Stanford University Press, 1993). In fact, by the time the Supreme
Court ruled in *Loving v. Virginia* (388 U.S. 1 [1967]) that antimiscegenation
laws were unconstitutional, thirty-eight states had enacted them, sixteen of
which were still in effect. See Leti Volpp, "American Mestizo: Filipinos and
Antimiscegenation Laws in California," *University of California at Davis Law
Review* 33 (2000).

22 Jennifer Ting has studied the formation of bachelor communities as queer
spaces. See her "Bachelor Society: Deviant Heterosexuality and Asian American Historiography," in *Privileging Positions: The Sites of Asian American
Studies*, eds. Gary Y. Okihiro, Marilyn Aquizola, Dorothy Fujita Rony, and
K. Scott Wong (Pullman: Washington State University Press, 1995), 271–79.

23 Magnuson Act, Act of 17 December 1943, chap. 344, §1, 57 Stat. 600.

24 *Brown v. Board of Education*, 347 U.S. 483, 489 (1954).

25 See Butler, *Bodies*. Writing about the "reality" of the body, Butler states:
"First, psychic projection confers boundaries and, hence, unity on the body
so that the very contours of the body are sites that vacillate between the
psychic and the material. Bodily contours and morphology are not merely
implicated in an irreducible tension between the psychic and the material
but *are* that tension" (66).

26 Frank Chin, Jeffery Paul Chan, Lawson Fusao Inada, and Shawn Wong, eds.,
Aiiieeeee! An Anthology of Asian-American Writers (Garden City, NY: Anchor
Books, 1975), x.

27 The psychic introjection and transformation of debilitating material inequi-

ties once external as "feelings" of inferiority and self-hate outlines a process of melancholic incorporation that various scholars of race are currently elaborating with extraordinary promise. See, for instance, José Esteban Muñoz, "Photographies of Mourning: Melancholia and Ambivalence in Van Der Zee, Mapplethorpe, and *Looking for Langston*," in Muñoz, *Disidentifications*, 57–74; Anne Anlin Cheng, "The Melancholy of Race," *Kenyon Review* 19.1 (1997): 49–61; David L. Eng and Shinhee Han, "A Dialogue on Racial Melancholia," *Psychoanalytic Dialogues* 10.4 (2000): 667–700; and David L. Eng and David Kazanjian, eds., *Loss* (forthcoming).

28 This debate between feminism and heroism is also very much alive in African American studies. For example, Ishmael Reed has attacked Toni Morrison's work in ways similar to the *Aiiieeeee!* group's critique of writers such as Kingston.

29 Sigmund Freud, "Femininity," in Freud, *Standard Edition*, 22:134.

30 Stanley Sue and Derald W. Sue, "Chinese-American Personality and Mental Health," *Amerasia Journal* 1.2 (July 1971): 42.

31 Louis Althusser, *Lenin and Philosophy and Other Essays*, trans. Ben Brewster (New York: Monthly Review Press, 1971), 162.

32 See W. E. B. Du Bois, *The Souls of Black Folk: W. E. B. Du Bois, Writings* (New York: Library of America, 1986), 372.

33 See two essays by Homi Bhabha, "Interrogating Identity: Frantz Fanon and the Postcolonial Prerogative" and "How Newness Enters the World: Postmodern Space, Postcolonial Times, and the Trials of Cultural Transmission," in *The Location of Culture* (New York: Routledge, 1994), 40–65, 212–35.

34 Maxine Hong Kingston, *The Woman Warrior: Memoirs of a Girlhood among Ghosts* (New York: Vintage, [1976] 1989), 5–6.

35 Abel, Christian, and Moglen, *Female Subjects*, 5.

36 Gayatri Chakravorty Spivak, "Negotiating the Structures of Violence," in *The Post-colonial Critic: Interviews, Strategies, Dialogues*, ed. Sarah Harasym (New York: Routledge, 1990), 150.

37 Wendy Brown, *States of Injury: Power and Freedom in Late Modernity* (Princeton: Princeton University Press, 1995). Brown writes: "Starkly accountable yet dramatically impotent, the late modern liberal subject quite literally seethes with *ressentiment*. . . . But in its attempt to displace its suffering, identity structured by *ressentiment* at the same time becomes invested in its own subjection. This investment lies not only in discovery of a site of blame for its hurt will, not only in its acquisition of recognition through its history of subjection (a recognition predicated on injury, now righteously revalued), but also in the satisfactions of revenge, which ceaselessly reenact even as they redistribute the injuries of marginalization and subordination in a liberal discursive order that alternately denies the very possibility of these things and blames those who experience them for their own condition. Identity politics structured by *ressentiment* reverse without subverting this blaming structure: they do not subject to critique the sovereign subject

of accountability that liberal individualism presupposes, nor the economy of inclusion and exclusion that liberalism establishes" (69–70).

38 See, for instance, the 1987 debate in African American studies aired in *Cultural Critique:* Barbara Christian, "The Race for Theory," *Cultural Critique* 6 (spring 1987): 1–63; and Henry Louis Gates, "Authority, (White) Power, and the (Black) Critic: It's All Greek to Me," *Cultural Critique* 7 (fall 1987): 19–46.

39 Maxine Hong Kingston, *China Men* (New York: Vintage, [1980] 1989), 138.

40 The quotation is from Walter Benjamin, "Theses on the Philosophy of History," in *Illuminations: Essays and Reflections,* ed. Hannah Arendt (New York: Schocken, 1969), 255.

41 Jacques Lacan, "The Meaning of the Phallus," in *Feminine Sexuality: Jacques Lacan and the École Freudienne,* eds. Juliet Mitchell and Jacqueline Rose (New York: Norton, 1985), 74–85.

42 See Oscar V. Campomanes, "Filipinos in the United States and Their Literature of Exile," in *Reading the Literatures of Asian America,"* eds. Shirley Geok-lin Lim and Amy Ling (Philadelphia: Temple University Press, 1992), 49–78.

43 See Fredric Jameson, *Postmodernism, or the Cultural Logic of Late Capitalism* (Durham: Duke University Press, 1991). Lowe in *Immigrant Acts,* for example, writes: "From roughly 1850 to World War II, Asian immigration was the site for the eruptions and resolutions of the contradictions between the national economy and the political state, and, from World War II onward, the locus of the contradictions between the nation-state and the global economy" (158–59).

ONE   *I've Been (Re)Working on the Railroad*

1 Maxine Hong Kingston, *China Men* (New York: Vintage, [1980] 1989); Frank Chin, *Donald Duk* (Minneapolis: Coffee House Press, 1991).

2 David Leiwei Li, "*China Men:* Maxine Hong Kingston and the American Canon," *American Literary History* 2.3 (fall 1990): 482.

3 Tom De Haven, "He's Been Dreaming on the Railroad," *New York Times Book Review,* 31 March 1991, 9.

4 In addition to railroads, sugar plantations, laundries, and restaurants, Chinese immigrants also found jobs in the mining industry, agriculture, grocery stores, and specialty shops. As in the railroad industry, laborers in these jobs often fell victim to poor working conditions and low wages. See Sucheng Chan, *Asian Americans: An Interpretive History* (Boston: Twayne, 1991), 25–42; and Victor G. Nee and Brett de Bary Nee, *Longtime Californ': A Documentary Study of an American Chinatown* (Stanford: Stanford University Press, 1972).

5 In the *re Ah Yup* (1F. Cas. 223 [C.C.D. Ca 1878]) court ruling, Chinese immigrants were deemed ineligible for citizenship because they were not "white." The first exclusion law against any racial group was the Chinese Exclusion

Act of 1882 (chap. 126, 22 Stat. 58), which targeted Chinese immigrant laborers. Subsequent legislation was enacted in attempts to exclude all Chinese from the United States (Act of 9 July 1884, chap. 220, 23 Stat. 115). The Geary Amendment (Act of 5 May 1892, chap. 60, 27 Stat. 25) extended Chinese exclusion for another ten years. Further exclusion acts were passed in 1902 (Act of 29 April 1902, chap. 641, 32 Stat. 176) and 1904 (Act of 27 April 1904, chap. 1630, 33 Stat. 428). Finally, the Johnson-Reed Act (Immigration Act of 1924, chap. 190, §131, 104 Stat. 4978) barred virtually all Asian immigration to the United States. These acts were not repealed until the Magnuson Act of 1943 (Act of 17 December 1943, chap. 344, §1, 57 Stat. 600), which instituted a small quota system that granted Chinese naturalization privileges. See Shirley Hune, "The Politics of Chinese Exclusion: Legislative-Executive Conflict 1876–1882," *Amerasia Journal* 9.1 (1982): 5–27; Sucheng Chan, "The Exclusion of Chinese Women, 1870–1943," in *Entry Denied: Exclusion and the Chinese Community in America, 1882–1943*, ed. Sucheng Chan (Philadelphia: Temple University Press, 1991), 94–146; Bill Ong Hing, *Making and Remaking Asian America through Immigration Policy, 1850–1900* (Stanford: Stanford University Press, 1993); and Lisa Lowe, "Immigration, Racialization, Citizenship," in *Immigrant Acts: On Asian American Cultural Politics* (Durham: Duke University Press, 1996), 1–36.

6 Robert M. Utley points out, "On May 10, 1869, a self-important and somewhat boozy array of frock-coated dignitaries gathered with several hundred rowdy laborers to drive the last spike in the Pacific Railroad. The site was Promontory Summit, Utah (not Promontory Point, 30 miles to the south). The last spike was an ordinary spike (not a 'golden' spike, which would have been crushed by a sledgehammer's blow)." See Robert M. Utley, "The Spike Wasn't Golden," *New York Times Book Review,* 12 December 1999: 10.

7 Roland Barthes, *Camera Lucida: Reflections on Photography,* trans. Richard Howard (New York: Hill and Wang, 1981), 65.

8 Walter Benjamin, "Theses on the Philosophy of History," in *Illuminations,* ed. Hannah Arendt (New York: Schocken, 1969), 255.

9 Kingston, *China Men,* 138.

10 Benjamin, "Theses," 255.

11 André Bazin, "The Ontology of the Photographic Image," in *What Is Cinema?,* trans. Hugh Gray (Berkeley: University of California Press, 1967), 1:13.

12 Christian Metz, "Photography and Fetish," in *The Critical Image: Essays on Contemporary Photography,* ed. Carol Squiers (Seattle: Bay Press, 1990), 155–64.

13 Walter Benjamin, "The Work of Art in the Age of Mechanical Reproduction," in *Illuminations,* 233.

14 Eduardo Cadava, *Words of Light: Theses on the Photography of History* (Princeton: Princeton University Press, 1997), 13–14.

15 See Rey Chow, "Walter Benjamin's Love Affair with Death," *New German Critique* 48 (fall 1989): 63–86. Chow provides another suitable place for us

to begin, observing that the vertiginous reproducibility of the visual image implicitly challenges any stable notion of the authentic or the real in photography. "Once the process of reproducibility has begun (and it has always already begun), Chow writes, " 'authenticity' itself is always *on the outside:* it does not really exist" (70; Chow's emphasis).

16 Cadava, *Words,* 8.

17 See, for instance, Kaja Silverman, *The Subject of Semiotics* (New York: Oxford University Press, 1983), 194–236.

18 Kaja Silverman, *The Threshold of the Visible World* (New York: Routledge, 1996), 125.

19 Jacques Lacan, *The Four Fundamental Concepts of Psycho-Analysis,* trans. Alan Sheridan (New York: Norton, 1981), 91.

20 In addition to Silverman's *Threshold,* see Jonathan Crary, *Techniques of the Observer: On Vision and Modernity in the Nineteenth Century* (Cambridge: MIT Press, 1990); Rosalind Krauss, *The Optical Unconscious* (Cambridge: MIT Press, 1993); and Martin Jay, *Downcast Eyes: The Denigration of Vision in Twentieth-Century French Thought* (Berkeley: University of California Press, 1993). In order to clarify the notion of a geometral point that is given in advance in any visual image, one need only think of an impressionist landscape. When the viewer of the landscape is standing too close or too far from the canvas, the painting appears only as a series of dots or blurs. It is only when the spectator occupies a position neither too close nor too far from the work—the "ideal" geometral point—that Monet's water lilies or the Rouen Cathedral, for example, appear to the human eye. The rather obvious optical positioning around which the impressionist work is organized provides, then, a lesson in perception that we can apply to photography and its reliance on the laws of Renaissance perspective. While the mimetic reality of the photographic image depends on an occluded geometral point from which the objects depicted seem to unfold effortlessly before our eyes, when thought of against the optical configuration of the impressionist landscape we come to understand the ideal location from where we can "get" the picture. Though seemingly unmarked and invisible in a Renaissance painting, the geometral point is nonetheless implicitly there—a pregiven position we must occupy in order to make sense of the picture, believe in its images, and invest in its reality. There are numerous examples from Renaissance painting in which the geometral point is visually encoded against a traditional Cartesian point of view. See, for instance, Jacques Lacan's reading of Holbein's *The Ambassadors* (1533) in *Four Fundamental Concepts,* 85–90. I discuss Lacan's reading of Holbein later in this chapter.

21 See Christian Metz, *The Imaginary Signifier: Psychoanalysis and the Cinema,* trans. Celia Britton, Annwyl Williams, Ben Brewster, and Alfred Guzzetti (Bloomington: Indiana University Press, 1977); Daniel Dayan, "The Tutor Code of Classical Cinema," in *Movies and Methods,* ed. Bill Nichols (Berkeley: University of California Press, 1976), 438–51; Stephen Heath, "Notes on Suture," *Screen* (winter 1977–78): 48–76; Jean-Pierre Oudart, "Cinema

and Suture," *Screen* (winter 1977–78): 35–47; and Laura Mulvey, *Visual and Other Pleasures* (Bloomington: Indiana University Press, 1989).

22 See Siegfried Kracauer, "Photography," trans. Thomas Y. Levin, *Critical Inquiry* 19.3 (spring 1993): 421–34.

23 Siegfried Kracauer, *History: Last Things before the Last* (Oxford: Oxford University Press, 1969), 191, quoted in Dagmar Barnouw, *Critical Realism: History, Photography, and the Work of Siegfried Kracauer* (Baltimore: Johns Hopkins University Press, 1994), 12–13.

24 Kracauer, "Photography," 425.

25 My analysis and deconstruction of the photograph's visual realism is indebted to Silverman's analysis of gaze, look, and screen in *Male Subjectivity at the Margins* (New York: Routledge, 1992); and *Threshold*.

26 Homi Bhabha, "The Other Question: Stereotype, Discrimination, and the Discourse of Colonialism," in *The Location of Culture* (New York: Routledge, 1994), 66.

27 Carol E. Neubauer, "Developing Ties to the Past: Photography and Other Sources of Information in Maxine Hong Kingston's *China Men*," *MELUS* 10.4 (winter 1983): 27; my emphasis.

28 See Ackbar Abbas, *Hong Kong: Culture and the Politics of Disappearance* (Minneapolis: University of Minnesota Press, 1997). Writing on the widespread refusal to recognize the existence of Hong Kong culture, Abbas notes that this "refusal to see what is there is an example of reverse hallucination, or what Sigmund Freud in his essay on Wilhelm Jensen's 'Gravida' called 'negative hallucination.' If hallucination means seeing ghosts and apparitions, that is, something that is not there, reverse hallucination means *not* seeing what *is* there" (6; Abbas's emphasis).

29 The Chinese called the United States "Gum Sahn" or "Gold Mountain." First called "Gum Sahn" because of the discovery of gold in California, "Gold Mountain" also suggests the notion of the United States as a land of opportunity.

30 Michel Foucault, *The Archaeology of Knowledge,* trans. A. M. Sheridan Smith (New York: Pantheon, 1972), 7.

31 King-Kok Cheung, *Articulate Silences: Hisaye Yamamoto, Maxine Hong Kingston, Joy Kogawa* (Ithaca: Cornell University Press, 1993), 112.

32 Silverman, *Threshold*, 182. See the discussion of *Camera Lucida* on pages 181–83, to which this argument is indexed.

33 Kracauer, "Photography," 425; Kracauer's emphasis.

34 Ibid., 432.

35 It seems important to note that Kingston reworks both Eastern and Western myths, legends, and fables, making a special effort to question both traditional American and Chinese points of view. Consequently, if myths, legends, and fables are those privileged cultural narratives that provide consistency to a society's conception of itself, then Kingston uses the vicissitudes of personal memory to displace these stories, which would create an imaginary community through the exclusion of sexual and racial minorities.

36 Lacan, *Four Fundamental Concepts*, 85–90. This skull is visible only when one looks at the painting anamorphically, that is, from the extreme edge of its frame.

37 The following biographies of the "Big Four" robber barons, whose names are still prominent and visible both inside and outside of California, are drawn from George Kraus, *High Road to Promontory: Building the Central Pacific (now the Southern Pacific) across the High Sierra* (Palo Alto, CA: American West, 1969), 294–97.

Collis P. Huntington (b. 22 October 1821, d. 13 August 1900), born in Harwinton, Litchfield County, Connecticut, in 1821, was the "most hated and longest lived of the Big Four" (294). Huntington began his business career as a general merchant in Oneonta, New York. Motivated by gold rush fever, he left Oneonta in 1849. Settling in Sacramento, he returned to his life as a merchant, opening a small store with a business partner, Mark Hopkins. By 1856, the Huntington and Hopkins store was one of the most prosperous on the West Coast. It was at Huntington and Hopkins that Theodore Judah convinced Huntington to invest in the transcontinental railroad. Huntington later claimed that he was largely responsible for bringing in the other three powerhouses who ultimately financed the railroad deal. Huntington's role in the railroad focused primarily on management and finance.

Mark Hopkins (b. 1 September 1813, d. 29 March 1878), born in Henderson, New York, began his career in 1825 as a clerk in a mercantile company in Niagara County, but he quickly worked his way up in the business world, becoming a leading partner in the company Hopkins and Hughes. In 1849, Hopkins moved to San Francisco, where he established a wholesale grocery business with E. H. Miller Jr., who later became secretary of the Central Pacific Railroad. He partnered with Huntington in 1855. No project of the Big Four commenced without his approval—his partners felt that nothing was "finished until Hopkins looked at it" (295).

Leland Stanford (b. 9 March 1824, d. 21 June 1893), born in Watervliet, New York, was the first president of the Central Pacific Railroad and governor of California. He is perhaps best known for the university he founded in memory of his only son. Stanford grew up in upstate New York, where he studied law and was admitted to practice in the Supreme Court of New York. In addition to the law, Stanford began his business career with a small horseradish and chestnut business that he ran with his brothers. His interest in the railroad was sparked in part by his father, who graded a part of the nation's first railroad between Albany and Schenectady. Following in the footsteps of his brothers, who later provided him a job in their store, Stanford headed west. Soon the Stanford brothers became members of the wealthy elite of the mining region. After several failed bids for public office, Stanford left for Washington, D.C., where he became a confidant of President Lincoln, exerting, many believe, a strong influence over Pacific coast policy. When he returned to California, he was nominated in for governor and overwhelmingly elected to a two-year term in 1861. Stanford's influence in government was the decisive factor that allowed him to join to the ranks of the Big Four (296).

Charles Crocker (b. 16 September 1822, d. 14 August 1888), born in Troy, New York, was already a successful merchant when he began working for the railroad. He began his business career as a paperboy in Troy. By the time he left for California in 1850, he had acquired enough business experience to open a dry goods store in Sacramento. In 1860, he was elected to the California legislature for a two-year term, but he served only one, choosing instead to focus on the development of the Pacific Railroad enterprise. He was considered the "ideal head" (296) of the Big Four, and it was under his direction that the railroad was completed seven years ahead of schedule. In addition to the Central Pacific Railroad, Crocker also helped build the Southern Pacific transcontinental line across the American Southwest.

38 Yen Le Espiritu, *Asian American Women and Men* (Thousand Oaks, CA: Sage, 1997), 17.

39 Chan, *Asian Americans*, 81.

40 Ronald Takaki, *Strangers from a Different Shore: A History of Asian Americans* (New York: Penguin, 1989), 85–86.

41 For a history of this consolidation of whiteness, see Alexander Saxton, *The Indispensable Enemy: Labor and the Anti-Chinese Movement in California* (Berkeley: University of California Press, 1971); and *The Rise and Fall of the White Republic: Class Politics and Mass Culture in Nineteenth-Century America* (New York: Verso, 1990). See also David R. Roediger, *The Wages of Whiteness: Race and the Making of the American Working Class* (New York: Verso, 1991); Ruth Frankenburg, *White Women, Race Matters: The Social Construction of Whiteness* (Minneapolis: University of Minnesota Press, 1993); and George Lipsitz, *The Possessive Investment in Whiteness: How White People Profit from Identity Politics* (Philadelphia: Temple University Press, 1998).

42 Low pay coupled with poor working conditions led to several strikes, one of the largest of which occurred in 1867. Chan writes in *Asian Americans* that "unhappy with their lot, 2,000 men digging tunnels in the high Sierras went on strike, demanding $40 a month, 10 hours of work a day for those laboring outdoors and eight hours for those inside the tunnels, an end to corporal punishment, and the freedom to leave whenever they desired. Their strike lasted a week—until their food ran out. The railroad company simply stopped bringing them rations, thus starving them back to work. The company also took the precaution of asking employment agencies to stand ready to supply it with black workers should the Chinese strike again" (81–82).

43 Kingston chronicles in "The Laws," the chapter following "The Grandfather of the Sierra Nevada Mountains," a long history of congressional and state exclusion acts directed against the Chinese. These laws and treaties formalized the legal disenfranchisement of Chinese immigrants from naturalization and citizenship precisely through, among other measures, the state-enforced separation of Chinese American male laborers from their wives and families.

44 Fae Myenne Ng, *Bone* (New York: Hyperion, 1993), 61.

45 Somewhere wafting through the Chinatown streets "comes what sounds like Julio Iglesias singing 'To All the Girls I Loved' in Cantonese" (59).

46 See Kracauer's 1927 essay "The Mass Ornament," trans. Barbara Correll and Jack Zipes, *New German Critique* 5 (spring 1975): 67–76. In this essay, Kracauer asserts that "the mass ornament is the aesthetic reflex of the rationality aspired to by the prevailing economic system" (70). Kracauer was one of the first critical theorists to suggest the monopolization of leisure time as a commodity for the purpose of distraction—what Horkheimer and Adorno label the "culture industry." In his pioneering 1929 study, *Die Angestellten* [The white-collared workers], Kracauer connects industrial regimentation with the leisure industry, describing the amusement spots of the bourgeoisie as "pleasure barracks." See Karsten Witte, "Introduction to Siegfried Kracauer's 'The Mass Ornament,' " *New German Critique* 5 (spring 1975): 64.

47 See, for example, the preface to Frank Chin, Jeffery Paul Chan, Lawson Fusao Inada, and Shawn Wong, eds., *Aiiieeeee! An Anthology of Asian-American Writers* (Garden City, NY: Anchor, 1975), ix–xx, as well as Chin's "Come All Ye Asian American Writers of the Real and Fake," in *The Big Aiiieeeee!: An Anthology of Chinese American and Japanese American Literature*, eds. Jeffrey Paul Chan, Frank Chin, Lawson Fusao Inada, and Shawn Wong (New York: Meridian, 1991), 1–92.

48 Judith Butler, *Bodies That Matter: On the Discursive Limits of "Sex"* (New York: Routledge, 1993), 223.

49 Chin et al., *Aiiieeeee!*, x.

50 See Butler, *Bodies*, 227.

51 For an elaboration on cultural atavism, see Rey Chow, "Where Have all the Natives Gone?" in *Writing Diaspora: Tactics of Intervention in Contemporary Cultural Studies* (Bloomington: Indiana University Press, 1993), 27–54.

52 See chapter 6, "The Dream-Work," of Sigmund Freud's *The Interpretation of Dreams*, in Sigmund Freud, *The Standard Edition of the Complete Psychological Works of Sigmund Freud*, ed. James Strachey (London: Hogarth, 1955), 4 and 5: 277–508.

53 See J. Laplanche and J.-B. Pontalis, *The Language of Psycho-Analysis*, trans. Donald Nicholson-Smith (New York: Norton, 1973), 125.

54 Silverman, *Threshold*, 180.

55 See Laplanche and Pontalis, *Language*, 111.

56 Ibid., 112. Laplanche and Pontalis note three main characteristics of Freud's theory:

> a. It is not lived experience in general that undergoes deferred revision but, specifically, whatever it has been impossible in the first instance to incorporate fully into a meaningful context. The traumatic event is the epitome of such unassimilated experience.
> b. Deferred revision is occasioned by events and situations, or by an organic maturation, which allow the subject to gain access to a new level of meaning and to rework his earlier experiences.

c. Human sexuality, with the peculiar unevenness of its temporal development, provides an eminently suitable field for the phenomenon of deferred action. (112)

57 See Louis Althusser, "Contradiction and Overdetermination: Notes for an Investigation," in *For Marx*, trans. Ben Brewster (New York: Verso, 1990), 87–116.

58 See Laplanche and Pontalis's entry "Phantasy (or Fantasy)," in *Language*, 314–18. See also their essay "Fantasy and the Origins of Sexuality," in *Formations of Fantasy*, eds. Victor Burgin, James Donald, and Cora Kaplan (New York: Methuen, 1986), 5–34.

59 Maxine Hong Kingston's *The Woman Warrior: Memoirs of a Girlhood among Ghosts* (New York: Vintage, [1976] 1989), won the National Book Award in 1976. It is by many accounts the most widely taught work of fiction by a living author on university campuses today. See L. A. Chung, "Chinese American Literary War," *San Francisco Chronicle*, 26 August 1991, D3–4. For a summary of Chin's criticisms of Kingston, see Frank Chin, Jeffrey Paul Chan, Lawson Fusao Inada, and Shawn Hsu Wong, "An Introduction to Chinese- and Japanese-American Literature," in Chin et al., *Aiiieeeee!*, 3–36. See also the editors' introduction to Chan et al., *The Big Aiiieeeee*, xi–xvi. In addition, see Frank Chin, "Backtalk," in *Counterpoint: Perspectives on Asian America*, ed. Emma Gee (Los Angeles: Asian American Studies Center, UCLA, 1976), 556–67; "Come All Ye Writers"; and "Uncle Frank's Fakebook of Fairy Tales for Asian American Moms and Dads," *Amerasia Journal* 18.2 (1992): 69–87.

60 The editors also write in *The Big Aiiieeeee!* about David Henry Hwang and *M. Butterfly*. They state that "the good Chinese man, at his best, is the fulfillment of white male homosexual fantasy, literally kissing white ass. Now Hwang and the stereotype are inextricably one" (xiii). Hwang's response was to dub Chin "the ayatollah of Asian America" (Chung, "Chinese American Literary War," D4).

61 Chan et al., *The Big Aiiieeeee!*, xii.

62 Chung, "Chinese American Literary War," D4.

63 Chin and Kingston came of age as contemporaries. Both were undergraduates at the University of California, Berkeley, in the 1960s.

64 Frank Chin and Jeffery Paul Chan, "Racist Love," in *Seeing through Shuck*, ed. Richard Kostelanetz (New York: Ballantine, 1972), 68.

65 Chan et al., *The Big Aiiieeeee!*, xiii.

66 Sau-ling Cynthia Wong, *Reading Asian American Literature: From Necessity to Extravagance* (Princeton: Princeton University Press, 1993), 153. Wong writes of Chin's *Donald Duk* that instead of focusing on the "intense contradictions involved in creating a Chinese American mobility myth around the symbol of the railroad, . . . after struggling for years with raw and impossible contradictions, Chin has decided to settle for a defanged version of Chinese American history and the simple warm glow of ethnic pride" (146, 153).

67 Robert Murray Davis, "West Meets East: A Conversation with Frank Chin," *Amerasia Journal* 24.1 (1998): 88–89.

68 Freud writes in "On the Mechanism of Paranoia": "After the stage of heterosexual object-choice has been reached, the homosexual tendencies are not, as might be supposed, done away with or brought to a stop; they are merely deflected from their sexual aim and applied to fresh uses. They now combine with portions of the ego-instincts and, as 'attached' components, help to constitute the social instincts, thus contributing an erotic factor to friendship and comradeship, to *esprit de corps* and to the love of mankind in general" (Freud, *Standard Edition*, 12:61).

TWO *Primal Scenes*

1 Report of Curtis B. Munson, "Japanese on the West Coast," attached to a memo from John Franklin Carter to President Roosevelt, 7 November 1941 Franklin Delano Roosevelt Library [(FDRI], PSF 106, Stimson, Commission on Wartime Relocation and Internment of Civilians [CWRIC] 3673–89; Munson's emphasis).

2 Memo from J. Edgar Hoover to Attorney General, 2 February 1942, FBI, CWRIC 5794.

3 Executive Order 9066, 19 February 1942, National Archives, General Records of the U.S. Government, Record Group 11.

4 Ronald Takaki, *Strangers from a Different Shore: A History of Asian Americans* (New York: Penguin, 1989), 387. Chapter 10 of *Strangers* and Sucheng Chan's *Asian Americans: An Interpretive History* (Boston: Twayne, 1991), chap. 7, contain detailed histories of Japanese American internment. For a comprehensive juridical history of the internment, see *Personal Justice Denied: Report of the Commission on Wartime Relocation and Internment of Civilians* (Washington, DC: Civil Liberties Public Education Fund; Seattle: University of Washington Press, 1997). For a visual history of the internment, see Deborah Gesensway and Mindy Roseman, *Beyond Words: Images from America's Concentration Camps* (Ithaca: Cornell University Press, 1987). Visual media, such as Rea Tajiri's stunning video *History and Memory* (Women Make Movies, New York, 1991), also explore the psychic impact of incarceration on the children of internees.

Although officials at the Department of Justice initially opposed the mass evacuation of Japanese Americans and its flagrant abrogation of civil liberties, proponents of "relocation" at the War Department strongly argued for this suspension of constitutional rights in the interests of national security and military necessity.

While one would expect that war panic against the Japanese would be most virulent in Hawai'i, the site of the Pearl Harbor bombing, the fact that 32 percent of Hawai'i's population was of Japanese descent made it impossible to evacuate them without destroying the islands' economy and the war effort. General Delos Emmons, the U.S. commander in Hawai'i, managed the military situation without ordering a mass evacuation, showing that order could be maintained without the abrogation of civil liberties. In Hawai'i, no acts of subversion occurred and due process was preserved.

Curiously enough, while the days following the United States' entry into World War II witnessed the seizure of weapons, radios, cameras, binoculars, and other instruments of surveillance from "enemy" aliens of Japanese, German, and Italian ancestry, only the Japanese, along with their American-born children, were subsequently evacuated to makeshift assembly centers and then incarcerated in ten concentration camps inland: Manzanar and Tule Lake in California; Minidoka in Idaho; Poston and Gila River in Arizona; Rohwer and Jerome in Arkansas; Amache in Colorado; Topaz in Utah; and Heart Mountain in Wyoming.

This egregious act of racial discrimination, FBI director J. Edgar Hoover later noted, was based primarily upon public and political pressure rather than factual data or any real threat of espionage on the part of individuals of Japanese descent. The lack of any factual basis for the internment was dismissed by various government reports and investigative agencies. At the heart of Executive Order 9066, then, was the assumption that Japanese Americans remained continuously loyal to Japan, their land of "origin," and thus were disloyal to the United States. To be a Japanese American during the war and after the promulgation of Executive Order 9066 was consequently to be constituted as an enemy of the state.

By contrasting "white" groups with the Japanese and relying on visual markers of race, Executive Order 9066 generated its own (il)logical consistencies. Indeed the court cases that tested the constitutionality of internment illustrate this point. *Hirabayashi v. U.S.*, 320 U.S. 81 (1943); *Yasui v. U.S.*, 320 U.S. 115 (1943); *Korematsu v. U.S.*, 323 U.S. 214 (1944); and *Ex Parte Endo*, 323 U.S. 283 (1944) challenged the constitutionality of detention and internment before the U.S. Supreme Court. While the Court found that the government could no longer detain Endo, it upheld Korematsu's conviction, holding in the case that "the exclusion of a single racial group [is] within the war powers of the Congress and of the President." Ironically, the *Korematsu* and *Endo* decisions were filed on the same day.

5 Telephone conversation between DeWitt and McCloy, 3 February 1942, National Archives and Records Service [NARS], Record Group 107, CWRIC 131–40. The conversation continues: "The same applies in practically the same way to alien Germans and alien Italians but due to the large number of Japanese in the State of California (approximately 93,000), larger than any other State in the Union, and the very definite war consciousness of the people of California, as far as pertains to the Japanese participation in the war, the question of the alien Japanese and all Japanese presents a problem in control, separate and distinct from that of the German and Italian."

6 Chan, 124. On 13 April 1943, General Dewitt defended the internment before a congressional committee (Testimony before House Naval Affairs Subcommittee, 13 April 1943, NARS, Record Group 338, CWRIC 1725–28):

GENERAL DEWITT: I have the mission of defending this coast and securing vital installations. The danger of the Japanese was, and is now,—if they are permitted to come back—espionage and sabotage. It makes no difference whether he is an American citizen, he is still Japanese. American citizenship does not necessarily determine loyalty.

MR. BATES: You draw a distinction between Japanese and Italians and Germans? We have a great number of Italians and Germans and we think they are fine citizens. There may be exceptions.

GENERAL DEWITT: You needn't worry about the Italians at all except in certain cases. Also, the same for the Germans except in individual cases. But we must worry about the Japanese all the time until he is wiped off the map. Sabotage and espionage will make problems as long as he is allowed in this area—problems which I don't want to have to worry about.

7 This quotation is taken from the television adaptation of Jeanne Wakatsuki Houston and James D. Houston's *Farewell to Manzanar* (1973), which was broadcast on 11 March 1976 on NBC. It is quoted in Darrell Y. Hamamoto, *Monitored Peril: Asian Americans and the Politics of TV Representation* (Minneapolis: University of Minnesota Press, 1994), 67.

8 Chan, *Asian Americans*, 136.

9 Arguing on behalf of the government and mandatory internment, the U.S. solicitor general stressed the "preventive" aspects of detention, which was being "undertaken to protect persons of Japanese ancestry from hostile public reception and to prevent potential racial outbreaks in society at large" (quoted in ibid., 138).

10 *Korematsu v. United States*, 323 U.S. 214 (1944). Sanda Mayzaw Lwin, at Columbia University, wrote a 1999 dissertation, "The Constitution of Asian America," in which she offers a notable analysis of the *Korematsu* case and John Okada's *No-No Boy*.

11 "How to Tell Your Friends from the Japs," *Time*, 22 December 1941, 33; "How to Tell Japs from the Chinese: Angry Citizens Victimize Allies with Emotional Outburst at Enemy," *Life*, 22 December 1941, 81–82.

12 The visual policing of the Japanese American racial image during World War II should not be characterized as an anomalous historical occurrence, the exigent result of war panic. This is an optic regime that not only affects all Americans of Asian descent but continues to persist in contemporary American society. One of the most alarming recent cases of this was the 1982 murder of the Chinese American Vincent Chin, who was beaten to death by two unemployed Detroit autoworkers who mistakenly assumed that he was Japanese. See William Wei's account of the murder of Vincent Chin in *The Asian American Movement* (Philadelphia: Temple University Press, 1993); and Christine Choy's and Renee Tajima-Pena's documentary film *Who Killed Vincent Chin?* (New York: Filmmakers Library, 1988).

13 Homi Bhabha, "The Other Question: Stereotype, Discrimination, and the Discourse of Colonialism," in *The Location of Culture* (London: Routledge, 1994), 66.

14 Lisa Lowe, *Immigrant Acts: On Asian American Cultural Politics* (Durham: Duke University Press, 1996), 18–19.

15 Writing about what Evelynn Hammonds terms the "politics of articulation," Ann Pellegrini makes the following remarks about the political theater of Anna Deveare Smith: "However tempting it might be to counter 'negative' images of blackness with 'positive' images, this political and psychological response to the deprivations of being identified from without cannot go all the distance. We can no more predict what actions or identifications 'positive' representations will give rise to than we can be certain to capture the all of us in 'our' would-be positive images. Can any campaign for 'positive' images reckon with the unconscious and its unpredictable uptake of 'the' image? Will 'our' images be any less normalizing than 'theirs'?" See Ann Pellegrini, *Performance Anxieties: Staging Psychoanalysis, Staging Race* (New York: Routledge, 1997), 81.

16 Lonny Kaneko, "The Shoyu Kid," *Amerasia Journal* 3.2 (1976): 1–9. The story is reprinted in Jeffrey Paul Chan, Frank Chin, Lawson Fusao Inada, and Shawn Hsu Wong, eds., *The Big Aiiieeeee: An Anthology of Chinese American and Japanese American Literature* (New York: Meridian, 1991), 304–13.

17 Frank Chin, in particular, often writes about white American male cinematic idols. In addition to *Donald Duk*, see his novel on Hollywood images, *Gunga Din Highway* (Minneapolis: Coffee House Press, 1994); and his short story "Riding the Rails with Chickencoop Slim," *Greenfield Review* 6.1–2 (1977): 80–89.

18 Jean Laplanche and Jean-Bertrand Pontalis, *The Language of Psycho-Analysis*, trans. Donald Nicholson-Smith (New York: Norton, 1973), 331–33.

19 Jacques Lacan, "The Mirror Stage as Formative of the Function of the I as Revealed in Psychoanalytic Experience," in *Écrits: A Selection*, trans. Alan Sheridan (New York: Norton, 1977), 1–7.

20 Jacques Lacan, *The Seminar of Jacques Lacan, Book II, The Ego in Freud's Theory and in the Technique of Psychoanalysis, 1954*, trans. Sylvana Tomaselli (New York: Norton, 1991), 54.

21 Kaja Silverman, *The Threshold of the Visible World* (New York: Routledge, 1996), 9–37. Silverman cites Freud's assertion that the ego is "first and foremost a bodily ego" to conclude that "our experience of 'self' is always circumscribed by and derived from the body" (9). It is through this brief but provocative statement in *The Ego and the Id*—as well as through a footnote in the body of its text describing the ego as derived from bodily sensations—that Silverman argues for not only a specular but a bodily (or "sensational") theory of the ego. Freud's states in his footnote that "the ego is ultimately derived from bodily sensations, chiefly from those springing from the surface of the body. It may thus be regarded as a mental projection of the surface of the body, besides, as we have seen above, representing the superficies

of the mental apparatus" (Sigmund Freud, *The Ego and the Id*, in *The Standard Edition of the Complete Psychological Works of Sigmund Freud*, ed. James Strachey [London: Hogarth, 1955], 19:26). Indeed, Lacan's theory of the mirror stage is commonly seen as the conceptual elaboration of the second part of this footnote, that the ego must "be regarded as a mental projection of the surface of the body."

22 Freud, *Ego*, 26.

23 As such, the imago must be understood as more than a mere reflection of the infant's specular corporeal outline; it is fundamentally an (unattainable) image of anticipated unity—what Jane Gallop has labeled, borrowing a grammatical term, "the future perfect." See Jane Gallop, *Reading Lacan* (Ithaca: Cornell University Press, 1985), 81.

24 Mikkel Borch-Jacobsen, *Lacan: The Absolute Master*, trans. Douglas Brick (Stanford: Stanford University Press, 1991), 49.

25 See Jacques Lacan, *The Four Fundamental Concepts of Psycho-Analysis*, trans. Alan Sheridan (New York: Norton, 1981), for his discussion of screen, look, and gaze. For an explication of these three Lacanian concepts, see Kaja Silverman, *Male Subjectivity at the Margins* (New York: Routledge, 1992), 125–56.

26 Lacan, *Four Fundamental Concepts*, Seminar XI, 106. Silverman argues in *Threshold*, chap. 4, that the gaze has for the past hundred years found in the camera its most influential metaphor. See also Jonathan Crary, *Techniques of the Observer* (Cambridge: MIT Press, 1990).

27 Silverman, *Threshold*, 10.

28 See Alan Read, *The Fact of Blackness: Frantz Fanon and Visual Representation* (Seattle: Bay Press, 1996); Diana Fuss, *Identification Papers* (New York: Routledge, 1995); and Bhabha, *The Location of Culture*.

29 Frantz Fanon, *Black Skin, White Masks*, trans. Charles Lam Markmann (New York: Grove, 1967), 109–10.

30 *Two Lies*, dir. Pamela Tom, UCLA Film School, Los Angeles, 1989. For a guide to independent Asian American cinema, see Russell Leong, ed., *Moving the Image: Independent Asian Pacific American Media Arts* (Los Angeles: Asian American Studies Center, UCLA, 1991).

31 See Monica Sone's *Nisei Daughter* (Seattle: University of Washington Press, 1953); and Rea Tajiri's film *Strawberry Fields* (Open City Films, New York, 1997), for eloquent testimonies to this purging of Japanese artifacts.

32 The "No-No boy" phenomenon, so well documented in John Okada's novel *No-No Boy* (Seattle: University of Washington Press, [1957] 1979), refers to President Roosevelt's 29 January 1943 directive offering interned Japanese American males the chance to volunteer for military combat. Prior to his induction, however, each internee first needed to submit to a loyalty oath, which was administered by military recruiters in the camps.

Questions 27 and 28 of the loyalty questionnaire became the ultimate litmus test for acceptable political allegiance and national identity: "Are you willing to serve in the armed forces of the United States on combat duty, wherever ordered? Will you swear unqualified allegiance to the United States of America and forswear any form of allegiance to the Japanese Emperor of any other foreign power or organization?" Sanda Mayzaw Lwin points out that for "*Issei,* Japanese-born U.S. residents whose 'ineradicable brownness' had precluded them from becoming citizens because of the 1790 'whites-only' naturalization law—and the alternate naturalization requisite for 'African' blood—to answer 'yes' would mean to renounce the one form of citizenship they possessed and thus render themselves stateless. For *Nisei,* American-born citizens of Japanese ancestry, the question assumed that their loyalties were already divided, and thus already interpellated them as treasonable subjects from the onset" (107). From a slightly different angle, the first question is ironic, to say the least, asking one to serve the nation even as one's constitutional rights have been abrogated and one has been jailed by the government. The second question is a no-win proposition. Answering yes or no served only to confirm the respondent as a disloyal subject, assuming an initial or subsequently forsworn allegiance to the Japanese emperor.

Nevertheless, answering yes to both questions provided the burden of proof necessary for military induction. Answering no confirmed what the U.S. government had suspected all along—that the presence of Japanese American bodies on national soil posed a dangerous threat to national security. This questionnaire, cast as a positive affirmation of one's allegiance to the nation, in fact, becomes an exercise in what Althusser terms "interpellation" and the production of bad subjects. See Louis Althusser, "Ideology and Ideological State Apparatuses," in *"Lenin and Philosophy" and Other Essays,* trans. Ben Brewster (New York: Monthly Review Press, 1971), 127–86. Put otherwise, the loyalty questionnaire might be described less as a juridical mechanism proving one's loyalty and more as a punitive legal exercise producing one's presumed treason.

See Leslie T. Hatamiya, *Righting a Wrong: Japanese Americans and the Passage of the Civil Liberties Act of 1988* (Stanford: Stanford University Press, 1993); and David O'Brien and Stephen S. Fugita, *The Japanese American Experience* (Bloomington: Indiana University Press, 1991).

33 Notice, of course, that all the Japanese Americans incarcerated in Minidoka are literally prisoners of war, and all are under suspicion of espionage. This ironic disavowal on the part of the three boys results in increasing psychic pressure as the story progresses.

Here I use the term *abject* in reference to its social, as well as its psychoanalytic, connotations. The abject signifies socially that devalued zone outside of subjecthood proper that nevertheless sustains sociality as a silenced but constitutive part of it. Psychoanalytically, it signifies that domain—Lacan's "real"—foreclosed through the barring of the primary signifier and the production of an unconscious and its prohibitions. See Judith Butler, *Bodies That Matter, On the Discursive Limits of "Sex"* (New York: Routledge, 1993) as well as her "Imitation and Gender Insubordination," in *The Les-*

bian and Gay Studies Reader, eds. Henry Abelove, Michèle Aina Barale, and David M. Halperin (New York: Routledge, 1993), 307–20. See also Julia Kristeva, *Powers of Horror: An Essay on Abjection* (New York: Columbia University Press, 1982); and Jean Laplanche and J.-B. Pontalis's entry on "foreclosure" in *The Language of Psycho-Analysis,* trans. Donald Nicholson-Smith (New York: Norton, 1973), 166–69, for a further elaboration of the abject.

34 Homi Bhabha, "Of Mimicry and Man: The Ambivalence of Colonial Discourse," *October* 28 (1984): 130; Bhabha's emphasis.

35 See Althusser, "Ideology," 127–186.

36 See Jacques Lacan, "Some Reflections on the Ego," *International Journal of Psycho-Analysis* 34 (1953): 11–17.

37 See Laura Mulvey, *Visual and Other Pleasures* (Bloomington: Indiana University Press, 1989).

38 The example of Sartre's voyeur is invoked in Lacan, *Four Fundamental Concepts,* 84.

39 Sau-ling Cynthia Wong, *Reading Asian American Literature: From Necessity to Extravagance* (Princeton: Princeton University Press, 1993), 100.

40 Jean Laplanche, *Life and Death in Psychoanalysis,* trans. Jeffrey Mehlman (Baltimore: Johns Hopkins University Press, 1976), 102. In *The Language of Psycho-Analysis,* Laplanche and Pontalis mention three primal fantasies, calling them original fantasies (*fantasmes originaires*) or fantasies of origin (*fantasmes des origines*): the primal scene, the seduction scene, and the castration scene. These three fantasies of origin, taken together, constitute an entire Oedipal history of the subject. Like myths, they claim to provide a representation of, and a solution to, the major enigmas that confront the child: "In the 'primal scene,' it is the origin of the subject that is represented; in seduction phantasies, it is the origin or emergence of sexuality; in castration phantasies, the origin of the distinction between the sexes" (332).

41 The "spying" infant cannot be in an actively voyeuristic position. The infant by definition occupies a passive role precisely because of its inability to understand or control the events it witnesses.

42 Lee Edelman, "Seeing Things: Representation, the Scene of Surveillance, and the Spectacle of Gay Male Sex," in *Inside/Out: Lesbian Theories, Gay Theories,* ed. Diana Fuss (New York: Routledge, 1991), 95.

43 Silverman, *Male Subjectivity,* 164.

44 Freud coined the term *stereotype plate* in his earliest writings in *The Interpretation of Dreams (Standard Edition,* vols. 4, 5). He returns repeatedly to this concept, most notably in "The Dynamics of Transference" (*Standard Edition,* 12:99–100). He discusses the concept of the readymade in chapter 6 of *The Interpretation of Dreams.*

45 Sigmund Freud, "Some Psychological Consequences of the Anatomical Distinction between the Sexes," in ibid., 19:241–60.

46 Silverman, *Male Subjectivity,* 165.

47 Sigmund Freud, "From the History of an Infantile Neurosis (The 'Wolf Man')," in Freud, *Standard Edition,* 17:1–122.

48 Lee Edelman writes: "Insofar as the participants in the primal scene are as yet undifferentiated sexually to the infant who observes them—both, that is, in the logic of Freudian theory, are seen as phallic—it is no small wonder that he has little difficulty in experiencing an identification with each of their positions; but insofar as that scene must thereafter bear traces of sodomitical phantasy and homosexual desire, it is small wonder that Freud has great difficulty indeed in allowing himself or his psychoanalytic practice to be implicated in this scene at all" ("Seeing Things," 101).

49 Ibid. Laplanche and Pontalis in *Language* define the primal scene as a "scene of sexual intercourse between the parents which the child observes, or infers on the basis of certain indications, and phantasies. It is generally interpreted by the child as an act of violence on the part of the father" (335). They go on to state the "the act of coitus is understood by the child as an aggression by the father in a sado-masochistic relationship; secondly, the scene gives rise to sexual excitation in the child while at the same time providing a basis of castration anxiety; thirdly, the child interprets what is going on, within the framework of an infantile sexual theory, as anal coitus" (335).

50 The emasculation of the Asian American male—a youngster in this instance—follows the strict logic of French active / Greek passive.

51 Teresa de Lauretis, *The Practice of Love: Lesbian Sexuality and Perverse Desire* (Bloomington: Indiana University Press, 1994), 82–83.

52 See also the installation work of artist Ik Joong Kang. At the Whitney Museum of American Art, Kang recently installed "8490 Days of Memory," a work with 8,490 squares of chocolate hung on foil-covered walls. This same number corresponds to the polished clear plastic cubes amassed on the floor below, under the feet of a solid chocolate-covered Douglas MacArthur. Each three-inch square on the wall consists of an insignia from the U.S. Army cast in relief. Each three-inch cube on the floor contains a memento from Kang's childhood—marbles, wind-up toys, and dice preserved in resin.

53 See R. Zamora Linmark, *Rolling the R's* (New York: Kaya Production, 1995); Shyam Selvadurai, *Funny Boy* (New York: Morrow, 1994); and Norman Wong, *Cultural Revolution* (New York: Persea, 1994).

54 Eve Kosofsky Sedgwick, "How to Bring Your Kids up Gay: The War on Effeminate Boys," in *Tendencies* (Durham: Duke University Press, 1993), 161.

55 For a feminist critique of Fanon, see Fuss, *Identification Papers*, as well as Gwen Bergner, "Who Is That Masked Woman? or the Role of Gender in Fanon's *Black Skin, White Masks*," *PMLA* 110.1 (January 1995): 75–88. For a queer critique of Fanon, see Lee Edelman, *Homographesis: Essays in Gay Literary and Cultural Theory* (New York: Routledge, 1994), 42–75.

56 Angela Y. Davis, *Women, Race, and Class* (New York: Vintage, 1983), 200.

THREE   *Heterosexuality in the Face of Whiteness*

1 For instance, Ralph Ellison's novel *Invisible Man* (New York: Random House, 1952); Christine Choy's *Out in Silence* (San Francisco: National Asian Ameri-

can Telecommunications Association, 1994), a documentary on AIDS in the Asian Pacific American community; and ACT UP's chant of queer affirmation and protest, "We're here, we're queer, get used to it!" are examples that collectively emphasize—even demand—the need for the disenfranchised subject to emerge into the domain of visibility and speech.

2 Kobena Mercer, "Skin Head Sex Thing," in *How Do I Look*, ed. Bad Object Choices (Seattle: Bay Press, 1991), 206. See also "White Like Who? Notes on the Other Race," a special issue of the *Village Voice*, 18 May 1993, 24–41. This special issue is a compendium of articles examining whiteness as an invisible racial identity.

3 Ping-hui Liao's article, "'Of Writing Words for Music Which Is Already Made': *Madama Butterfly, Turandot*, and Orientalism," *Cultural Critique* 16 (fall 1990): 31–59, provides an excellent summary of Puccini's opera and its critical antecedents. According to Liao, the opera was originally based upon a drama, *Naughty Anthony*, written by American playwright David Belasco (see *Six Plays: Madame Butterfly, Du Barry, The Darling of the Gods, Adrea, The Girl of the Golden West, The Return of Peter Grimm* [Boston: Little Brown, 1928]). Belasco adapted the story from a novella by American author John Luther Long (see *Madame Butterfly, Purple Eyes, A Gentleman of Japan and a Lady, Kito, Glory* [New York: Century, 1898]). The original story line is apparently based on the actual suicide of a Japanese geisha, a story notably recorded by the French writer Pierre Loti in *Madame Chrysanthème* (Paris: Calmann-Levy, [1887] 1922).

4 David Henry Hwang, *M. Butterfly* (New York: Plume, 1988), 91.

5 See, for example, Gabrielle Cody's article, "David Hwang's *M. Butterfly*: Perpetuating the Misogynist Myth," *Theatre* 20.2 (spring 1989): 24–27; and John Louis DiGaetani's interview with the playwright, "*M. Butterfly*: An Interview with David Henry Hwang," *Drama Review* 33.3 (fall 1989): 141–53.

6 Majorie Garber, *Vested Interests: Cross-Dressing and Cultural Anxiety* (New York: Harper Perennial, 1992), 243; Garber's emphasis.

7 Here Garber quotes Hwang.

8 Judith Butler, *Bodies That Matter: On the Discursive Limits of "Sex,"* (New York: Routledge, 1993), 18; Butler's emphasis.

9 Ibid., 182; my emphasis.

10 Ibid.

11 Eve Sedgwick, "White Glasses," in *Tendencies* (Durham: Duke University Press, 1993), 255.

12 Frank Rich, "*M. Butterfly*: A Story of a Strange Love, Conflict, and Betrayal," *New York Times*, 21 March 1988, C13.

13 Moira Hodgson, "*M. Butterfly*," *Nation*, 23 April 1988, 577.

14 See Miriam Horn's review of *M. Butterfly*, "The Mesmerizing Power of Racial Myths," *U.S. News and World Report*, 28 March 1988, 52–53. In this article, Horn compares Hwang to African American film director Spike Lee. For an excellent summary of the material conditions prohibiting the Asian American artist from full participation in the American mainstream of artistic

production, see Sau-ling Cynthia Wong's *Reading Asian American Literature: From Necessity to Extravagance* (Princeton: Princeton University Press, 1993), chap. 4.

15 John Simon, "Finding Your Song," *New York*, 11 April 1988, 117.

16 In "An Actor Despairs," *New York*, 24 October 1988, 145–46, which Simon wrote after *M. Butterfly* won the Tony Award, he retracts his earlier statement and responds to the issue of white masculinity: "While sharing in the shame and heartbreak of René Gallimard as embarrassingly well conveyed by Lithgow, I let the quality of the play slip out of my focus" (146). For an analysis of Simon's admission of a vexed (dis)identification with Gallimard's failed white manhood, see Angela Pao, "The Critic and the Butterfly: Sociocultural Contexts and the Reception of David Henry Hwang's *M. Butterfly*," *Amerasia Journal* 18.3 (1992): 1–16.

17 For a similar debate on the use of yellowface by a white actor, see Yoko Yoshikawa's analysis of the *Miss Saigon* controversy, "The Heat Is on *Miss Saigon* Coalition: Organizing across Race and Sexuality," in *The State of Asian America: Activism and Resistance in the 1990s*, ed. Karin Aguilar–San Juan (Boston: South End, 1994), 275–94.

18 Sigmund Freud, "The Dissection of the Psychical Personality," in *The Standard Edition of the Complete Psychological Works of Sigmund Freud*, ed. James Strachey (London: Hogarth, 1955), 22:79.

19 Sigmund Freud, *The Ego and the Id*, in Freud, *Standard Edition*, 19:18.

20 Sigmund Freud, "Splitting of the Ego in the Defensive Process," in Freud, *Standard Edition*, 23:275.

21 Ibid., 276.

22 I place *castration* in quotation marks since one can technically be castrated only when one loses something that one once had. The idea of female castration is problematic, since the woman never had a penis to lose in the first place. Freud's conflation of female penis envy (and the notion of clitoris as an inferior penis) with loss and castration is both slippery and overdetermined. I thank David Hirsch for discussing this issue with me.

23 Freud, "Splitting of the Ego," 277.

24 Ibid., 275–76.

25 Indeed, *M. Butterfly* was based on the actual story of a low-level attaché in the French Foreign Service, Bernard Boursicot, and a Chinese opera diva, Shi Pei Pu, who had an on-again, off-again affair for nearly eighteen years (from about 1965 to 1983). Shi Pei Pu regularly dressed as a man but confided to Boursicot that she was, in fact, a woman who had been raised as a boy by her family. During the course of their relationship, Boursicot not only "sired" a son but passed on several hundred documents from the French embassies in Beijing and Ulan Bator, Mongolia, to the Chinese authorities. In 1983, after Boursicot had returned and Shi Pei Pu had emigrated to France, they were both charged with espionage. During various medical examinations resulting from the espionage charges, French officials discovered that Shi Pei Pu was a man, despite Boursicot's belief to the contrary. In 1987, Boursicot

and Shi Pei Pu were given presidential pardons due to the inconsequential nature of the stolen documents as well as the embarrassment this unimportant legal case caused the Chinese and French governments. The story of Boursicot and Shi Pei Pu is chronicled by Joyce Wadler in *Liaison* (New York: Bantam, 1993).

26 See Robert J. Corber, *Homosexuality in Cold War America* (Durham: Duke University Press, 1997); and Lee Edelman, *Homographesis: Essays in Gay Literary and Cultural Theory* (New York: Routledge, 1994), esp. chap. 9.

27 Commenting on this crossing of homosexuality and racialization, Edelman notes in *Homographesis* that "the historical pressure upon the postwar American national self-image found displaced articulation in the phobic positioning of homosexual activity as the proximate cause of perceived danger to the nation at a time of unprecedented concern about the possibility of national—and global—destruction. Revising late nineteenth-century arguments about racial degeneration and bringing them to bear upon mid-twentieth-century social and political conflicts, historically deployed readings envisioning male homosexuality in terms of the abjection associated with the men's room could complain of the threat homosexuality posed to the continuity of civilization itself" (168).

28 I do, of course, make ironic reference to this abduction of Gallimard into heterosexuality and whiteness over and against the hysterical accusations of those who would say that homosexuality is given over to the logic of recruitment in its "reproductive" affiliative capacities.

29 Sigmund Freud, "Fetishism," in Freud, *Standard Edition*, 21:154.

30 It is interesting to note that Freud ends "Fetishism" with a gesture toward a race-psychological parallel to this psychic mechanism of denial and projection: the Chinese custom of foot binding, of "mutilating the female foot and then revering it like a fetish after it has been mutilated" (157). "The Chinese male wants to thank the woman for having submitted to being castrated" (157), Freud claims. Here, he seems to raise this racial example only to further his assertions of fetishism's role in the anatomical distinction between the (white) sexes.

31 Kaja Silverman, *The Threshold of the Visible World* (New York: Routledge, 1996), 31.

32 Here I am allowing a certain slippage from *Asian* to *Asian American* not only because Hwang's text functions within the politics of Asian America but also because, to many a Western eye, Asians and Asian Americans all "look alike."

33 Richard Fung, "Looking for My Penis: The Eroticized Asian in Gay Porn Video," in *How Do I Look?* ed. Bad Object Choices (Seattle: Bay Press, 1991), 153.

34 Lisa Lowe, *Immigrant Acts: On Asian American Cultural Politics* (Durham: Duke University Press, 1996), 151.

35 Kaja Silverman, "The Lacanian Phallus," *differences: A Journal of Feminist Cultural Studies* 4.1 (spring 1992): 113.

36 This scene suggests that Renée neutralizes the gender of the phallus. As Jane Gallop notes in *Reading Lacan* (Ithaca: Cornell University Press, 1985), the typographical error concerning the definite article *la*, which marks the "phallus" in the French publication of Lacan's "La Signification du phallus," speaks to a breakdown in symbolic structuration: "If 'the phallic signifier is intrinsically neutral,' then the signifier 'phallus,' the word in language, might be either feminine or masculine, epicene" (137).

37 Eve Sedgwick, for example, argues that the homosocial order annexes the figure of woman as the conduit through which homosexual desire is channeled. See *Between Men: English Literature and Male Homosocial Desire* (New York: Columbia University Press, 1985).

38 Freud, "Fetishism," 154.

39 Ibid., 153.

40 See Freud's discussion of anaclitic and narcissistic love in "On Narcissism: An Introduction," in Freud, *Standard Edition*, 14:87–91. In this essay, Freud names homosexuals, females, children, cats, and criminals as exemplary narcissists. See also Judith Butler's excellent discussion of normative heterosexuality as a melancholic renunciation of homosexual desire in *Gender Trouble: Feminism and the Subversion of Identity* (New York: Routledge, 1993), 57–72 and *The Psychic Life of Power: Theories in Subjection* (Stanford: Stanford University Press, 1997), 132–50.

41 A suitable parallel can be drawn from Freud's admonition in *The Ego and the Id* that, although the superego comes about through an abjection of homosexuality, it cannot ultimately enforce this prohibition, from which it is produced.

42 Earl Jackson Jr., "Scandalous Subjects: Robert Glück's Embodied Narratives," *differences: A Journal of Feminist Cultural Studies* 3.2 (summer 1991): 121.

43 In an earlier reading of the drama, I explored the material conditions around which Rice Queens might choose to pass. The identitarian bent with which I approached this first reading of *M. Butterfly* remains crucial in debates on identity-based politics. See my "In the Shadows of a Diva: Committing Homosexuality in David Henry Hwang's *M. Butterfly*," *Amerasia Journal* 20.1 (1994): 93–116. I hope that the current reading of *M. Butterfly* provides a supplementary angle from which to merge my arguments on the material and psychoanalytic levels.

44 Freud, "Fetishism," 156.

45 Mark Chiang, "A White Thing: Fetishism and Paranoia in the Nation," paper presented at the annual conference of the Association of Asian American Studies, University of Michigan, Ann Arbor, April 1994, 5. I thank Mark Chiang for allowing me to quote from his manuscript.

46 Lacan, in "Signification of the Phallus" (in *Écrits: A Selection*, trans. Alan Sheridan [New York: Norton, 1977], 281–91), states: "But one may, simply by reference to the function of the phallus, indicate the structures that will govern the relations between the sexes.

"Let us say that these relations will turn around a 'to be' and a 'to have,' which, by referring to a signifier, the phallus, have the opposed effect, on the one hand, of giving reality to the subject in this signifier, and, on the other, of derealizing the relations to be signified" (289).

47 As Lacan points out: "It should not be forgotten that the organ [the penis] that assumes this signifying function [of the phallus] takes on the value of a fetish" (ibid., 290).

48 Freud, "Splitting of the Ego," 276.

FOUR *Male Hysteria—Real and Imagined—in* Eat a Bowl of Tea *and* Pangs of Love

1 Some prominent female hysterics in Asian American literature include Miss Sasagawara in Hisaye Yamamoto's "The Legend of Miss Sasagawara," in *Seventeen Syllables and Other Stories* (Latham, NY: Kitchen Table/Women of Color Press, 1988), 20–33; Hualing Nieh's split narrator Mulberry/Peach in *Mulberry and Peach: Two Women of China,* trans. Jane Parish Yang with Linda Lappin (Boston: Beacon, 1981); the narrator in Wendy Law-Yone's *The Coffin Tree* (Boston: Beacon, 1983); and Jessica Hagedorn's Baby Alacran in *Dogeaters* (New York: Pantheon, 1990).

2 Maxine Hong Kingston, *The Woman Warrior: Memoirs of a Girlhood among Ghosts* (New York: Vintage, [1976] 1989), 181–82.

3 Louis Chu, *Eat a Bowl of Tea* (New York: Lyle Stuart, [1961] 1990); David Wong Louie, *Pangs of Love* (New York: Knopf, 1991).

4 For a brief overview of the history of female hysteria, see Charles Bernheimer, "Introduction: Part One," in *In Dora's Case: Freud—Hysteria—Feminism,* eds. Charles Bernheimer and Claire Kahane, 2d ed. (New York: Columbia University Press, 1985) 1–18. For a more detailed history of female hysteria, see Ilza Vieth's *Hysteria: The History of a Disease* (Chicago: University of Chicago Press, 1965). For a psychoanalytic account of female hysteria, see Monique David-Menard's *Hysteria from Freud to Lacan: Body and Language in Psychoanalysis,* trans. Catherine Porter (Ithaca: Cornell University Press, 1989).

5 Magnuson Act, Act of 17 December 1943, chap. 344, §1, 57 Stat. 600; and War Brides Act, Act of 28 December 1945, Pub. L. No. 271, 59 Stat. 659. Sucheng Chan notes that the 1945 War Brides Act, which "had initially excluded veterans of Asian ancestry, was amended in 1947 to include them. That fact enabled GIs to marry in Asia and to bring their brides back to the United States, where they started families. From the late 1940s through the 1950s and the first half of the 1960s, the number of Asian women entering the country exceeded the number of men." *Asian Americans: An Interpretive History* (Boston: Twayne, 1991), 140.

6 Gayatri Chakravorty Spivak, "Scattered Speculations on the Question of Culture Studies," in *Outside in the Teaching Machine* (New York: Routledge, 1993), 255–84; "Culture," in *A Critique of Postcolonial Reason: Toward a His-*

tory of the Vanishing Present (Cambridge: Harvard University Press, 1999), 312–421. Spivak defines the "new immigrant" in relation to the continuing influx of immigrants since the Immigration and Nationality Act of 1 October 1965—as those "groups escaping decolonization one way or the other" (393). *New immigrant* refers primarily to immigrants from Asia, the Caribbean, Central America, and Mexico. See also Lisa Lowe, *Immigrant Acts: On Asian American Cultural Politics* (Durham: Duke University Press, 1996); and Aiwha Ong, *Flexible Citizenship: The Cultural Logic of Transnationality* (Durham: Duke University Press, 1999).

7 Slavoj Žižek, *The Sublime Object of Ideology* (New York: Verso, 1989), 113.

8 See Bernheimer, "Introduction," on which the following historical summary of female hysteria draws.

9 Gerard Wajeman, *Le Maître et l'hystérique* (Paris: Navarin, 1982), 127.

10 Even as late as 1855, for instance, the *Dictionnaire de médecine* by Littré and Robin continued to deny the possibility of a male diagnosis of hysteria: "If one does not want to confuse hysteria with a great many other illnesses, one cannot locate the originary locus of this affliction in the brain. One can also not accept that such hysteria could be observed in the male sex: hysteria is an illness that is peculiar to the female sex" (Emile Littré and Albert Robin, *Dictionnaire de médecine* [Paris: J. B. Baillière, 1855]). It was not until 1878, with the publication of the fully revised fourteenth edition of the *Dictionnaire de médecine,* that this entry was emended, leaving out the claim that hysteria could not be observed in the male sex. Quoted in Ursula Link-Herr, " 'Male Hysteria': A Discourse Analysis," *Cultural Critique* 15 (spring 1990): 203.

11 See Jean-Martin Charcot, *Lectures on the Diseases of the Nervous System,* trans. George Sigerson (London: New Syndenham Society, 1877). See also Mark S. Micale, "Charcot and the Idea of Hysteria in the Male: Gender, Mental Science, and Medical Diagnosis in Late Nineteenth-Century France," *Medical History* 34 (1990): 363–411.

12 Sigmund Freud, "Observation of a Severe Case of Hemi-Anaesthesia in a Hysterical Male," in *The Standard Edition of the Complete Psychological Works of Sigmund Freud,* ed. James Strachey (London: Hogarth, 1955), 1: 25. Indeed, Freud's first medical lecture upon returning to Vienna from Charcot's clinic specifically concerned male rather than female hysteria. Daniel Boyarin writes that it is "well known that what most aroused the ire of the Viennese medical audience that heard Freud's first lecture upon returning from Charcot was the fact that it was about *male* hysteria" ("Freud's Baby, Fleiss's Maybe: Homophobia, Anti-Semitism, and the Invention of the Oedipus," *GLQ: A Journal of Lesbian and Gay Studies* 2.1–2 [1995]: 118; Boyarin's emphasis).

13 Jacques Lacan, "Kanzer Seminar at Yale University," trans. Barbara Johnson (1975), quoted in Shoshana Felman, *What Does a Woman Want? Reading and Sexual Difference* (Baltimore: John Hopkins University Press, 1993), 101.

14 Josef Breuer and Sigmund Freud, "On the Psychical Mechanism of Hysteri-

cal Phenomena: Preliminary Communication," in *Studies on Hysteria*, trans. James Strachey (New York: Basic Books, 1961), 7.

15 Ibid. Freud tells us that the most common memories of sexual seduction are female reminiscences of paternal seduction. It was the high incidence of female patients claiming seduction by the father that led Freud to posit the category of false, or screen, memories.

16 Ibid., 86.

17 Jacqueline Rose, "Dora: Fragment of an Analysis," in Bernheimer and Kahane, *In Dora's Case*, 138.

18 See Freud, *Standard Edition*, 1:262, in which Freud describes himself as a male hysteric.

19 For a history of male hysteria and Jewish identity, see Sander Gilman, *The Case of Sigmund Freud: Medicine and Identity at the Fin de Siècle* (Baltimore: Johns Hopkins University Press, 1993; Jonathan Geller, "'A Glance on the Nose': Freud's Inscription of Jewish Difference," *American Imago* 49 (1992): 427–44; and Ann Pellegrini, *Performance Anxieties: Staging Psychoanalysis, Staging Race* (New York: Routledge, 1997). For an analysis of male hysteria in relation to the traumas of modernity and industrialization, see Neil Hertz, "Medusa's Head: Male Hysteria under Political Pressure," *Representations* 4 (fall 1983): 26–54; Lynne Kirby, "Male Hysteria and Early Cinema," *Camera Obscura: A Journal of Feminism and Film Theory* 17 (1988): 113–31; Paul Smith, *Clint Eastwood: A Cultural Production* (Minneapolis: University of Minnesota Press, 1993); and Paul Smith, "Vas," *Camera Obscura: A Journal of Feminism and Film Theory* 17 (1988): 89–111.

20 See Hélène Cixous and Catherine Clément, "The Untenable," in Bernheimer and Kahane, *In Dora's Case*, 276–93. This essay is a dialogue between Cixous and Clément. As such, subsequent citations from this dialogue will be attributed to the specific speaker.

21 Philip Rieff, Introduction to *Dora: An Analysis of a Case of Hysteria*, ed. Philip Rieff (New York: Collier, 1963), 10.

22 In an increasingly industrial society, Bernheimer comments in "Introduction," "the Victorian woman was looked up to as representative of the purity, order, and serenity of earlier, less anxious times. Gentle, submissive, naive, and good, she was also expected to be strong in her righteousness, perfectly controlled in her decorous conduct, and skilled in her domestic managerial capacities. Faced with this conflict, numerous Victorian women developed unconscious defensive strategies whereby they disavowed the intense anger and aggressive impulses for which the culture gave them no outlet. Thus were generated the conversion reactions, prevalent throughout the latter part of the nineteenth century, whereby women transformed their repressed hostility and desire into physical symptoms that simultaneously acknowledged and disowned those feelings" (5–6).

23 In another respect, this refusal is politically ambivalent insofar as it is at least partly, if not mostly, unconscious. As such, this protest paradoxically marks the inability to protest as well.

24 Jane Gallop, "Keys to Dora," in Bernheimer and Kahane, *In Dora's Case*, 203.

25 See Louis Althusser, *"Lenin and Philosophy" and Other Essays*, trans. Ben Brewster (New York: Monthly Review Press, 1971), 174–75.

26 Slavoj Žižek, *For They Know Not What They Do: Enjoyment as a Political Factor* (New York: Verso, 1991), 101.

27 Quoted in Henry Abelove, "Freud, Male Homosexuality, and the Americans," in *The Lesbian and Gay Studies Reader*, ed. Henry Abelove, Michèle Aina Barale, and David Halperin (New York: Routledge, 1993), 387.

28 Smith, "Vas," 109.

29 Smith, *Clint Eastwood*, 170.

30 Link-Herr, "Male Hysteria," 216.

31 Jane Gallop offers an incisive analysis of class difference in female hysteria. She writes: "One of psychoanalysis's consistent errors is to reduce everything to a family paradigm. Sociopolitical questions are always brought back to the model father–mother–child. Class conflict and revolution are understood as a repetition of parent–child relations. This has always been the pernicious apoliticism of psychoanalysis. It has also been hard to argue against without totally rejecting psychoanalysis, since it is based upon the fundamental notion that everything we do as adults must repeat some infantile wish, and for most of us, the infantile world was the family. What is necessary to get beyond the dilemma is a recognition that the closed, cellular model of the family used in such psychoanalytic thinking is an idealization, a secondary revision of the family. The family never was, in any of Freud's texts, completely closed off from questions of economic class. And the most insistent locus of that intrusion into the family circle (intrusion of the symbolic into the imaginary) is the maid/governess/nurse. As Cixous says, 'She is the hole in the social cell' " ("Keys," 213).

32 The racial subject as the "native question" is expressed in Žižek's *The Sublime Object of Ideology* when the author observes that the mainstream media's coverage of the 1988 presidential election insistently configured Jesse Jackson's initial political successes by asking "What does Jackson really want?" Žižek continues: "The conclusion that we are here dealing with racism is further confirmed by the fact that this '*Che vuoi?*' erupts most violently in the purest, so to say distilled form of racism, in anti-Semitism: in the anti-Semitic perspective, the Jew is precisely a person about whom it is never clear 'what he really wants'—that is, his actions are always suspected of being guided by some hidden motives" (114).

33 The first immigration exclusion law directed against Chinese immigrants was passed in 1882 (Chinese Exclusion Act, chap. 126, 22 Stat. 58). Exclusion was subsequently renewed by Congress as well as extended to other Asian immigrant groups in 1892 (Act of 5 May 1892, chap. 60, 27 Stat. 25); 1902 (Act of 29 April 1902, chap. 641, 32 Stat. 176); and 1917 (Act of 5 February 1917, chap. 29, 39 Stat. 874). It was extended indefinitely in 1924 (Immigration Act of 1924, chap. 190, §131, 104 Stat. 4978). In addition, the Tydings-McDuffie Act (Act of 24 March 1934, 48 Stat. 456) restricted Filipino immi-

gration to fifty individuals a year. It was not until 1943, in response to a political and military alliance between China and the United States during World War II, that Congress repealed these discriminatory laws and legally paved the way for Chinese women to enter the country with the War Brides Act of 1945 (Act of 28 December 1945, Pub. L, No. 271, 59 Stat. 659). For a history of this exclusion, as well as a description of antimiscegenation laws and laws barring the entry of Chinese wives (such as the Page Act Law, Act of 18 February 1875, chap. 80, 18 Stat. 318), see Sucheng Chan's *Asian Americans: An Interpretive History* (Boston: Twayne, 1991); and Bill Ong Hing, *Making and Remaking Asian America through Immigration Policy, 1850–1990* (Stanford: Stanford University Press, 1993).

34 Even the suggestion that Ben Loy's eroded manhood is the result of organic causes, the dissipated result of too many prostitutes and venereal disease, takes on a racialized inflection. The prostitutes Ben Loy frequents before marriage are all white women, their whiteness a metonymic inflection of the mainstream community that unmans the Chinese American male.

35 Sigmund Freud, "Femininity," in Freud, *Standard Edition*, 22:134.

36 Richard Fung, "Looking for My Penis: The Eroticized Asian in Gay Porn Video," in *How Do I Look?* ed. Bad Object Choices (Seattle: Bay Press, 1991), 153.

37 *Eat a Bowl of Tea,* dir. Wayne Wang (New York: American Playhouse, 1989).

38 William Shakespeare, *Othello, the Moor of Venice* (New York: Penguin, 1971).

39 Marita Sturken, *Tangled Memories: The Vietnam War, the AIDS Epidemic, and the Politics of Remembering* (Berkeley: University of California Press, 1997), 73. Departing from Sturken, Sanda Mayzaw Lwin writes about Ichiro and the wounded Kenji in John Okada's novel *No-No Boy:* "Although both men were born on 'the dirt of America,' in Ichiro's eyes, Kenji's stump provides visible proof not only of his military service—but also of his right as a full-fledged citizen to claim America as his land. Ironically, it is his partial limb—the stump—that Ichiro reads as a sign of full membership in the U.S. nation." See "The Constitution of Asian America," Ph.D. diss., Columbia University, 1999, 122. This discussion of the U.S. military also brings to mind the segregated 442nd regiment of Japanese American soldiers during World War II, the most highly decorated battalion and the battalion that suffered the most casualties.

40 Victor Burgin, *In/Different Spaces: Place and Memory in Visual Culture* (Berkeley: University of California Press, 1996), 130.

41 Edward W. Said, "Secular Criticism," in *The World, the Text, and the Critic* (Cambridge: Harvard University Press, 1983), 17.

42 Sau-ling Cynthia Wong, "Chinese/Asian American Men in the 1990s: Displacement, Impersonation, Paternity, and Extinction in David Wong Louie's *Pangs of Love,*" in *Privileging Positions: The Sites of Asian American Studies,* eds. Gary Y. Okihiro, Marilyn Alquizola, Dorothy Fujita Rony, and K. Scott Wong (Pullman: Washington State University Press, 1995), 187–88.

43 Wong uses the original *Aiiieeeee!* introduction from 1975 to analyze the

concept of an "ever-evolving Asian American culture unencumbered by expectations of 'authenticity.'" In the era of the Asian American model minority—the era of Asian American citizenship—this promise seems to remain unfulfilled. In a current Asian American era no longer under the threat of biological extinction, the *Aiiieeeee!* group has insistently turned to the idea of cultural authenticity and biological purity. Indeed, the publication of Chin et al.'s *The Big Aiiieeeee!* in 1991 witnessed the insistent return to (heterosexual) debates about "realness" and "fakeness" in Asian America, a topic explored in the epilogue.

44 Jeffery Chan, introduction to the 1979 edition of *Eat a Bowl of Tea*, 5.

45 Not all of Louie's short stories are set in the multicultural 1980s, although nine of eleven are.

46 In fact, the term *Chinatown*, the ghettoized urban communities that initially formed in response to racial discrimination, no longer adequately describe Chinese American demographic patterns. See Timothy Fong's study of Monterey Park in *The First Suburban Chinatown: The Remaking of Monterey Park, California* (Philadelphia: Temple University Press, 1994).

47 Manini Samarth, "Affirmations: Speaking the Self into Being," *Parnassus Poetry in Review* 17.1 (1992): 99.

48 For an exploration of this dynamic of racial melancholia and assimilation, see David L. Eng and Shinhee Han, "A Dialogue on Racial Melancholia," *Psychoanalytic Dialogues* 10.4 (2000): 667–700.

49 Bob H. Suzuki, "Education and the Socialization of Asian Americans: A Revisionist Analysis of the 'Model Minority' Thesis," *Amerasia Journal* 4.2 (1977): 23–51. See also Mari J. Matsuda, "We Will Not Be Used. Are Asian-Americans the Racial Bourgeoisie?" in *Where is Your Body? And Other Essays on Race, Gender, and the Law* (Boston: Beacon Press, 1996), 149–59.

50 Homi Bhabha, "Of Mimicry and Man: The Ambivalence of Colonial Discourse," *October* 28 (spring 1984): 126, 130; Bhabha's emphasis.

EPILOGUE *Out Here and Over There*

1 For a summary of the sojourner and model minority theses, see Sucheng Chan, *Asian Americans: An Interpretive History* (Boston: Twayne, 1991). It is worth considering how the 1965 Immigration and Nationality Act, which facilitated an explosion in Asian American immigration, contributed to the historical rise of the model-minority myth in the late 1960s. To what extent, one might ask, does 1965 provide a pivotal moment in which the image of Asian Americans as "alien" (sojourners, the yellow peril) shifted into a more common stereotype of Asian Americans as "whiter than white" (the model minority)? To what extent did this shift occur earlier in relation to *Brown v. Board of Education* and its juridical proclamation of a color-blind society?

2 The diaspora debate in Asian American studies is now a heated one, and the place of transnational issues within the field is the subject of wide deliberation. In the late 1990s, the question of diaspora became *the* ques-

tion gripping Asian American studies on its twenty-fifth anniversary in the academy. This chapter intervenes by exploring how queerness functions in this debate. For the diaspora debate, see *Amerasia Journal* 22.1–2 (1995), a special issue on "Thinking Theory in Asian American Studies," and *Amerasia Journal* 22.3 (1996), a special issue on "Transnationalism, Media, and Asian American Studies." In this chapter, I use *diaspora* in a rather capacious manner to encompass several meanings and contemporary phenomena: the global scattering of peoples of Asian origin; the shifting critical emphasis from domestic to global in the study of nationalism and nation-states; the transnational movement of both economic, cultural, and intellectual capital; the global commodification of sexuality; the transnational displacement of flexible labor; and the increasing permeability of national borders through electronic media, communications, and international travel. While recognizing the historical specificites of these various issues and trends, my hope is to provide some speculations that may serve to anchor future investigations of diaspora and queerness in Asian American studies.

3 A quick survey of recent book titles in Asian American studies—including my own—illustrates this Asian America phenomenon. For instance, see Emma Gee, *Counterpoint: Perspectives on Asian America* (Los Angeles: Asian American Studies Center, UCLA, 1976); Roger Daniels, *Asian America: Chinese and Japanese in the United States since 1850* (Seattle: University of Washington Press, 1988); Bill Ong Hing, *Making and Remaking Asian America through Immigration Policy: 1850–1990* (Stanford: Stanford University Press, 1993); Karin Aguilar–San Juan, ed., *The State of Asian America: Activism and Resistance in the 1990s* (Boston: South End Press, 1994); and Lane Hirabayashi, ed., *Teaching Asian America: Diversity and the Problem of Community* (Boulder: Rowman and Littlefield, 1997). We might consider the term *Asian America* along with spatial terminology in other ethnic studies fields. Scholars in ethnic studies do not, for example, use the term *African America* or *Latino/Chicano America* with any notable frequency. However, the term *Black America* in African American studies and *Aztlán* in Latino/Chicano studies may gesture toward a set of concerns similar to those invoked by *Asian America*, warranting a more thorough comparison.

4 Sau-ling Cynthia Wong, "Denationalization Reconsidered: Asian American Cultural Criticism at a Theoretical Crossroads," *Amerasia Journal* 21.1–2 (1995): 4. Against this idea of landlessness and psychic dispossession of home, how might we think about the history of alien-land laws that barred Asian Americans from owning property and current stereotypes of Asians and Asian Americans as voracious consumers and collectors of "prime" national real estate?

5 Oscar V. Campomanes, "Filipinos in the United States and Their Literature of Exile," in *Reading the Literatures of Asian America*," eds. Shirley Geok-lin Lim and Amy Ling (Philadelphia: Temple University Press, 1992), 51.

6 If social affirmation is unrealizable for queers, then "in" and "out" of the closet is equally nebulous. The closet becomes an impossibly blurred space

of private concern and public regulation. This continual blurring of in and out—and of public and private space—divests queer subjects of access to traditional notions of citizenship (e.g., the right to privacy) in a bourgeois ordering of the nation-state and public sphere. See Jürgen Habermas's *Structural Transformation of the Public Sphere: An Inquiry into a Category of Bourgeois Society*, trans. Thomas Burger (Cambridge: MIT Press, 1989). See also Bruce Robbins, ed., *The Phantom Public Sphere* (Minneapolis: University of Minnesota Press, 1993), for critical readings of Habermas and the public sphere in relation to queer and feminist issues.

7 *Paris Is Burning*, dir. Jennie Livingston (New York: Off-White Productions, 1991).

8 This loss of home is a function not only of queerness but of racism and poverty. Livingston's film is exemplary insofar as these three axes of social difference are highlighted in their multiple crossings.

9 See, for example, Lauren Berlant and Elizabeth Freeman, "Queer Nationality," in Lauren Berlant, *The Queen of America Goes to Washington City: Essays on Sex and Citizenship* (Durham: Duke University Press, 1997), 145–73; and Lisa Duggan, "Queering the State," in Lisa Duggan and Nan D. Hunter, *Sex: Sexual Dissent and Political Culture* (New York: Routledge, 1995), 179–93.

10 Khachig Tölölyan, "The Nation-State and Its Others: In Lieu of a Preface," *Diaspora: A Journal of Transnational Studies* 1.1 (spring 1991): 4–5.

11 JeeYeun Lee, "Toward a Queer Korean American Diaspora," in *Q & A: Queer in Asian America*, eds. David L. Eng and Alice Y. Hom (Philadelphia: Temple University Press, 1998), 194.

12 See Martin Manalansan, "In the Shadows of Stonewall: Gay Transnational Politics and the Diasporic Dilemma," in *The Politics of Culture in the Shadow of Capital*, eds. Lisa Lowe and David Lloyd (Durham: Duke University Press, 1997), 485–505; and Gayatri Gopinath, "Nostalgia, Desire, Diaspora: South Asian Sexualities in Motion," *positions: east asia cultures critique* 5.2 (fall 1997): 467–89.

13 See Yen Le Espiritu, *Asian American Panethnicity: Bridging Institutions and Identities* (Philadelphia: Temple University Press, 1992); and William Wei, *The Asian American Movement* (Philadelphia: Temple University Press, 1993), for their historical accounts of the emergence of the Asian American movement and the development of Asian American studies within the academy.

14 Michael Omi and Dana Takagi, "Thinking Theory in Asian American Studies," *Amerasia Journal* 21.1–2 (1995): xii.

15 Frank Chin, Jeffery Paul Chan, Lawson Fusao Inada, and Shawn Wong, preface to *Aiiieeeee! An Anthology of Asian-American Writers*, eds. Frank Chin, Jeffery Paul Chan, Lawson Fusao Inada, and Shawn Wong (Garden City, NY: Anchor, 1975), x.

16 The key question here is how public agency and the nation-state, which are constituted as male, depend upon the possession and control of the popu-

larly devalued private realm of the home, which is constituted as female and homosexual. The seamless narration of the nation is thus dependent upon subordinating and disciplining the feminine and homosexual to the masculine. See Nancy Fraser's analysis of Habermas's public sphere in relation to gender, "Rethinking the Public Sphere: A Contribution to the Critique of Actually Existing Democracy" in Robbins, *Phantom Public Sphere*, 1–32. See also in the same volume Michael Warner's queer analysis, "The Mass Public and the Mass Subject" (234–56).

17 Chin et al., *Aiiieeeee!* x.

18 It is important to remember the historical roots of the term *Asian American:* it has always served as a coalitional label under which different Asian groups have come together for the promotion of common interests and for purposes of political representation, economic action, and cultural identification (e.g., in census counts, voting issues, and cultural and social services funding). As a label, *Asian American* implies a certain unified identity that works to smooth over diverse racial, ethnic, and national backgrounds, languages, sexualities, and religions.

19 Jeffrey Paul Chan, Frank Chin, Lawson Fusao Inada, and Shawn Wong, introduction to *The Big Aiiieeeee! An Anthology of Chinese American and Japanese American Literature* (New York: Meridian, 1991), xiii.

20 The phrase "devoid of manhood" is from Frank Chin and Jeffery Paul Chan, "Racist Love," in *Seeing through Shuck*, ed. Richard Kostelanetz (New York: Ballantine, 1972), 68.

21 See King-Kok Cheung, "The Woman Warrior versus The Chinaman Pacific: Must a Chinese American Critic Choose between Feminism and Heroism?" in *Conflicts in Feminism*, eds. Marriane Hirsch and Evelyn Fox Keller (New York: Routledge, 1990), 234–51, for an excellent discussion of the feminism/heroism debate in Asian American studies.

22 Chin and Chan, "Racist Love," 68.

23 The paternal complicities of nationalist projects are most incisively critiqued by feminists in postcolonial studies such as Rey Chow, Chandra Mohanty, and Gayatri Chakravorty Spivak. Much of this critique still needs to be absorbed in Asian American studies.

24 In highlighting the private/public contradiction of the domestic, I intend to claim both realms for Asian Americans and queers and not privilege one over the other. The issue of private/public that I engage here in relation to the national terrain is expanded in the final section to include a discussion of private/public in relation to the global arena. In terms of claiming the public sphere on both the domestic and diasporic levels, one might consider the concept of oppositional public spheres, what Fraser, in "Rethinking the Public Sphere," calls subaltern counterpublics.

25 This claim of vexed hyphenation is not a difficult one to substantiate. Pick up any mainstream—even Asian American—newspaper or magazine to see how the hyphen appears with confounding arbitrariness.

26 While many non-Western ethnic groups have tenuous claims on the nation,

the persistent mainstream configuration of Asian Americans as exterior to the nation-state takes on particular historical dimensions and distinctions through the orthographic hyphen. This debate has not, to my knowledge, been as widely deliberated in other fields of ethnic studies.

27 The mistaken perception of Chinese American Vincent Chin for a Japanese autoworker is only one of many unfortunate manifestations of this phenomenon. In 1982, Chin was murdered by two unemployed Detroit autoworkers who mistook him for a Japanese.

28 Risking the hyphen would also force us to confront the status of *American* in the term *Asian American,* making us consider American studies outside its domestic locale and in multiple spaces. While there has been a long historical antagonism between East Asian Studies—perceived as orientalist—and Asian American studies, any serious consideration of *Asian* in *Asian American* would warrant the theoretical linking of these two fields.

29 Sucheta Mazumdar, "Asian American Studies and Asian Studies: Rethinking Roots," in *Asian Americans: Comparative and Global Perspectives,* eds. Shirley Hune, Hyung-chan Kim, Stephen S. Fugita, and Amy Ling (Pullman: Washington State University Press, 1991), 29–44. It might be useful to note that as a group that has experienced the longest and most specific legacy of racial exclusion from the United States, it would be impossible to understand the legal status of Asian Americans outside a transnational model of racialization. How do we bring together current shifts in immigration patterns with the hyphen debate on alienness?

The sojourner paradigm of Asian American settlement and the status of the legal citizen-subject of the U.S. nation-state were at odds from the nineteenth century until the 1943–65 period. Prior to the Magnuson Act (Act of 17 December 1943, chap. 344, §1, 57 Stat. 600), the McCarran-Walter Act (Act of 27 June 1952, chap. 477, 66 Stat. 163), and the Immigration and Nationality Act (Act of 1 October 1965, Pub. L. No. 89-236, 79 Stat. 911), race was the determining factor for exclusion laws that prevented the unification of non-European families and the naturalization of Asians. The first of these restrictions, the Chinese Exclusion Act of 1882 (Chinese Exclusion Act, chap. 126, 22 Stat. 58), was passed in response to a national economic recession and the perception of Chinese immigrants as unassimilable coolie labor. The 1882 act was followed by similar renewals in 1892 (Act of 5 May 1892, chap. 60, 27 Stat. 25), 1902 (Act of 29 April 1902, chap. 641, 32 Stat. 176), 1907 (Act of 2 March 1907, chap. 2534, §3, 34 Stat. 1228), and 1917 (Act of 5 February 1917, chap. 29, 39 Stat. 874), which also expanded exclusion to other Asian immigrant groups. The 1924 Immigration Act (Immigration Act of 1924, chap. 190, §131, 104 Stat. 4978) extended these provisions indefinitely while establishing immigration quotas for Northern European nations alone.

30 Wong, "Denationalization," 3.

31 See, for example, Carlos Bulosan's 1943 novel *America Is in the Heart* (Seattle: University of Washington Press, 1973), for a narrative of American school

missionaries and their teaching of nationalist ideology. In chapter 9, for example, the protagonist learns about Lincoln, "a Poor boy [who] became President of the United States!" and who "died for a black person" (69–70).

32 See Lisa Lowe, *Immigrant Acts: On Asian American Cultural Politics* (Durham: Duke University Press, 1996), 159.

33 Jenny Sharpe, "Is the United States Postcolonial? Transnationalism, Immigration, and Race," *Diaspora* 4 (fall 1995): 188.

34 Satellite people (a.k.a. "Astronauts") maintain residences in several countries, traveling back and forth in accordance with immigration residency requirements and job demands. Parachute children, the offspring of satellite people, are left alone in the United States for schooling and separated from their parents for long periods. Reverse settlers are Asian Americans who emigrate to Asia for job-related economic opportunities. See Aihwa Ong, *Flexible Citizenship: The Cultural Logic of Transnationality* (Durham: Duke University Press, 1999).

35 The September 1996 passage of the Illegal Immigration Reform and Immigrant Responsibility Act (much of which went into effect on 1 April 1997), Pub. L. No. 104-208, 110 Stat. 3009-546, is but one unanalyzed effect. The increase in Asian American immigration from outside of East Asia (China, Japan, and Korea) and the Philippines is another.

36 Saskia Sassen, "Whose City Is It? Globalization and the Formation of New Claims," *Public Culture* 8 (1996): 213.

37 The national anxiety produced by contemporary global formations of capital and labor have caused nation-states to clamp down on their borders—literally and figuratively—both in the form of patrolling national boundaries and the form of patrolling what constitutes good citizenship. In the United States, this focus on borders, for instance, has resulted not only in the prevention of illegal immigrants and immigrants of color from entering the nation but in the criminalization of African Americans, poor people, single mothers (welfare reform), and even Asian/American lobbyists. See Saskia Sassen, "Beyond Sovereignty: Immigration Policy Making Today," *Social Justice* 23 (fall 1996): 9–19.

38 Lisa Lowe, "Heterogeneity, Hybridity, Multiplicity: Asian American Differences," in Lowe, *Immigrant Acts,* 83.

39 *Amerasia Journal* is one of the oldest serial publications in the field of Asian American studies. Founded at Yale University, it is now housed at UCLA's Center for Asian American Studies.

40 Dana Takagi, "Maiden Voyage: Excursions into Sexuality and Identity Politics in Asian America," *Amerasia Journal* 20.1 (1994): 2.

41 I use *gay* and *lesbian* to describe the largely identity-based political and academic movements that arose after Stonewall in response to the dominant, pathologizing medico-legal discourse of the "homosexual." In its publicness, as Rosalind Morris suggests, the notion of gay is often conflated with the issue of same-sex practices—practices that are often thought to be

symptomatic of identity. I differentiate *gay* and *lesbian* from the term *queer*, which I believe eschews a political platform based exclusively on sexual identity and practices, and the polarization of homo- and heterosexuality. Use of the term *queer* is not just generational; as Michael Warner points out, "'queer' gets a critical edge by defining itself against the normal rather than the heterosexual" (Introduction to *Fear of a Queer Planet: Queer Politics and Social Theory*, ed. Michael Warner [Minneapolis: University of Minnesota Press, 1993], xxvi). Initially a designation of terror and shame, *queer* in contemporary usage has been resignified in a rather open and capacious context—one that can be used simultaneously to discuss the politics of the personal, to question a spectrum of personal identities, to act against normalizing ideologies, and to resist the historical terror of social phobia and violence. We must remember that *gay, lesbian,* and *queer* are not mutually exclusive terms. Gayness might provide an ideal, though not exclusive, grounds for queer practices, and queers can often be "lesbians and gays in other contexts—as for example where leverage can be gained through bourgeois propriety, or through minority-rights discourse, or through more gender-marked language (it probably won't replace lesbian feminism)" (Warner, *Queer Planet*, xxviii). While *queer* has been used as a shorthand term to name a population of individuals with a stake in nonnormative, oppositional politics, the term also harbors homogenizing impulses that serve to erase some of the racial and gendered differences (lesbian feminism being one example) that I explore in this chapter.

42 Omi and Takagi, "Thinking Theory," xiii.

43 Certainly not immune to similar accusations concerning the co-optation of special rights, members of mainstream gay and lesbian organizations must think through the particular political difficulties and contradictory agendas that national issues like gay marriage and affirmative action pose, both for individual queers of color who hold multiple affiliations with various political causes and for the politics of coalition building. The consideration of Asian American identity in a queer and diasporic context is complicated by mainstream gay and lesbian activism's resistance to theorizing itself outside of U.S. national borders. That the dominant focus of current gay and lesbian activism is on domestic issues and the claiming of equal rights obscures the international genealogy of queer activism and its reliance on the global. In claiming equal rights and access to the queer nation, queer activism reifies the U.S. nation-state as the privileged site for oppositional politics in ways reminiscent of the Asian American cultural nationalist project, which calls for vigilant interrogation.

44 See Masao Miyoshi, "A Borderless World? From Colonialism to Transnationalism and the Decline of the Nation-State," *Critical Inquiry* 19 (1993): 726–51, for a concise summary of the economic and political shifts in the 1980s that allowed for the rampant spread of multinational capital and the global restructuring of these economic resources as transnational institutions.

45 However, given the current mainstreaming of the gay and lesbian movement and the waning public attention to the AIDS crisis, the future of queer activism looks rather bleak.

46 The gay and lesbian liberation movement that emerged following the Stonewall era was largely based on a politics restricted to sexual identity and practices. The new queer social movements are often based, instead, on the critique of identity politics and the discursive production of the subject. Queer activism's critique of the subject and its reorganization of coalitional interests along the lines of political goals needs to be considered in the context of racial differences.

47 *The Wedding Banquet*, dir. Ang Lee (Taipei: Central Motion Pictures Corporation, 1993); R. Zamora Linmark, *Rolling the R's* (New York: Kaya Productions, 1995).

48 See filmmaker Richard Fung's "Looking for My Penis: The Eroticized Asian in Gay Porn Video," in *How Do I Look?* ed. Bad Object Choices (Seattle: Bay Press, 1991), 145–60. Fung writes that in Western society "the Asian man is defined by a striking absence down there. And if Asian men have no sexuality, how can we have homosexuality?" (148). In the mainstream heterosexual community, Asian American men have had to contend with the pervasive stereotype of themselves as the "emasculated sissy" (Frank Chin's Charlie Chan and Fu Manchu syndrome). These mainstream portrayals of enervated Asian American members recirculate within gay communities, where queer Asian American men find themselves repositioned as passive and feminized "bottoms"—impotent Cio-Cio-Sans plucked from the orientalized stages of *Madama Butterfly*.

49 David L. Eng, "*The Wedding Banquet:* You're Not Invited and Some Other Ancillary Thoughts," *Artspiral* 7 (fall 1993): 8–10.

50 Mark Chiang, "Coming out into the Global System: Postmodern Patriarchies and Transnational Sexualities in *The Wedding Banquet*," in *Q & A: Queer in Asian America*," eds. David L. Eng and Alice Y. Hom (Philadelphia: Temple University Press, 1998), 383.

51 Chiang adds that the "multicultural, non-heterosexual family formed by Wai-Tung and Simon at the end of the film is in sharp contrast to the representation of women's liberation offered to Wei-Wei. Although it is unclear what kind of arrangement she and Wai Tung will eventually come to, the decision to keep the baby drastically reduces her options, foreclosing the possibility of withdrawal from the global system" (ibid., 384).

52 Leslie Sklair labels this class of global citizen the transnational capitalist class. See Leslie Sklair, *Sociology of the Global System*, 2d ed. (Baltimore: Johns Hopkins University Press, 1995).

53 Wong, "Denationalization," 17; Wong's emphasis.

54 Chandan Reddy, "History, Allegory, Sexuality: The Minors of Linmark's *Rolling the R's*." Paper presented at the annual conference of the American Studies Association, Kansas City, Missouri, 31 October 1996. I thank Chandan Reddy for allowing me to quote from his essay.

BIBLIOGRAPHY

Films

Eat a Bowl of Tea. 1989. Directed by Wayne Wang. New York: American Playhouse.

History and Memory. 1991. Directed by Rea Tajiri. New York: Women Make Movies.

M. Butterfly. 1993. Directed by David Cronenberg. Burbank: Warner Home Video.

Out in Silence. 1994. Directed by Christine Choy. San Francisco: National Asian American Telecommunications Association.

Paris Is Burning. 1991. Directed by Jennie Livingston. New York: Off-White Productions.

Strawberry Fields. 1997. Directed by Rea Tajiri. Los Angeles: Phaedra Cinema.

Two Lies. 1989. Directed by Pamela Tom. Los Angeles: University of California at Los Angeles Film School.

The Wedding Banquet. 1993. Directed by Ang Lee. Taipei: Central Motion Pictures Corporation.

Who Killed Vincent Chin? 1988. Directed by Christine Choy and Renee Tajima-Pena. New York: Filmmakers Library.

Government Documents, Statutes, and Legal Cases

Act of 18 February 1875, chap. 80, 18 Stat. 318 (Page Act Law).

In re Ah Yup, 1F. Cas. 223 (c.c.d. Ca 1878).

Chinese Exclusion Act, chap. 126, 22 Stat. 58 (1882).

Act of 9 July 1884, chap. 220, 23 Stat. 115.

Act of 5 May 1892, chap. 60, 27 Stat. 25 (Geary Amendment).

Plessy v. Ferguson, 163 U.S. 537 (1896).

Act of 29 April 1902, chap. 641, 32 Stat. 176.

Act of 27 April 1904, chap. 1630, 33 Stat. 428.

Act of 2 March 1907, chap. 2534, §3, 34 Stat. 1228 (Gentleman's Agreement).

Act of 5 February 1917, chap. 29, 39 Stat. 874.

Immigration Act of 1924, chap. 190, §131, 104 Stat. 4978 (Johnson-Reed Act).

Act of 24 March 1934, 48 Stat. 456 (Tydings-McDuffie Act).

Report by Curtis B. Munson, "Japanese on the West Coast." Attached to memo from John Franklin Carter to President Roosevelt, 7 November 1941. FDRL, PSF 106, Stimson, CWRIC 3673–89.

Memo from J. Edgar Hoover to Attorney General, 2 February 1942. FBI, CWRIC 5794.

Telephone conversation between DeWitt and McCloy, 3 February 1942. NARS, Record Group 107, CWRIC 131–40.

Executive Order 9066 (19 February 1942), National Archives, General Records of the U.S. Government, Record Group 11.

President Franklin D. Roosevelt's (No-No Boy) Loyalty Oath, 29 January 1943.

General DeWitt, testimony before House Naval Affairs Subcommittee, 13 April 1943. NARS, Record Group 338, CWRIC 1725–28.

Hirabayashi v. U.S., 320 U.S. 81 (1943).

Yasui v. U.S., 320 U.S. 115 (1943).

Act of 17 December 1943, chap. 344, §1, 57 Stat. 600 (Magnuson Act).

Korematsu v. U.S., 323 U.S. 214 (1944).

Ex Parte Endo, 323 U.S. 283 (1944).

Act of 28 December 1945, Pub. L. No. 271, 59 Stat. 659 (War Brides Act).

Act of 27 June 1952, chap. 477, 66 Stat. 163 (McCarran-Walter Act/Immigration and Nationality Act of 1952).

Brown v. Board of Education, 347 U.S. 483, 489 (1954).

Act of 1 October 1965, Pub. L. No. 89-236, 79 Stat. 911 (Hart-Geller Act/Immigration and Nationality Act Amendments).

Loving v. Virginia, 388 U.S. 1 (1967).

Illegal Immigration Reform and Immigrant Responsibility Act of 1996, Pub. L. No. 104–208, 110 Stat. 3009-546.

Published Sources

Abbas, Ackbar. *Hong Kong: Culture and the Politics of Disappearance.* Minneapolis: University of Minnesota Press, 1997.

Abel, Elizabeth, Barbara Christian, and Helene Moglen, eds. *Female Subjects in Black and White: Race, Psychoanalysis, Feminism.* Berkeley: University of California Press, 1997.

Abelove, Henry. "Freud, Male Homosexuality, and the Americans." In *The Lesbian and Gay Studies Reader,* edited by Henry Abelove, Michèle Aina Barale, and David Halperin, 381–93. New York: Routledge, 1993.

Aguilar-San Juan, Karin, ed. *The State of Asian America: Activism and Resistance in the 1990s.* Boston: South End Press, 1994.

Alarcón, Norma. "The Theoretical Subject(s) of *This Bridge Called My Back* and Anglo-American Feminism." In *Making Face, Making Soul: Haciendo Caras,* edited by Gloria Anzaldúa, 356–69. San Francisco: Aunt Lute, 1990.

Althusser, Louis. *"Lenin and Philosophy" and Other Essays.* Translated by Ben Brewster. New York: Monthly Review Press, 1971.

Althusser, Louis. *For Marx.* Translated by Ben Brewster. New York: Verso, 1990.

Barthes, Roland. *Camera Lucida: Reflections on Photography.* Translated by Richard Howard. New York: Hill and Wang, 1981.

Bazin, André. "The Ontology of the Photographic Image." In *What Is Cinema?* Translated by Hugh Gray, 1:9–16. Berkeley: University of California Press, 1967.

Belasco, David. *Six Plays: Madame Butterfly, Du Barry, The Darling of the Gods, Adrea, The Girl of the Golden West, The Return of Peter Grimm.* Boston: Little, Brown, 1928.

Benjamin, Walter. "Theses on the Philosophy of History." In *Illuminations: Essays and Reflections,* edited by Hannah Arendt, 253–64. New York: Schocken, 1969.

Benjamin, Walter. "The Work of Art in the Age of Mechanical Reproduction." In *Illuminations: Essays and Reflections,* edited by Hannah Arendt, 217–51. New York: Schocken, 1969.

Bergner, Gwen. "Who Is That Masked Woman? or the Role of Gender in Fanon's *Black Skin, White Masks.*" *PMLA* 110.1 (January 1995): 75–88.

Berlant, Lauren, and Elizabeth Freeman. "Queer Nationality." In Lauren Berlant, *The Queen of America Goes to Washington City: Essays on Sex and Citizenship,* 145–73. Durham: Duke University Press, 1997.

Bernheimer, Charles. Introduction to part 1 of *In Dora's Case: Freud—Hysteria—Feminism,* 2d ed., edited by Charles Bernheimer and Claire Kahane, 1–18. New York: Columbia University Press, 1985.

Bernheimer, Charles, and Claire Kahane, eds. *In Dora's Case: Freud—Hysteria—Feminism.* 2d ed. New York: Columbia University Press, 1985.

Bhabha, Homi. *The Location of Culture.* New York: Routledge, 1994.

Bhabha, Homi. "Of Mimicry and Man: The Ambivalence of Colonial Discourse." *October* 28 (1984): 125–33.

Borch-Jacobsen, Mikkel. *Lacan: The Absolute Master.* Translated by Douglas Brick. Stanford: Stanford University Press, 1991.

Boyarin, Daniel. "Freud's Baby, Fliess's Maybe: Homophobia, Anti-Semitism, and the Invention of Oedipus." *GLQ: A Journal of Lesbian and Gay Studies* 2.1–2 (winter-spring 1995): 115–47.

Breuer, Josef, and Sigmund Freud. "On the Psychical Mechanism of Hysterical Phenomena: Preliminary Communication." In *Studies on Hysteria.* Translated by James Strachey, 3–17. New York: Basic Books, 1961.

Brown, Wendy. *States of Injury: Power and Freedom in Late Modernity.* Princeton: Princeton University Press, 1995.

Bruno, Giuliana. "Ramble City: Postmodernism and *Blade Runner.*" In *Alien Zone: Cultural Theory and Contemporary Science Fiction,* ed. Annette Kuhn (London: Verso, 1990).

Bulosan, Carlos. *America Is in the Heart.* Seattle: University of Washington Press, [1943] 1973.

Burgin, Victor. *In/Different Spaces: Place and Memory in Visual Culture.* Berkeley: University of California Press, 1996.

Butler, Judith. "Against Proper Objects." *differences: A Journal of Feminist Cultural Studies* 6.2–3 (summer-fall 1994): 1–26.

Butler, Judith. *Bodies That Matter: On the Discursive Limits of "Sex."* New York: Routledge, 1993.

Butler, Judith. "Imitation and Gender Insubordination." In *The Lesbian and Gay Studies Reader,* edited by Henry Abelove, Michèle Aina Barale, and David M. Halperin, 307–20. New York: Routledge, 1993.

Butler, Judith. *The Psychic Life of Power: Theories in Subjection.* Stanford: Stanford University Press, 1997.

Cadava, Eduardo. *Words of Light: Theses on the Photography of History.* Princeton: Princeton University Press, 1997.

Campomanes, Oscar V. "Filipinos in the United States and Their Literature of Exile." In *Reading the Literatures of Asian America,* edited by Shirley Geok-lin Lim and Amy Ling, 49–78. Philadelphia: Temple University Press, 1992.

Chan, Jeffery. Introduction to the 1979 edition of Louie Chu, *Eat a Bowl of Tea,* 1–5. New York: Lyle Stuart, [1961] 1990.

Chan, Jeffery Paul, Frank Chin, Lawson Fusao Inada, and Shawn Wong, eds. *The Big Aiiieeeee! An Anthology of Chinese American and Japanese American Literature.* New York: Meridian, 1991.

Chan, Jeffrey Paul, Frank Chin, Lawson Fusao Inada, and Shawn Wong. Introduction to *The Big Aiiieeeee! An Anthology of Chinese American and Japanese American Literature,* edited by Jeffrey Paul Chan, Frank Chin, Lawson Fusao Inada, and Shawn Wong, xi–xvi. New York: Meridian, 1991.

Chan, Sucheng. *Asian Americans: An Interpretive History.* Boston: Twayne, 1991.

Chan, Sucheng, ed. *Entry Denied: Exclusion and the Chinese Community in America, 1882–1943.* Philadelphia: Temple University Press, 1991.

Chan, Sucheng. "The Exclusion of Chinese Women, 1870–1943." In *Entry Denied: Exclusion and the Chinese Community in America, 1882–1943,* edited by Sucheng Chan, 94–146. Philadelphia: Temple University Press, 1991.

Charcot, Jean-Martin. *Lectures on the Diseases of the Nervous System.* Trans. George Sigerson. London: New Sydenham Society, 1877.

Cheng, Anne Anlin. "The Melancholy of Race." *Kenyon Review* 19.1 (1997): 49–61.

Cheng, Anne Anlin. *The Melancholy of Race.* New York: Oxford University Press, forthcoming 2001.

Cheung, King-Kok. *Articulate Silences: Hisaye Yamamoto, Maxine Hong Kingston, Joy Kogawa.* Ithaca: Cornell University Press, 1993.

Cheung, King-Kok. "The Woman Warrior versus The Chinaman Pacific: Must a Chinese American Critic Choose between Feminism and Heroism?" In *Conflicts in Feminism,* edited by Marianne Hirsch and Evelyn Fox Keller, 234–51. New York: Routledge, 1990.

Chiang, Mark. "Coming out into the Global System: Postmodern Patriarchies and Transnational Sexualities in *The Wedding Banquet.*" In *Q & A: Queer in Asian America,* edited by David L. Eng and Alice Y. Hom, 374–95. Philadelphia: Temple University Press, 1998.

Chiang, Mark. "A White Thing: Fetishism and Paranoia in the Nation." Paper presented at the annual conference of the Association of Asian American Studies, University of Michigan, Ann Arbor, April 1994.

Chin, Frank. "Backtalk." In *Counterpoint: Perspectives on Asian America,* edited by Emma Gee, 556–67. Los Angeles: Asian America Studies Center, UCLA, 1976.

Chin, Frank. "Come All Ye Asian Writers of the Real and the Fake." In *The Big Aiiieeeee! An Anthology of Chinese American and Japanese American Literature,* edited by Jeffery Paul Chan, Frank Chin, Lawson Fusao Inada, and Shawn Wong, 1–92. New York: Meridian 1991.

Chin, Frank. *Donald Duk.* Minneapolis: Coffee House Press, 1991.

Chin, Frank. *Gunga Din Highway.* Minneapolis, Coffee House Press, 1994.

Chin, Frank. "Riding the Rails with Chickencoop Slim." *Greenfield Review* 6.1–2 (1977): 80–89.

Chin, Frank. "Uncle Frank's Fakebook of Fairy Tales for Asian American Moms and Dads." *Amerasia Journal* 18.2 (1992): 69–87.

Chin, Frank, and Jeffery Paul Chan. "Racist Love." In *Seeing through Shuck,* edited by Richard Kostelanetz, 65–79. New York: Ballantine, 1972.

Chin, Frank, Jeffery Paul Chan, Lawson Fusao Inada, and Shawn Wong, eds. *Aiiieeeee! An Anthology of Asian-American Writers.* Garden City, NY: Anchor, 1975.

Chin, Frank, Jeffery Paul Chan, Lawson Fusao Inada, and Shawn Wong. Preface to *Aiiieeeee! An Anthology of Asian-American Writers,* edited by Frank Chin, Jeffery Paul Chan, Lawson Fusao Inada, and Shawn Wong, ix–xx. Garden City, NY: Anchor, 1975.

Chow, Rey. "Walter Benjamin's Love Affair with Death." *New German Critique* 48 (fall 1989): 63–86.

Chow, Rey. "Where Have All the Natives Gone?" In *Writing Diaspora: Tactics of Intervention in Contemporary Cultural Studies,* 27–54. Bloomington: Indiana University Press, 1993.

Christian, Barbara. "The Race for Theory." *Cultural Critique* 6 (spring 1987): 1–63.

Chu, Louis. *Eat a Bowl of Tea.* New York: Lyle Stuart, [1961] 1990.

Chung, L. A. "Chinese American Literary War." *San Francisco Chronicle,* 26 August 1991, D3–4.

Cixous, Hélène, and Catherine Clément. "The Untenable." In *In Dora's Case: Freud—Hysteria—Feminism,* 2d ed., edited by Charles Bernheimer and Claire Kahane, 276–293. New York: Columbia University Press, 1985.

Cody Gabrielle. "David Hwang's *M. Butterfly:* Perpetuating the Misogynist Myth." *Theatre* 20.2 (spring 1989): 24–27.

Corber, Robert J. *Homosexuality in Cold War America.* Durham: Duke University Press, 1997.

Crary, Jonathan. *Techniques of the Observer: On Vision and Modernity in the Nineteenth Century.* Cambridge: MIT Press, 1990.

Daniels, Roger. *Asian America: Chinese and Japanese in the United States since 1850.* Seattle: University of Washington Press, 1988.

David-Menard, Monique. *Hysteria from Freud to Lacan: Body and Language in Psychoanalysis*. Translated by Catherine Porter. Ithaca: Cornell University Press, 1989.

Davis, Angela Y. *Women, Race, and Class*. New York: Vintage, 1983.

Davis, Robert Murray. "West Meets East: A Conversation with Frank Chin." *Amerasia Journal* 24:1 (1998): 87–103.

Dayan, Daniel. "The Tutor Code of Classical Cinema." In *Movies and Methods*, edited by Bill Nichols, 438–51. Berkeley: University of California Press, 1976.

De Haven, Tom. "He's Been Dreaming on the Railroad." *New York Times Book Review*, 31 March 1991, 9.

de Lauretis, Teresa. *The Practice of Love: Lesbian Sexuality and Perverse Desire*. Bloomington: Indiana University Press, 1994.

DiGaetani, John Louis. "*M. Butterfly*: An Interview with David Henry Hwang." *Drama Review* 33.3 (fall 1989): 141–53.

Doane, Mary Ann. *Femme Fatales: Feminism, Film Theory, Psychoanalysis*. New York: Routledge, 1991.

Du Bois, W. E. B. *The Souls of Black Folk: W. E. B. Du Bois, Writings*. New York: Library of America, 1986.

Duggan, Lisa. "Queering the State." In Lisa Duggan and Nan D. Hunter, *Sex: Sexual Dissent and Political Culture*, 179–93. New York: Routledge, 1995.

Edelman, Lee. *Homographesis: Essays in Gay Literary and Cultural Theory*. New York: Routledge, 1994.

Edelman, Lee. "Seeing Things: Representation, the Scene of Surveillance, and the Spectacle of Gay Male Sex." In *Inside/Out: Lesbian Theories, Gay Theories*, edited by Diana Fuss, 93–116. New York: Routledge, 1991.

Ellison, Ralph. *Invisible Man*. New York: Random House, 1952.

Eng, David L. "In the Shadows of a Diva: Committing Homosexuality in David Henry Hwang's *M. Butterfly*." *Amerasia Journal* 20.1 (1994): 93–116.

Eng, David L. "*The Wedding Banquet*: You're Not Invited and Some Other Ancillary Thoughts." *Artspiral* 7 (fall 1993): 8–10.

Eng, David L., and Shinhee Han. "A Dialogue on Racial Melancholia." In *Psychoanalytic Dialogues* 10.4 (2000): 667–700.

Eng, David L., and Alice Y. Hom, eds. *Q & A: Queer in Asian America*. Philadelphia: Temple University Press, 1998.

Eng, David L., and David Kazanjian, eds. *Loss*. Forthcoming.

Espiritu, Yen Le. *Asian American Panethnicity: Bridging Institutions and Identities*. Philadelphia: Temple University Press, 1992.

Espiritu, Yen Le. *Asian American Women and Men*. Thousand Oaks, CA: Sage, 1997.

Fanon, Frantz. *Black Skin, White Masks*. Translated by Charles Lam Markmann. New York: Grove, 1967.

Felman, Shoshana. *What Does a Woman Want? Reading and Sexual Difference*. Baltimore: Johns Hopkins University Press, 1993.

Fong, Timothy. *The First Suburban Chinatown: The Remaking of Monterey Park, California*. Philadelphia: Temple University Press, 1994.

Foucault, Michel. *The Archaeology of Knowledge and The Discourse on Language.* Translated by A. M. Sheridan Smith. New York: Pantheon, 1972.

Frankenburg, Ruth. *White Women, Race Matters: The Social Construction of Whiteness.* Minneapolis: University of Minnesota Press, 1993.

Fraser, Nancy. "Rethinking the Public Sphere: A Contribution to the Critique of Actually Existing Democracy." In *The Phantom Public Sphere,* edited by Bruce Robbins, 1–32. Minneapolis: University of Minnesota Press, 1993.

Freud, Sigmund. "The Dissection of the Psychical Personality." In *The Standard Edition of the Complete Psychological Works of Sigmund Freud.* Edited by James Strachey, 22:57–80. London: Hogarth, 1955. First published in 1933.

Freud, Sigmund. "The Dynamics of Transference." In *The Standard Edition of the Complete Psychological Works of Sigmund Freud.* Edited by James Strachey, 12:97–108. London: Hogarth, 1955. First published in 1912.

Freud, Sigmund. *The Ego and the Id.* In *The Standard Edition of the Complete Psychological Works of Sigmund Freud.* Edited by James Strachey, 19:1–59. London: Hogarth, 1955. First published in 1923.

Freud, Sigmund. "Feminity." In *The Standard Edition of the Complete Psychological Works of Sigmund Freud.* Edited by James Strachey, 22:112–35. London: Hogarth, 1955. First published in 1933.

Freud, Sigmund. "Fetishism." In *The Standard Edition of the Complete Psychological Works of Sigmund Freud.* Edited by James Strachey, 21:152–57. London: Hogarth, 1955. First published in 1927.

Freud, Sigmund. "From the History of an Infantile Neurosis (The 'Wolf Man')." In *The Standard Edition of the Complete Psychological Works of Sigmund Freud.* Edited by James Strachey, 17:1–122. London: Hogarth, 1955. First published in 1918.

Freud, Sigmund. *The Interpretation of Dreams.* In *The Standard Edition of the Complete Psychological Works of Sigmund Freud.* Edited by James Strachey, vols. 4–5. London: Hogarth, 1955. First published in 1900.

Freud, Sigmund. "Observation of a Severe Case of Hemi-Anaesthesia in a Hysterial Male. In *The Standard Edition of the Complete Psychological Works of Sigmund Freud.* Edited by James Strachey, 1:23–31. London: Hogarth, 1955. First published in 1886.

Freud, Sigmund. "On Narcissism: An Introduction." In *The Standard Edition of the Complete Psychological Works of Sigmund Freud.* Edited by James Strachey, 14:67–103. London: Hogarth, 1955. First published in 1914.

Freud, Sigmund. "Some Psychological Consequences of the Anatomical Distinction between the Sexes." In *The Standard Edition of the Complete Psychological Works of Sigmund Freud.* Edited by James Strachey, 19:241–60. London: Hogarth, 1955. First published in 1925.

Freud, Sigmund. "Splitting of the Ego in the Defensive Process." In *The Standard Edition of the Complete Psychological Works of Sigmund Freud.* Edited by James Strachey, 23:271–78. London: Hogarth, 1955. First published in 1938.

Freud, Sigmund. *Totem and Taboo: Some Points of Agreement between the Mental Life of Savages and Neurotics.* In *The Standard Edition of the Complete Psycho-*

logical Works of Sigmund Freud. Edited by James Strachey, 13:1–161. London: Hogarth, 1955. First published in 1912–13.

Fung, Richard. "Looking for My Penis: The Eroticized Asian in Gay Porn Video." In *How Do I Look?* edited by Bad Object Choices, 145–68. Seattle: Bay Press, 1991.

Fuss, Diana. *Identification Papers.* New York: Routledge, 1993.

Gallop, Jane. "Keys to Dora." In *In Dora's Case: Freud—Hysteria—Feminism,* 2d ed., edited by Charles Bernheimer and Claire Kahane, 200–220. New York: Columbia University Press, 1985.

Gallop, Jane. *Reading Lacan.* Ithaca: Cornell University Press, 1985.

Garber, Majorie. *Vested Interests: Cross-Dressing and Cultural Anxiety.* New York: Harper Perennial, 1992.

Gates, Henry Louis. "Authority, (White) Power, and the (Black) Critic: It's All Greek to Me." *Cultural Critique* 7 (fall 1987): 19–46.

Gee, Emma. *Counterpoint: Perspectives on Asian America.* Los Angeles: Asian American Studies Center, UCLA 1976.

Geller, Jonathan. "'A Glance on the Nose': Freud's Inscription of Jewish Difference." *American Imago* 49 (1992): 427–44.

Gesensway, Deborah, and Mindy Roseman. *Beyond Words: Images from America's Concentration Camps.* Ithaca: Cornell University Press, 1987.

Gilman, Sander. *The Case of Sigmund Freud: Medicine and Identity at the Fin de Siècle.* Baltimore: Johns Hopkins University Press, 1993.

Gilman, Sander. *The Jew's Body.* New York: Routledge, 1991.

Gopinath, Gayatri. "Nostalgia, Desire, Diaspora: South Asian Sexualities in Motion." *positions: east asia cultures critique* 5.2 (fall 1997): 467–89.

Habermas, Jürgen. *Structural Transformation of the Public Sphere: An Inquiry into a Category of Bourgeois Society.* Translated by Thomas Burger. Cambridge: MIT Press, 1989.

Hagedorn, Jessica. *Dogeaters.* New York: Pantheon, 1990.

Hamamoto, Darrell Y. *Monitored Peril: Asian Americans and the Politics of TV Representation.* Minneapolis: University of Minnesota Press, 1994.

Hartman, Saidiya V. *Scenes of Subjection: Terror, Slavery, and Self-Making in Nineteenth-Century America.* New York: Oxford University Press, 1997.

Hatamiya, Leslie T. *Righting a Wrong: Japanese Americans and the Passage of the Civil Liberties Act of 1988.* Stanford: Stanford University Press, 1993.

Heath, Stephen. "Notes on Suture." *Screen* (winter 1977–78): 48–76.

Hertz, Neil. "Medusa's Head: Male Hysteria under Political Pressure. *Representations* 4 (fall 1983): 26–54.

Hing, Bill Ong. *Making and Remaking Asian America through Immigration Policy, 1850–1990.* Stanford: Stanford University Press, 1993.

Hirabayashi, Lane, ed. *Teaching Asian America: Diversity and the Problem of Community.* Boulder: Rowman and Littlefield, 1997.

Hodgson, Moira. "*M. Butterfly.*" *Nation,* 23 April 1988, 577.

Horn, Miriam. "The Mesmerizing Power of Racial Myths." *U.S. News and World Report,* 28 March 1988, 52–53.

Hune, Shirley. "The Politics of Chinese Exclusion: Legislative-Executive Conflict, 1876–1882." *Amerasia Journal* 9.1 (1982): 5–27.

Hwang, David Henry. *M. Butterfly*. New York: Plume, 1989.

Jackson, Earl, Jr. "Scandalous Subjects: Robert Glück's Embodied Narratives." *differences: A Journal of Feminist Cultural Studies* 3.2 (summer 1991): 112–34.

Jameson, Fredric. *Postmodernism, or the Cultural Logic of Late Capitalism*. Durham: Duke University Press, 1991.

Jay, Martin. *Downcast Eyes: The Denigration of Vision in Twentieth-Century French Thought*. Berkeley: University of California Press, 1993.

Kaneko, Lonny. "The Shoyu Kid." *Amerasia Journal* 3.2 (1976): 1–9.

Kazanjian, David. "Notarizing Knowledge: Paranoia and Civility in Freud and Lacan." *Qui Parle* 7.1 (fall-winter 1993): 102–39.

Kim, Elaine H. *Asian American Literature: An Introduction to the Writers and Their Social Context*. Philadelphia: Temple University Press, 1982.

Kingston, Maxine Hong. *China Men*. New York: Vintage, [1980] 1989.

Kingston, Maxine Hong. *The Woman Warrior: Memoirs of a Girlhood among Ghosts*. New York: Vintage, [1976] 1989.

Kirby, Lynne. "Male Hysteria and Early Cinema." *Camera Obscura: A Journal of Feminism and Film Theory* 17 (1988): 113–31.

Kracauer, Siegfried. *Die Angestellten (The White Collared Workers): Aus dem neusten Deutschland*. Vol. 1. Frankfurt: Suhrkamp, 1971.

Kracauer, Siegfried. *History: Last Things before the Last*. Oxford: Oxford University Press, 1969.

Kracauer, Siegfried. "The Mass Ornament." Translated by Barbara Correll and Jack Zipes. *New German Critique* 5 (spring 1975): 67–76. First published in 1927.

Kracauer, Siegfried. "Photography." Translated by Thomas Y. Levin. *Critical Inquiry* 19.3 (spring 1993): 421–34.

Kraus, George. *High Road to Promontory: Building the Central Pacific (Now the Southern Pacific) across the High Sierra*. Palo Alto: American West, 1969.

Krauss, Rosalind. *The Optical Unconscious*. Cambridge: MIT Press, 1993.

Kristeva, Julia. *Powers of Horror: An Essay on Abjection*. New York: Columbia University Press, 1982.

Lacan, Jacques. *The Four Fundamental Concepts of Psycho-Analysis*. Translated by Alan Sheridan. New York: Norton, 1981.

Lacan, Jacques. "Kanzer Seminar at Yale University." Translated by Barbara Johnson, 1975.

Lacan, Jacques. "The Meaning of the Phallus." In *Feminine Sexuality: Jacques Lacan and the École Freudienne*, edited by Juliet Mitchell and Jacqueline Rose, 74–85. New York: Norton, 1985. First published in 1958.

Lacan, Jacques. "The Mirror Stage as Formative of the Function of the I as Revealed in Psychoanalytic Experience." In *Écrits: A Selection*. Translated by Alan Sheridan, 1–7. New York: Norton, 1991. First published in 1949.

Lacan, Jacques. *The Seminar of Jacques Lacan. Book II, The Ego in Freud's Theory and the Technique of Psychoanalysis, 1954–55.* Translated by Sylvana Tomaselli. New York: Norton, 1991.

Lacan, Jacques. "The Signification of the Phallus." In *Écrits: A Selection.* Edited by Alan Sheridan, 281–91. New York: Norton, 1977. First published in 1958.

Lacan, Jacques. "Some Reflections on the Ego." *International Journal of Psychoanalysis* 34 (1953): 11–17.

Lane, Christopher, ed. *The Psychoanalysis of Race.* New York: Columbia University Press, 1998.

Laplanche, Jean. *Life and Death in Psychoanalysis.* Translated with an introduction by Jeffrey Mehlman. Baltimore: Johns Hopkins University Press, 1976.

Laplanche, J., and J. B. Pontalis. *The Language of Psycho-Analysis.* Translated by Donald Nicholson-Smith. New York: Norton, 1973.

Laplanche, Jean, and Jean-Bertrand Pontalis. "Fantasy and the Origins of Sexuality." In *Formations of Fantasy,* edited by Victor Burgin, James Donald, and Cora Kaplan, 5–34. London: Methuen, 1986.

Law Yone, Wendy. *The Coffin Tree.* Boston: Beacon Press, 1983.

Lee, JeeYeun. "Toward a Queer Korean American Diaspora." In *Q & A: Queer in Asian America,* edited by David L. Eng and Alice Y. Hom, 185–209. Philadelphia: Temple University Press, 1998.

Lee, Robert G. *Orientals: Asian Americans in Popular Culture.* Philadelphia: Temple University Press, 1999.

Leong, Russell, ed. *Amerasia Journal* 22.3 (1996). Special issue, "Transnationalism, Media, and Asian American Studies."

Leong, Russell, ed. *Moving the Image: Independent Asian Pacific American Media Arts.* Los Angeles: Asian American Studies Center, UCLA, 1991.

Li, David Leiwei. "*China Men:* Maxine Hong Kingston and the American Canon." *American Literary History* 2.3 (fall 1990): 482–502.

Li, David Leiwei. *Imagining the Nation: Asian American Literature and Cultural Consent.* Stanford: Stanford University Press, 1998.

Liao, Ping-hui. "'Of Writing Words for Music Which Is Already Made': *Madama Butterfly, Turandot,* and Orientalism." *Cultural Critique* 16 (fall 1990): 31–59.

Linmark, R. Zamora. *Rolling the R's.* New York: Kaya Production, 1995.

Link-Herr, Ursula. "'Male Hysteria': A Discourse Analysis." *Cultural Critique* 15 (spring 1990): 191–220.

Lipsitz, George. *The Possessive Investment in Whiteness: How White People Profit from Identity Politics.* Philadelphia: Temple University Press, 1998.

Littré, Emile, and Albert Robin. *Dictionnaire de médecine.* Paris: J.B. Baillière, 1855.

Long, John Luther. *Madame Butterfly, Purple Eyes, A Gentleman of Japan and a Lady, Kito, Glory.* New York: Century, 1898.

Loti, Pierre. *Madame Chrysanthème.* Paris: Calmann-Levy, [1887] 1922.

Louie, David Wong. *Pangs of Love.* New York: Knopf, 1991.

Lowe, Lisa. "Heterogeneity, Hybridity, Multiplicity: Asian American Differences." In *Immigrant Acts: On Asian American Cultural Politics,* 60–83. Durham: Duke University Press, 1996.

Lowe, Lisa. *Immigrant Acts: On Asian American Cultural Politics*. Durham: Duke University Press, 1996.

Lwin, Sanda Mayzaw. "The Constitution of Asian America." Ph.D. diss., Columbia University, 1999.

Manalansan, Martin. "In the Shadows of Stonewall: Gay Transnational Politics and the Diasporic Dilemma." In *The Politics of Culture in the Shadow of Capital*, edited by Lisa Lowe and David Lloyd, 485–505. Durham: Duke University Press, 1997.

Mapa, Alec. "I Remember Mapa." In *O Solo Homo: The New Queer Performance*, edited by Holly Hughes and David Román, 199–228. New York: Grove, 1988.

Matsuda, Mari J. "We Will Not Be Used. Are Asian-Americans the Racial Bourgeoisie?" In *Where is Your Body? And Other Essays on Race, Gender, and the Law*, 149–159. Boston: Beacon, 1996.

Mazumdar, Sucheta. "Asian American Studies and Asian Studies: Rethinking Roots." In *Asian Americans: Comparative and Global Perspectives*, edited by Shirley Hune, Hyung-chan Kim, Stephen S. Fugita, and Amy Ling, 29–44. Pullman: Washington State University Press, 1991.

Mercer, Kobena. "Skin Head Sex Thing." In *How Do I Look?* edited by Bad Object Choices, 169–222. Seattle: Bay Press, 1991.

Metz, Christian. *The Imaginary Signifier: Psychoanalysis and the Cinema*. Translated by Celia Britton, Annwyl Williams, Ben Brewster, and Alfred Guzzetti. Bloomington: Indiana University Press, 1977.

Metz, Christian. "Photography and the Fetish." In *The Critical Image: Essays on Contemporary Photography*, edited by Carol Squires, 155–64. Seattle: Bay Press, 1990.

Micale, Mark S. "Charcot and the Idea of Hysteria in the Male: Gender, Mental Science, and Medical Diagnosis in Late Nineteenth-Century France." *Medical History* 34 (1990): 363–411.

Miyoshi, Masao. "A Borderless World? From Colonialism to Transnationalism and the Decline of the Nation-State." *Critical Inquiry* 19 (1993): 726–51.

Moy, James S. *Marginal Sites: Staging the Chinese in America*. Iowa City: University of Iowa Press, 1993.

Mulvey, Laura. *Visual and Other Pleasures*. Bloomington: Indiana University Press, 1989.

Muñoz, José Esteban. *Disidentifications: Queers of Color and the Performance of Politics*. Minneapolis: University of Minnesota Press, 1999.

Nee, Victor G., and Brett de Bary Nee. *Longtime Californ': A Documentary Study of an American Chinatown*. Stanford: Stanford University Press, 1972.

Neubauer, Carol E. "Developing Ties to the Past: Photography and Other Sources of Information in Maxine Hong Kingston's *China Men*." *MELUS* 10.4 (winter 1983): 17–36.

Ng, Fae Myenne. *Bone*. New York: Hyperion, 1993.

Nieh, Hualing. *Mulberry and Peach: Two Women of China*. Translated by Jane Parish Yang with Linda Lappin. Boston: Beacon, 1981.

O'Brien David, and Stephen S. Fugita. *The Japanese American Experience*. Bloomington: Indiana University Press, 1991.

Okada, John. *No-No Boy*. Seattle: University of Washington Press, [1957] 1993.

Omi, Michael, and Dana Takagi, eds. *Amerasia Journal* 21.1–2 (1995). Special issue, "Thinking Theory in Asian American Studies."

Ong, Aihwa. *Flexible Citizenship: The Cultural Logic of Transnationality*. Durham: Duke University Press, 1999.

Oudart, Jean-Pierre. "Cinema and Suture." *Screen* (winter 1977–78): 35–47.

Palumbo-Liu, David. *Asian/American: Historical Crossings of a Racial Frontier*. Stanford: Stanford University Press, 1999.

Pellegrini, Ann. *Performance Anxieties: Staging Psychoanalysis, Staging Race*. New York: Routledge, 1997.

Personal Justice Denied: Report of the Commission on Wartime Relocation and Internment of Civilians. Washington, DC: Civil Liberties Public Education Fund; Seattle: University of Washington Press, 1997.

Phillips, Adam. "Keep It Moving: Commentary on Judith Butler." In Judith Butler, *The Psychic Life of Power: Theories in Subjection*, 151–59. Stanford: Stanford University Press, 1997.

Read, Alan. *The Fact of Blackness: Frantz Fanon and Visual Representation*. Seattle: Bay Press, 1996.

Reddy, Chandan. "History, Allegory, Sexuality: The Minors of Linmark's *Rolling the R's*." Paper presented at the annual conference of the American Studies Association, Kansas City, Missouri, 31 October 1996.

Rich, Frank. "*M. Butterfly*, a Story of a Strange Love, Conflict, and Betrayal." *New York Times*, 21 March 1988, C13.

Rieff, Philip. Introduction to *Dora: An Analysis of a Case of Hysteria*, edited by Philip Rieff, 7–20. New York: Collier, 1963.

Robbins, Bruce, ed. *The Phantom Public Sphere*. Minneapolis: University of Minnesota Press, 1993.

Roediger, David E. *The Wages of Whiteness: Race and the Making of the American Working Class*. New York: Verso, 1991.

Rose, Jacqueline. "Dora: Fragment of an Analysis." In *In Dora's Case: Freud—Hysteria—Feminism*, 2d ed., edited by Charles Bernheimer and Claire Kahane, 128–148. New York: Columbia University Press, 1985.

Said, Edward. "Secular Criticism." In *The World, the Text, and the Critic*, 1–30. Cambridge: Harvard University Press, 1983.

Samarth, Manini. "Affirmations: Speaking the Self into Being." *Parnassus Poetry in Review* 17.1 (1992): 88–101.

Sassen, Saskia. "Beyond Sovereignty: Immigration Policy Making Today." *Social Justice* 23 (fall 1996): 9–19.

Sassen, Saskia. "Whose City Is It? Globalization and the Formation of New Claims." *Public Culture* 8 (1996): 205–23.

Saxton, Alexander. *The Indispensable Enemy: Labor and the Anti-Chinese Movement in California*. Berkeley: University of California Press, 1971.

Saxton, Alexander. *The Rise and Fall of the White Republic: Class Politics and Mass Culture in Nineteenth-Century America*. New York: Verso, 1990.

Sedgwick, Eve Kosofsky. *Between Men: English Literature and Male Homosocial Desire*. New York: Columbia University Press, 1985.

Sedgwick, Eve Kosofsky. "How to Bring Your Kids Up Gay: The War on Effeminate Boys." In *Tendencies*, 154–64. Durham: Duke University Press, 1993.

Sedgwick, Eve Kosofsky. "White Glasses." In *Tendencies*, 252–66. Durham: Duke University Press, 1993.

Selvadurai, Shyam. *Funny Boy*. New York: William Morrow, 1994.

Shakespeare, William. *Othello, the Moor of Venice*. New York: Penguin, 1971.

Sharpe, Jenny. "Is the United States Postcolonial? Transnationalism, Immigration, and Race." *Diaspora* 4 (fall 1995): 181–99.

Silverman, Kaja. "The Lacanian Phallus." *differences: A Journal of Feminist Cultural Studies* 4.1 (spring 1992): 84–115.

Silverman, Kaja. *Male Subjectivity at the Margins*. New York: Routledge, 1992.

Silverman, Kaja. *The Subject of Semiotics*. New York: Oxford University Press, 1983.

Silverman, Kaja. *The Threshold of the Visible World*. New York: Routledge, 1996.

Simon, John. "An Actor Despairs." *New York*, 24 October 1988, 145–46.

Simon, John. "Finding Your Song." *New York*, 11 April 1988, 117.

Sklair, Leslie. *Sociology of the Global System*. 2d ed. Baltimore: Johns Hopkins University Press, 1995.

Smith, Paul. *Clint Eastwood: A Cultural Production*. Minneapolis: University of Minnesota Press, 1993.

Smith, Paul. "Vas." *Camera Obscura: A Journal of Feminism and Film Theory* 17 (1988): 89–111.

Sone, Monica. *Nisei Daughter*. Seattle: University of Washington Press, 1953.

Spivak, Gayatri Chakravorty. "Culture." In *A Critique of Postcolonial Reason: Toward a History of the Vanishing Present*, 312–421. Cambridge: Harvard University Press, 1999.

Spivak, Gayatri Chakravorty. "Negotiating the Structures of Violence." *In The Post-colonial Critic: Interviews, Strategies, Dialogues*, edited by Sarah Harasym, 138–51. New York: Routledge, 1990.

Spivak, Gayatri Chakravorty. "Scattered Speculations on the Question of Culture Studies." In *Outside in the Teaching Machine*, 255–84. New York: Routledge, 1993.

Sturken, Marita. *Tangled Memories: The Vietnam War, the AIDS Epidemic, and the Politics of Remembering*. Berkeley: University of California Press, 1997.

Sue, Stanley, and Derald W. Sue. "Chinese-American Personality and Mental Health." *Amerasia Journal* 1.2 (1971): 36–49.

Suzuki, Bob H. "Education and the Socialization of Asian Americans: A Revisionist Analysis of the 'Model Minority' Thesis." *Amerasia Journal* 4.2 (1977): 23–51.

Takagi, Dana. "Maiden Voyage: Excursions into Sexuality and Identity Politics in Asian America." *Amerasia Journal* 20.1 (1994): 1–17.

Takaki, Ronald. *Strangers from a Different Shore: A History of Asian Americans.* New York: Penguin, 1989.

Tate, Claudia. *Psychoanalysis and Black Novels: Desire and the Protocols of Race.* New York: Oxford University Press, 1998.

Ting, Jennifer. "Bachelor Society: Deviant Heterosexuality and Asian American Historiography." In *Privileging Positions: The Sites of Asian American Studies,* edited by Gary Y. Okihiro, Marilyn Aquizola, Dorothy Fujita Rony, and K. Scott Wong, 271–79. Pullman: Washington State University Press, 1995.

Tölölyan, Khachig. "The Nation-State and Its Others: In Lieu of a Preface." *Diaspora: A Journal of Transnational Studies* 1.1 (spring 1991): 3–7.

Utley, Robert M. "The Spike Wasn't Golden." *New York Times Book Review,* 12 December 1999, 10.

Vieth, Ilza. *Hysteria: The History of a Disease.* Chicago: University of Chicago Press, 1965.

Village Voice. "White Like Who? Notes on the Other Race." Special Issue, 18 May 1993.

Volpp, Leti. "American Mestizo: Filipinos and Antimicegenation Laws in California." *University of California at Davis Law Review* 33 (forthcoming 2000).

Wadler, Joyce. *Liaison.* New York: Bantam, 1993.

Wajeman, Gerard. *Le Maitre et l'hystérique.* Paris: Navarin, 1982.

Warner, Michael. Introduction to *Fear of a Queer Planet: Queer Politics and Social Theory,* edited by Michael Warner, vii–xxxi. Minneapolis: University of Minnesota Press, 1993.

Warner, Michael. "The Mass Public and the Mass Subject." In *The Phantom Public Sphere,* edited by Bruce Robbins, 234–56. Minneapolis: University of Minnesota Press, 1993.

Wei, William. *The Asian American Movement.* Philadelphia: Temple University Press, 1993.

Witte, Karsten. "Introduction to Siegfried Kracauer's 'The Mass Ornament.'" *New German Critique* 5 (spring 1975): 59–66.

Wong, Norman. *Cultural Revolution.* New York: Persea, 1994.

Wong, Sau-ling Cynthia. "Chinese/Asian American Men in the 1990s: Displacement, Impersonation, Paternity, and Extinction in David Wong Louie's *Pangs of Love.*" In *Privileging Positions: The Sites of Asian American Studies,* edited by Gary Y. Okihiro, Marilyn Alquizola, Dorothy Fujita Rony, and K. Scott Wong, 181–91. Pullman: Washington State University Press, 1995.

Wong, Sau-ling Cynthia. "Denationalization Reconsidered: Asian American Cultural Criticism at a Theoretical Crossroads." *Amerasia Journal* 21.1–2 (1995): 1–27.

Wong, Sau-ling Cynthia. *Reading Asian American Literature: From Necessity to Extravagance.* Princeton: Princeton University Press, 1993.

Yamamoto, Hisaye. "The Legend of Miss Sasagawara." In *"Seventeen Syllables" and Other Stories,* 20–33. Latham, NY: Kitchen Table, Women of Color Press, 1988.

Yamamoto, Traise. *Masking Selves, Making Subjects: Japanese American Women, Identity, and the Body*. Berkeley: University of California Press, 1999.

Yoshikawa, Yoko. "The Heat Is on *Miss Saigon* Coalition: Organizing across Race and Sexuality." In *The State of Asian America: Activism and Resistance in the 1990s*, edited by Karin Aguilar-San Juan, 275–94. Boston: South End, 1994.

Žižek, Slavoj. *The Sublime Object of Ideology*. New York: Verso, 1989.

Žižek, Slavoj. *For They Know Not What They Do: Enjoyment as a Political Factor*. New York: Verso, 1991.

INDEX

Abbas, Ackbar, 237 n.28
Abel, Elizabeth, 20
Abject, 143, 247–48 n.33
Affiliation vs. filiation, 190–93, 197, 200, 202, 207, 221
African American studies: feminism vs. heroism debate in, 233 n.28
Agency. *See* Subjectivity: and agency
Aiiieeeee! group (Chan, Chin, Inada, Wong), 1, 20–21, 23, 31, 72; heterosexism and sexism of, 21, 90, 92, 136, 191, 208–11, 241 n.60
Alarcón, Norma, 5
Althusser, Louis, 23, 83; interpellation, 119, 141, 176, 246–47 n.32
Archive, 49–50, 67. *See also* Foucault, Michel
Asian America: location of, 204–5
Asian American(s): cultural nationalism, 20–21, 92–93, 208–11; definition of, 102, 252 n.32, 262 n.18; hyphenated identity of, 211–15, 260 n.3, 262 n.18, 262–63 n.26, 263 n.29 *See also Aiiieeeee!* group; Subjectivity: split
Asian American studies movement: feminism vs. heroism debate in, 15; history of, 208–11, 212–13, 217–19; and Marxism, 15, 208–9; and poststructuralist theory, 26–28; and psychoanalysis, 19–24, 28; and queerness, 216–20; sociological emphasis of, 19–22; and Women's and Queer studies,

16. *See also Aiiieeeee!* group; Chin, Frank; Kingston, Maxine Hong
Assimilation, 180–81, 185–87, 193, 194–95, 199, 203, 204; contradictions of, 21–22; and psychic health, 167–68. *See also* Chu, Louis; Hysteria; Impotence; Louie, David Wong; "Marginal Man"

Barthes, Roland, 36, 38–40, 44, 56, 79–80, 212; punctum, 54–55, studium, 54
Bazin, André, 38
Benjamin, Walter, 36, 38–39, 65, 69, 75, 76, 81, 83, 86, 90, 91, 102. *See also* Photography: and history, and memory
Bernheimer, Charles, 171, 256 n.22
Beyond the Pleasure Principle (Freud), 56
Bhabha, Homi, 24, 119; on mimicry, 201–2; stereotype, 30, 37, 44, 56–57, 109
Blade Runner (film; Scott), 36, 63
Big Four (Crocker, Hopkins, Huntington, Stanford), 61, 65, 238–39 n.37; labor practices of, 61–63, 239 n.42. *See also* Promontory Summit; Transcontinental Railroad
Body: Japanese-American, 105–10, 137; materiality of, 184–87; mutilation of, 117; speaking through, 172–73. *See also* Fetishism; Hysteria; Lacan, Jacques: mirror-stage;

Body (*continued*)
  Primal scene; Silverman, Kaja:
  self-same body
Bone (Ng), 67
Borch-Jacobsen, Mikkel, 113
Boyarin, Daniel, 173, 179, 230 n.12,
  255 n.12
Breuer, Joseph, 196
Brown, Wendy, 26, 233–34 n.37
Brown v. Board of Education, 20, 169,
  193, 198, 259 n.1
Bruno, Giuliana, 35
Burgin, Victor, 188, 231 n.13
Butler Judith, 13, 27, 70–71, 141, 160,
  162, 232 n.25

Cadava, Eduardo, 39
Campomanes, Oscar V., 204–5
Capitalism: global, 169, 264 n.37;
  and nation-state; 33–34; racialized
  foundation of U.S., 61–63. *See also*
  Globalization; Labor; Nation-state
Central Pacific Railroad. *See* Trans-
  continental Railroad
Chan, Jeffery, 191–92
Chan, Sucheng, 61–62, 105, 254 n.5
Charcot, Jean-Martin, 171, 178
Cheung, King-Kok, 15–16, 51, 97
Chiang, Mark, 164, 222, 266 n.51
Chin, Frank, 21, 29, 30; *Donald Duk*,
  35–37, 45, 69–103; heterosexism
  and sexism of, 90–91, 92–98, 136,
  204; relationship to Maxine Hong
  Kingston, 90–103, 241 n.63. *See
  also Aiiieeeee!* group
Chin, Vincent, 244 n.12, 263 n.27
China Men (Kingston), 35–37, 45–67,
  69, 86, 90–92, 98–103, 237 n.35,
  239 n.43
Chinatown: as bachelor community,
  17–18, 32, 168–69, 180, 181, 183,
  189–92, 196, 198, 259 n.46
Chinese American(s): during internment, 107–10; male laborers,

16–17, 35–37, 61–64, 109, 137, 169,
  234 n.4
Chow, Rey, 235–36 n.15
Christian, Barbara, 20
Citizenship: Asian American, 180–
  82, 193–95, 200, 202–3, 221; and
  Asian-American males, 16–19,
  34, 36; contradictions of, 65–67;
  and heterosexuality, 182. *See also*
  Law(s): immigration/exclusion;
  Lowe, Lisa; Paper sons
Cixous, Hélène, 179, 187, 257 n.31;
  and Catherine Clément, 174–77
Cold War, 147–49; and homosexuality, 148; and immigration,
  169. *See also* Law(s): immigra-
  tion/exclusion
Colonialism, 134; fantasies of, 1–4,
  138, 147–49, 151, 153, 158–60; and
  psychoanalysis, 9–10, 148–49;
  symbolic ideals of, 164–66. See
  also *M. Butterfly; Totem and Taboo*
Corber, Robert, 148
Cronenberg, David: *M. Butterfly*,
  140
Cultural Revolution (Wong), 135
Culture, 33–34

Davis, Angela Y., 136
De Haven, Tom, 36
de Lauretis, Teresa, 132–33
Deferred action. See *Nachträglichkeit*
Democracy: and education, 74–77,
  88–89, 167–68, 226–27; ideals
  of, 22, 148. *See also* Althusser,
  Louis: interpellation; Citizenship;
  Equivalence, Abstract; Laws(s):
  immigration/exclusion
Dewitt, John L., 105, 243–44 nn. 5–6
Diaspora, 204–28, 259–60 n.2;
  definition of, 206–7; exile and
  emergence vs. immigration and
  settlement, 33, 205; and queerness,
  204–27, 265 n.43

"Dissection of the Psychical Personality, The" (Freud), 145
Doane, Mary Ann, 230 n.12
Donald Duk (Chin), 35–37, 45, 69–103
Dreamwork, 30, 69, 74, 77–84, 86–89, 91, 94–97; and preconscious, 78–79. *See also* Memory; *Nachträglichkeit*
Du Bois, W. E. B., 24

Eat a Bowl of Tea (film; Chu), 32, 168, 179–93, 198, 204
Economics. *See* Capitalism; Globalization; Labor; Model minority myth
Edelman, Lee, 129, 148, 249 n.48, 252 n.27
Education. *See* Democracy
Ego and the Id, The (Freud), 145, 253 n.41
Emasculation/feminization, 102; of Asian American males, 1–4, 16–18, 64, 72–74, 75, 98, 180–81, 183; and hysteria, 178–81; through racialization, 49, 64, 72–74, 150–51, 184, 249 n.50; through U.S. immigration law, 92, 99–100. *See also* Chin, Frank; Fetishism: castration, racial; Hwang, David Henry
Equivalence: abstract, 23, 26–27, 36, 76, 85, 109–10, 134, 135, 169–70, 181–82, 185, 198, 203, 213, 224, 226. *See also* Citizenship; Democracy
Espiritu, Yen Le, 61
Ethnicity. *See* Race and ethnicity
Ethnic studies, 4, 19. *See also* Asian American studies movement
Executive Order 9066, 105, 243–44 n.4. *See also* Internment

Fanon, Frantz, 115–17, 136
Farewell to Manzanar (Houston), 105, 116
Felman, Shoshana, 173

Feminism: and psychoanalysis, 14
Feminization. *See* Emasculation/feminization
Fetishism, 2–3, 32, 144, 146–47, 150–66; and female castration, 146, 150, 153, 251 n.22; and homosexuality, 157–61; and racial castration, 2–3, 150–66
"Fetishism" (Freud), 2, 32, 146, 150, 161–62
Filiation: vs. affiliation. *See* Affiliation vs. filiation
Filipino Americans, 204–5, 225, 228
Four Fundamental Concepts of Psychoanalysis (Lacan), 43–44, 59, 114–15
Fraser, Nancy, 262 n.24
Freud, Sigmund, 33, 79–81, 111, 125–29, 130–31, 144, 153, 154, 157, 170, 171–73, 177–78, 255–56 n.15; *Beyond the Pleasure Principle*, 56; "The Dissection of the Psychical Personality," 145; *The Ego and the Id*, 145, 253 n.41; "Fetishism," 2, 32, 146, 150, 161–62; *Group Psychology and Analysis of the Ego*, 25, 96; *Interpretation of Dreams*, 77–79; "Observation of a Severe Case of Hemi-Anaesthesia in a Hysterical Male," 171, 255 n.12; "On the Mechanism of Paranoia," 96; "On Narcissism," 10–13, 96; "Some Psychological Consequences of the Anatomical Distinction Between the Sexes," 128; "Splitting of the Ego in the Defensive Process," 145–47, 148; *Totem and Taboo*, 6–13, 76; "Wolf Man," 128. *See also* Dreamwork; Fetishism; Hysteria; *Nachträglichkeit*; Oedipus complex; Primal scene; Unconscious
Foucault, Michel, 49–50, 51
Fung, Richard, 1, 14, 151, 184, 266 n.48
Funny Boy (Selvadurai), 135
Fuss, Diana, 25; on Fanon, 6, 9, 22

Gallop, Jane, 176, 246 n.23, 253 n.36, 257 n.31
Garber, Marjorie, 139–41
Gay and Lesbian studies. *See* Queer studies
Geller, Jonathan, 230 n.12
Genthe, Arnold, vii, 68
Gilman, Sander, 230 n.12
Globalization, 206–8, 212–14, 218–20, 222–23. *See also* Diaspora; Multiculturalism; Universalism
Golden Spike ceremony. *See* Promontory Summit
Group Psychology and Analysis of the Ego (Freud), 25, 96

Hawai'i, 224, 242 n.4
Heterosexuality. *See* Sexuality
Hippocrates, 170. *See also* Hysteria
Historical materialism. *See* Benjamin, Walter; Kracauer, Siegfried
History: alternative, 35–36, 81–89, 91; dominant, 75–77, 100–101, 181; production of, 75–76; repression of, 181; and the visual, 36. *See also* Image-repertoire; Silverman, Kaja: productive look
Hodgson, Moira, 143
Home. *See* Nation-state: as home
Homosexuality. *See* Sexuality
Hopkins, Mark. *See* Big Four
Horn, Miriam, 250 n.15
Humanism. *See* Democracy; Equality: abstract
Huntington, Collis P. *See* Big Four
Hwang, David Henry, 2, 31, 204; *M. Butterfly*, 1–4, 5–31–32, 138–66, 241 n.60, 251–52 n.25
Hysteria: and the body, 188; female, 167–68, 170–77, 255–56 n.15; male, 168, 170–71, 173, 177–203, 255 nn.10, 12, 258 n.34; and Oedipal complex, 177–78; as psychic protest, 174–77, 181; racial, 181–

203; and sexual difference, 173; spatial, 180–81, 196–203; and the unconscious, 171–72. *See also* Žižek, Slavoj

Identification, 111–17; fiction of, 20–28; historical constraints of, 133–34; and identity, 25–28; and the nation, 23, 74–75. *See also* Lacan, Jacques: mirror-stage
Image-repertoire, 69, 80–89; re-signification of, 57, 69–71, 89–91, 102, 220, 221, 224, 227. *See also* Dreamwork; Silverman, Kaja: productive look
Immigration: "new immigrant," 169, 254–55 n.6. *See also* Law(s): immigration/exclusion
Imperialism. *See* Colonialism
Impotence, 180–81, 187, 189, 195. *See also* Assimilation; Hysteria
Internment, 30–31, 104–36; and Chinese Americans, 106; and Japanese Americans, 104–10, 118–19, 136, 247–48 n.33; justifications for, 104–6, 242–44 nn. 4–6, 9
Internal exile, 188, 197–98
Interpretation of Dreams (Freud), 77–79

Jackson, Earl, Jr., 160
Jameson, Fredric, 33
Japanese American(s): during internment, 104–9, 117–36

Kang, Ik Joong, 249 n.52
Kazanjian, David, 9, 10
Kingston, Maxine Hong, 21, 30, 204; *China Men*, 35–37, 45–67, 69, 86, 90–92, 98–103, 237 n.35, 239 n.43; kinship, 221–24; *Woman Warrior, The: A Memoir of Girlhood among Ghosts*, 24–25, 167–68, 241 n.59. *See also* Diaspora; Paternity; Patriarchal privilege

Kirby, Lynne, 178
Kracauer, Siegfried, 42, 55, 240 n.46.
  See also Photography: and history,
  and memory

Labor: Chinese immigrant, 16–17, 36,
  61–64, 109, 137, 169, 234 n.4; and
  gender, 222; gendered, 216; racialized, 61–63, 85, 179, 216; white,
  63. *See also* Lowe, Lisa
Lacan, Jacques, 120, 173; *Four Fundamental Concepts of Psychoanalysis,*
  43–44, 59, 114–15; gaze, 43, 114,
  123; geometral point, 41, 236 n.20;
  given-to-be-seen, 37, 43–45, 51–
  64, 69, 77–78, 80, 83–84, 86, 87,
  89, 91–92, 94, 98, 101; look, 43;
  mirror stage, 31, 74, 111–17, 133,
  246 n.23; name-of-the-Father, 31;
  screen, 43, 44, 74, 86, 92, 114, 117,
  136; signification of the phallus,
  164, 253–54 n.46
Laplanche, Jean, and Jean-Bertrand
  Pontalis, 79–80; on primal scene,
  111, 125–26, 130, 240–41 n.56, 248
  n.40, 249 n.49
Law(s): alien-land, 260 n.4; antimiscegenation, 17–18, 232 n. 1;
  Chinese Exclusion Act of 1882,
  263 n.29; *Ex Parte Endo,* 243–44
  n.4; Gentleman's Agreement, 229
  n.5; immigration/exclusion, 17–
  18, 92, 168–70, 180, 182, 234–35
  n.5, 257–58, n.33; Immigration and
  Nationality Act of 1965, 169, 193,
  213, 259 n.1, 263 n.9; *In re Ah Yup,*
  234–35 n.5; *Korematsu v. United
  States,* 105–6; liberalizaton of, 193,
  213; *Loving v. Virginia,* 232 n.21;
  Magnuson Act of 1943, 18, 169,
  234–35 n. 5, 263 n.29; McCarran-
  Walter Act of 1952, 169; National
  Origins Law, 168; Page Act Law
  of 1875, 17; Tydings-McDuffie Act
  of 1934, 257–58 n.33; War Brides

Act, 169, 180, 254 n.5, 257–58 n.33;
  1790 Naturalization Act, 232 n.18;
  1924 Immigration Act, 263 n.29
Lee, JeeYeun, 207
Lévi-Strauss, Claude, 174
Li, David Leiwei, 35–36
Liberia, 48
Louie, David Wong, 32, 168, 193–203,
  204, 259 n.45
Lowe, Lisa, 16–18, 23, 34, 62, 66,
  85, 109, 169–70, 213, 215, 216, 231
  n.18, 234 n.43
Lwin, Sanda Mayzaw, 188, 258 n.39

M. Butterfly (Hwang), 1–4, 5, 31–32,
  138–66, 241 n.60, 251–52 n.25;
  reviews of, 143–45
Madama Butterfly (opera; Puccini),
  138, 144, 147, 158, 160, 165, 220,
  250 n.3, 266 n.48
Manifest Destiny, 61, 85
Mapa, Alec, 90
"Marginal Man," 21–22, 24
Masculinity: Asian American, 1–4,
  14–17, 93–96, 120–24, 132–33, 135–
  36, 151–53, 157–59, 180–203; black,
  150–51; white, 110–11, 118–20, 123,
  143–44, 147–49, 151–66
Mazumdar, Sucheta, 212
McCloy, John J., 105, 243 n.5. *See also*
  Internment
Melancholia: and race, 75, 199, 232–
  33 n.27
Melting pot. *See* Assimilation
Memory, 30; and history, 55, 63–65,
  91; unreliability of, 53–54, 56–58,
  69. *See also* Photography
Mercer, Kobena, 138
Metz, Christian, 38
Mimicry. *See* Bhabha, Homi; Primal
  scene
Minidoka concentration camp. *See*
  Internment; Kaneko, Lonny
Miscegenation, 194–95. *See also*
  Paternity

Model minority myth, 24, 169, 193, 194, 198–99, 203–4, 227, 259 n.1; as used against blacks and latinos, 199
Moglen, Helene, 20
Morris, Rosalind, 264–65 n.41
Multiculturalism, 193–203. *See also* Assimilation; Diaspora; Universalism
Mulvey, Laura, 71, 123
Munson, Curtis B., 104. *See also* Internment

Nachträglichkeit (deferred action), 79–81, 125–29. *See also* Dreamwork
Nation-state: and Asian Americans, 111, 206, 211; and culture, 33–34; and global capitalism, 214, 264 n.37; as home, 204–2, 223–24, 261–62 n.16, 262 n.24; and nuclear family, 92, 180; and racialized labor, 170. *See also* Capitalism; Democracy; Equivalence: abstract
Neoimperialism: U.S., 148–49. *See also* Colonialism
Neubauer, Carol E., 45
Ngai, Mae, 231–32 n.18
No-No Boy (Okada), 188
"No-No Boy" phenomenon, 118, 246 n.32. *See also* Internment

"Observation of a Severe Case of Hemi-Anaesthesia in a Hysterical Male" (Freud), 171, 255 n.12
Oedipus complex, 11–12; negative, 128, 130–31; positive, 128–29, 131, 154
"On the Mechanism of Paranoia" (Freud), 96
"On Narcissism" (Freud), 10–13, 96
Othello (Shakespeare), 179–80, 187

Pacific Islander(s), 225
Pangs of Love. See Louie, David Wong
Paper sons, 67, 102, 190. *See also* Archive; Citizenship; Foucault, Michel
Paris is Burning (film; Livingston), 205–6, 261 n.8
Paternity, 99–101, 152–57, 190–98, 200. *See also* Patriarchal privilege
Patriarchal privilege, 153–55, 161–66, 190–93, 196, 222. *See also* Paternity
Pellegrini, Ann, 14, 230 n.12, 245 n.15
Phallus: having/being, 164–65; vs. penis, 155–56. *See also* Fetish; Hwang, David Henry; Silverman, Kaja
Phillips, Adam, 167, 176
Photography: and citizenship, 66–67; and history, 42, 55, 63–66, 84–89, 91; as lamination, 39–40; and memory, 54–58, 63–65; pose, 45–46; "reality effect," 30, 36, 38–39; suture, 41–42
Popular culture: 69–72, 110–11, 118–20, 226–27
Primal scene, 31, 111, 125–33, 248 n.41, 249 n.48
Promontory Summit, 30, 60, 63, 64, 66–67, 84–86, 88–89, 97, 104, 235 n.6. *See also* Big Four; Transcontinental Railroad
Psychoanalysis: and colonialism, 9–10, 148–49; and race, 4–15, 20

Queer Nation, 205–6
Queer studies: and activism, 265 n.45, 266 n.46; and Asian American studies, 216–20; and childhood, 128–36, 154, 226–28; as critical methodology; 215–19; vs. gay and lesbian, 264–65 n.41; and psychoanalysis, 14. *See also* Sexuality

Race and ethnicity: and sexuality, 2, 15–19, 92, 94–102, 111, 124, 129–36, 137–38, 141–44, 150–52, 157–61, 168, 202, 216. *See also* Chinese

American(s); Citizenship; Filipino American(s); Japanese American(s); Labor; Pacific Islander(s); Sexuality; Vietnamese American(s)
Racial castration. *See* Fetishism
Racism: internalization of, 20–21, 72–73, 81
Reddy, Chandan, 225
Rice Queen, 158–59, 220, 253 n.43. *See also* Colonialism
Rich, Frank, 143
Robber Barons. *See* Big Four
Rolling the R's (Linmark), 33, 135, 220, 224–28
Roosevelt, Franklin Delano, 105. *See also* Internment
Rose, Jacqueline, 172
Rubin, Gayle, 174

Said, Edward, 190
Samarth, Manini, 194
Sassen, Saskia, 214
Sedgwick, Eve, 135, 142, 253 n.37
Self-hatred. *See* Racism: internalization of
Sexuality: compulsory heterosexuality, 13, 94–98, 127–29, 141–42, 165, 205, 210; heterosexuality and domestic, 33, 148, 210–11; heterosexuality and whiteness, 5–15, 139–45; homosexuality, 10–15, 95–96, 135, 202, 242 n.68, 252 n.28; homosexuality and communism, 148; homosexuality and diaspora, 33, 204–8, 215–28, 260–61 n.6; invisibility of heterosexuality, 142; and racial difference, 2, 5–15, 92, 94–102, 111, 124, 129–36, 137–38, 141–44, 150–52, 157–61, 198, 202, 216; sexual difference, 51, 127, 179; sexual passing, 158–61. *See also* Cold War; Hwang, David Henry; Race: sexuality
"Shoyu Kid, The" (Kaneko), 30, 105, 110–11, 117–36, 204, 228

Silverman, Kaja, 41, 44, 54, 56, 59, 98–99, 150–51, 246 n.26; linguistic and paternal castration, 154–55; productive look, 57, 80, 87; self-same body, 111, 112–15, 130–31, 245–46 n.21. *See also* Fetish; Phallus
Simon, John, 143, 251 n.16
Sklair, Leslie, 266 n.52
Smith, Paul, 177–78
"Some Psychological Consequences of the Anatomical Distinction Between the Sexes" (Freud), 128
Spivak, Gayatri Chakravorty, 25, 169, 254–55 n.6
"Splitting of the Ego in the Defensive Process" (Freud), 145–47, 148
Stanford, Leland. *See* Big Four
Stereotype, 49, 56, 106, 109. *See also* Bhabha, Homi
Sturken, Marita, 187–188
Subjectivity: and agency, 25–28, 98, 189; split, 72–74, 201–3, 209, 211–15; and subject, 24–28; and subjection, 119, 123, 213. *See also* Althusser, Louis: interpellation
Sue, Derald, and Stanley Sue, 21–23. *See also* "Marginal Man"
Suzuki, Bob H., 199–200

Taiwan, 48, 221
Takagi, Dana Y., 215–16; and Michael Omi, 217–19
Takaki, Ronald, 61–62
Tate, Claudia, 25
Timaeus (Plato), 170
Tölölyan, Khachig, 206–7
Totem and Taboo (Freud), 6–13, 76
Transcontinental Railroad, 16–17, 30, 36, 60, 61–63, 84, 102–3. *See also* Big Four; Promontory Summit
Two Lies (film; Tom), 116–17

Unconscious: and dreamwork, 78–79; and hysteria, 171–72

Union Pacific Railroad. *See* Transcontinental Railroad

Universalism, 185–88, 198–99, 203.
See also Assimilation; Multiculturalism

Utley, Robert M., 235 n.6

Vietnamese American(s), 225
Visuality: and alterity, 79–80; and
gender, 51; and history; 81–89; and
queerness, 121–24, 148, 249–50
n.1; and race, 49, 104; and race
and sexuality, 122–24; relationship
of identity to, 36–37, 135. *See also*
Photography; Sexuality: sexual
difference

Wajeman, Gerard, 171
Warner, Michael, 264–65 n.41
Wedding Banquet, The (film; Lee), 33,
220–24

Whiteness: historical development of,
63, 85; invisibility of, 138, 141–44.
See also Race/ethnicity
Williams, Raymond: structure of
feeling, 198
*Woman Warrior, The: A Memoir of
Girlhood among Ghosts* (Kingston),
24–25, 167–68, 241 n.59
Wong, Sau-ling Cynthia, 93, 98, 124,
130, 190–91, 194, 204, 212, 224,
241 n.66, 258–59 n.43

Yellow fever, 158–59. *See also* Colonialism
Yellow Peril: myth of, 24, 168–69,
199, 203, 204, 259 n.1

Žižek, Slavoj, 170, 257 n.32; hysteria
as failed interpellation, 176–77

David L. Eng is Assistant Professor of English and
Comparative Literature at Columbia University and coeditor
of *Q & A: Queer in Asian America*.

Library of Congress Cataloging-in-Publication Data
Eng, David L.
Racial castration : managing masculinity in Asian America / David L. Eng.
p. cm. — (Perverse modernities)
Includes bibliographical references and index.
ISBN 0-8223-2631-0 (cloth : alk. paper) — ISBN 0-8223-2636-1 (pbk. : alk. paper)
1. Asian Americans—Race identity.   2. Masculinity—United States.
3. Sex role—United States.   4. Race—Psychological aspects.
5. American literature—Asian American authors—History and criticism.
6. Asian Americans in literature.   I. Title.   II. Series.
E184.06 E53 2001
305.38'895073—dc21   00-057807